FEELING FILM: AFFECT
AUTHENTICITY IN POPULAR CINEMA

Cinema has the capacity to enflame our passions, to arouse our pity, to inspire our love. *Feeling Film: Affect and Authenticity in Popular Cinema* is a book that examines the emotional encounters found in contemporary popular cinema cultures. Examining melodrama, *film noir*, comic book franchises, cult indie movies and romantic comedy within the context of a Jungian-informed psychology and contemporary movements in film-philosophy, this book considers the various kinds of feelings engendered by our everyday engagements with cinema.

Greg Singh questions the popular idea of what cinema is, and considers what happens during the anticipation and act of watching a movie, through to the act of sharing our feelings about it, the reviewing process and repeat-viewing practices. *Feeling Film: Affect and Authenticity in Popular Cinema* does this through a critique of purely textual approaches, offering a model which emphasises lived, warm (embodied and inhabited) psychological relationships between the viewer and the viewed. It extends the narrative action of cinema beyond the duration of the screening into realms of anticipation and afterlife, in particular providing insight into the tertiary and participatory practices afforded through rich media engagement. In rethinking the everyday, co-productive relationship between viewer and viewed from this perspective, *Feeling Film: Affect and Authenticity in Popular Cinema* reinstates the importance of feelings as a central concern for film theory.

What emerges from this study is a re-engagement of the place of emotion, affect and feeling in film theory and criticism. In reconsidering the duration of the cinematic encounter, *Feeling Film: Affect and Authenticity in Popular Cinema* makes a significant contribution to the understanding of the intersubjective relationship between viewer and viewed. It takes post-Jungian criticism into the realms of post-cinema technologies and reignites the dialogue between depth psychology and the study of images as they appear to, and for, us. This book will make essential reading for those interested in the relationship between film and aspects of depth psychology, for film and philosophy students at advanced undergraduate and postgraduate levels, and for film and cinema academics and cinephiles.

Greg Singh is Lecturer in Media and Communications at the University of Stirling. He is the author of *Film After Jung: Post-Jungian approaches to film theory* (Routledge, 2009).

FEELING FILM: AFFECT AND AUTHENTICITY IN POPULAR CINEMA

Greg Singh

Routledge
Taylor & Francis Group

LONDON AND NEW YORK

First published 2014
by Routledge
27 Church Road, Hove, East Sussex, BN3 2FA

and by Routledge
711 Third Avenue, New York, NY 10017

Routledge is an imprint of the Taylor & Francis Group, an informa business

© 2014 Greg Singh

British Library Cataloguing in Publication Data
A catalogue record for this book is available from the British Library

Library of Congress Cataloging in Publication Data
Singh, Gregory Matthew, 1976-
Feeling film : affect and authenticity in popular cinema / Greg Singh.
pages cm
Includes bibliographical references and index.
Includes filmography.
ISBN 978-0-415-49635-3 (978-0-415-49636-0) 1. Motion pictures--Psychological
aspects. 2. Motion picture audiences--Psychological aspects. 3. Jungian psychology. I.
Title.
PN1995.9..E46S58 2014
791.4301--dc23
2013031225

ISBN: 978-0-415-49635-3 (hbk)
ISBN: 978-0-415-49636-0 (pbk)
ISBN: 978-1-315-81745-3 (ebk)

Typeset in Times
by Saxon Graphics Ltd, Derby

Printed and bound in Great Britain by
TJ International Ltd, Padstow, Cornwall

CONTENTS

FOREWORD

Initially, *Feeling Film* might seem a slightly curious title for this book. It is not as though film is alive, nor does it have a body, and yet one of the many intriguing aspects of watching a film is that we treat it as though it *is* almost real, as though the characters on the screen are actual flesh and blood. Of course, films are not unique in the way they evoke emotional responses in us, and it is striking how the characters we meet in the cinema are reminiscent of the people we meet in our dreams. As in the cinema, so too in our sleep we respond to the images of the imagination as though they had a physical substance to them: an observation that led Christian Metz to refer to cinema as a waking delusion.

While, of course, cinema audiences know that neither films nor dreams are 'real' in a material sense, both nonetheless retain the capacity to encapsulate a certain psychological reality. We see this in the way they elicit strong emotional responses, almost as though something in our inner lives is being stirred into action through the passage of image and sound. While watching film, and also while dreaming, these imaginary images come to mean something that is psychologically significant, and this is because these fantasy images represent the quintessence of psychological reality – which is to say, they contain and encapsulate the missing essence (the missing fifth essence) of our psychological existence. These fantasy-images are the connection between our inner lives and the outer world, and, like the rainbow bridge of Norse mythology *Bilrost*, cinema offers us a shimmering connection between the present moment and the lived existence of our lives. In doing so, it spans the gap between audience and screen and offers a way to cross the crevasse of anxiety that so readily threatens to swallow up our dreams.

One of the insights offered by the Jungian view of the world is that the division between the world of imagination and the physicality of the outer world is not as rigid as it often appears. Jung realised that the material world was in fact overlaid by a series of unconscious projections and fantasies. It follows from that insight that our understanding of the arts, of myth and religion, and other shared cultural experiences are coloured with the projection of unspoken and unknown unconscious contents; the hidden patterns that we find in the world and the connections we make are as much the product of unconscious processes as they are the results of intentional conscious investigation. In this way, the unknown aspects of our personal psychologies shade and shape the ways we understand our personal relationships, our society and our culture.

This raises the interesting question as to how it is possible to recognise such unconscious material and the role it plays as it continues to influence our understanding of ourselves and our relationships. A partial answer to this question is that when we experience such unconscious contents they are characterised by a strong affect. These affects can be so powerful that they invade our ego, and when they do so something that is curious, and yet significant, happens. The conscious part of ourselves believes we are behaving in a reasonable and rational manner, when in reality we have been overwhelmed by affects and are in the grip of something profoundly unconscious. When this happens, a temporary and rather unstable bridge is formed in which momentarily it becomes impossible to distinguish between what are rational and non-rational thoughts and between ideas and feelings. We briefly lose track of what is 'real' and what is not, and the cinema seems able to shift us into this liminal territory in a particularly effective manner. When we are on this bridge, it is the felt and embodied image that provides us with a means to understand, to encapsulate and hold what the intellect alone is unable to comprehend. It is through that awareness of embodied affect that we gain access to our own interiority.

Another of Jung's contributions was to ascribe to feelings the same evaluative function as thoughts. Intuitively, we know this, and the English language is full of expressions that encapsulate this insight. We say we have a good or bad feeling about a situation, we comment that something doesn't feel right, or that it felt good to achieve something. We 'feel' our way with a situation or a relationship. However, feelings, like thinking, can lead us astray. Sometimes a feeling can become attached to the 'wrong' situation – something that ordinarily we wouldn't find troubling becomes a source of considerable anxiety or stress. Just as our thoughts can be faulty, so too we can have feelings that become attached to the 'wrong' person, object or experience. Again, this takes us into a liminal space, in which our personal psychology becomes enmeshed with the outer environment.

Of course, feelings are much more nuanced than this compressed account suggests. Crucially, feelings are embodied experiences, in which our bodies respond to our conscious feelings and also to our unconscious ones. If we notice the ways we respond to situations physically, then we can also become aware of the unconscious messages that our bodies are encoding. Often this takes the form of some type of pain, trauma or distress. This is something that psychotherapists are particularly familiar with and it is gradually become more widely apparent that mind–body systems are something where our current understanding is partial. There is a pressing need to formulate new frameworks and devise fresh ways of articulating these insights and the attendant problems they raise.

Culturally, we are on the brink of seeing how important it is to recognise the way in which our thoughts and feelings and the conscious and unconscious parts of ourselves interact with each other. This is quite a challenge for academic theory in the humanities, as historically it has approached the objects of its study in a somewhat detached manner, sometimes emphasising the cohesive nature of texts, at other times their unstable qualities. One of the important contributions of *Feeling Film* is the way it demonstrates that the very conceptualisation of something as a text is unstable. This is not just a post-postmodern observation in which the image is seen is part of an unstable chain of signifiers, signifieds and referents with their attendant paratextual qualities. Rather, this is a dissolution of the text and it is one which is concerned with how the psychological meaning of the cinema is less about the film itself and more our relationship with it. Just as with dreams whose meanings are personal and tailor-made, so too the meanings and values we find in the popular media are much more personal and bespoke than is generally realised.

While not dealt with head-on, this is nonetheless a theme that permeates *Feeling Film*. Greg Singh brings a rich and intuitive understanding to his accounts of 'warmth' in both the act of watching film and in the attendant cinephilia which envelops and interweaves with the experience. Singh also derives a great warmth from his enjoyment of critical theory, and there is a joyful playfulness in his writing that is palpable as he explores interconnections and dissonances between theory, the enjoyment of films and the contributions that analytical writing can make. As a reader, you cannot help but bask in some of the reflected pleasure – the warm glow of someone on the hunt to understand their own experiences as a means though which to connect to something more general, that has cultural and social significance.

This is not just about 'feeling film' but instead it is to show us as readers what a feeling theory is. I do not mean by this to imply this book is a theory of feeling, though to some extent it is that too; I want to suggest that *Feeling Film* marks an important step in film theory. This is because, rather than seeing thinking and feeling as opposites, this book demonstrates the ways in which they exist in relationship with each other and how both have a central role to play in scholarship. One of the remnants of the grand theories of the semiotic, structuralist and Lacanian inflected film theory of the last century has been to foreground the conceptual and structural over the experiential. While being richly analytical, *Feeling Film* shows how a careful and theoretically informed approach can be both perceptive and apperceptive, which, as this book's title suggests, is an authentic and affective way to approach scholarly inquiry. As Jung was apt to remark, all major ideas find their origins in the unconscious. That is another way of saying that nothing is just conscious or indeed just unconscious. This book manages to discern the delicate traces of the one on the other, and in so doing it shows how both illuminate and amplify their objects of interest.

Jungian typological theory regards thinking and feeling as though they existed on a continuum in which each of us as an individual uses both orientations while at the same time retaining a clear preference for one over the other. Yet Greg Singh shows how thinking and feeling interweave. In his writing they become different strands of understanding that come together to combine and relate in subtle ways.

In so doing, he succeeds in bringing out the underlying patterns of our experiences of film. This offers a series of powerful insights as we come to see that the theory Greg Singh develops actually embodies a mode of analysis and understanding within itself. There is a good reason why the research output of a scholar is referred to as a *corpus*. This is lived theory, which draws on lived experiences. The series of reflections that take place throughout this book are not reifying but instead act to clarify and illuminate personal, collective, theoretical and experiential concerns: they hold the object and subject together, not in equal measure but in dialogue and discussion. *Feeling Film* proves an affective account of the ways that theory can enrich our appreciation of why it is that the movies matter so much to us. In so doing, like the cinema itself, this book offers a bridge and a walkway between the conscious act of watching a film to the pleasurable and often unconscious process of making meaning.

Luke Hockley
Professor of Media Analysis
University of Bedfordshire

ACKNOWLEDGEMENTS

As with all kinds of solo projects, this book comes at the end of a lengthy and collaborative dialogue with friends, colleagues and relations whose support and friendship have been of crucial importance to me. There are many people whom I wish to thank, first and foremost Janice and my girls for (amongst so many other things) allowing me to build a big shed in the garden to write in.

Some of the material in this book was developed as part of my doctoral research, so I'd like to extend my gratitude to colleagues and mentors in the Department of Film, Theatre and Television at the University of Reading where I spent many happy years as a postgraduate researcher. In particular, I want to thank Simone Knox for her generosity and the meticulous attention to detail in her reading of the very early drafts of this book. Thanks also to Lisa Purse for her comments which went a long way in shaping my approach to this study, and, of course, thanks to Jonathan Bignell for his years of support as my supervisor at the Department. I ought to mention the Arts and Humanities Research Council for their financial support of that doctoral research, out of which many of the ideas for this book first came about.

I wish to thank my fellow post-Jungian thinkers, and in particular Luke Hockley for his kind support, particularly in the closing months of the writing-up process and in generously lending this book his sage opening words.

Other people to whom I owe a debt of gratitude for their kind words and support of all descriptions over the last five years include: Susan Alexander, Helena Bassil-Morozow, Mark Bould, Havi Carell, Alan Cholodenko, Robert Consoli and the Digital Media team at the University of Hull's Scarborough Campus, Kathrina Glitre, Chris Hauke, John Mullarky, Humberto Perez-Blanco, David Sorfa and Greg Tuck.

Finally, a big thank you to my publisher Kate Hawes and her dedicated team at Routledge. Kate has always shown faith in my work and I am very grateful for her ongoing support.

INTRODUCTION

If a modern reader thinks of a film projected in darkness, the film
has nonetheless been projected.
(Gilles Deleuze, *The Fold: Leibniz and the Baroque*, 2006: 30)

Feeling Film is a book that illuminates the relationship between popular cinema
and feelings, revealing the often hidden emotional work of cinema. It bridges the
gap between film studies and the rarefied world of the philosophy and psychology
of different kinds of feelings: expression, perception, affect and emotion. To me,
psychology, in many ways like cinema and, indeed, philosophy, is about
understanding the world in which human beings happen to live. The untidy
contiguity of consciousness and world raises important questions about how
people, at both personal and collective levels, express that understanding in
cultural production. At a fundamental level, psychology is concerned with human
feelings about and within the world, and, from a post-Jungian, depth position, it is
concerned with the overlapping personal and collective experience; that is, self-
identity and intersubjectivity within cultures and communities. In its classical
Jungian sense, analytical psychology contributes to our understanding of what
feelings are; taking them into account, showing their importance. In its post-
Jungian variety, psychology acknowledges the interplay of social and political
impacts upon the formation of identity and connectivity. Rather ironically, whether
one believes in the psyche as an assemblage of identity and sense of self in the
world of relationships and things, or affords it little importance (whether thinking
about psyche in its collective or personal, in a Freudian, Jungian or Lévi-Straussian
sense), one need not rely upon the notion of psyche in order to understand the role
of psychology in the relationship between human consciousness, the products of
popular culture and the world. Likewise, currents in phenomenology which
emphasise this relationship share a common pathway with depth psychology in
particular, in its quest to uncover the underlying matrices that lend human existence
its meaningfulness.

I realise the controversial gravity of such comments. In many ways, I am
referring to psyche here as a way of articulating what in popular discourse might

1

be described as the 'mind' – that aggregation of identity, personality, memories and thoughts that we often associate with a sense of the self in our day-to-day lives. As a conceptual framework, therefore, the idea of psyche seems crucial to an understanding of human consciousness. Nevertheless, it stands, somewhat irresistibly, that one does not even need to presume that the mind is the central object of investigation in order to appreciate psychology's importance. Indeed, somewhat in common with some contemporary Jungian and post-Jungian approaches, this book argues for a more holistic approach to the mind in its relationship with human feelings, taking cues from both existential phenomenology and depth psychology. Its theoretical and practical contribution to an understanding of perception, cognition, affect, emotion and so on in relation to cinema lends this approach its academic and philosophical weight.

This approach to psychology is a critical approach, and I suppose that, given my training in cultural studies and humanistic traditions common to many film and media studies scholars, I sometimes tend to treat things with suspicion almost out of habit. I should make it clear that I do not reject outright the existence of mind and psyche within psychological investigation, nor do I claim for them a diminished importance as conceptual elements in the history of thought. In fact, as shall become apparent, my integration of consciousness (the mind, the body) and world (the body, the environment), profoundly influenced by the existential phenomenologist Maurice Merleau-Ponty and his followers, shapes my view of what psychology is and can do – both more generally and in the service of furthering an understanding of the cinematic encounter. I do, however, think that this preamble is necessary – a micro-philosophy of psychology, if you like – to bring out the importance of psychology, and depth psychology in particular, to this study. If minds and psyche(s) do indeed exist, they appear to and for the layperson at an everyday level as feelings of various sorts (and also, of course, as thoughts, although, as we shall see, the terms 'feeling' and 'thinking' overlap considerably in depth psychology as much as they do in everyday life). This is a subjective set of the encounter with and within the world to which I will return frequently throughout this book, in the light of contemporary phenomenology especially, which takes this appearance of feelings as an aspect of consciousness and whole-body perceptiveness quite different to more traditional assumptions of the Cartesian *cogito*. Indeed, it is the very nature of the subjectivity of feelings, and how this feeling of having a feeling is perceived and expressed through cinema and our encounters with it, that led me to realise the importance of a robust psychology in dealing with cinema and screen cultures in the first place.

This line of thought follows on, in many ways, from the ideas that I set out in my first book, *Film After Jung: Post-Jungian Approaches to Film Theory*. There, I outlined a number of interstices between depth psychology as a theoretical framework and various strands discernible in any history of film theory: notions of film art, of the *auteur*, the influence of structuralism, psychoanalysis, historical materialism, and the more contemporary turn towards film-phenomenology. I do not mind admitting here (as I did during the course of the book itself) that *Film*

After Jung is in some ways an unfinished effort. Of course it is, and necessarily so. At the time of its writing, *Film After Jung* was a work that combined its disciplinary materials and thematic strands in a necessarily original and idiosyncratic way. It did so because previous critical writing that shared its themes of a specifically psychological inquiry within film studies was relatively scarce then. In short, I was reaching into the dark; there was very little light in an expanse of interdisciplinary space, a space in which I had to roam and find myself.

Having said this, I do not apologise at all for its existence. For all its mishaps, misshapes and philosophical tangents, *Film After Jung* made some modest, but I think important, contributions to the field of post-Jungian film scholarship. In the process, it allowed me the space to think and write at length about a subject that fascinates me and has a growing audience of like-minded (not to mention open-minded) academics, clinicians and filmmakers who are interested in the relationship between cinema, its ability to communicate feelings, and traditions in depth psychology which regard our feelings as human beings with all the due seriousness and care they deserve.

The present book does take some of the theoretical materials discussed and expanded in *Film After Jung* and uses them in various ways to deliberate the connections between popular cinema and feelings. However, it should be noted that this book is not a sequel or a direct follow-on, and the reader is not asked to go away and understand my other book before reading this one. Likewise, some of the concerns of depth psychology are indeed concerns of *Feeling Film*, but the reader is not required to have specialised knowledge of depth psychology nor, perhaps more importantly, to subscribe to its disciplinary and clinical frameworks. A book with such ambitions I leave for other specialists and talented minds to conceive. This book does something quite different.

About the structure and themes of this book

There are two broadly interconnected sections to this book, each with its own short introductory chapter. The first section, titled 'Feelings, identification and the problematics of cinema' addresses a perennial theme of film criticism. Any brief scan of popular film reviews will uncover an often celebrated discourse concerning the power of good characterisation to enable the viewer to 'get inside the mind' of the main characters, to 'identify' with them, to 'sympathise' with them, to aspire to 'be' them. This is all familiar ground, and yet it mobilises a presupposition that this is what film does, or indeed is even capable of doing. My charge is that such discourses (sometimes painfully reproduced in serious academic film study, including, on occasion, my own) short-circuit the argument that what the film is doing is nothing of the sort, but that, if there is any kind of identification or sympathy to be had, the important part of the equation is who or what is doing the identifying and sympathising.

This is you or I, the viewer, obviously. Less obviously, the complex indeterminate space between viewer and viewed seems to be doing much of the work of 'identifying' or 'sympathising' for us. That is, the relationship between viewer and viewed is itself an active intermediary, working at various levels (that we might here provisionally identify as psychological, phenomenological, cultural and socio-political) to render the cinematic encounter and realise the perceptual field within which empathy and meaningful connections may occur in time. The first section of this book, therefore, is dedicated to addressing this indeterminate space between viewer and viewed. In particular, this section discusses the cinematic encounter through the contextual and epistemic spaces of repeated viewing (of a favourite film, perhaps), extratextual encounters (with publicity about film stars, for example, or marketing materials for the films themselves) and through adaptation, transmedial story-worlds and narrative experiences.

There are perhaps two key points worth raising here. First, because of the emphasis I place upon transmediality and what viewers do with the cinematic materials we consume and the experiences of cinema we share, this study inevitably takes the view that the cinematic is not a matter of just watching film texts and interpreting them. This is not to say that I am somehow 'anti' close textual analysis. In fact, as I go on to discuss below, I make much use of this method to open up the various cinematic encounters discussed throughout, and, in my view, it forms an indispensable strategy for understanding cinema. However, as with many contemporary approaches to film, the current study engages *context* as a crucial part in the shaping of the cinematic encounter. Admittedly, I have therefore set myself quite an ambitious task to take into account currents in film theory and the political implications of contemporary digital media cultures. In addition to this, in seeking to redress the traditional problematic emphasis within screen theory upon the ocular, I include discussion on what I see as important interventions from the perspective of existential theory, in the tradition of Sartre occasionally, but more frequently and in particular the work of Merleau-Ponty and other contemporary phenomenologists. My second point here, related to the first, is that I place emphasis on the importance of the notion of an indeterminate cinematic space – a space which is related in a number of ways to the psychological space I referred to in *Film After Jung* as the 'Image'. Note the capital 'I' in this term, to denote the difference between images that are viewed on screen, images that come to mind during the viewing process, and the Image: the co-creational indeterminate psychological relation between viewer and viewed. This is an ambiguous and dialectical tension of affect, emotion and expression between viewer and viewed. I say more about this in the first couple of chapters, continuing the discussion in the second section of this book, in relation to spectacle, embodiment and the cinematic glance.

My position, one in which the Image stands as a figural and phenomenological descriptor for the encounter with cinema, has been refined since *Film After Jung* to a great extent by the subsequent work done in the area of depth psychology and film analysis, and I wish briefly to refer the reader here to two significant strands of work that relate to this notion. Both of these strands address what might be termed the 'Third Image' of the encounter with cinema. Media analyst and psychotherapist Luke Hockley presented a paper at *Screen* 2009 titled 'Cinema and the Psychotherapeutic: In-Between the Screen and the Viewer', in which he discussed the Third Image at length, defining it as 'a participatory, fluid and emergent thing' between viewer and viewed.[1] This almost-materialist account of the matrix of relations in the encounter with cinema, based partly on Hockley's observations of reflective encounters in the therapy clinic, is crucial as it opens up for the non-specialist the complexity of how psychodynamics work in the cinematic encounter. What we know about cinema and our relationship with it we *already know*, before we can account for it. It suggests a co-creational meaning-making process that is pre-representational, and therefore pre-linguistic – a different kind of knowing that might be described as feelings of various sorts.[2]

This is a turn of thought that finds a ready home in the contemporary field of film-philosophy: several commentators are now acknowledging the ability of cinema to go beyond the immediate realm of informatics; that is, culturally circulated and available knowledge of production, analysis and interpretation. Damian Sutton, for example, has recently noted this of the Deleuzian strand of thinking on film, quoting from Deleuze's highly influential *Cinema 2* book: 'Above all, Deleuze held that cinema is a prelinguistic regime of signs from which language, narrative, and the subject are created, and that the "life or the afterlife of cinema depends on its internal struggle with [this] informatics"' (2009: 22). In other words, we may say that cinema springs forth from a pre-linguistic world of feelings (felt as signs, and as meaningful encounters, and identified in Deleuzian thought as informatics) and enters into a struggle with how it is viewed in a world, by subjects themselves shaped by this informatics. Cinema has an all-at-once interior struggle with this informatics as well as undergoing the struggle between the world and how it is viewed; and, of course, as we encounter cinema, we undergo a corresponding struggle. These struggles are the very stuff of the psychologically indeterminate space of the cinematic encounter, and this is a theme taken up again in the second part of this book in relation to a Pontean whole-body perception and what phenomenologist Don Ihde has described as technological encounters that are 'encounters with much wider and deeper notions of who we are. They are the full range of our desires and imaginations' (Ihde 2002: xii).

The second strand of work in depth psychology and film analysis has come from filmmaker, cultural theorist and Jungian analyst Christopher Hauke, who delivered a paper on the Third Image at the *Screen* conference in July 2009. In 'Movies and the Third Image', Hauke offered a disquisition of six kinds of Third Image, and, in doing so, explored further the elements of meaning-making that relate to our fluctuating awareness of what is happening on-screen and off-screen during the cinematic encounter. It does not do Hauke's work the justice it deserves to outline briefly here, but I think that for me (and the most influential aspect of his approach to my own work) his description of 'talking up the image' as a kind of Third Image is a productive aspect of the cinematic encounter in contemporary screen cultures, and a rich way of engaging how narrative develops and grows beyond the duration of a film screening. In 'talking up the film', people often find personal meanings in their encounters with a film, but that encounter endures; it lives on in what I describe as an afterlife of cinema, in our shared thoughts and discussions, critiques and reviews, and in our repeated viewings.

The idea that there are different kinds of Third Image provides a particularly useful model, as it allows the film theorist to be more precise about what aspect of the Third Image is being addressed when thinking through the fluctuating indeterminacy that accompanies such a theoretical framework. Far from being imprecise or 'woolly', I would argue that it is this peculiar admixture of indeterminacy twinned with analytical precision that can enrich the analytical process, revealing for us other, 'unlooked-for' dimensions of the viewer and the viewed, as Hockley has put it. For Hauke's model, and in relation to Hockley's work in his recent book *Somatic Cinema* (2013),[3] this Third Image approach underscores what I see as the existential encounter of the all-at-once in cinema: that being with and towards cinema might be considered an always-already aspect of the cinematic encounter; a sometimes non-conscious aspect that infiltrates conscious experience through the phenomenon of various kinds of feelings. It is this aspect of these theorists' work that I pick up on in my own approach, with some caveats I now outline below.

Although very much part of the same 'movement' in film theory, the present study departs from depth-psychology positions in a number of ways. Most obviously, it constitutes a departure through my use of Merleau-Ponty's phenomenology and the subsequent (and recent) work done in this area in film-philosophy (most notably, Carel 2011; Tuck 2007, 2011; and Sobchack 1992, 2004, 2011). Also of importance here is the philosophy of Gottfried Leibniz (until recently, a relatively overlooked thinker for cinematic studies), whose work went on to influence, among others, David Hume, Immanuel Kant and Bertrand Russell. In this book, I am particularly concerned with his notion of 'little perceptions': an aspect of his work that has in recent years been taken up with force in film theory and philosophy, especially in approaches undertaken by French philosopher Gilles Deleuze and his followers. In the first section of this book, I distinguish the micro-moment perception of close details in an encounter with a film (such as gesture, frame transition, etc.) from a set of competing elements within a frame and momentary encounters with them (including aesthetic framework, shot composition, camera movement, etc.). I also distinguish both kinds of phenomena from a wider contextual network of references, symbols, reflexivity and what Althusser referred to as 'problematics'; in this context, what questions are enabled to be asked of a film, such as 'what is this film about?', 'who is in it?', 'what does this or that film mean?' or 'what is the filmmaker trying to say here?'; a specific manifestation of the informatics of criticism in popular cinema culture. Importantly, although these levels are distinguishable, they are not completely discrete, and a number of aspects overlap considerably. For example, a camera movement is an attentive element that can also be regarded as a gestural micro-moment, and also as a reflection of a filmmaker's style. Robert Altman, for example, is a filmmaker whose use of zoom is well known, but the meaning of that phenomenon may be felt rippling throughout all three identified phenomenal levels of the cinematic encounter (micro-moment, competing elements, contextual network).

Therefore, having to distinguish these kinds of phenomena is not without its problems, and the main task of the second section of this book is to identify and work with a suspended dialectical relationship between micro-moments, sets of competing elements and contextual networks in the context of whole-body perceptive encounters. Therefore, much of what follows in the second section, 'The surround of cinema', works to complicate the foundational premises of the first section. This is rightly so, as in this section I develop the notion of a 'cinematic afterlife' within the duration of feeling extending through time, through multiple and competing access points and economic models of viewing independent of the discretion of micro-moment, set and network. The notion of a cinematic afterlife, to which I devote a chapter in the second section, allows the phenomenon of duration in the cinematic encounter to burst forth in an uncanny, momentary flux, therefore necessitating the need for a dialectical suspension between the three phenomenal levels mentioned. But I am already getting ahead of myself ...

A note on terminology

Although I go into some detail concerning definitions and use of key terms in my critical analysis during the book, I thought it expedient to provide a note here on why I choose to use certain terms, how I use them, and in what context. For example, when most people use the term 'film' in everyday conversation, they do not usually mean celluloid film run through a projector and projected onto a canvas screen. Often when they do, the use of the term comes with an explanatory proviso. What they do tend to mean is a feature film of a specific (90 minutes plus) length, sometimes watched at a cinema theatre, sometimes at home on television or occasionally on a home PC or laptop (often utilising the larger screen of a widescreen TV for monitoring). With the fairly recent arrival of utile broadband provision in the UK, the speed of which enables users to stream HD-quality video into their homes, even ownership of carrier media is not a necessity. Whereas the term 'film', therefore, carries with it specific conventional connotations associated with feature films, it generally assumes the act of viewing them in a variety of contexts.

Before the reader accuses me of jumping on a new media bandwagon, I should stress that very often the current case is that most people rely on carrier media (DVD and so on) such that contemporary definitions of cinephilia (put simply, the love of, or an excessive interest in, cinema) rely upon various practices of archiving, collecting and sharing in a broader media culture that feeds into and from the media industry's secondary markets. The briefest scan of the scholarship on cinema industry (Caldwell 2004a; Elsaesser 2002; Lewis 2002; McDonald 2007; Meehan 2008; Ross 2008; Wasko 1994, 2003) as well as industry literature itself (screenonline.org.uk; Robertson 2003; noci.com; *Film Journal International*; Freeman 2009; Compaine and Gomery 2000; Davison 2004; Maltby 2003; Neale and Smith 1998; McDonald and Wasko 2008) would reveal that this is no secret: the film industry relies upon secondary markets for its stability and growth. This very straightforward (although, to an extent, somewhat mechanical) economics forms a general industrial context within which to think about the arguments put forward in this study.

I have tried to avoid using the term 'film' to describe the phenomena discussed in this book, although there may be times when I use it deliberately to invoke the physical carrier medium of celluloid film and the projection phenomenon. At other times, it slips in surreptitiously, and I suppose one could put this down to habit. I should not apologise for these slips, however: go to any academic conference on 'film' and one can find plenty of examples where the speakers are referring not to film but to something altogether different. It is an extension of the everyday use of the term, and whilst inaccurate in the sense of defining the objects of inquiry, it is wholly accurate in another sense of reflecting what we are talking about and what is generally understood about 'film' in the popular imagination. As Deleuze so sharply observes in the above epigraph, the use of the word 'film' evokes associations with the physical spaces in which we encounter movies – it is already projected, psychologically speaking, in the personal and collective imagination, as are our engagements with it. Generally, in this book 'film' refers to feature-length popular cinema, viewed in a variety of technological, social, economic and material contexts.

This is why I have opted to use the term 'cinema' to denote the processes and acts of feature film consumption, in common with many theorists working in the field of cinema studies today, although two more important provisos are necessary to express how exactly I employ the term in this book. First, and somewhat ironically I suppose, I would like to turn to the idea of 'television'. John Caldwell has written at length on the subject of the co-existence of old and new media. He insists in 'Convergence Television: Aggregating Form and Repurposing Content in the Culture of Conglomeration', for example, that one of the main omissions from nostalgia-saturated histories of audio-visual technology and consumption is the 'one persistent and nagging bridge between old and new media: television' (2004a: 70). Television is a ubiquitous form, ostensibly laying down patterns and ground rules at various stages of the production/exhibition/consumption process that other domestic and cinematic formats have since either appropriated or approximated in the convergence of different media platforms and cultures. This is, as Caldwell correctly points out, a bit of an inconvenience for new media historiographers, because television ought not to still exist in the forms that it does according to logical 'accelerator/brake' teleology (see, for example, Winston 1986, 1996 and 1998). Broadcast television, and in particular public service broadcasters in the UK such as the BBC, continue to play a key role in content provision not only for first-run broadcast but also for niche television channels, online streaming and video on demand (VoD) services. This, of course, extends worldwide, and a growing number of the BBC's co-productions are the result of collaborations with other 'quality TV' providers such as HBO and the Discovery Channel.

Caldwell's 'nagging bridge' has proved a thorn in the side of not only professional academic writers but also my own undergraduate students in the last few years. In discussions of their own average weekly screen time and associated viewing activity, they have shown in seminar workshops a tendency to deride Caldwell's 'nagging bridge' statement as outdated or erroneous because it does not sit neatly with their own experiences and recent media use. TV as a physical presence in the living room is, in many common accounts, essentially a monitor to screen material imported from other platforms – DVD, videogame consoles and YouTube included. I would argue that, rather than Caldwell erring (and I should in fairness extend this courtesy to my students), the idea of what television is and does in the popular imagination is boxed-off as a discrete institutional phenomenon, with its specific rules, identity and usage. Well, it does perform such roles in the media ecology, but, as I will argue in some detail (in particular, towards the end of this book), the idea of 'televisuality' as a philosophical and phenomenological agent of inquiry opens out for the critic new ways of identifying, approaching and defining what we might think of as 'cinema' and the 'cinematic'.[4]

Turning toward my use of the term 'cinema', and I would like to pre-empt any accusations that I may have forgotten about medium-specificity: broadly speaking, the notion that each medium performs its own functionality, has its own essential capabilities and whose effects, therefore, can only ever be simulated by another medium. It is true that I do not wish to dwell too heavily upon this question as it is broad enough to warrant its own study, but it is a relevant one and therefore I reserve special mention of it here and follow up in relevant chapters. One possible brief answer to the medium-specificity question would be to think through how industry synergy, media technology convergence and transmediality are all working in concert to shape consumer practices and to forge entertainment experiences that are found across spaces, screens and uses. Thinking about medium-specificity as a strategy for the categorisation of discrete phenomena and encounters would be a nonsense under such conditions, other than as a theoretically artificial construct for analytical purposes.[5] This feeds into the notion that such standardisation of transmedial experiences across a whole range of access points and platforms is leading to a sophisticated commodification of the experience itself, beyond anything that has been written about concerning the commodification of content.

The question of thinking through what it is we do when we go to see a movie is, as I see it, a negative dialectic that works in retrospect to unpack what it is we *imagine* we are watching and doing. After all, the act of describing what we loved or hated about a particular film often comes with an adjoined comment about extratextual aspects of the encounter: how expensive the ticket was, the quality of the print/projection, the relative good or bad positioning of the allocated seat, the noises other people made during the screening and so on. Sometimes this extra-textual matter is so tightly bound within the whole experience that we might not differentiate these aspects. Cinema in this respect becomes a thing we do, rather than (merely) a thing we view. As Thomas Elsaesser has described in detail in his essay on the blockbuster, 'Everything Connects, but Not Everything Goes':

> Why do we go to the movies, rather than watch individual films? The micro-levels of pleasure highlight, among other things, the fact that as scholars we may have much at stake in the distinction between 'film-as-text' and 'film-as-event', but as audiences we evidently have quite pragmatically resolved one of the central but rarely asked questions of film studies, which is not whether a film is 'art' or 'entertainment', but whether films are 'products' or 'services'.
>
> (2002: 13–14)

Here, Elsaesser identifies the differences between film as a product (a discrete commodity) and film as a service (a commodified experience), making the distinction between viewing a film and going to the movies. This differentiation is a vital one, as it outlines how the encounter between viewer and viewed is a battleground for industrial efforts not only to commodify the content that we seek as consumers, but also to commodify the viewing experience and therefore the viewer themselves. I return to this theme in the second section of the book.

Another pre-emptive defence that I would like to offer the reader is to explain that I am *not* attempting to argue for a homogenised media ecosystem. I fully recognise that qualitative differences exist and occur between different media, whether conceived of as physical, technological, experiential or whatever. These differences remain an important source of tension, struggle and industrial drive, and one would like to believe that such differences provide a well-spring for creativity in moving image arts, in one way or another. However, as I argue throughout the second section of this book, in order for film theory to move forward and face the challenges presented by a fast-changing, 'mashed-up' media landscape, it would need to reconsider the implications of migrating and repurposed content from platform to platform, context to context. Most notably in relation to this, the cinematic seems to have incorporated the televisual, just as the televisual seems to have incorporated the cinematic.

In the repetitive forms of encounter with screens that I discuss at various points in this book, an intense and ingrained interactive viewership characteristic of specifically *televisual* viewing has migrated to the cinematic in its various guises and platforms. This may be for a number of related reasons (whether industrial, stylistic, technological, etc.), but I think that primary among them is an experiential shift: the apparent erosion of material and qualitative differences between viewing platforms and the extended narrative encounter that takes place over time and across various access points. This goes some way to giving the cinematic a newer, somewhat different 'feel' – access to an expansive world of the film that was probably always present in film cultures, but has become more perceptible because of the 'sheer plenitude of narrative' that contemporary popular cinema has to offer, to borrow a phrase from Paul Lunenfeld (2004). It ought to be pointed out, however, that I do not abandon altogether the idea of viewing the film as a discrete whole text, or disregard the notion of 'going to the movies' as an enjoyable and looked-for cultural practice. Obviously, people still enjoy viewing a film as a film, as well as the rather ritualistic way to engage with the attributes of cinema as consumption spaces. On the contrary, I have previously published on some aspects of this kind of cinephilia (2011), and I return to these aspects where appropriate throughout the book. My point here is that the contextual kinds of cinematic encounter that I have described above are shaped by, and feed back into, the act of viewing a film. The *appearance* of such disassemblage of narrative and text within the media ecosystem is of crucial importance in understanding the complex relationship between viewer and viewed.

I started this introduction discussing 'feelings', and so I think it only fitting to round off by addressing my use of this term, although I should point out that Chapters 1 and 2 will deal with this in some detail. In the book *Film After Jung*, I discussed in detail the work of Hugo Münsterberg, an early proponent of film theory who offered a psychology-led approach to the idea of film and film-viewing. Münsterberg stated that there are four mental operations that are key to uncovering the relationship between screen and spectator: 'The photoplay tells us the human story by overcoming the forms of the outer world, namely, space, time, and causality, and by adjusting the events to the forms of the inner world, namely, attention, memory, imagination and emotion' (1999: 402). This approach informs my position in the most general sense, on the idea of feelings in the relationship between viewer and viewed: the space that is occupied between the embodied psychological world and the exterior material environment is 'felt' rather subject-ively as 'feelings' in what Münsterberg has classed as the correspondence of mental operations and experience of the world. This seems to make cinema an ideal candidate for thinking through the expressive potential of cultural production from a psychological perspective. To take this to its logical conclusion, one might say that, for Münsterberg, cinema is psychomimetic and might reveal something of the motivation behind the perceptive expression that cinema has to offer about human being and its relationships with and in the world. Furthermore, it stretches the definitions by which we are bound in terms of what 'feeling' might be.

For example, strictly speaking, in traditional psychological models such as Münsterberg's, attention is a cognitive mental process and is only feeling in the sense that perception is momentarily focused in the psychic economy. This approach to attention in the economy of viewing and viewed, however, does provide a guideline to thinking through a mimetic system, a doubling, that occurs in the viewing encounter, and for which there are a number of strands in film theory that have more recently and forcefully taken up psychological approaches. I return to the idea of doubling as a theme of sorts throughout the first section of this book in depth (repeated viewing, adaptation, self-reflexive viewing, the doubled gaze), and in the second section of this book (particularly in relation to the cinematic surround, the notion of the cinematic glance, and the existential–phenomenological concept of the all-around-all-at-once). However, I think it would be useful to note Elsaesser here once more, and his discussion of the encounter with the blockbuster film as an example of how (in my reading of him, at least) this approach stands up in contemporary theory. He states that:

> Such films [blockbusters] systematically 'double' the levels of their referentiality, making us aware that we exist in two places at once: watching a movie and remembering ourselves watching a movie. But instead of 'breaking the illusion', the split actually deepens our fascination.
>
> (2002: 20)

This fascination, this *mimesis* of reflection, reflexivity and spatial occupation in the encounter with cinema, is tied in with what might be described as 'feelings', and is how I will employ the term henceforth, and, in the broadest sense, as a description of these phenomenal registers. Obviously, this very broad notion of feelings to cover experiences associated with emotions, with affects, with ideas and with thinking of certain kinds in the cinematic encounter is highly problematic if left as it is, and admittedly as I use it here the term is quite obtuse. This is why, in what follows in the Introduction to Part I and in Chapter 1, a detailed discussion of feelings as experiential description in both everyday and technically distinct uses will clarify what I mean by this, and how various particular manifestations of feelings are productive in articulating the subtleties and complexities of the cinematic encounter. What is crucial to bear in mind for now, in relation to Elsaesser's point in particular, is the relationship that such a notion of feeling has with the idea of doubling: that his notion of doubling, and that feeling of doubling in the cinematic encounter, is, in various ways, a kind of mimesis or movement between viewer and viewed; in Deleuzian terms, a projected film through thinking, a thought-film. The cinematic encounter is never one thing only. It relies heavily on the imagination of filmmakers and film-viewers, on the predominant styles and currents in cinema and innovations in technologies. To put it in phenomenological terms, following the work of Sobchack and also of Tuck in particular, the enfolding of perception–expression in that encounter is what I would identify with the cinephilic, mimetic doubling that Elsaesser notes in his work.

My contention, and my argument throughout this book, is that this doubling feeling within the indeterminate, warm (as in embodied, inhabited, lived) psychological space between viewer and viewed, endures through repeated viewing in popular film cultural practice, through knowing intertextual practice and endless quotations in conventional content, through remaking and branding in industrial filmmaking, and through our everyday 'talking up' of the movies.

Notes

1 Subsequently published with revisions as 'The Third Image: Depth Psychology and the Cinematic Experience', in Hauke, C. and L. Hockley (eds) *Jung and Film 2*, Hove:

Routledge, 2011; and touched upon in detail in 'Losing the Plot: A Story of Individuation and the Movies', *Quadrant* XXXX: 1 (Winter 2010).

2 In personal correspondence with Hockley, he has pointed out to me that recent work in the field of neuroscience has shown that perceptions exist before language. Although outside of the immediate realm of this study and perhaps not definitive in its findings, such research is worthy of note as it corresponds fairly closely with the assertions found in Jungian film scholarship and contemporary film-philosophy of pre-linguistic, wild communication, deep unconscious understanding and whole-body perception.

3 At the time of writing, this project was at manuscript stage.

4 Of course, Caldwell (1995) uses this term specifically to address the innovative presence of the televisual in the history of new media and visual cultures, as well as the qualitative specificity and style of television, in interesting ways in his book *Televisuality: Style, Crisis and Authority in American Television*. I will address this other use of 'televisuality' in my discussion in Part II of this book.

5 Although, as I discuss presently, it should be highlighted here that medium-specificity is nonetheless meaningful for all its artificial construction. It plays a very important role in the discursive functions of marketing, audiences, critical engagement and production planning. It is a rather circular argument, but acknowledging the existence of medium-specificity as a construct crucially allows for its material presence as a system with technological, industrial, commercial and stylistic aspects.

Part I

FEELINGS, IDENTIFICATION AND THE PROBLEMATICS OF CINEMA

INTRODUCTION TO PART I

The emotional work of cinema: intersubjectivity, affective properties and emotional states

> The cinema provokes us to see, to feel, to sense, and finally to think *differently*, and while this induces Deleuze to write his two volumes, those volumes in turn compel us to return to the cinema, to see its images in the light of our own captivity to the rituals of representation, the philosophical-narrative program we have been running.
>
> (Greg Flaxman, Introduction to *The Brain Is the Screen: Deleuze and the Philosophy of Cinema*, 2000: 3)

> As cinema makes manifest, we are moved when affects provide access to knowledge, when they reach into its very fabric, enacting a passage of unconscious experiences, a transfer of states of mind, feelings and moods. The moving image is thus not only a language of mental motion, but also a language for emotion – a moody, atmospheric way to fashion affects in transmittable fabrics.
>
> (Giuliana Bruno, 'Pleats of Matter, Folds of the Soul', 2010: 227)

This section of *Feeling Film* looks at the role of feelings in the cinematic encounter and, more specifically, seeks to address feelings as a crucial part of how the viewer engages the cinematic experience both in the moment and over time. One way in which feelings may be described is in their status as affective properties or emotional states. For a cultural form such as cinema, which is so crucially tied-in with telling human stories and concerned with attempts at expressing human emotion, particularly in its popular forms, it seems vitally important to address the question of affect and emotion. Necessarily, recent film theory has sought to account for the affective and emotional properties of the cinematic encounter through various psychoanalytic and philosophical frameworks, and this current study discusses such work in some detail at various points. However, to begin, I would like to think through these topics in relation to formulations of affect in depth psychology, in addition to these other frameworks, in order to consider the role of warm, lived psychological reality as a foundational aspect of the cinematic encounter. In this sense, I am invoking warmth as a way of describing the embodied and inhabited world of psychology; an 'inner' world that is both with and in the outer world. This is not to say that approaches in depth psychology cannot deal with cold realities and feelings: it is worth pointing out that I am not using the term 'warm' to describe warm, fuzzy feelings and that sense of cathartic bliss sometimes popularly associated with warmth; I am really attempting to engage with the psychological realities of embodied spaces, and the imagined and fantasy spaces that are co-created with them. Depth psychology has a lot to offer film studies in this regard especially, perhaps, as affect as a concept, particularly in its embodied aspects, is a crucial question in clinical practice and much debate in the analytical tradition has been devoted to it. It is an approach to psychology, following the early pioneering work of Bleuler, Jung and others, that takes into account an understanding of the role of the unconscious. As Hockley puts it, the term 'depth psychology' is a suggestive one 'in the way it hints that underneath the conscious part of the psyche there are unknown regions that have the capacity and power to influence the behaviour of the whole person' (2013: in press). Some of these 'regions' are highly personal in nature, others collective, and there is considerable overlap and reciprocation between the two at a deep, structural level. As we shall see, this inclusion of depth psychology is discussed in a critical form, in relation to philosophical debates on cinema and, in particular, phenomenological approaches to the moving image.

As Luke Hockley notes in his book *Frames of Mind* (2007), Jung formulated a typology for the psychological functions of personality fairly early on in his career. Although he was to move on to other concerns in his later period, Jung tended to return to these types throughout his work, and there are several instances within that corpus, as well as in that of his followers – the post-Jungians – where these functions retain a position of importance in identifying and working with normal pathologies of human thought and behaviour. These functions signify a psychology of the elements of personality that reach far beyond thought and behaviour, however, and here, following both Jung (1964, 1998) and Hockley, I outline this typology in order to give the reader a sense of where it might lie in relation to contemporary thinking on affect and the cinematic encounter.

For Jung, there are four psychological functions. Sensation tells us that something is; thinking tells us about the thing; intuition tells us about its potential (becoming, where it might lead); and feeling is an operation of evaluation about the thing (reflection, how we feel about it). The reader may note here that these types align fairly closely with the concerns of Greg Flaxman's statement on cinema in the above epigraph. Although Flaxman is pointing to a rather different philosophical tradition – that of Deleuze – nonetheless, most of the elements are present in his address. His statement that '[t]he cinema provokes us to see, to feel, to sense, and finally to think *differently*' already mentions three of Jung's terms, whereas the last part of the statement, in a 'return to cinema', evokes, in my mind at least, the idea of intuition; a compulsion to return and to see (with fresh eyes, so to speak) the potentialities of cinema and, in turn, ourselves. Although radically differing in many ways, the Deleuzian cinema project and Jung's depth psychology tradition share some common ground, and I would like the introduction to the first part of this book to address this commonality.

The importance of affect for contemporary cinema theory

It seems to me that what these two areas of thought have in common is their concern with the importance of affect. Indeed, as Christopher Hauke points out, '[i]t is impossible to imagine the beginnings of psychoanalysis without the concept of affect' (2000: 227). One may equally argue that it is impossible to regard Deleuze's cinema project without the same concept. Indeed, the latter half of his *Cinema 1* book (2004) is devoted to his thinking on affectivity, affect as an entity and the 'affection-image'. Problems begin to arise when we start to dig into what, exactly, Jung and others working with depth psychology mean by the term 'affect'. In particular, because the terms 'emotion' and 'affect' are synonymous and often used interchangeably in Jungian and post-Jungian thought, it is difficult to pinpoint their meanings exactly. Compounded with this, is the often-held view in depth psychology approaches that both emotion and affect – either, if they mean the same thing – are kinds of feelings in the typology of psychological functions, but that they differ from feelings in the ways that we encounter and experience them.

Hockley (2007: 39) states that the blending of the terms 'emotion' and 'affect' in Jungian thought, in their differentiation from 'feeling' as an evaluative response, is useful for redressing an imbalance in traditions of film theory – in particular, the screen theory of the 1970s, with its primacy of the ocular–specular and its emphasis on the ideological production of cine-subjectivity – which seemed to place little importance on emotion other than, perhaps, as a cathartic form of distraction. I would agree that in identifying feeling as an evaluative response, different to emotion and affect, Jungian thought refits film criticism with the tools for according feeling the same importance in the critical process as thinking and analysing – often accorded rational (and therefore sometimes deemed more valuable) status as critical faculties. However, the frequency with which 'emotion' and 'affect' are homogenised in Jungian and post-Jungian theory is often confusing.

For example, the entry on 'affect' from Samuels, Shorter and Plaut's *Critical Dictionary of Jungian Analysis* describes it as: '[s]ynonymous with emotion; feeling of sufficient intensity to cause nervous agitation or other obvious psychomotor disturbances. One has command over feeling, whereas affect intrudes against one's will and can only be repressed with difficulty [...]' (1986: 11). The reader should note that, even in the encyclopaedic entry here, not only are the terms 'emotion' and 'affect' stated as being synonymous, but, in further describing what they are, a switch is made without notice, giving the impression that the two phenomena are indeed one and the same. Even more confusingly, they are described as 'feeling of sufficient intensity' in one phrase and different to feeling in the next. I disagree with this interchangeability on a number of philosophical and phenomenological points which I elaborate below. Indeed, we see disagreement within psychology theory: even in Jung's own early writings, there seem to be grounds for inferring that depth psychology does not always use the terms synonymously. He wrote that:

> Affectivity, comprising all affects and quasi affective processes, is an inclusive concept which covers all non-intellectual psychic processes such as volition, feeling, suggestibility, attention etc. It is a psychic factor that exerts as much influence on the psyche as on the body.
>
> (Jung, cited in Hockley 2007: 41)

As Hockley notes, Jung is here defining affectivity as encompassing emotion (as well as feeling), but he seems to be indicating that affect is different in that it is somehow embodied differently to emotion. In order that the confusion of terms does not detract from the usefulness of the post-Jungian conception of emotion and affect, we need to unpack what emotions and affects are, the qualities common to both, their relation to the notion of feeling as a reflective and evaluative experience, and the ways in which these terms describe quite different phenomenological inhabitations in their relationship with each other. Here I briefly outline some key interventions from Jungian and post-Jungian thought, noting the preponderance for interchanging emotion and affect, and offer the reader some thoughts on reinterpreting the dynamic of feeling in this theoretical tradition, in light of contemporary phenomenology and film-philosophy.

To start with, Jung notes in 'Approaching the Unconscious' (1964: 49) that the common usage of the term 'feeling' can denote *sentiments* (as in feeling anxious, troubled or elated), or a definition of an *opinion* (Jung's own example from official communications here: 'The President feels ... '), or even an *expression of intuition* (for example, Han Solo's frequent use of the phrase 'I've a bad feeling about this' in the *Star Wars* film franchise). To summarise, Jung generally uses the term 'feeling' in contrast to the term 'thinking', as a way of describing a judgement of value, although he also notes the common ground between thinking and feeling as ordering functions – 'making sense' of the world and evaluating its meaning. Indeed, John Izod has written on Jung's definition of feeling, remarking that feeling is 'a process that imparts a definite value to a given content in the mind: one likes or dislikes it. It is a subjective process which, in expressing a sort of valuation, functions as a form of judgement' (2006: 3–4). As such, feeling should be taken as equivalent to the thinking process in terms of its importance in ordinary cognitive operations. This is no less important for considering the kinds of feelings that are produced and co-created through the cinematic encounter.

This definition is very different to Jung's definition of 'affects' which, if the term has a common usage, would tend to describe how one feels in a bodily sense (butterflies in the stomach, intrusive feelings beyond one's immediate control, feelings of which we are not quite fully aware), as well as intuitively (again, Han Solo, feelings as they are becoming), which would suggest similarities with feelings in the Jungian typology. In depth psychology, however, the term 'affect' takes on a rather different resonance, and Jung gave many different formulations of affect in his long career. Essentially, however, these definitions may be summarised by noting one or two here, along with their implications. For example, he wrote in 1964 that 'I regard affect on the one hand as a psychic feeling-state and on the other as a physiological innervations-state, each of which has a cumulative, reciprocal effect on the other' (cited in Hockley 2007: 41).

Confusingly, this version of affect seems to have as much in common with Jung's concept of sensation with its links to perception in the manner of physical sense-perception (or what C. T. Stewart (2008) has termed a reciprocity to 'life stimulus') as it does with feeling in Jung's evaluative sense of the term. It ought to be pointed out that there do exist significant distinctions between what the two terms signify. Sensation is perhaps more typically identifiable in terms of engaging environmental detail, structuring our responses to experience of the world and helping us to order it. Affect tends to signify a more unconscious feeling-function in that it has the capacity to let content erupt into the conscious (a process known in psychotherapy as 'invasion') but also serves the purpose of managing the permeability between conscious and unconscious material.[1] In my view, however, there are several ways in which the Jungian notions of sensation and affect are brought together in terms of physical feeling, and, as such, the Jungian take on affect (in its classical configuration, at least) enables us to think of it as going some way outside of the realms of emotion, even as it allows for a dynamic relationship between the two phenomena. Indeed, C. T. Stewart – a veteran of some decades in the field of clinical depth psychology – wrote a book-length study devoted to the role of affectivity in pathological conditions, and the dynamics of affect and feeling. Stewart writes that:

> Jung understood that 'the essential basis of our personality is affectivity' [...] which I take to mean that the primary motivational system in humans, the energy behind all agency, is to be found in the innate affects. But these archetypal mechanisms need a human container in which to unfold, and a human other through which they can be mirrored and responded to.
>
> (2008: 5)[2]

This approach to intersubjective relations finds some common ground with the post-Deleuzian emphasis on the notion of the 'fold' – for example, as stated in the above epigraph, Giuliana Bruno's notion of the moving image as an 'atmospheric way to fashion affects in transmittable fabrics' (2010: 227). That affect operates as 'an extensive form of *contact*: a transmission that communicates in different spaces, and does so tangibly' (2010: 214 [emphasis in original]).[3] Stewart's approach to affectivity is also similar in some ways to the Sartrean modelling of intersubjectivity as set out by film theorist Tarje Laine (2007), in that Stewart's model accommodates an intersubjective mutual recognition process. However, it should be noted here that Laine would probably argue that the 'mirrored' aspect of mutual recognition needs to occur in order that any kind of affectivity can unfold in the first place. Additionally, the human container mentioned by Stewart runs counter to the existential notion of the unutterably alone but in- and of-the-world subject in whose existence as a conscious body enables such unfolding through mutual recognition of an other. Laine writes that:

> Emotional experience is [...] not to be found in the external world or in the 'essence' of the subject, but in the texture of the whole intersubjective operation. This means that self, emotion and meaning are always and already both external and internal phenomenon [sic.]: it is through emotion in and through which the subject and the social world intertwine.
>
> (2007: 119)

In the final section of this Introduction to Part I, I return to the idea of the intersubjective encounter, in relation to the notion of the fold, as it is crucial to my position on affectivity and the operations of feeling. For now, I would like to note that I do not wish to dwell on the 'archetypal' aspect of the post-Jungian formulation of affect and intersubjectivity, instead bearing in mind Stewart's take on the idea of affects as a fundamentally dialectical movement. He suggests a 'happy dialectic' of self and world that enables us to move beyond and towards a more material, embodied and actualised model of intersubjective encounter, a transcendent movement that proves extremely productive in thinking about the relationship between viewer and viewed.

'Having' feelings, and being 'had' by them

One way to elaborate upon this is in rethinking affectivity not merely as an operation that springs from within but as kinds of feelings that are mobilised through such 'energetic orienting and apprehension' responses to, within and for the world. To return to classical writing on the subject, Jung states that:

> Emotion, incidentally, is not an activity of the individual but is something that happens to him. [...] [O]ne behaves more or less like a primitive, who is not only the passive victim of his affects but also singularly incapable of moral judgement.
>
> (1998: 91)

Aside from potential links to developmental and evolutionary psychology here,[4] what seems to be going on when one feels affectivity is not only that we 'have' feelings but also that we are 'had' by them. In other words, feelings can lie beyond our control – that we are caught out by them, caught up with them, taken by surprise or otherwise possessed by them when they invade our conscious lives. Laine's take on the work of Steven Shaviro's 'somatic film theory' is of particular interest on this: 'Film images "catch" the spectators directly, in a state of prereflective, bodily affect, rather than through a reflective cognitive processing'

(2007: 111). So it appears that we are 'had' by our feelings, as much as we 'have' them, when we engage in the act of viewing film. This approach also suggests that, once again, emotion is an evaluative operation, which implies that at least some reflection is involved for feelings' articulation as feelings, and is echoed again by Jung when he suggests that emotions are 'elemental outbursts' and that '[a]ffects are not "made" or wilfully produced; they simply happen' (1998: 215). We might as well add here that they happen 'to us', but that in our reflecting practices (our 'feelings' on the matter) we tend to articulate our responses as identifiable emotional objects, with certain meanings and values attributed to them. Therefore, affectivity has pre-reflective, reflective and post-reflective aspects that are integral to our intersubjectivity.

This is where the importance of affectivity for contemporary theories of cinema pulls into focus. Images, like affects, 'happen' to the viewer, albeit in a crucially reciprocal and co-productive relationship between viewer and viewed. Shaviro, for example, writing in *The Cinematic Body* (1993), suggests that '[i]mages literally assault the spectator, leaving him or her no space for reflection [...] Perception has become unconscious. It is neither spontaneously active nor freely receptive, but radically passive, the suffering of a violence perpetrated against the eye' (1993: 49–50).

There is a sense in Shaviro's statement here that cine-spectatorship is a little unidirectional, and there is much to disagree about in his statement, particularly in light of depth psychology's 'happy dialectic' of self and world. Again, however, there is scope for further investigation. This tendency to write about film as 'happening' to us, particularly in its efficiency as a mode of affect, has been present in film theory for decades. Rudolf Arnheim, for example, wrote in *Film as Art* (1957) that '[w]hen the eyes and ears are prevented from perceiving meaningful order, they can only react to the brutal signals of immediate satisfaction' (1957: 7). When he wrote this, Arnheim was looking back upon his early writing to recontextualise it as the writings of an enthusiastic 'monomaniac', in later years transformed into a 'stray customer, who gratefully enjoys – a few times a year – the screen performances of intelligent artists' (1957: 2). In other words, his early thoughts on the ideological formation of film were revised, underpinned by an acceptance of the place and importance in theory of viewing pleasure.

However, this mellowing did not reflect a completely forgiving attitude towards industrialised filmmaking, as the above statement attests. What Arnheim is expressing here are his feelings about the lowest common denominator films – popular cinema – as 'brutal' and 'unintelligent', but also highly enjoyable. It should be noted here that this is one of the reasons why this book concentrates upon popular cinema rather than other kinds of cinema – with a couple of exceptions, the films discussed are those most likely to reach the most people, are most likely to have been made with a popular audience in mind (i.e. low-risk, familiar, conventional, 'apolitical') and are most likely to evoke feelings in terms of what I would term the problematics of popular cinema. These problematics, following Althusser's notion of the problematics of culture (in *For Marx*, 1977), allow for certain questions that may be asked, and enable certain modes of analysis at the expense of alternatives. He states that '[t]his problematic is *itself an answer, no longer to its own internal questions – problems – but to the objective problems posed* for ideology *by its time*' (1977: 67, note 30 [emphasis in original]). So, questions such as 'what is this film about?', 'who is in it?', 'what does this or that film mean?' or 'what is the filmmaker trying to say here?' employ hermeneutic frameworks relevant to their time (i.e. *our* time) that are naturalised through the conventions of genre, authorship, interpretation, technicity, ephemeral consumer goods (and their consumption) and marketing strategies. As I wrote in *Film After Jung*, these questions, present in even the most banal plot summary offered in daily tabloid film reviews, proliferate at the expense of what might be more immediate political and ideological analyses in popular film culture. Therefore, one might say, this kind of filmmaking encourages certain kinds of pleasurable consumption, evoking its audience to 'feel' by seeing in a specific way; to evaluate emotional objects and to respond to the affectivity involved in the act of viewing through a culturally privileged ocular–specular way of looking.

About this book, Part I: problematics of cinema

Although at first it may seem that there are three elements to the notion of 'the feeling of having a feeling' (working backwards here: feelings, having them, and the feeling of having them), there are, in fact, four. The first is feelings, and, as discussed, one way to think about this term is by employing the term in the same sense as found in depth psychology. I return to this question frequently throughout the book, but, beginning in Chapter 1, I outline a provisional definition of what 'feelings' might mean in relation to cinema, its cultures and its acts of viewing, particularly in relation to the Deleuzian schools of film-philosophy and the tradition of perception (a kind of feeling) handed down from Leibniz. More specifically, we can say that feelings in the cinematic encounter are negotiated through a specific cultural privileging of the ocular and specular; that is, the most readily accessible traditional accounts of cinema-going involve looking and seeing, the gaze and its curiosity. Whilst it is true to say that vision is a primary mover in the production and shaping of the moving image, as well as for its interpretation, it should certainly not be granted an essential primacy.

On this subject, I am reminded of a discussion that took place following Vivian Sobchack's keynote talk at the inaugural Film-Philosophy conference at the University of the West of England in July of 2008. Then, as Sobchack had just finished talking through her phenomenological reading of Derek Jarman's *Blue*, the inevitable question emerged in the Q&A about *Blue*'s disruption of the primacy of the visual – highlighting what film-phenomenologists have been saying for quite some time now about cinema in general. Sound, music, noise – these were all conceded to be by far the more 'immersive' qualities in the audio-visual equation. With a film such as *Blue*, which uses the neat trick of screening a static[5] blank, blue field for its duration, and over which a soundtrack featuring various events takes over as a narrativising force, the viewer has the feeling of starting to 'see things' in the blueness, even after a relatively short viewing time. The film undoes the association of the visual as some sort of prime signifier of reality: seeing is believing, as they say, but perceiving is feeling – even as those 'feelings' we may speak of are not necessarily 'visual' in origin or even exist because of an external, visual sensory stimulus; they are a subjective evaluation of our whole-body viewing experience. Don Ihde, in *Bodies in Technology* (2002), offers a lengthy, robust critical account from a Pontean phenomenological perspective on the 'cultural habit' of visualism in late modernity, which lends veracity to the idea that acoustemology[6] has an important role to play in the gauging of encounters with audio-visual technologies. Even so, those kinds of feelings, in relation to the cinematic encounter, are fundamentally tied in to the idea of an image – what we 'see' as much as how we 'feel', in a co-productive relationship. This visualism therefore proves remarkably persistent in terms of cultural references to cinema, and what may be gleaned or 'had' from the cinematic encounter.

In the work of Gilles Deleuze, and in particular his two *Cinema* books, an approach is pieced together that allows the critic to fully account for the cultural primacy of the visual. This is important, as it allows the critic to rethink cultural conventions and problematics without having to rely on them in order to formulate a theory of cinema or having to rest upon the simple presuppositions of ocular–specular approaches (the resulting psychoanalytic correlation between viewer and viewed based upon distance and loss, and a cine-subjectivity based upon the specular psychoanalytic concepts of voyeurism and narcissism). Such an approach would be philosophically erroneous as well as critically disengaged. In my view, it would amount to an academic laziness ripe for commercial exploitation and political disavowal, no less. I am not alone in thinking this. As Damian Sutton has recently noted:

> Deleuze argues that one does not adopt a theory and then look for films that appear to support it. To do so suggests an agency other than cinema is at work on cinema, working cinema over. The nadir of this practice can be seen whenever the critical analysis of a film becomes a leisure pursuit and whenever interpretive practices become desirable as a facet of cinema as commodity.
>
> (2009: 19)

This reading of Deleuze not only bolsters the idea of a problematics of cinema, and the limitation of allowable or avowable questions (and therefore predetermines what we might think cinema *is*), but also cuts to the political centre of the problem: the commodification of problematics and their interpretation as 'criticism'. Indeed, this is echoed by Greg Flaxman:

> Historicism, spectator studies, cultural studies, and cognitivism have come to dominate the field. The result is a peculiar, and peculiarly

fashionable, absence of debate – about what film is, about its difference from other arts, about its effect on thought, about the way its images can be distinguished – in which a set of traditional assumptions quietly cement themselves.

(2000: 7–8)

This, together with the commodification of problematics as well as the casualisation of academic film studies, has led to what Catherine Constable (2005), Slavoj Žižek (1999) and others have noted as a crisis in film theory that reflects a wider crisis in theory as a whole.

Chapter 1 begins to address this by discussing other ways in which we may think about the process of the way we feel through the cinematic encounter. Post-Theory seems to want to abandon the idea that theory can be productive, and this much I have already commented on at length in *Film After Jung*, but it is a problem worth looking at from the perspective of this study too. The problem with this, as I see it, is that, in discarding Lacanian-driven Screen Theory, many so-called Post-Theorists have tended to disengage from what I would describe as a living and lived 'warm' psychology of the cinematic encounter, even as many of the same theorists fully accept cognitivist accounts of film-viewing as somehow more valuable to film scholarship than other psychological approaches. This is quite apart from the additional abandoning of a political theory system – an anti-political move characteristic of much Post-Theory rhetoric. Having written about this anti-politics in *Film After Jung*, I am reluctant to attend to this problem again here, as it may seem that I am retreading an old theoretical tyre. However, it seems that, judging by such recent accounts as offered by Sutton, Flaxman, Constable, Žižek and others in the film-philosophy movement, the problem is, if anything, getting worse. Part I of this book is an attempt to engage the problem of Post-Theory head-on, the chapters rearticulating the criticisms found in film-philosophy to deal with the specific problems of feelings in the act of viewing, cinematic proxemics and cinephilia.

The second element in the notion of 'the feeling of having a feeling' is that of 'having', which in this instance alludes to some kind of possession, appropriation or apprehension of a feeling. Perhaps the idea of 'having' relates to all three. This will form part of the discussion in the opening chapter, enabling me to reconsider, throughout the first part of this book, the third element in the title, 'feelings'. This is a reprise of the first element perhaps, only now mediated through the notion of 'having' one, and being the object of 'feeling' in the sense that it is in some way removed or mediated in the conscious awareness of the person doing the 'having'. That, more than anything perhaps, gives us the notion that it has something to do with duration, in that it might take time to register a feeling that one is 'having a feeling'. Furthermore and as already discussed in this Introduction to Part I, the opening chapter will also regard the way that the person 'having' the feeling is also 'had' by it: the fourth, 'interior' element in the notion of 'the feeling of having a feeling'.

One way to flag up the importance of this possession of a feeling (as well as one's possession by a feeling), and the recognition that one is 'having a feeling', stems from the way that the notion of intersubjectivity has taken on a crucial role in contemporary film-philosophy. Tarje Laine (2007), writing from a Sartrean existentialist perspective, has noted this in relation to what I would call the co-creational indeterminate space between viewer and viewed, where the psychologically 'warm' feeling of having a feeling occurs. In fact, Laine goes further in suggesting that we can interrogate received notions of the cinematic by rethinking such co-relational spaces as 'in-between' space. She writes:

> The 'cinematic' emerges from an intersubjective 'in-between' space, since the cinematic experience is much more immediate, much more dependent on the existence of others, and much more socially conditioned than assumed in theories that operate within the ocular-specular paradigm only (such as psychoanalysis).
>
> (2007: 10)

Indeed, we can identifiably describe this 'ocular–specular paradigm' as a problematic of film studies itself. In addition to the kinds of institutional questions that I outlined in the Introduction to this book, following Althusserian perspectives on the notion of problematics in cinematic production and consumption, the discipline itself has incorporated its own problematics, through conventions of commodification and casualisation. Absolutely tied in with the ocular–specular is the key idea that has, in the course of perhaps 40 years, promulgated the myth of the essential primacy of the visual in film studies: the notion of identification. This is the basic assumption that Chapters 2 and 3 attempt to break down.

In fact, we already have, through Flaxman, a means of breaking down the problematic of identification; this is evident in the above epigraph. He suggests, following Deleuze, that we as viewers and as a collective viewing culture – again the primacy of the specular programme implicit in my turn of phrase, which I fully acknowledge – are captivated by and captive to the 'rituals of representation' that emerge through the academicised (in the sense of populist) interpretation of what we are seeing and feeling when we watch a film. Flaxman resorts to a computing analogy, a favourite of many of the cognitivist film theorists as it happens, in that we have been running a 'philosophical-narrative program', enabling the appearance of these rituals as psychologically relevant and, philosophically speaking, part of our cultural heritage(s), our epistemological project in Western thought. That project, privileging the individuated trajectory of subjects and subjectivity manifested in this scenario as the culture of interpretation and of review, is a fast-track way back to the privileged ocular–specular of the centred and authorial subject. It is a return to the problematic of viewing and interpretation.

In order to resolve the ocular–specular problem (at least theoretically, if not institutionally), Laine employs the concept of intersubjectivity to revitalise the idea of the importance of the viewing spectator in relation to the viewed. She uses this model, in which the self is constituted through recognition by the Other even as the Other's consciousness is recognised by one's own, to emphasise that, '[c]inema spectatorship is an intrinsically reciprocal practice that is constitutive of subjectivity'. To realise this is to 'move outside of the intrapsychic model of earlier moments in film theory where the concept of spectatorship is often structured by the diametrically opposed but complementary positions of subject and object, active and passive, seer and seen' (2007: 32). This perspective on how to deal with the cultural primacy of the ocular–specular crucially starts to shift theory away from the binaries of inside/outside, subject/object, seeing/being.

However, I should point out that Laine states that these binaries are 'traditional, dialectical poles' (2007: 10), and I believe that in this she is, to a degree, erroneous. I understand how Laine has drawn her conclusion critiquing 'dialectics': the dyadic opposition, a binary of antimonies or opposites, of interior and exterior is an artificial separation of the co-relational productivity of each. In addition, the recognition of consciousness by consciousness, the Sartrean position on being, is contingent upon another consciousness within the co-relation of recognition. This has, in many ways, similarities to my own approach, although it should be noted that I am not writing from a particularly Sartrean perspective, but rather in the tradition of a Pontean existential phenomenology. However, if I am reading Laine's position accurately, she appears to misconceive the dialectic (because she follows Sartre on this, perhaps) as a collapsing force, where I would describe it, after Merleau-Ponty's 'hyperdialectic', as a suspension of struggle, an opening out or bursting forth; a dynamic between interior and exterior, consciousness and Other consciousness. This is, essentially, dialectics-without-synthesis, the kernel of which can be discerned in Merleau-Ponty's vitriolic response to Sartre's Stalinist political leanings, *Adventures of The Dialectic*. Here, he writes in the Epilogue that:

> The dialectic does not, as Sartre claims, provide finality, that is to say, the presence of the whole in that which, by its nature, exists in separate parts; rather, it provides the global and primordial cohesion of a field of experience wherein each element opens onto the others. [...] The natural and human world is unique [...] because we are imitatable and participatable through each other in this relationship with it.
>
> (1973: 204)

Indeed, Merleau-Ponty's thinking on this extended to the ways in which, intersubjectively, the 'work' of being, the 'action' of the encounter, is never experienced as fully finished. In *Phenomenology of Perception* (2002), he developed this idea further:

> The world is already constituted, but also never completely constituted; in the first case we are acted upon, in the second we are open to an infinite

number of possibilities. But this analysis is still abstract, for we exist in both ways at once.

(2002: 527)

Having said this, Laine's model of intersubjectivity is particularly accommodating when it comes to the notion of an 'in-between' space, common to both of our approaches, and in particular to the emphasis we as theorists both place on the body and the embodied nature of emotion and thought. This is because, drawing from Sartre's existentialism, Laine argues that human consciousness is always consciousness of the world, that '[e]motion is an orientation towards the world and an embodiment of the world and it cannot be reduced to one or the other. This is why emotional processes resonate with cultural meanings, even though they are individually embodied' (2007: 18).

Where I depart from Laine is in her insistence upon a separation of outside ('the position from which the subject is seen') and the inside ('the position from which the subject looks'). This separation seems artificial somehow: even as we know that interior and exterior spaces are 'felt' differently (in other words, one's evaluations of these kinds of spaces differ), the creaturely existence of being bodies and engaging in the field of experience allows the subject to form itself and know itself and its place in the world *as of the world*. For, as Laine herself states, this relationship of selfhood and world is epitomised in the kind of dynamics that occur in the cinematic encounter: 'In the cinematic experience, the relationship between the film and the spectator is based on the mutual capacity for and possession of experience through common structures of embodied vision' (2007: 25). This makes the intersubjective approach to cinema eminently useful for thinking through the dynamics of viewer and viewed, in relation to the traditional phenomenological concerns of perception and being more generally.

The fundamental difference between emotional objects that we view on a screen (images designed to evoke a feeling-response – and to this we may add soundtrack and musical score) and affective responses within the dynamic of viewing and viewed might at first seem to wholly complicate Merleau-Ponty's suggestion of an 'imitatability' and a 'participatability' in the intersubjective encounter with others within the world. This difference may be described first of all as the functionality of counterparts in the political register of film-viewing: essential to understanding what kind of feeling we address when we describe that an image gives us a feeling. This is because although it would be a nonsense to deny the existence of the image (merely) as image, it would equally be nonsensical, as if in radical response to this, to deny that such an image has meaning ascribed to it within cultural interaction. Describing image (merely) as image (moving or otherwise) allows us to entertain the notion that a prelinguistic and affective meaning-making can and does occur for and within the act of viewing, even as cultural meanings can and are ascribed to images. This affective response is attributable to what Sobchack has called an instance of 'wild communication' (1992: 4) and partakes of the prereflective notion of affectivity discussed previously. The difference between

29

this and emotional objectivity, by and for which in the act of viewing the viewer attributes meaning to an image (or sequence, or set, or extratextual phenomenon), also starts to reveal what we might mean by 'having' a feeling.

In fact, we can go back to Merleau-Ponty here and his thinking on the subject in *Sense and Nonsense* (1964). In that book, he links the notion of intersubjectivity and the cinema with the act of meaning-making in an explicit way: 'A movie has meaning in the same way that a thing does: neither of them speaks to an isolated understanding; rather, both appeal to our power tacitly to decipher the world or men and to coexist with them' (1964: 58). Essentially, this attitude to the occurrence of meaning-making phenomena in the in-between of viewer and viewed allows us to return to the notion of representation and image, but from a very different theoretical direction – to borrow Sobchack's phrase, a 'wild' communication. Here, the reader will find it useful if I clarify exactly how I use phenomenology and its concomitant terms in the context of the contemporary cinematic encounter, especially in the light of Sobchack's film-phenomenology, and the existential phenomenology of Merleau-Ponty.

As phenomenology is concerned with appearances, so it lends itself to the idea that it can reveal much in the textual material that appears to us in the act of viewing film; that, in a sense, its primary concern is the image, representation. As the quote from Merleau-Ponty above suggests, the phenomenology of film is little different to the phenomenology of things because its primary concern is the perception and understanding of the world and being-in-the-world. Problems of representation obviously play an important role here, in that popular moving images most often attempt to reflect or show human action (whether fictional or not). The more important aspect of Merleau-Ponty's observation here is the implication that film operates within a process of ongoing meaning-making, the *ambiguity* of such narrative operations forming the anthropocentric view that underscores Sobchack's oeuvre: of, to and for human vision and intersubjective co-production of meaning.

It is true that phenomenology as a method can reveal the hidden elements of a representation in its apparency, the way it appears to us in the act of viewing. As a method, it can help film theory move beyond what appears for us as immediate to the text and into the means by which such encounters endure beyond the text's momentary duration. They endure for us and through us (as viewers, as members of the audience) as acts of narration; as the 'action' of narrative in telling and retelling. Chapter 2 explores an instance of how representational meaning-making occurs within a feature film's textual material, and also beyond its textual limits: stretched 'onto' other texts through consensual meanings, reflexive filmmaking, production strategies and the tertiary practices of popular film cultures (where this study encounters and flirts with notions of fandom, cinephilia and star studies). Chapter 3, with its case studies in the representation and encounter with representations of masculinity in contemporary cinema, takes this notion further in terms of one of the key historical themes of critical film studies – gender politics.

Chapter 2 seeks to appraise and move beyond alternative models to that of the traditional projection/identification model of psychoanalytic film theory in order to question the notion of a fixed or mechanistic relation between viewer and viewed. In particular, I seek to critically engage the role of the contemporary trend in synergistic business practices concerning cinematic releases of literary adaptations. There are many franchises that spring to mind here: *Harry Potter*, *Twilight* and *Chronicles of Narnia* are all brand names that embody what I would describe as a 'cinematic surround'. Their popularity seems to defy imagination; a popularity that seems to define the *most popular* of popular cinema today. I address some of these concerns later in the book, but, for this chapter, I concentrate most of my analysis on the question of adaptation, and the vast changes in narrative encounter and characterisation that occur through relatively small incremental changes and cosmetic alterations within the process. I achieve this through a case study on *The Girl with the Dragon Tattoo* – the first part of the Millennium franchise making waves in global cinema even as I write this. It is a particularly useful case study, because it is the subject of multiple adaptation doubling: a translation process from the first of a trilogy of Swedish novels (Stieg Larsson, 2005) to English (2008); an adaptation into a six-part TV mini-series for Swedish TV (the whole trilogy coming under the title *Millennium*, subsequently available on DVD and Blu-Ray release in Region 2), which was restructured as a Swedish/Danish co-production film trilogy (*The Girl with the Dragon Tattoo*, Oplev, 2009, and *The Girl Who Played with Fire* and *The Girl Who Kicked the Hornet's Nest*, both Alfredson, 2009), restructured as and subsequently remade as a Hollywood business concern (the first instalment directed by Fincher, 2011). I will discuss this case through engaging the notion of cinephilia (in short, the love of, or an excessive interest in, cinema) as an ongoing, psychologically 'warm' process of co-creation and meaningfulness, relating this to the captivating potentialities of cinema-going, the vicissitudes of narrative, affectivity and being 'had' by one's feelings.

It should be noted that the three case studies chosen for Chapter 3 – mainly concentrating on *The Wrestler* (Aronofsky, US, 2008) and *Into the Wild* (Penn, US, 2007), but also investigating *Zidane: A 21st Century Portrait* (Gordon/ Parreno, Fr./Ice., 2006) and *Click* (Coraci, US, 2006) – should not be taken as isolated examples in my reading of them. Whilst writing papers on *Into the Wild* and *Click*, I encountered *The Wrestler* and *Zidane: A 21st Century Portrait* for the first time when I saw them back-to-back (on DVD), and my impression of the effect of doing so was startling. The 'action' of the narrative that I was able to bring to the act of viewing these films was something akin to what in television studies is known as 'flow' and 'overflow': emphasising the way that texts can be porous, malleable and, most certainly, *not* fixed; flowing on from each other, one to the next. Thus, Chapter 3 explores the phenomena of time, change and movement in the intersubjective encounter with cinema, the action of narrative. Here, these phenomena, eminently repeatable in the ways cinema is produced and consumed more generally, are given a personal treatment in relation to the particular emotional objects under discussion and my own cinephilic, affective responses to the films, a strategy that I continue to employ in Part II. These themes are also connected through a critical phenomenological look at one of the recurrent themes of film theory – the gendered gaze – and the gendered on-screen spaces that seem to double or mimic a semblance of real life in a cinematic virtual reality.

To begin the current section, however, I engage the notion of feelings through the unfinished dialectic of being together, being apart in the cinematic encounter: exploring how Leibniz's notion of little perceptions can illuminate the ripples of affect that occur in the cinematic encounter, and how having feelings and being had by them are two sides of the same dialectical phenomenon of being together, being apart. I do this through investigating repeated viewings of different versions of Spielberg's *Close Encounters of the Third Kind* (US, 1977), noting the subjective sets of encounters at the level of micro-moments, competing elements and contextual networks at play.

Notes

1 I'm indebted to Luke Hockley for pointing towards these issues in *Somatic Cinema*, and following up with some explanatory details in personal correspondence. I refer the reader to his detailed and insightful discussion of invasion in the cinematic experience in the final chapter of that book.
2 This particular take on affect relies somewhat heavily on the Jungian notion of archetype, and I fully acknowledge this connection. Whereas this notion is foundational in most types of Jungian thought, it was the subject of some discussion in *Film After Jung*, and I opt to leave this connection as an endnote in this particular instance as it falls some way outside of the course of my argument on intersubjectivity here. There is, however, some ground for further work on the role of archetype in intersubjective relations.
3 See also Deleuze 2006; Mullarkey 2010.
4 Links to which I have not the space to devote, although interested readers would do well to see Adler 1956; Bjorklund and Hernandez Blasi 2005; Ellis and Bjorklund 2005; Fordham 1994; Hillman 1960; Michel and Moore 1995; and Samuels et al. 1986 for different approaches to, and critiques of, these disciplinary fields.
5 It should be noted, however, that in film-phenomenology dealing with projected celluloid, this appearance of stasis is, in actuality, still a 'moving' picture because of the mechanical movement of celluloid throught the projection unit. It is also moving in some fundamentally embodied ways through our engagement with it as viewers – the subject of the following discussion.
6 See, in particular, the work of Anahid Kassabian (2001, 2013).

1

THE FEELING OF HAVING
A FEELING

Cinema and Leibniz's 'little perceptions'

Noticeable perceptions arise by degrees from ones which are too minute to be noticed. To think otherwise is to be ignorant of the immeasurable fineness of things, which always and everywhere involves an actual infinity.

(G. W. Von Leibniz, *New Essays on Human Understanding*, cited in Hergenhahn 2009: 188)

Can one speak of the affect? Does not what one says about it concern the periphery of the phenomenon, mere ripples at the furthest remove from the centre, which remains unknown to us?

(André Green, *The Fabric of Affect in the Psycho-Analytic Discourse*, 1999: 3)

In his classic essay on *photogenie*, 'The Essence of Cinema' (1978), Jean Epstein notes that during a film viewing somewhat incidental moments seem to push through the screen, to punctuate the encounter with a meaningfulness quite apart from that found in moments of overt spectacle. These incidental moments of *photogenie* tend to have the most emotional impact on the cinema-goer; they might be thought of as the 'nourishment of the film'. That is, moments incidental to the overall conscious intentionality of the filmmaker, as well as nominally incidental to the film's narrative trajectory. Despite their incidental nature, however, these cinephilic moments are fundamentally important to the film's storytelling strategies, its formal make-up and its stylistic attitude, and therefore the viewer's encounter with it. Furthermore, these moments are incidental for another reason: in the popular imagination, they are not as often noted as part of the general 'flavour' of the film. That is to say, these moments may have an impact on an individual during the course of viewing and even possibly afterwards in the way that the viewer retells the film and his/her response to it. However, they do not, by and large, feature in the collective discourse on the film; they do not last in popular memory (nor, in fact, do they perhaps need to).

This metaphor is suggestive of Leibniz and his notion of the 'immeasurable fineness of things'; an implication that cinema reflects for us the way human perception is made up of both the noticeable and incidental. It also brings forth, in Epstein's metaphor of flavour and nourishment in the cinematic encounter, a relationship between the perceptible and imperceptible – a notion that Christian Metz (1977) explored in his discussion of *trucage* in cinema; that cinema is one vast *trucage* or 'trick', and that cinema reveals for us the relation between the spectacular and the subtle in cultural experience.

These issues raise a number of points concerning the discrepancy between individual instances of viewing, collective discourse in the popular imagination, and how the narrative image of the film (to borrow a phrase from Stephen Heath 1975a, 1975b, 1981; and Ellis 1992) tends to be composed of more general ideas of spectacle and emotional impact garnered from ephemera such as marketing materials, poster art, trailers and the popular review system. This is not to say that the two notions (individual instance and popular imagination) are wholly autonomous or disconnected: as already noted in the Introduction to Part I, Tarje Laine (2007: 18) has written that 'emotional processes resonate with cultural meanings, even though they are individually embodied'. I return to the relationship between these two phenomena (the cultural and the individual experience of film viewing) in the next two chapters, and to narrative image, in particular, in the final chapter of this book. They are, however, different. Epstein states that 'When a dish is too peppery, it is the pepper that you are most conscious of, but it isn't the pepper that nourishes you' (1978: 25). The 'nourishment' that Epstein speaks of is the feeling about cinema; the 'pepper' is the overall impression of the film in the popular imagination; superficially rendered perhaps, but the stuff of cinema's problematics. This 'flavour' of film can be found in all kinds of examples from popular cinema and, to my mind, is exemplary in Steven Spielberg's *Close Encounters of the Third Kind* (US, 1977).

I have chosen this example, and specifically the Ultimate Edition DVD version, for several reasons.[1] The multiple versions of the same film in the box-set enable close comparative viewing, and the DVD itself as a medium provides a value for money when viewed repeatedly (therefore repeated viewing is also encouraged through its form). The rhythm of the film – realist filmmaking techniques, the relatively slow pace of plotting, everydayness punctuated with moments of spectacle – lends the film to cinephilic practices of viewing. Finally, it exemplifies, in contemporary Hollywood product, what I call a dialectic of being together, being apart: a dialectic that emerges through narrative devices such as characterisation and 'the journey', but also through cinematic micro-moments and competing elements within the frame at given times. Its particular rendering of togetherness–apartness is a reflection of a more general trend in popular film narrative forms. Through engaging with this notion, we may start to unpick the intersubjective, co-productive 'in-between' space of viewer and viewed discussed in depth in the introduction to this section. I go into some detail regarding this in the *Close Encounters* narrative below, but further expand upon this notion in Chapters 2 and 3.

In one scene early on in *Close Encounters*, air traffic controllers are negotiating a near-collision between an aeroplane and a UFO in real time. There is an element that appears to 'leap' from the screen during the course of the unfolding narrative in this scene: the uncommon element of overlapping dialogue. It has this appearance because overlapping of dialogue is relatively rare and certainly unconventional in Hollywood. As I will go on to discuss in more detail, the competition between visual and *mise-en-scène* elements co-existing within the frame and on the audio track here is immediately noticeable. The 'pepper' of *Close Encounters* in this case, to borrow from Epstein's 'condiments of cinema' idea, is the spectacular climax of the entire film, which overwhelms the narrative composition of the film and towards which most critical attention has been directed. However, the 'nourishment' of the film, the characterisation implicit in the everyday gestures and exchanges within domestic or work settings throughout its course, is still evident in the scenes that seem, as they play out at least, incidental and 'natural'. Thus, as noted in some detail in the Introduction to Part I, the idea of the primacy of the visual is a difficult one to sustain, as the subjective, emotional elements of response seem to mislead us into an unsuspecting difficulty in sorting out the film's presence in order of meaningful importance. That is to say, we are unsure of how we feel (evaluate, express judgement on affect) about scenes where conventional rules in popular filmmaking practice are transgressed in such an irreverent way.

This chapter seeks to build further understanding on the 'un-sureness' and ambiguity of meaningful cinematic encounters. *Close Encounters* is typical of latter New Hollywood's spectacular intentionality; it draws emphasis towards the technicity of special effects, the individuation narrative of the protagonists. However, if emphasis is being drawn *towards* something, then an irresistible possibility is dangled before us: it is being *drawn away* from something else. In what follows, I conduct a close textual reading (by having had a 'close encounter with' the *Close Encounter* DVDs) to elaborate Epstein's ideas of the discrepancies between cinematic nourishment and condiment, and develop Metz's distinction of perceptible and imperceptible *trucages* to reveal the dialectical relationship between the two. To begin this process, however, I would like to note in passing the two statements in the epigraph to this chapter, as they are of immediate concern for the methodological and theoretical frameworks for this strategy of work. I return to these in some detail later in the chapter. For now, it is enough to relate the following.

The incidental moments of *photogenie* which Epstein so eloquently fuses into the nourishment metaphor arise from minute changes in the relationship between viewer and viewed, and have affinity with Gottfried Leibniz's notion of the 'immeasurable fineness' of perception. The most important of these changes, for the purposes of this study at least, would be a change in the degree of meaningfulness for the viewer. Certain moments, like the one described above concerning overlapping dialogue, deliver an impact not immediately noticeable, but arise from the granular details built up over a brief duration of time. The fineness of these details should not go unnoticed – in fact, it is their fineness that reveals to us how meaningfulness is conducted within the confines of the scene in question. This also has some intriguing implications concerning André Green's statement on the ripples of affect: what may be ordinarily articulated about one's feelings concerning the cinematic phenomenon are articulations of thinking-feeling (to borrow Jung's terminology), or reflections at the periphery of what is felt about it. Even noticing, let alone articulating, the granularity of detail at the centre of the phenomenon would be, if Green is to be taken seriously, an almost-impossibility. What follows (here, as well as in close analysis of further examples in the following chapters) is an attempt to engage such cinematic granularity at the periphery (the 'ripples') and express it in terms that explore the meaningfulness embodied in the fine detail. It also starts to unpick the dialectic of together–apart articulated at various levels of the film's narrative and textual strategies that might also be felt in the proxemics of viewer and viewed.[2]

The scene is set in a busy air traffic control centre. As expected in such settings, the atmosphere is one of controlled hustle – there are multiple dialogues occurring as background noise. A first air traffic controller receives a call from a pilot, at first reporting nothing untoward; he then spots an object on his radar screen that is not accounted for and reports this information – an Unidentified Flying Object. This exchange is witnessed by another controller who sits in the foreground, seemingly not contributing to the exchange until the first controller asks that he check something. Another controller leans over to see what is happening, and a supervisor notices the dialogue exchange between controller and pilot and gets involved; his glances toward the radar screen and the controller indicate concern as the dialogue continues between controller, pilot and the operator at 'areas 31'. Over this exchange, the supervisor and the two other controllers suddenly engage in a discussion about the UFO. There is no difference in the level of audibility between the first exchange and the second – both are given parity in their volume and audibility, suggesting that both are of equal importance in terms of telling the story.

At this point an electronic alarm sounds, accompanied by an extreme close-up of the message flashing on the radar screen which reads: 'CONFLICT ALERT'. There is then a cut to a close-up of the first controller, responding to the alert, in which he tells the pilot to take evasive action; the camera tracks backwards to include the supervisor in the shot, and pulls him into focus as he begins to tell the second controller to call the 'recon wing'. The camera continues to track backwards to include the second controller, who pulls into focus as he makes the call. The next shot establishes other controllers in the room and their disengagement from their own stations to see what is happening. This is followed by a return to the action, with a shot of the controllers and their reaction to what is happening on the radar screen. The next shot is of what we might assume to be a senior member of staff, given his authoritative demeanour and comparative senior age, in close-up asking the controller to ask the pilot if he wants to make an official report. This is followed by a wider shot, which includes all of the controllers and supervisors involved, plus some of the other controllers who have joined them. As the first controller asks the pilot and the operators at 'areas 31' whether they want to file a report, the characters are seen reflected in the radar screen. The scene ends with none of the characters involved wanting to file a report.

The last few shots in this scene are of real importance concerning André Green's notion of the 'ripples' of affect. Both the reflection of figures in the radar screen and the reluctance of characters to file a report have consequences in terms of, respectively, the film's textual strategies (the repeated theme of together–apart, mediated via screens and artworks such as sculpture and chalk drawing) and the film's narrative conceits regarding the relationship of men with authority and bureaucracy (and the wilful disregard of both in one's life). What is most interesting about this notion of affective 'ripples' is the way in which a causal relationship is built up in retrospect, implying that the meaningfulness is encountered through residual elements on the periphery of some authentic, centred experience. I would argue that, in taking in the film's textual strategies and narrative conceits, we may start to unpick that notion of an authentic centre, to rethink the 'periphery' as an indeterminate, meaningful site of encounter, rather than (as implied by many notions of centre–periphery in cultural theory) a comparatively impoverished cinematic experience. This is largely because these 'peripheral' encounters, the after-effects of viewing, are largely how the cinematic encounter appears to and for us as viewers. Of course, this way of thinking about the significance of the incidental, the meaningfulness of the details as they build incrementally towards the sense of an holistic encounter, overturns what is often considered a hierarchical structure of narrative meaning. Here, I am thinking primarily about Roland Barthes and his idea of cardinal points of narrative, but that in the detail of reading (as well as in the relationship between the reader and the read) the functions of narrative are transformed into a lexicon of interpenetrating meanings, senses and signifiers.[3] I return to these two kinds of affective 'ripples' in the final section of this chapter, but in what follows it should become relatively clear where these elements of together–apart and disregard for authority manifest in *Close Encounters*. To begin, I offer the reader a brief summary of the plot.

Re-vision: close encounters with DVD trucages[4]

After investigating a power shortage, municipal line worker Roy Neary (Richard Dreyfuss) has an encounter with a UFO, and thereafter receives nagging visions of a mountain that he's never seen. Investigating further, he meets a woman called Jillian (Melinda Dillon) and her son Barry, who have also had alien encounters and give accounts of similar visions. Roy's obsession with the encounter and his visions lead him into emotional turmoil, as he repeatedly gives in to an urge to sculpt his visionary mountain. This puts a strain on his marriage to Ronnie (Teri Garr), whose initial concern for her husband's well-being turns to exasperation and, finally, flight, as she leaves with their three children. The nagging visions lead Roy and Jillian to an actual mountain, which is being used as an alien landing site by the US military, and a team of French scientists led by Lacombe (François Truffaut). Barry has been abducted by the aliens, and after a spectacular scene involving the scientists' attempts to communicate with the alien mothership, it opens, revealing the aliens as child-like creatures. Barry is returned to Jillian safely. Several astronauts have been trained to travel with the aliens, but the aliens choose Roy to accompany them, instead of the military personnel.

Some interpretative questions and statements concerning the chosen text immediately come to mind following this summary of the plot. These have deliberately been left general and obtuse here, in order to tease out the analysis, and present for its theorising what Althusserian approaches to film interpretation would refer to as the film's 'problematics': ideologically contained questions that may be asked of the film, according to the norms and accepted standards of film review in popular culture. These questions, in relation to this film, might be articulated as follows.

Is *Close Encounters* really a film about visitors from another planet, or do the aliens represent something else – that is, as is popularly understood with many of Spielberg's films, do the unknown or misunderstood characters work as a metaphor for race, children, or some other marginalised group in modern societies? Is it actually a film about the underlying unity of man, and the eternal goals that we 'all' share, namely, inner peace, fulfilment of desire, pursuit of happiness, family, destiny? Is it a film about the redemption of an alienated and emasculated Middle-American lower-middle class – if we (the homogenised, lowest common denominator audience; 'we, the people') all pursue our own dreams, we can achieve success and overcome social barriers such as economic privation, disen-franchisement and so on? Is it about the breakdown of traditional family and work structures (Roy is not his own boss, is suspicious of authority, and is uncomfortable with conventional work hierarchies, as well as his responsibilities as a father)? Perhaps *Close Encounters* highlights the playful (and selfish) escapist fantasies of a man undergoing an emotional breakdown?

These questions are, of course, a representation of the problematics of the film, and not necessarily answerable, nor, for that matter, is there an urgent need to answer them. As problematics, they set up the contextual framework of references necessary to understanding the cultural meaning of the film itself and reveal some of the ideological and political implications that appear to us in the intersubjective space of viewer and viewed as narrative, textual and extratextual elements. It is useful to signpost these problematics here in order to keep in mind the most memorable discourses that exist both within the film's textual and narrative make-up and in the popular imagination about the film. Of course, *Close Encounters* is not the only film in which and about which this occurs, and one might speculate with confidence at the systemic use of problematics in popular cinema more generally, given the prominence of Spielberg's work in the Hollywood system. With this in mind, some of the detailed analysis in the following chapters will examine such systemic contextual frameworks. For now, I will discuss these operational and systemic observations in the immediate case study.

There are several points in this film that are particularly memorable purely because they intentionally seek the viewer's attention, provoking such interpretative questions: these include the sight of thousands of people in Dharmsala, India, pointing to the sky in unison, or the climactic landing of the alien mothership in the final scene. These spectacles also extend through aural textual elements: the film's signature five-note musical motif running throughout. These key spectacles are the textual, audio-visual make-up of the film, and are the raw materials for cultural commentary.[5]

Things become complex when one considers what constitutes the spectacular scenes of the film itself and other textual elements between these spectacles. For example, in the original theatrical release of this film, the climax has Roy stepping into a bright light as he enters the mothership. The closing scene inside of the mothership in the *Special Edition* (released in cinema theatres in 1980) was a contractual compromise between Spielberg and Columbia, where Spielberg agreed to shoot the scene if Columbia would finance a re-edit and allow Spielberg to revise existing material and add extra material to the original theatrical release. One way of describing these textual additions would be to think of them as footage newly inserted into an existing, or original, film text, furnishing the unfinished work of a film. Furthermore, such additions as these are often placed in an existing film for commercial or marketing purposes, hence the term 'special edition' here.

One such addition was the insertion of an entire scene: the forced-perspective shot of the SS *Cotopaxi* freighter in what is supposed to be the Gobi desert. It adds to the original text because it is another memorable, spectacular moment, but it is additional for other reasons. Specifically, it is a later insert for the *Special Edition* and therefore undermines the notion of a 'pure' or 'original' *Close Encounters*. Certainly, from an authorial argument, one might say that this is compromised from the very beginning. Spielberg has, by his own admission in the documentary DVD special feature and on the DVD liner notes, stated that the *Special Edition* compromised the imaginative speculation of the original theatrical release. It is an instance of studio interference in authorial intentionality. In other ways, however, the *Special Edition* exerts more authorial control because of the additions of scenes such as the *Cotopaxi* scene. This is complicated by the fact that one can now easily access information on this addition: information is included on techniques used to create the shot in the 'making-of' documentary in the DVD special features, for example. Such ease of access in popular cultural contexts inevitably leads to a more detailed 'common knowledge' of a film's production, and this kind of knowledge is an addition to the kind of knowledge a viewer accumulates both through the act of viewing and in the retelling of that encounter.[6] Once again, it should be noted that this film is not an isolated case in cultural production – these kinds of knowledge have been described in philosophy as well as in literary and film theory. I will give brief outlines of three such interrelated descriptions (Derrida's *supplement*, Genette's *paratext* and Metz's *trucage*) to note their importance in the way that signifiers of value, such as DVD extras and extratextual information on deleted or added scenes in the *Close Encounters*

Ultimate Edition box-set, provide the setting for the film's contemporary problematics and, ultimately, help shape meaningful encounters between viewer and viewed.

To borrow a useful phrase, such additions are species of 'supplementary' text in Derridean terms: 'The supplement adds itself, it is a surplus, a plenitude enriching another plenitude, the *fullest measure* of presence' – intervening, filling in a figurative void, as if there were something missing in an originary utterance (1992: 83). This creates something of an ambiguity in the status of an 'original' text, a 'whole' body (or indeed bodies) of work, because the original theatrical release was already 'full': the supplement itself does not supply a lack, but is added to a cultural object already identifiable as whole *as if there were something missing*. This whole object, this central phenomenon, is retrofitted in the cinematic encounter because of the emanations (or ripples) of affective and meaningful material. The addition of the supplement makes the original, in retrospect, seem un-whole (and therefore, one may speculate, not as valuable as the *Special Edition*). I return to this ambiguity in Chapter 6, where these problems of supersession (originality, innovation and the process of continually adding commodities) extend the duration of the cinematic encounter more generally as an 'action' of narrative. Of course, it may be that such ambiguous evaluative retrofitting goes against the grain of this additive work, such that the original, unaltered release of a film becomes sought after and desirable in itself. Here one might think of differences in the 1983 and 1997 releases of *Return of the Jedi* (Marquand, US), where added CGI special effects to the re-release were seen in fan circles as excessive and an artistic devaluation of the film. In the case under discussion here, there is an institutional anxiety of missing returns, even as most films undergoing such treatment could be considered the most successful in terms of turning in a profit, and therefore indicate that a surplus profit *could* be made. There also seems to be a need to increase box-office receipts (themselves 'supplemented' through sales of secondary products such as DVD and so forth) for which the *Special Edition*, in a supply-side economic model of cinematic production, enables a presence of authoritative or otherwise, authentic, spectacle.

One can also think about this anxiety of not-lack following Marx in the *Grundrisse* and in *Capital* as an appearance-form, a (meaningful) surplus (and an embodiment of surplus value) to a central phenomenon of the film that we somehow can never get to without first seeking out or adding textual or cultural material. This is because the retrofit of the supplement has the appearance-form of added value, supplanting any value that may be regarded inherent in the film itself (insofar as it ever had inherent value) with a commodity value or commodity-identity; this is especially in the case of contemporary dynamics of narrative worlds whose access points are spread through several media platforms, and the transmedial information concerning its boundaries itself appears boundless – a plenitude-enriched plenitude. Thus the ripples of affect to which Green refers are (somewhat ironically) central to the encounter, as this is how the film appears to and for us; even as they are *also* supplementary or incidental or surplus to the requirements of a film as film.

Alternatively, such additions may be thought of as 'paratexts', following Gerard Genette (1997): any (literary) text is rarely presented in an unadorned state and is accompanied by productions that enable a text's presence to be felt within a public domain. Packaging, marketing materials, reviews and so on exist to promote the text's presence, selling it and supplementing the meaning-making process in the act of consumption. The commodity-identity of such textual elements has therefore been implied in the contexts of critical philosophy and in literary theory, and may be extended here to include contemporary remediated film. I return to such themes as a subject of discussion in Chapter 2, where a consideration of the implications for such phenomena upon narrative experience and a theory of meaningfulness in relation to contemporary cinephilia will be discussed in depth. For now, one may say that the term *trucage* can be used to both describe such phenomena and facilitate a theoretical application in the textual analysis. Here, the term *trucage* is employed following Christian Metz's conception as a kind of 'trick'; sometimes highly visible, at others conceived as perceptible or imperceptible phantasmagoria. This concept may be usefully engaged in a number of ways when thinking through cinephilia and dialectical meaningfulness in film culture, and here I am going to employ it to explore the complex interaction between spectacle, narrative and encounter.

Metz's ideas on the special effect, in his 1977 essay '*Trucage* and the Film', examine effects within the *mise-en-scène* and in the cinematography at play with conventions of genre. He writes that '[i]n classical cinema (diegetic cinema), a detailed and coded procedure which is part of the *cinematographic establishment* prescribes the different types of relationships which the spectator can have with *trucage*' (1977: 663 [emphasis in original]). These relationships can be extended, especially given the technological and cultural innovations in the world of cinema since 1977, to the audience's changing relationship with the screen and the recontextualisation of that relationship through certain expectations of the form and its capabilities. DVD, for example, is, after all, a format largely marketed upon its non-linear accessibility and its data storage capacity, allowing more material and added features to be included in a single unit of production.[7] At the risk of stretching the point, perhaps, *trucage* is, therefore, a concept that may be applied to the carrier media being discussed (whether projected film, DVD, mobile media or online).

More useful, perhaps, is Metz's idea that considers the *trucage* not only as the manipulation of the elements within the frame, but also as comments upon the form itself: 'It is in fact essential to know that cinema in its entirety is, in a sense, a vast *trucage*' (1977: 670). What is meant here is a more generalised version of Landon's 'aesthetics of ambivalence' (1992): a suspension of disbelief that what is being viewed is a true representation of real events as filmed, but that spectacular elements push the boundaries of realistic representation to the point of wonderment. Metz's concept is generalised, because it encompasses a general trick that negotiates, for example, the invisible, but nonetheless perceptible, *trucage* of montage editing as an effect (something found in most filmmaking, where we see the effect of a cut between shots, for example, but not the cut itself which lies between the two frames), as well as the complicity of the viewer in engaging such perceptibility.

Importantly, Metz writes about extratextual materials within film culture, such as film reviews, academic criticism, poster art, marketing materials, cross-promotion and so forth, that enable idiosyncratic readings of films, within the context of corporate choosing. He implies that the space of knowledge within film culture is of the utmost importance in enabling *trucages* as signifiers of value in the act of consumption, rather than in the act of 'merely' viewing a film. This extradiegetic textuality of a film, a textuality which lies beyond the world of the film, its characters and its plot elements, is a fundamental part of the consumption process, and *trucages* that are not perceptible other than through the dissemination of information on their existence (whether through discussion or supplementary productions such as documentaries, or in the case of the *Close Encounters Ultimate Edition* DVD, liner notes and interviews with Spielberg himself in the special features) become sites of meaning and value exchange. Thus the political effects of the problematics of cinema may be said to be fundamentally economic in the forms they take; they provide the terms for 'added value', particularly for fans and cinephiles perhaps, where specialist knowledge of a certain film or director's work is often felt to be important.

Metz writes that the consumer 'may *know* [the *trucage*] by having read of it in a film journal, but it is of little import, if he has not noticed it, whether he knows it or not (it is even better if he does not know)' (1977: 663 [emphasis in original]). Typically in contemporary film culture, this is achieved through DVD commentary, special features, or word of mouth on blogs, although, of course, in the case of big budget science fiction films like *Close Encounters*, on-screen, visible *trucages* play a crucial role in driving the topic of retelling. The act of viewing and the act of retelling a film (whether from a producer or consumer point of view) are therefore quite separate, though intertwined, elements of cultural experience, and help shape an encounter with film in fundamental ways.

This might extend beyond authorial intention (whilst at the same time enabling the consumption of authorship as an embodiment of exchange value, a brand) to encompass predominant views in film culture, ideological productions and incidental cinephilic fascinations (the aforementioned 'nourishment' of the film). This aspect of the concept of cinephilia, of an excessive knowledge of or about a given film, has arguably moved on in the age of DVD, but if anything is more urgent. In respect of 'reading' the DVD text as an entity, the consumer has been acculturated to certain expectations – for example, DVD 'extras'. The disappointment of the DVD enthusiast who receives a mail-order DVD copy of a favourite film, only to discover that it 'has no extras', is a vivid image, and one which reflects upon the changing contemporary audience dynamic – their reading of the text in terms of monetary *value* and its elision with cultural value in the sense of there being a notable edition of the film made available on DVD. Therefore, contrary to Metz's reading of perceptibility, it is reasonable to assume that it is even better if the consumer *does* know.

A vivid example of perceptible, but invisible, *trucage* can be found in the DVD version of *Close Encounters*. In an early domestic scene, in the original theatrical edition, Roy is seen playing with the train set. A musical box plays 'When You Wish upon a Star', a song made famous as a Jiminy Cricket number from the Disney feature *Pinocchio* (Luske and Sharpsteen, US, 1940), while Roy is clearly preoccupied with playing, as well as watching the television with his children. Ronnie takes responsibility for sending the children to bed, before taking a phone call from Roy's bosses at work. The emphasis seems to be located, in this scene, upon Roy and his preoccupations rather than his position within the family (which appears to be that of an emotionally neglectful father).

In the *Special Edition*, the same scene opens with an establishing shot of identical suburban condominiums at night. By the inclusion of this shot, already the meaning of the scene takes on a different nuance. The close-up of the music box, with its intertextual reference to *Pinocchio*, is replaced with a contextual reference to surburbia: the family home is one of discrete standards (size and shape, but also moral and cultural) and functionality rather than a place of commune or fantasy. Although both the toy and the housing represent kinds of realist context, they are different: the *Pinocchio* reference is familiar, the music box kitsch; by contrast, the housing shot suggests a more socially aware realism, one that, while not at odds with domesticity, nevertheless points towards the social roles of the family, to familial economy and its myriad political structures of responsibility and repression, rather than the emotional needs of the individual. The kitschy celebration of knowing one's pleasure, the 'second tear' of kitsch in Milan Kundera's words (1984), or Mary Ann Doane's notion in cinephilia of loving film for a second time (2002), is palpable in the first edition in this example. The *Pinocchio* musical reference is a deliberately nostalgic one and, as shall be discussed, returns as a motif later in the film (in the mountain sculpture scene and over the closing credits). In the *Special Edition*, the re-edit featuring establishing shots of suburban housing moves the film away from first order nostalgia, and, as shall become clear, enables Roy Neary as a character to 'rediscover' the inner child, instead of knowingly living it all along. Typical of Spielberg's later films, it is the journey of discovery that comes to the fore through this re-vision. The *Special Edition* establishing shot does just as it suggests: *establishing* a context through which the rest of the scene is cued to be read.

The establishing shot then cuts to an internal medium two-shot of Roy's son asking him to help with his maths homework. Roy replies that he graduated so that he didn't have to do maths problems, but then proceeds to attempt to explain what a fraction is. Even though there is plenty of evidence here that Roy is not that interested in his son's problems (his demeanour is impatient, bored even), he nevertheless makes a failed attempt to address them. There is also less evidence in this edition that it is he, and not his son, who would rather play with the train set. In this edition, they are *both* sitting by it.

This is extended to the following shot, where Ronnie reminds Roy about a promise he made to take the family out to see a movie and to play 'goofy golf'. The accompanying racket of one of the younger children in the background, repeatedly hitting a doll against the side of a playpen, is mixed with Ronnie's complaints about Roy's mess on the breakfast table and Roy's verbal consideration of what film would be most suitable to go to see: a reprise of the textual strategy of multiple competing elements and overlapping dialogue from the earlier air traffic controller scene. What is interesting here is that Roy settles on *Pinocchio*, the reference verbalised rather than obliquely made through a diegetic song, as in the first edition. The effect of this is remarkably different to that of the first edition's intertextual reference. The verbalisation in the *Special Edition* marks Roy's nostalgia for his own childhood, as opposed to a seeming inability to put it aside. Thus, while the escapism of the final scene is justifiable in the *Special Edition* for its emphasis on the fulfilment of one man's destiny, it is a rather more serious caesura, as it marks Roy's rupture from his own family. In the first edition, that rupture is already present in Roy's natural preoccupation.

The change in the way the different scenarios, via the manipulation of editing, shot choices and differences in narrative material, engage the viewer is related to the way the availability of problematics changes as a result. This can be additionally demonstrated in changes in verbal material. For example, Roy's phone call in this scene differs markedly in the two editions. In the first edition, the voice on the other end is authoritarian and monotone, suggesting that he is a known insubordinate who needs to be told specific instructions in order to keep his attention from straying. Roy hears the following message:

> Neary. Listen to me now. Get over to the Gilmore substation. We've lost power up and down the line. There's a drain on the primary voltage.

In the *Special Edition*, the voice is rather more incredulous and panicked, a plea for Roy to act, suggesting that his character is much more capable and responsible in his work:

> Neary. The [incoherent] director reports a [frantic mumbling] ... We're losing power across the grid! Has the outage hit you yet? ... Neary? ... Neary?!

Both versions of the conversation end in blackout, with the children cheering in the background. Only repeated viewings, comparative analysis and what Roger Cardinal (1986) describes as a 'panoramic perception' of events and meanings can bring out the full measure of these textual differences, much like the viewing practice of the cinephile.[8] The important point to establish here is the way that such relatively small changes can produce such significant changes in the enunciation of narrative and affective 'ripples' as a result.

As a result of the changes to the telephone conversation, other conclusions about Roy's character are enabled and foreclosed. Instead of a boss who is in control of the situation and confident in telling Roy what is happening, he becomes a boss who is out of control and seems to be pleading with Roy to solve the problem. This switch suggests a characterisation that, because of Roy's subsequent behaviour, may be read as changed from one of wilful insubordinate to a simplified case of misconduct. Subsequent meanings that are available to the viewer are thus foreclosed, rather like a butterfly effect, whose airborne winged ripples can be felt elsewhere as hurricanes. For example, when Roy takes the family out in the middle of the night to show them the alien aircraft, Ronnie shows compassion for, and attraction to, Roy's youthful enthusiasm: a reaction that turns to frustration and then fear later on in the film. Roy's reaction to Ronnie is rather telling here: he looks to the sky mid-kiss, slightly mischievously, preoccupied as he is with his alien sighting, rather than his wife's passion. It is a manifestation of the together–apartness running throughout this film, both thematically and stylistically – aspects to which I shall return in detail momentarily.

Roy's simple gesture is an indication that his attention is being drawn elsewhere. Although physically occupied with the act of kissing (he performs this act satisfactorily as far as the viewer is concerned, because Ronnie reciprocates), as his eyes look upwards, his thoughts are no longer on his own physical activity or Ronnie's physical presence. One cannot say for certain exactly what is going on in his thoughts, but, in keeping with his characterisation so far, what is apparent is that Roy's preoccupations do not lie with his role as father and husband, but to a certain extent with self-gratification and the pursuit of ideas at the expense of conventional familial responsibility. Physically, Roy and Ronnie are together, but emotionally they are very much apart. This is made apparent and materialised through Roy's gesture and suggests a complex dialectical relationship that involves characterisation and plot, a particular viewing strategy to read the meaning in the gesture (in this case, the repeated viewings of a fan or the additional viewings of a completist cinephile) and casual viewers' extradiegetic knowledge of the film.

The feeling of having: being together, being apart and the ripples of affect

The scene just described is a vivid example of the visual, textual and narrative motif of togetherness–apartness in this film. In a general sense, there are two ways that the dialectic of being together, being apart manifests itself in *Close Encounters*. First, it does this in the way that characters, objects and elements of the world of the film are placed in relation to each other within the frame and in montage. As in the domestic scene described above, the overall impression of such elements in relation to each other may be extended into ideological formations of human relationships, manipulated by such *trucages* as editing, shot emphasis, duration and choice. The differences between the two versions of this scene as discussed revise the entire framework upon which characterisation is built, and therefore fundamentally alter the choice of problematics available at the end of the film. Revisionism, it thus seems, is not reserved for explicit revision and remaster regimes in digital cinema today but had already occured in more subtle ways in earlier examples of New Hollywood, such as the *Close Encounters Special Edition*.[9]

The first edition, with its emphasis on Roy's rather self-absorbed personality crisis, tends to highlight an individuation narrative, in which the crisis of masculinity Roy faces in the loss of his job and family is offset by the fulfilment of his personal destiny to be chosen by the aliens to accompany them. His man-child persona is both amplified to the point of selfishness and disintegrated to the point of reversal: his journey is one from man-child to child-man. It seems that abandoning one's responsibilities is fine, as long as one is participating in a 'great adventure' and the pursuit of happiness. The *Special Edition* is very much concerned with the trope of wonderment: here Roy's familial role is at the centre of the narrative's concerns, his recapturing of the 'inner child' (a familiar trope in Spielberg's cinema) in a gesture of warm nostalgia and memory.

Second, togetherness–apartness manifests in the way that this spatial relation of characters, objects and elements of the world of the film can be articulated further to the audience, and the psycho-phenomenological interplay that occurs in the potentiality of the narrative dynamic as a result. The following is an example to help illustrate this dialectic of togetherness–apartness apparent in the experience of this film. Here, it is worth noting the different visio-spatial elements competing for attention, particularly in the manner in which the scene has been edited and then revised.

At one point in the film, roughly two-thirds through, Roy suffers what appears to be a breakdown of sorts, as a result of his insistent visions, gripped in an intense fantasy of visions and revelations. He has a compulsion to sculpt what he sees, using everyday objects (such as shaving foam and mashed potato). As he hastily gathers building materials from the garden (bricks, fencing, dustbins, shrubs and cement) to sculpt a giant version of his mountain in the living room, Ronnie escapes with their children. He completes his task, the television blaring a little too loudly, drawing the viewer's attention to it very much in imitation of such sonic inconsistencies as found in latter-period French New Wave.[10] Having solicited part of the focus upon the television, it allows what is shown on it to viably compete for viewer attention, when there are other things happening simultaneously (both in audio and visual terms). *Days of Our Lives*, a long-running American daytime soap that would presumably be familiar to a popular audience in the US, features on the TV set in the foreground of the shot, providing additional evidence of everydayness. Its own diegetic soundtrack acts as a score for the scene, conveying a sense of realism but through its levels of mediation (a television on screen) lending the scene something of a layered distanciation. The loudness and tinniness of the music tends to grate rather than emotionally embellish. Here, Spielberg enhances this distanciation by incorporating everyday mess: in particular, the two cans of Budweiser left at the foreground of the shot are prominent features, alongside the daytime TV programme.

Roy moves to the window and, visibly exhausted through his efforts, stares at the everyday events outside. He has been engaged in a struggle to comprehend and master his vision, to find meaning in it, and indeed in his own life. Ironically, however, he becomes upset by the realisation that his obsessive and erratic behaviour has chased away his wife and children. One can see this in Dreyfuss' performance – as he stares out of his window, Roy is distracted by the familiar and everyday activities going on in the suburban setting: a group of youths play baseball; a father and son wash the family car; a family enjoys an afternoon together in the garden. All are simple, familiar pleasures, now denied Roy because of the constant pressure to express his vision of the mountain. As he turns back towards the mountain sculpture, his resentment is displayed, a visible grimace in his face. Cut off from the outside world and trapped in his own world of broken domesticity, he appears to be coming apart: apart from the world and apart inside, his identity and status as a father in tatters.

As the set-up returns to the interior of Roy's living room, however, a temporal rupture has occurred. The Budweiser cans have disappeared, only to be replaced by a Budweiser commercial playing loudly on the TV. This is in no uncertain terms a product placement, typically justified in filmmaking through a need to produce a verisimilitudinal representation of real life, but here, to an extent, it draws attention towards the televisual presence in the scene. Roy then walks into frame, at the start of a phone conversation with Ronnie. Both phenomena (the cut and the act of speaking on the telephone) clearly demarcate an ellipsis in time. Roy had to cross the room, clear up the empty beer cans and dial the number during the millisecond edit itself. However, the Budweiser commercial had started playing before the edit, indicating that no time had lapsed. Is this, then, a case of undisclosed product placement for its own sake? Can this rupture be justified in filmic terms?

The Budweiser cans are so prominent that it is difficult to believe their place-ment was not deliberate. Indeed, their presence helps to orient the viewer through Roy's desperation in realising his actions have destroyed the familial setting of the home: clearly, he has been enjoying a beer or two whilst setting about his work. Such incidental appearance and disappearance does have an impact on the scene more generally. For, as well as punctuating the scene with a realist aesthetic, the prominence of the Budweiser cans in the foreground of the frame, followed by the prominence of the Budweiser commercial in the aural make-up of the scene, allows attention to be equally dispersed over various audio and visual cues in a direct way. It prepares the viewer for what is to follow in the scene, invoking what Torben Grodal (1997) has described as 'enaction' – the viewers' physiological and psychological readiness for action, tempered with the knowledge that such physical readiness need not be used physically.[11]

In this section of the scene, the emphasis lies on competing elements within frame and soundscape, simultaneously. The sculpture features strongly in the background, obviously, engaging some attention mainly through its incongruent status as matter-out-of-place. The foreground is dominated by the television broadcast, now playing a (fictional, diegetic) news story about a toxic cloud, and borrowing real newscasters (ABC's Howard K. Smith) to give it a sense of belonging in the real world. Most interesting of all, however, is the interplay between all of the elements: they are far from discrete, each reinforcing the other. This extends to Roy's conversation. It is difficult to make out all of the conversation, as his dialogue overlaps the noisy commercial and newscast: a continuation of the textual strategies of overlapping dialogue discussed earlier. When the mountain appears on the TV, viewing eyes are encouraged to flit between the two and then towards Roy, in anticipation (perhaps, hope) that he will notice the duplication and realise that his visions are real.

Almost immediately after his conversation ceases, he notices the mountain on the TV, and the non-diegetic score springs into action, enabling an aural cue of significance. Musicologically speaking, this score is similar in many ways to that found in *Pinocchio*: the musical motif is not quite the same as 'When You Wish upon a Star', but the tone and sentiment are striking in similarity. This is, I would argue, significant for its enacting of a moment of discovery, an emotional cue that may be followed to aid in the understanding of meaning being conveyed. It is also a replay of the kitschy elements of nostalgia that accompany the overt references to *Pinocchio* earlier in the film. There is a cut to a shot of Jillian, who is watching the same newscast in her hotel room. She is surrounded by her drawings of the mountain, and she appears relieved, affirmed that she is not going mad and that the mountain is a real place. Importantly, and perhaps significantly for the intratextual reference to realist aesthetics and verisimilitude in this scene, both she and Roy now believe the mountain is real, because they have seen it on the news.

The complexity of this scene cannot be overestimated. The depth of frame composition, as well as the sound design overall, allows the performances to tie together the competing elements, in both physical and narrative space. The happenstance that both Roy and Jillian are watching the same news report at the same time is revelatory in narrative terms: Roy's own realisation that he has been cut off from the world of being a father is replaced at once with a moment of connectedness with a woman he barely knows and yet feels bonded to, through their shared experiences.

Jillian, for her part, has had her status as mother wrenched from her by the alien abduction of her son. The TV, a medium sometimes traditionally associated with the atomisation of audience experiences in popular and academic discourse, here becomes a tool of induction. The mediation process brings Roy and Jillian together in ways that their prior physical meeting did not – and allows their brief and fantastic fleshly encounter towards the end of the film. What is ironic here in terms of mediated encounters is the fact that the newscast within the diegesis is a phoney – the physical mountain may exist, but the story of the toxic cloud is a ruse: a government cover-up to prevent the public from witnessing the landing of the mothership.

Upon repeated viewings of this film, it is difficult to feel positive about this outcome. Roy effectively abdicates his responsibility as a husband and father, eschewing it in favour of a vision, a fantasy that he hopes will validate his life. The evocation of moral ambiguity here, as well as aesthetic of ambivalence, is a powerful one: he is living out a fantasy that his wife is all too aware of, but one that is realistic and perhaps feels more real to him than his everyday life does. The two kisses featured in the film differ in Roy's engagement with them. The first, with Ronnie, is consciously performing the role of husband, whereas the second, with Jillian, is performed out of a need to fulfil the role of adventurer, and one may say that it deliberately seeks to be more juvenile in its ambitions. The first is, somewhat ironically because of its context in an expression of married love, more infantile, reflecting as it does Roy's relationship with Ronnie more generally. He even goes as far as to tell her on the phone that he is an adult but only as far as 'adulthood' exists. Thereby, this leaves open the possibility that, even though desperate to share those everyday experiences together with his family as an adult, he would much prefer to be apart, both emotionally and geographically, despite his protestations. In the end, his ambiguous status demonstrates an open dialectical togetherness–apartness: an intertwining that cannot be undone. Thus, the signifi-cant effects at the periphery of minute changes at the centre are profound, all the more so for being tightly bound in a movement that takes in narrative devices, textual strategies and contextual frameworks all at once. What starts as a rather incidental gesture, a movement, a focus, ends up as something altogether bigger, spectacular and memorable: ripples become waves, drops become oceans.

Cinema, ripples and the 'immeasurable fineness of things'

When Leibniz, in his preface to *New Essays on Human Understanding*, wrote of 'little perceptions', he used the example of the roar of the sea, which is made up of hundreds of thousands of imperceptible dashes of water on rock. As little perceptions accumulate, so we become aware of them, and this awareness Leibniz called 'apperception'. This may be applied fairly straightforwardly to the cinematic encounter, both generally and specifically to our example: in the gradual accumulative experience of micro-moments of close details (a character's gesture, a particular edit, an instance of music); in the set of competing elements within a frame and momentary encounters with them (use of sentimental music, depth of field, camera movement); and also through a wider contextual network of references ('When You Wish upon a Star' intertextual references, ephemeral marketing materials, 'making-of' documentaries and so forth). The threshold of awareness, I would argue, is itself an expression of affect – a 'tonality', as André Green would put it – that resonates through the narrative image of a film. The threshold itself is an indeterminate limen, a field of affective experience, or a continuum existing between conscious and unconscious perception where the embodied state of a subject plays a crucial role in perceiving and making sense of that which it encounters in the world. In this Leibnizian model of perception, any perceptions below the aggregate of little perceptions, the threshold of awareness, remain unconscious. This threshold, itself not located at a specific or general site in the psychic economy precisely because it partakes of both conscious and unconscious elements, is more akin to an instance of flux or momentary duration in phenomenological terms – a family member of the Derridean supplement. However, as the threshold (where or whenever that might be) is crossed, so a transcendence occurs at a psychological level whereby consciousness of and in the world becomes apparent to the body-subject. As one becomes aware of the cinematic object(s) encountered, so one begins to 'make sense' of the film. One begins to feel a certain way about it in making a critical judgement upon it. At what point this aggregate reaches a critical mass or a tipping point is unclear – of course, Leibniz is not around to comment on cinema – but one might speculate that such a point is variable and always liminal. It is contingent upon set, setting and so on, upon the precise details of the cinematic encounter and the *ripple* into conscious awareness – the ripple, which itself might, after all, be the most important element in the cinematic encounter, yet is still contingent upon the consciousness of the viewer; what is brought to that encounter in the act of viewing and what lives on beyond the duration of the screening in the imagination and in the retelling.

I say this because I would argue that the example discussed in detail in this chapter allows us to re-imagine the ambiguous state of the cinematic encounter as a psychologically warm, lived encounter that takes in this apparent accumulation of perceptions, this 'apperception'. This suggests to me a rather more holistic model than many film theorists are perhaps willing to fully acknowledge: a model that engages both the thing that is encountered (the film) and the mode of our encounter (the cinematic) which partakes of embodied subjectivity (consciousness). Furthermore, it suggests that there are moments in the aesthetic experience, as Mikel Dufrenne suggests in his book *The Phenomenology of Aesthetic Experience*, when the field of affectivity, the tonality of affect, becomes a *totality* of affect in a holistic or plenary sense:

> Instead of being determined from without, affective qualities involve a certain way of relating themselves to each other, a manner of constituting themselves as a totality – in short, a capacity for affecting *themselves*. As a consequence, the affective qualities into which the atmosphere of an aesthetic object is resolved become anthropomorphic.
>
> (1973: 442 [emphasis in original])

More accurately, perhaps, and as I suggested in the Introduction to Part I, we might describe this phenomenon as *anthropocentric*: to and for human perception and expression (as affectivity). I address this in more depth in Part II. However, these ideas concerning moving pictures, being moved by films, and the physical movement of bodies both on-screen and off feed back to Leibniz's model of apperception on a cultural-contextual level, in the fine, gradual awareness of narrative patterns that emerge through encounters with the film and its supplementary paratexts in time. As Jennifer M. Barker describes in *The Tactile*

Eye, 'These expressive, affective qualities of the film and the viewer's affective responses are, in fact, two sides of a single structure that exists in the space between film and viewer, which we discover by making ourselves vulnerable to the film' (2009: 148). I would argue further that this space of play, of a single structure between viewer and viewed, extends through cultural viewing practices as well as the dissemination of the narrative image of the film through paratextual means, such as those described in my example above (repeated viewing and so forth), and will be the subject of in-depth discussion in Chapter 2 (in relation to adaptation). The gradual fineness of cinema, then, is certainly in its emergence as a text, but also has grounding in the more general cultural encounters between viewer and viewed. This is how we tell our stories and how those stories are retold: in personal and cultural ripples of affect.

To summarise, the analysis of the material discussed in this chapter brings into focus a number of issues that are of immediate concern for this book. Namely, the dialectic of meaningfulness that is facilitated through such jostling moments of togetherness–apartness, the 'nourishment' of the film and the 'rippling' of affect through narrative themes and the viewing encounter is a complex issue that is not easily addressed in the space of a single chapter. The complexity of this issue is compounded through the revisionist attempts to both satisfy the demands of the studio financing the film (e.g. Columbia's insistence) and artistic adventures into re-imagining the journey of the main protagonist. What occurs as a direct result of these interventions on the 'original' theatrical release is the existence of two very different films; films that come about because of technological reshaping, and shifts that are discernible through cinephilic viewing practices that are themselves in turn facilitated through viewing technologies. Not directly determinist but nonetheless palpable shifts facilitated through moving-image technologies (on both production and consumption sides, in this case), the example of *Close Encounters* makes visible and palpable the more nuanced and subtle relationship between Hollywood and the mobilisation of technologies. Much of the remainder of this book seeks to address this issue and, in particular, those aspects of cinematic meaningfulness that engage the knowing pleasures of contemporary audio-visual consumption, the 'intrinsically nostalgic' aspects of popular cinema consumption that actively seek out such pleasurable spaces. Chapter 2 does this by engaging dimensions of these ripples of affect within the context of particular cinematic encounters with film adaptations, the franchising of transmedial narratives and the incremental changes produced in some of the more perennial concerns of film criticism – namely, narrative, characterisation and gender representation.

Notes

1 The version I use for this chapter is the 30th Anniversary Ultimate Edition DVD box-set. It contains three discs, each carrying a different version of the film. Included are the original theatrical version, the Special Edition and the Director's Cut. Although released on video in 1998, this edition was first made available on DVD in this form in

2007. As a secondary product, it therefore constitutes contemporary Hollywood output, with its tendencies towards revisionism and reliance on the financial returns of secondary products and sequels, and this box-set is notable for inclusion of historical product as well as production notes and special features interviews with Spielberg himself.

2 A theme to which I return to in some detail in Chapter 2.

3 A subject to which I return to in detail in Chapter 6.

4 Elements of this section are discussed briefly in my chapter 'Cinephilia; or, Looking For Meaningfulness in Encounters with Cinema' in Hauke, C. and L. Hockley (eds) (2010) *Jung and Film II: The Return*, Hove: Routledge. This reading was first outlined in a paper titled 'Being Together, Being Apart; Or, *Close Encounters* and the Bits between the Bits', presented at 'Screen', University of Glasgow, July 2009.

5 For further references to the kinds of discourses generated in academic engagement with *Close Encounters*, see Vivian Sobchack (1991), whose engagement with several similar genre movies of the latter New Hollywood period identifies a fascinating preoccupation with the shifting roles of fatherhood and masculinity. I return to this theme in the following chapter, to discuss aspects of shifting masculinity in the representation of cinematic time, change and duration. Of less concern are the recent, rather encyclopaedic accounts of Spielberg's work, which all include entries and/or commentary on *Close Encounters* to varying degrees: Warren Buckland 2006; Lester D. Friedman 2006; Andrew M. Gordon 2008; and Nigel Morris 2007. One should also, perhaps, add to these, Mark Bould's eloquent and brutally honest critique of all four accounts in his review essay 'Nothing Much to Phone Home About (with Exceptions): Four Books on Spielberg' (2008).

6 It is certainly worth noting here that the different kinds of value abstracted from special effects in film production and consumption have been the subject of commentary for quite some time now. I refer the reader to Herbert Schiller (1996) and his essay on the political economy of special effects in *Information Inequality: The Deepening Social Crisis in America*.

7 DVD has also been historically marketed on its increased fidelity capabilities, although it should be noted here that such fidelity is relative (Blu-Ray and HD are marketed using similar tropes) and philosophically dubious (the term 'fidelity' implies a fidelity to something, an original, the real, etc.). I open up this discussion of fidelity in relation to film adaptation in Chapter 2.

8 Incidentally, a related intervention in television studies content analysis has been put forward by James Walters in his essay 'Repeat Viewings: Television Analysis in the DVD Age', in Bennett and Brown (eds) (2008). Here, Walters emphasises the attention to detail that may be brought forth through repeat viewings of DVD material.

9 This is not to say that revisionism is exclusive to New Hollywood, nor indeed to Hollywood generally. My point here is rather more that the opportunities exist, through careful repeat viewing on newer portable formats and carrier media, to notice the revisions in films. Nor is this necessarily a technological determinist view: it suggests a technological pattern that owes much to existing cinephilic practices perhaps, as much as it determines or facilitates ways of viewing. An example of digital revisionism is given in my chapter 'Cinephilia; Or, Meaningfulness in the Encounter with Cinema' (2010). It discusses in detail how the character of Han Solo is fundamentally revised in the digital remaster of *Star Wars*. Further discussions of this alteration of character in the revision processes that accompany adaptation are included in Chapters 2 and 3.

10 For example, Jean-Luc Godard's *Two or Three Things I Know About Her* (*2 ou 3 choses que je sais d'elle*, Fr., 1967) includes a scene in which an alarmingly loud telephone rings for what seems like an interminable time, whilst nothing else happens in the scene. The presence of François Truffaut in *Close Encounters* enables a further

cultural link to the French New Wave. It should be noted, however, that many such references in this film are stylistic, rather than especially cultural or political, and this is consistent with the fairly widely known respect that Spielberg reserves for the New Wave filmmakers.

11 Of course, there is the possibility that the cans' disappearance was a continuity error or some other production mistake. I would, however, defend my particular analysis of the scene, because, even if a mistake, the cans *do* disappear, significantly altering the nuance of the scene, however slightly.

2

BUTTERFLY AFFECTS

Incremental narrative changes and compound representations in contemporary film and adaptation

The tortured genius and the celebrity recluse are two archetypes by which the popular imagination appears incurably enthralled. They occupy extreme but ambiguous positions in the social firmament, simultaneously familiar and unknowable, often winning our sympathy even as they fail our understanding. Working as Mephistophelean morality tales, they reassuringly remind us that exceptional talent can be an affliction as well as a gift and that sometimes the price of success is one that we – the average, the normal, the unchosen – would not wish to pay.

(Andrew Anthony, 'Bobby Fischer: From Prodigy to Pariah', *Observer*, May 2011)

The point is to ask why many people go to the cinema when they are not obliged to, how they manage to 'assimilate' the rules of this game which is exceedingly complex and historically fairly new, how they themselves become cogs of the institution. For anyone who asks this question, 'loving the cinema' and 'understanding film' are no more than two closely mingled aspects of one vast socio-psychical machinery.

(Christian Metz, 1986: 80)

In the previous chapter, I discussed aspects of cinematic meaningfulness that engage the knowing pleasures of contemporary audio-visual consumption through ripples of affect. These ripples occur, via the act of viewing (in the intersubjective relationship between viewer and viewed), in competing elements at the levels of audio-visual composition, narrative unfolding and extratextual engagement, and in cinematic apperception – a derivative of what Leibniz described as 'the immeasurable fineness of things'. What emerged through the close analysis of *Close Encounters of the Third Kind* was that apparent 'intrinsically nostalgic' aspects of popular cinema consumption actively seek out pleasurable spaces of encounter through the rippling of affect. Furthermore, these affective ripples seem to embody the very fabric of cinematic material that constitutes a proxemics of cinema, even occupying the spaces in-between the fine threads of this fabric – a dialectic of being together, being apart in the psychological and epistemic activity of viewer and viewed; an 'unfinished work' or open dialectic that is suspended and, psychologically speaking, warm.

This materiality presents to and for us, the viewer, a sense of meaningfulness that goes beyond specific meanings and certainly beyond the notion of specific on-screen content working alone to produce meaning. One aspect of this set of phenomena that was not discussed in detail, but ran as a parallel meta-argument throughout the chapter in relation to that specific case study, was the knock-on effect of such interplay between instances of affect at the various levels upon representations of identity and, in particular, masculinity's shifting place within domestic and familial life. Roy Neary, an 'everyman' character, is, even at the most superficial level of narrative, struggling with his competing roles as worker, father, husband and man-child/child-man.

If it seems a little far-fetched to make such conclusive statements about *Close Encounters* as a viewed narrative, it probably has something to do with the conflation of generic iconographies and possibilities associated with two quite distinct film genres that the film draws from: science fiction and family melodrama. These genres, Vivian Sobchack (1991) notes in her essay 'Child/Alien/Father: Patriarchal Crisis and Generic Exchange', are 'previously distinct sites' that have become congruent or contiguous in New Hollywood output. She states that:

> [t]he exotic, decadent and alien spatio-temporal fields of the horror and SF film have geographically conflated with the familiar and familial spatio-temporal field of the family melodrama. What was once a distinctly displaced 'There' has now been replaced 'Here' – and 'Then' and 'When' have been condensed as 'Now'. The time and place of horror and anxiety, wonder and hope, have been brought back into the American home.
>
> (1991: 5)

In this, Sobchack claims that *Close Encounters* provides the first context in latter New Hollywood in which the disenfranchised father is refigured as a 'starchild' innocent: a transcoding of 'American bourgeois culture's *lack of effectivity* into *child-like innocence*, and its *failed aggressivity* into a *transcendent victimization*' (1991: 15 [emphasis in original]). In *Close Encounters*, failed paternity is transcended through its conflation with child-like innocence and contempt for power and authority; a highly ambiguous and contradictory homology of powerful vulnerability.[1] 'Real' issues of disenfranchisement and disempowerment are thus negated through the film's dubious redemption narrative. The current and subsequent chapters seek to engage this particular characteristic of film narrative in more contemporary contexts, as it appears to be a crucial vehicle for political representation and recognition in contemporary popular cinema. Cinematic masculinity, particularly in its popular narrative forms, which extends such existential phenomena of togetherness–apartness through its ambiguous status, will be the main subject of Chapters 3 and 4. The current chapter will examine affective properties of the cinematic encounter as they ripple through the transmedial landscapes of contemporary popular culture, engaging the production of compound representations more generally (with some focus on gender representations) and the incremental changes that occur as a result of this transmedia storytelling.

To begin, it ought to be noted that the ripples of affect in the cinematic encounter not only characterise the in-between-ness of cinema but reveal an expansion of that psychologically warm space into the extratextual world of stardom, fandom and the different kinds of knowledge that accompany such identities and identifications. Therefore, we may say that the cinematic encounter involves the recognition of convention (in narratives, archetypes, the unfolding of narrative through time, change and causality). Chapter 3 will locate such aspects in the phenomena of representation and recognition in the contemporary text *The Wrestler* (Aaronofsky, US, 2008), whilst also recognising in Adam's Sandler's character Michael Newman in *Click* (Coraci, US, 2006) the means by which celebrity on-screen persona leaks out into the real world of affective interpersonal relations, and considers the related textual concerns of gender, performance and *mise-en-scène* as vehicles for the representation of transcendence in Sean Penn's *Into the Wild* (US, 2007). There are many ways to speculate on *The Wrestler*'s global box-office and critical success, and we might say that one of those speculative engagements would include the film's premise as a metacomeback movie as a powerful box-office draw. It seems to pull together such momentous forms of viewing and storytelling into focus as epistemic dimensions of cinematic time, change and causality. Of course, these notions of the metacomeback, in relation to the Mickey Rourke/Ram combination of character and actor (and importantly, Marisa Tomei's extraordinary performance as Pam/Cassidy), are not isolated, and we may identify similar phenomena in wider contexts of celebrity, narrative and meaningfulness.

In the above epigraph, for example, Andrew Anthony's recent remarks about Bobby Fischer, the elusive chess grand master, echo through celebrity culture and stretch through time to engage archetypical tropes of heroism and genius in public figures within all fields of public life, familiar tropes that tend to be generally admired and valued in Western societies. The Faustian or Mephistophelean trade-off – a unique attribute or combination of attributes that one possesses exacts a terrible toll in one way or another – is a familiar narrative that provides for us a segue from Christian morality into secular accounts of pathology and psychological disquiet. Indeed, as we shall see in my example of Stieg Larsson's Millennium Trilogy, the character of Lisbeth Salander is a powerful fictional example of the overdetermined archetypicality under discussion: an enthralling, tortured and reclusive character, whose exceptional gifts of eidetic memory, puzzle-solving genius and street smarts (including, crucially, a stunning dress sense) must be paid for elsewhere in her life. It seems particularly overdetermined in this case, in that

Lisbeth is diagnosed with several pathological conditions (by men in authority) and, quite apart from these assessments, at the very least appears to be somehow autistic, a bit like the popular myths about the *idiot savant* as trapped genius – a trope exploited to critical and popular success (and possibly ethical dubiousness) by *Rain Man* (Levinson, US, 1988) and *Shine* (Hicks, Aus., 1996). This condition of trade-off, emotional coldness and suffering is complicated through the motifs associated with ambiguous sexuality, violence, extreme misogyny (at the institutional and personal level) and revenge fantasy detailed throughout the Millennium narrative. Indeed, Larsson's damning critique of the regulation of women in society more broadly, and his attempts to reveal the violent nature of such regulation at all levels of culture and politics, may be summed up in the literal translation of the title of his first Millennium novel, *Män som hatar kvinnor*: 'Men who hate women'.[2] The mythological narratives of real *people* (celebrities and actors such as Rourke, Noomi Rapace and Rooney Mara), film *characters* (The Ram, Lisbeth Salander), and the way *the two are frequently elided* (The Ram/Rourke, Lisbeth/Rapace/Mara), is a powerful psychological base through which cinematic encounters provide for us as viewers a dialectical structure of proxemics: a being together, being apart. In this sense, celebrity is an instance of such dialectics where the suspension forms the psychosocial ground for mythologies to emerge.

So far, we have seen how this sense of being together, being apart in the intersubjective encounter operates through comparative repeated viewing (of revised cinematic texts), and, as we shall see in Chapter 3, it operates through the phenomenon of conventions of stardom, fandom and cinematic representation. Looking forward to Part II of this book, we will also see how these aspects of cinematic encounter engage masculinity both in representational ways and in ways that are metatextual: that is, the textual and extratextual material itself seems to both embody and interrogate gendered notions of the encounter, even as the texts themselves seem to communicate meaningful commentary upon the very notions of gender and public image. This may be so in relation to films like *The Wrestler* – a single-film example, and I will argue as much – but might we also think this through in a more general sense? Is *The Wrestler* an isolated case? Can we say anything about it concerning the unfolding of cinematic encounters across time and through migrating content more generally? And what, if anything, might we say about femininity in this scenario? Irresistibly, the language available to describe the rippling of affect seems to describe phenomena that, in other contexts, may be thought of as 'feminine' – all of the notions that I have pointed to have rounded, enveloping, soft characteristics traditionally associated with femininity: rippling, enfolding, pleats, warm psychology, anima and so forth.

We will see that these 'feminine' traits are eminently applicable to encounters with *The Wrestler*, its narrative, its stars and its engagements with spaces of extra-textual knowledge. That film, although on first appearances an isolated filmic object concerning a historical genre traditionally considered very 'masculine' (the wrestling picture, which it references more than emulates, perhaps), connects with and ripples out into a larger cinematic encounter in psychologically warm ways. But what happens when these aspects of the cinematic encounter are stretched across media forms considered very different in the popular imagination (a literary adaptation film), and across global industrial spaces (Hollywood remakes of the products of what might be described as national cinemas)? And what happens when these aspects are given determinedly 'feminine' narrative connections? Does this make a difference to the way affect ripples through time, change and causality?

Although industrial filmmaking may be argued to have always employed vertical and horizontal integration of one species or another, in the blockbuster age such phenomena are increasingly commonplace, and synergistic business practices in popular global cinema industries are *de rigueur* strategies for widening profit margins. There are some obvious reasons for this (profit, awards, recognition) as well as not so obvious reasons (articulated in Screen Theory notions of an ideologically produced cine-subject, for instance), both of which have been articulated time and again in film theory. It should be noted that there are some telling tendencies in orthodox film studies that allow us to engage the political economy of such strategies. As Peter Krämer (2005: 125) puts it:

> It is a truism that Hollywood is in the business of making money, and the trade press as well as much reporting about cinema in newspapers and film magazines, on television and the Internet pays close attention to the amounts of money films earn at the American box office as well as their chart rankings, and, to a lesser extent, to the costs of movie production and marketing and the profits or losses generated by a movie's release.

This is in sharp relief with much attention in film studies (particularly in the UK's *Movie* tradition rather more so than, perhaps, the *Screen* tradition) which often steers clear of such financial matters, instead concentrating on individual films and their textual concerns, perhaps catering towards cultural studies approaches to modes of representation or meaning-making. Budgetary matters are sometimes given over to discussion in light of production values, or production tasks and their associated costs (e.g. the role of product placement in financing the catering or vehicle logistics of a shoot). Some canonical film studies in the US deal with the mechanical economics of global and popular cinema[3] and, whilst useful, tend to only deal with individual instances of films that illustrate particular trends in industrial production, or at the box office. There are some important exceptions or complementary approaches to these (for example, Grainge 2008; Miller et al. 2005; McDonald and Wasko 2008). However, whilst I would argue that both of these tendencies are useful in the analysis of cinema, and indeed I draw upon both kinds of approach to film in the current study, the recognition that Krämer brings to the table that alternative approaches and methods for the study of film are being formulated for the needs of twenty-first-century film scholarship is a valuable one, especially in relation to the idea of a literary adaptation film and subsequent remediations and remakes.

Faithfulness, fidelity and adaptation; or, 'I've been had':
låt den rätte komma in

I have already mentioned the Millennium Trilogy, a series of novels written by Stieg Larsson, a Swedish novelist and radical journalist. Now widely reported in wiki sources, imdb.com and numerous fan sites, Larsson's posthumous literary output has ignited the imagination of audiences. It has also mobilised the film, TV, tourism and fashion industries' collective resources to turn Larsson's (arguably, radical, though at times highly problematic) literary feminist critique of the violent regulation of women through institutional, constitutional and political means into a multi-million-dollar synergistic phenomenon. One might argue that Larsson's novels, the subsequent adaptations of his work[4] and industrial tie-ins to this EU (cross-promotion through a capsule collection at Swedish fashion outlet H&M, the Millennium tour of Stockholm, to cite a couple of examples) are part of a freakishly successful one-off phenomenon. However, the recent rise in popularity of Swedish and other Scandinavian output in the UK (the Danish–Swedish co-production *The Killing*, BBC4 2011–2012, and *Borgen*, BBC4 2012), as well as UK co-productions set in Sweden (*Wallander* 2005–present, a Yellow Bird/Canal+ Swedish language co-production was remade as the Kenneth Branagh vehicle *Wallander*, BBC4 2008–2010), suggest that such success is part of a wider pattern of global interest in Swedish and Scandinavian narratives and their market potential, and in serialised literary (or televisual) adaptations more generally.

Indeed, the Swedish vampire novel *Let the Right One In* (John Ajvide Lindqvist, *Låt den rätte komma in*, 2004) was a successful adaptation into a Swedish-language film (Alfredson, 2008) and subsequent US remake (*Let Me In*, Reeves, 2010) but departed somewhat in generic terms from the above successes, which can all to some extent be recognised as crime thrillers or murder mysteries of one sort or another. What is interesting about the *Let the Right One In* phenomenon is that it seems to be something of an anomaly: according to Rochelle Wright (2010), both the novel and film versions of the story gained considerable critical and favourable attention because of the novelty of a Swedish vampire story. She writes that:

> In the English-speaking world, vampire narratives, both literary and cinematic, have long been a staple of popular culture. What accounts, then, for the particular success of this film, not least in an international context? One crucial factor [...] is that *Let the Right One In* seamlessly merges several apparently disparate genres to create a hybrid form that appeals to widely divergent audiences.
>
> (2010: 56)

It is worth noting here, of course, that in many contemporary national cinemas, films seem to merge several genres seamlessly – Sweden doesn't seem to be a special case in this regard, and it could well be that a part of its international appeal stems from the lack of distinction from other settings where harsh winters can set in, and emotional distance between a film's characters seems to reflect the cold climate. However, I would say that in this case it is the novelty of a Swedish vampire story (set in a specific time and place: Stockholm suburbs, 1981/1982, Arctic winter) in a culture that doesn't seem to have a particularly indigenous vampire mythology (although, as Wright acknowledges, Sweden is as captivated by Central European vampire mythology in general and vampire films in particular as is the English-speaking world) that produces the raw materials for word-of-mouth buzz and global syndication. If this weren't enough, *Let the Right One In* engages in a genre hybridity exercise that enables it to become novel in other, less location-specific ways that add to these marketable materials. As Wright continues:

> A detailed analysis of the film demonstrates how it simultaneously draws on and departs from common themes and motifs of indigenous Swedish film as well as vampire film tradition, combining elements of the horror film, the coming-of-age story and the realistic socio-psychological drama to create a unique mix of the innovative and the familiar.
>
> (2010: 56)

This generic hybridity has much in common with the always-already hybrid tendencies of the Hollywood blockbuster, as noted previously in the case of hybridised family melodrama and science fiction in New Hollywood, so there is little surprise in the story's suitability for adaptation in that context. Furthermore, the recently renewed global interest in vampire narratives, sparked by the *Twilight* franchise, as well as that of *True Blood* amongst others, provides further market context within which such adaptations can thrive.[5] Finally, if we take Wright's view that *Let the Right One In* is, at its core, optimistic, we can further elaborate that popular cinema's fascination with outsider status (from antihero vigilante, to the outlaw gangster and the western's lone gunman) seems a good fit for *Let the Right One In*'s core message: '[...] that outsider status can be counteracted through empathy and mutual support, a theme that is hardly typical of vampire films but resonates across genre boundaries and audience groups' (2010: 62). Indeed, she notes that a plethora of recent output in Swedish cinema reflects a concern for children and other vulnerable figures, and their questionable outsider status:

> The motif of the bullied, isolated or 'different' child or adolescent, while atypical of the vampire genre, is a commonplace in recent Swedish film, examined from varying perspectives in works such as *Fucking Åmål/ Show Me Love* (Moodysson, 1998), a lesbian coming-of-age/coming-out story; *Före stormen/Before the Storm* (Parsa, 2000), where seventh-grader Leo [...] is bullied at school; *Gitarrmongot/The Guitar Mongoloid* (Östlund, 2004), in which the titular character has Down's syndrome;

and *Ping-pongkingen/The King of Ping Pong* (Jonsson, 2008), which explores status and hierarchy among boys in their early teens.

(Wright 2010: 58)

Taken as a whole, this cycle of films, culminating in the *Let the Right One In* books and filmic adaptations, affords the necessary thematic (as well as, one might say, cultural and economic) conditions for current Swedish film products to carry through into transnational markets. Equally, these examples seem to resonate with certain hybridising tendencies already noted in Hollywood melodrama (see Sobchack, 1991) that might suggest transcultural taste for such narratives. The repeated motifs in Swedish literature and film of the child as bullied, isolated and different are not exclusive to Swedish film by any means, but find common ground in the character of Lisbeth Salander in the Millennium Trilogy, who embodies aspects of all three attributes. In flashback sequences, we witness a young Lisbeth in a revenge attack on her abusive father, as well as scenes in which she was incarcerated in a mental institution as a teenager. Most of the action takes place with Lisbeth as an adult, but there are a number of interesting points on characterisation to note here: she is notably physically quite small (4' 11") for an adult, and has a 'boyish' frame; she has the status of legally incompetent, similar in many ways to the legal status of a minor; and she is repeatedly treated as naive, which provides the context in which she proves herself to be capable and gifted. In this sense, then, we may see the Millenium Trilogy as both a critique of the treatment of women and also importantly as a critical allegory of the political, legal and moral status of children and other groups accorded diminished responsibility. Overdetermined and effectively multiplied through the savagery and relentlessness of her violent treatment at the hands of men and male-run authority throughout the trilogy, these motifs express through Lisbeth a radical potential for critique but, as I will argue, form the basis for thinking through shifting availability of problematics through the rippling of affective properties in adaptation across the Millennium story-world.

What needs to be noted at this point are a number of common philosophical errors in the discourse concerning adaptation, remakes, sequelisations and other kinds of transmedial repetition. Chief among these errors is the notion of originality of a source text and the faithfulness or 'fidelity' of subsequent material to that 'original'. This is important because it is frequently found in both popular and academic discourse on the subject, even though several specialist studies have been conducted in relation to the relative and cultural values of perceived 'originality' and 'fidelity'. A brief scan of such studies reveals the importance of the subject for contemporary film studies, particularly because of the sheer number of recent book-length studies and anthologies on the question of adaptation and fidelity.[6] As shall be discussed in depth, such studies acknowledge fidelity arguments as difficult to dislodge from popular discourse, even though such arguments are largely cosmetic and lend little to the understanding of meaningful engagements with the texts themselves. As an introduction to this problem, this may be addressed through noting an example of academic engagement with the Hollywood remake (*Let Me In*) of the aforementioned example (*Låt den rätte komma in*).

In their essay, 'Faithful to a Fault: Was it Really Necessary to Remake "Let the Right One In" in English?', Kevin Taylor Anderson and Salman Hameed note with some pleasure how the US remake *Let Me In* '[...] remained true to the style and content of the original film' (2010: para. 1). Immediately, this raises a number of familiar points. First, that faithfulness of adaptations or remakes is a pleasurable notion – that is to say, a matter of feeling in the evaluative sense, and in the sense of emotional attachment to the contents of a narrative world and any changes rendered through adaptation. Second, that the evaluation of such fidelity marks out a source text as an 'original', against which adaptations are measured. Third, that some of the criteria employed to measure fidelity are comparable styles and contents. Very often, of course, adaptations are valued according to this comparison, but a valid point that Anderson and Hameed make (one of very few in their review) is that if the style and content are a 'carbon-copy' of an 'original', then what is the point in remaking in the first place? This is where Anderson and Hameed's argument starts to falter: style and content are not the only means by which remakes are judged, and, indeed, fidelity to a perceived original is not necessarily the goal of a remake. It may be true, on one hand, that producers risk alienating a ready-made audience if their output discernibly departs from source material. However, on the other hand, the shifting contexts involved in adaptation will invariably affect the production choices available, as well as the material outcomes of such choices. So, the medium of adaptation, differing industrial systems of filmmaking and release in varied global territories, and cultural differences and difficulties in translating any culturally specific references are some of the elements that will impact upon style and content, as well as produce myriad other small textual and cultural differences that engender something of a 'butterfly affect' of recognition, pleasure and dissatisfaction in the reception of an adaptation. In addition, the authors note (2010: para. 2) that:

> If the remake was done simply to make more money, then one could have imagined the American filmmakers possibly selling out and sacrificing the bleak, contemplative tone of the Swedish version for either the teen romance of the Twilight films or the gorefest of remade foreign horror films. But admirably, the filmmakers resisted the temptation.

There are a number of things that may be said against this statement. First, the suggestion that remakes are done simply to make more money is probably not as true as one might at first speculate: the notion of US 'art film' carries with it certain kudos in terms of its perceived difference to 'mainstream' fare, and in cultural terms can serve as a way of bolstering a director's name against future projects which carry a much higher production budget and therefore a higher risk threshold. This has in recent years been played out in the commercial and critical popularity of the Sundance festival in particular and the resurgence of the US indie film more generally. In addition, the implication here of a conflation of generalised 'Americanisation' of film and a 'cheapening' effect where filmmakers seek out spaces where the money is, is highly problematic and is challenged through the notion (and practice) of American indie film.

Second, in relation to filmmakers' 'admirable' intentions, it is difficult to discern precise production intentions without both interviewing the filmmakers themselves and analysing comparable adaptations where production choices are clearly different or clearly similar. In this case, it seems that one of the intentions to remake *Let the Right One In* is firmly situated in the marketability of a cult text and the creation of a new cult text with secondary and tertiary market value.[7] In this context, it doesn't seem to matter that initial box-office takings were around a third of the production budget – as Michael Allen (2003) has pointed out, historically, Hollywood output has been repeatedly used to promote technical innovations (sometimes previously untested with audiences), and as several critics have pointed out (Klinger 2006; McDonald 2007; and numerous others in McDonald and Wasko 2008), secondary and tertiary markets are where real profit margins are expanded. Given the limited nature of 'cult' theatrical releases, and the numerous ways that 'cult' is built virally through carrier media and file sharing, it should come as little surprise to discover the poor box-office performance of *Let Me In*. On the contrary, a box-office success at this stage could have been detrimental to its cult status.

Third, whilst thinking through the idea of a perceived difference to the 'mainstream' (and, in their statement, Anderson and Hameed explicitly evoke the fannish notion of 'selling out'), it is useful to note the concept of distinction in sociology (e.g. Bourdieu 1984; De Certeau 1984, 1986) and in fan studies.[8] The ideas on distinction and fidelity that academic adaptation studies sets itself up to interrogate and critique are reproduced somewhat in Anderson and Hameed's account.

Finally, as the authors go on to write, the mentions of religion and evil are more explicit in the US remake and are basically the sum of changes from the Swedish version, but such changes amount to fairly 'minor' plot changes. One might argue that such changes are crucial to the representational make-up of the film, its perceived audience and desired reception. As we have seen in Chapter 1, what appear to be relatively minor changes in plot have the potential to transform the affective properties of the encounter with the narrative, as well as result in compound changes of characterisation and representational politics across an entire story arc. One such relatively minor change that Anderson and Hameed do not mention in their review, but which deserves mention here because of its close relation to this final point, is the representation of gender in the different instances of the story. In the Swedish film version, it is somewhat obvious (perhaps more so in the context of repeated viewing) that Eli (Lina Leandersson) is not a girl, as she first appears. Not only is she a vampire (a demonic being immeasurably older than she appears), but also she was a boy when she was human, before being changed into a vampire. As Wright observes, this is evident through a brief glimpse of genital scarring that bear the marks of castration. This is made more explicit in the novel version, where a flashback account of an obscure ritual turns a 12-year-old boy, Eli, into the vampire he becomes. This is further borne out in the Swedish title of the novel and film, *Låt den rätte komma in*, where *rätte* can only refer to a male (2010: 61). This may go some way to the justification of title change in the remake: a pre-emptive strategy to avoid such comparisons.

It may seem rather petty to berate Anderson and Hameed for adhering to the notion of fidelity, and likewise to note the minor (perhaps rather cosmetic) changes between versions of adaptation in this case, the implications of which may be obvious to fans or cinephiles, and relatively unimportant to a popular audience. However, my point isn't so much to critique these particular reviewers as to use this case to illuminate the ways in which discourse on adaptation, particularly in relation to faithfulness to a perceived original, is a highly contentious philosophical point that reveals the underlying psychological attachments and affective properties that cinematic encounters evoke.

Many theorists and commentators have addressed such philosophical quandaries on the notion of fidelity and the discourses such a notion arouses. I have noted a number of recent and contemporary interventions above, and I now give a brief outline of what I consider the most important for the current study: Frederic Jameson, whose careful outlining of philosophical problems associated with adaptation (2011) is illustrated through discussion of Stanislaw Lem's novel *Solaris* (1961) and the subsequent film adaptation (Tarkovsky, USSR, 1972).[9] He does not mention Steven Soderbergh's version (US, 2002), which is in some ways a shame, because the temptation here would be to think of Soderbergh remaking Tarkovsky (because these versions have in common their expressive medium – film), a notion complicated through the much more perceptible narrative relationship between the novel and each of the two films than that between the two films themselves. It opens up a complex dialectic in the qualitative peculiarities of medium-specific storytelling (to which I shall return momentarily) and other forms of 'likeness' and 'closeness' that are not beholden to notions of the media under question. Each instance of adaptation suggests its own fascination with the narrative material, regardless of chronology of production, or of medium. In other words, cinephiles may very well hold the two film versions in comparison, but they have just as much difference as they have in common; and both share common ground with Lem's source text, whilst adding innovations peculiar to their own instance.

In such circumstances, the issue of fidelity becomes something of an obstacle, rather than an illuminating critical device as it is usually framed in popular (and sometimes academic) discourse. In his two essay collections, *What Is Cinema?* (1967), André Bazin sought to illuminate (amongst other things) the role of fidelity in cinema adaptations. Then as now, literature-to-film adaptations were a frequent concern of cinema as an industry; then as now, very often the qualitative differences afforded each medium were regulated culturally according to a hierarchy of cultural value. This sometimes coincides with chronological publication (the novel often comes first, so it sets the standards by which film adaptations are measured: 'it's not as good/detailed/clever as the book') and very often coincides with a perceived seriousness of the novel as a storytelling form and the trivialisation of cinema as inferior (evaluative statements such as 'it leaves little to the imagination' and so on). This is a familiar evaluative trope in film cultures. As Whelehan suggests in her co-authored book *Adaptations: From Text to Screen, Screen to Text* (Cartmell and Whelehan 1999: 3):

> For many people the comparison of a novel and its film version results in an almost unconscious prioritizing of the fictional origin over the resulting film, and so the main purpose of comparison becomes the measurement of the success of the film in its capacity to realize what are held to be the core meanings and values of the originary text.

However, Bazin's concern, even as he recognised such evaluations (and in some ways did little to repudiate them, illustrating the comparative artistic and ontological possibilities of cinema, theatre, painting and literature), argued for a much more organic affiliation between source material and the undeniably powerful transpositional properties of cinema. Whereas 'Fidelity meant respect for the spirit of the novel', and this strategy tended to be the rule of thumb, this did not necessarily exclude the possibility that a film might embody a greater artistic achievement than its literary source material. For example, in volume 2 of *What Is Cinema?*, Bazin wrote of the film adaptations of Robert Bresson:

> Fidelity is here the temporal affinity between film-maker and novelist, a deeply sympathetic understanding. Instead of presenting itself as a substitute, the film is intended to take its place alongside the book – to make a pair with it, like twin stars.
>
> (1967b: 141)

Clearly, here, fidelity is a matter of closeness and of respectful observation of another form's material affordances and constraints, but does not partake of the faithfulness that is normally attributed to it in film cultures. Recently, Dudley Andrew (2010) has written on Bazin's approach to adaptation and fidelity, situating it in what he describes as a kind of postmodern applauding of the horizontal proliferation of texts (2010: 127). He goes on to write that:

> Taken as one cultural form growing not in isolation but amidst many others, cinema absorbs or grabs what it needs from its neighbours, often giving something back in an ecology of the 'life of forms'. Complexity increased when one recognizes that forms evolve at different rates [...]
>
> (2010: 130)

This ecological view of media forms relates closely to the origins of the term 'adaptation', in the biodiversity sense of evolutionary science: just as life forms adapt, so do cultural forms. They adapt 'because of' environmental concerns, whether industrial, political, economic and so forth, and adapt 'to' technological, artistic and other specific instances that provide the material affordances and constraints that enable certain production choices to be made and certain problematics to be raised. Instances of cultural form may also innovate in their particular fields and both recognise and push against conventional standards of form and flow and content. This ecology, therefore, represents an account (among the many offered through film studies, including Screen Theory, political economy and film-philosophy[10]) that contributes to an understanding of the success of films, and the various criteria employed in judging that success. Part of this evaluative process, of course, is connected with the way people feel 'about' a film. If the film is an adaptation, the cultural temptation always seems to judge the film according to the 'success' of the adaptation (its fidelity – whether fidelity as a notion is judged to be 'faithful' or perhaps in terms of another kind of 'likeness' or 'closeness' à la Bazin). Success is also commonly measured in terms of a perceived and felt inherent 'quality', and has its own associations with the notions of distinction and taste.

Adaptation, relative autonomy and connoisseurship in transmedial cinema

In her book *Beyond the Multiplex* (2006), Barbara Klinger notes that one of the key evaluative judgements between different screen media, in popular culture as well as in academia, tends to highlight perceived differences in quality. She writes:

> The big-screen performance is marked as authentic, as representing bona fide cinema. By contrast, video is characterized not only as inauthentic and ersatz but also as a regrettable triumph of convenience over art that disturbs the communion between viewer and film and interferes with judgments of quality.
>
> (2006: 2)

Whereas, perhaps, there are issues of medium-specificity that need to be addressed in terms of transmedial storytelling, issues to which qualitative differences between different media forms remain important, Klinger's recognition of the widespread use of secondary media as a cinematic form is crucial in the contemporary mediascape. Her championing of home exhibition is important for a number of reasons (to which I devote detailed discussion in Chapters 5 and 6), but here specifically for the reason that adaptation from one medium to the next is not a simple daisy-chain of translation and copying. Certainly, in relation to these aspects of value-laden judgements that Klinger identifies, we may add that each operation of adaptation of a media property (whether pre-planned in a high-concept fashion or licensed to specialist media producers for adaptation) is an additive process as well as a multiplying one. If there are qualitative differences between specific media forms, and if the processes within specific media operations (publishing, TV production, local film production, Hollywood) produce availability of some choices whilst providing material constraints upon others, then we might say that questions of 'fidelity' are most visible in the popular imagination through the operations of industrial media production.

Where there are multiple texts to consider (the popular practice of producing literary and film trilogies), and additive tendencies in the synergistic practice of media production (televisual spin-offs, as well as their opposite number, the relatively rare television-to-film adaptation or transfer), there are somewhat obvious questions related to the discourses of fidelity. Such is the case with the two Swedish literary adaptations referred to above.

Methodological problems soon emerge when tackling such hugely successful media properties, as such expansive story-worlds (particularly within the realms of fan cultures) carry with them concomitant experience designs (partly drawn from media and business convergences, partly drawn from the activities of fans themselves). The first questions might be framed as follows: what is being analysed and how does one go about analysing it? The 'what' question in these cases would be differences between one version and another. This presents a problem that relates to the 'method' question: differences in adaptation invariably enter debates on fidelity, faithfulness and origin.

The cinephilic tendency perhaps most readily affiliated with fandom in relation to the reception of adaptation is the tendency to 'spot the difference' between versions of texts within a transmedial story-world. Whereas this tendency may be exploited to great effect when it comes to close textual analysis (indeed, Chapter 1's analysis of the different versions of *Close Encounters of the Third Kind* bears this out somewhat), I believe that merely cataloguing and listing the many differences between the various texts under question (which, in an exhaustive attempt, would take up most of the current chapter and reveal little concerning the rippling of affect through promulgation of media property in transmedial and convergent forms) would be problematic. It would both reproduce to a certain extent the fidelity issue that is supposedly under critique, and furthermore display the descriptive tendencies of fannish discourses of distinction and authenticity that operate in the cultural life of both fans and the texts they know and use. By themselves, both are examples of the problematics of cinema that contribute little to the understanding of the intersubjective being together, being apart-ness of the cinematic encounter.

In fact, one of the key places that prompted me to take a more detailed look at the above two cases (*Let the Right One In* and the Millennium Trilogy) was the detailed fan study of *Star Wars* cultures conducted by Will Brooker over the course of several publications (1997, 1999, 2002, 2009). In his book-length study, *Using the Force*, for example, he argued that:

On one level, *Star Wars* does not belong solely to Lucas anymore; its characters and stories have escaped the original text and grown up with the fans, who have developed their own very firm ideas of what *Star Wars* is and is not about.

(2002: 77)

Brooker's statement displays a way of understanding cinema and its connections with other aspects of popular culture that, whilst not necessarily a 'new' way of understanding, does illustrate the lengths to which fans are prepared to go in order that the ownership of a media property be appropriated and 'felt' by the fans themselves. At the same time, copyright and international intellectual property law places legal ownership of such properties firmly in the hands of corporate copyright holders. This contradiction presents film scholarship with a number of problems; two specifically are of immediate concern here – problems that are again nothing particularly new, but have taken on a different shade in recent years and are a matter of urgency for film theorists. First, the contradiction itself spells out the unresolved theoretical issue of relative autonomy in Althusserian film theory. The second problem related to this is that of commodity-identity, to which I shall return momentarily. It is not the task of this study to retread the old problem of relative autonomy specifically, but it is worth flagging up some of the key components of this problem, including some of the reasons for its disappearance from the theoretical map, in order to set up the second problem of commodity-identity, particularly in relation to the notion of an 'invested' viewing.

The Althusserian approach to cinema as a structuring system of signification formed the principal theoretical framework to address what Treddell (2002) describes as the approach to meaning as an 'oppressive relation' between audience and text. For Althusserian film theory, the cine-subject is a function of cinema as a signifying system, but cine-subjectivity (as with all subjectivity) is most often felt as coherently autonomous. The 'subjective' is therefore a sensation of autonomy framed within a relativity that addresses ('interpellates') the individual in a capitalist ideological position, within a system of production that is determined by economics in the last instance. Even though Althusser states that the economic is the 'last instance', which under capitalist relations of production is typical, nevertheless the experience within the social formation of this determination is never quite resolved (1977: 113). It is an internal contradiction which, for Althusser, negotiates the problem of economism but, for his detractors, becomes a problem of agency: the relation between economic base and cultural superstructure either collapses into economic determinism or allows for a full autonomy. One particular question seemed to be crucial for 1970s film theory and led to debates on the relevance of Athusserian structuralism: Althusser evaded the question of the hierarchy of instances – that social and cultural movements were, in the last instance, ultimately determined by the economic relations of production – rather than answered it. This is why, for example, influential critics of the

Wisconsin School such as Bordwell et al. (1985) abandoned the idea of relative autonomy in spectatorial relations as inherently unstable.

Writing at the end of the 1970s from a neo-Marxist perspective, Paul Hirst, in *On Law and Ideology*, was even more damning of Althusser's notion of interpellation. Lapsley and Westlake usefully summarise Hirst's argument as follows:

> If ideology functions by constituting individuals as subjects through interpellation, which involves misrecognition, then it can only do so by virtue of there being a pre-existing subject who can misrecognise him or herself. In short, the notion of interpellation assumes what it aims to explain.
>
> (1988: 14)

This was to prove the most far-reaching criticism of Althusser's approach within the discourse of film theory. Althusser had attempted to eliminate the humanist notion of the autonomy of the subject as an intending, discerning individual, by suggesting that the subject's beliefs, intentions and so on are the effects – not causes – of social practices. In these effects, however, are certain attributes of agency that allow for individual instances of understanding, evaluation and interpretation. The desires and pleasures frequently experienced through historical examples and within subjective reactions to filmic representation testify to this very contradiction. Although some theorists addressed these aspects of internal contradiction and struggle, 'those taking up Althusser's conception of ideology within film theory were slow to appreciate these aspects of his work, a failure that resulted in fatal flaws in early attempts to theorise the relation of the spectator to film' (Lapsley and Westlake 1988: 15). The text itself was not the univocal determination of spectator response, as this response inevitably drew from other forces within the social formation, alongside the misrecognition process informed by the effect of subjectivity.

The second, related question of 'felt' ownership in film culture is not merely a question of legality or, for that matter, even morality, but one of empowerment through commodity-identity and cultural meaningfulness. It is therefore, in a sense not so far removed from the Althusserian problem of relative autonomy, in that it is ideological in its reproduction of commodity relations between producer and consumer, in the construction of a felt sense of subjectivity and consumer agency; and ultimately, one could argue, in that this felt sense of agency is the appearance-form of empowered consumption 'misrecognised' as emancipation through consumer choice and 'invested' viewing. The cultural appropriation of textual signifiers, narrative tropes and expanded universes of popular and cult media properties has meant that fandom in particular has taken a potent place in the market share of cinematic consumption. This is important when one considers the integration of textual, market and intertextual presence of a film's narrative. The unresolved problem of relative autonomy has, as I will argue, left a residue in both the heart of the movie business, in its production processes and market research, its franchises and their audiences, and on its peripheries, in the various encounters and spaces of film culture that lie on the margins of business and are staged in the homes and technologies of consumers.

Related to this, Michele Pierson's work (1999a, 2002) usefully centres on the specialised knowledge afforded the connoisseur or 'buff', and she suggests that the desire of the buff to cultivate technical knowledge about the way cinematic spectacle is produced is a desire to break from the rather old-fashioned institutional (and academic) convention of the cinematic spectator as passive consumer and to engage fully with the acts, viewing, collecting and retelling as living and lived experiences. This helps the film theorist to rethink rather outdated models of viewing and meaning-making, fixed temporally and spatially in the movie theatre and during the film screening.

Barbara Klinger (2006), for example, synthesises a number of relevant methodologies to consider the phenomenon of film reception in its afterlife in secondary markets. Klinger's approach is essentially a reception study, but she also takes in political economy, audience research, textual analysis and cultural theory in order to fully ground the place of viewing acts in contemporary, technologised domestic settings and engage the discourses of film culture as lived, cine-literate practices. She states that:

> Although the dynamics of household viewing may not replicate the psychic parameters of spectatorship in the motion picture theater, certain home film cultures suggest that passion for the cinema is not anomalous within domestic space. [...] The home has been equipped and acculturated to produce its own kind of connoisseurship, its own brand of fascinations.
>
> (2006: 55)

Another such theoretical approach, that of Vivian Sobchack (1992, 2004) and others (e.g. Barker 2009; Marks 2000), considers the phenomenological implications of the relationship between viewer and viewed in the act of film-viewing. However, to put this into the context of a cine-literate viewing-and-telling practice, it would be useful to recall the above epigraph written by Christian Metz and his account of cinephilic levels of cine-engagement in even the most casual of viewing practices.

Indeed, what Metz is alluding to here is the manner in which viewing habits are instituted as part of the cinematic apparatus, and that, depending on one's interpretation of this institution, spectators are inculcated into a fixed ideological position of which they have limited awareness, if any at all; and that this instituting phenomenon is brought about at least partly through the formal aspects of (especially narrative) film, together with the psychical apparatus of spectators and the viewing contexts within which that spectatorship occurs. Of course, this approach is perhaps not as sustainable as it was once viewed in the orthodoxy of film theory. The break from the convention of passivity in film culture that Pierson implies may be found in the desire of even the most casual viewing audiences to demand of their film-related products the extratextual elements with which they may interact and which the technological developments of domestic cinema demand. For example, as Klinger (2006: 61) points out regarding the DVD:

> DVD extras and a sense of a DVD aesthetic have already become a prime feature of film culture. This is especially visible in the case of younger generations of viewers attracted to both blockbusters and technology and for newspaper and magazine columnists covering home releases who routinely refer to certain films (particularly those heavy on special effects) as 'perfect' DVD movies.

Thus, Pierson's film buff breaks from the convention of passivity in the age of DVD and beyond, and this desire is articulated in the shared practices and expertise of a highly cine-literate popular film culture, whose characteristics refit the idea of cinephilia as an ongoing, psychologically and culturally 'warm' process, in addition to being highly conversant with technological developments. This is, importantly, a sense of propriety that is felt by the consumer though not perhaps, as Cubitt (1991) and Wasko (1994) have written, under conditions of their own choosing.

This has been a subject touched upon in film studies by several recent book-length works. For example, Carolyn Jess-Cooke (2009) discusses the impact of corporate diversification upon the cultural reception of film sequels. She writes that:

> Choice is always carefully controlled and defined by distinct boundaries. The main method by which choice is controlled lies in the repetitious circularity of narrative 'worlds', which circulate and recycle a narrative across multiple plot possibilities, characters/avatars, intertexts and discourses.
>
> (2009: 86)

However, it is Pierson who also points to the articulation of ideology in this choice-desire, by returning to Adorno and his concept of 'culture industry': 'He also saw in this desire the work of ideology, which simply functions to reproduce more appreciative consumers without bringing them any closer to having "even the slightest influence" on the production process' (2002: 8). There are a couple of facets of Adorno's position (a position that Pierson does not necessarily subscribe to, incidentally) that should be noted here. The most important of these for this study, perhaps, is the assumption that consumers have any desire or intention to have an influence on production in the first place. This is not as straightforward as it first appears, first because specific fannish and cultish pleasures are sometimes associated with passive appreciation, and second because the interaction that participation culture involves provides its own pleasures that may (or may not) affect primary production, and that participation's appearance-form suggests that effectiveness upon primary production is not a criterion of importance in fan cultures. In terms of commodity-identity, it seems that the important element is in the discursive 'taking part' in Jess-Cooke's 'repetitious circularity of narrative "worlds"': in the *participation* itself.

The remainder of this chapter will discuss the reinforcement of commodity-identity through such participatory forms of cult production and fan interaction as meaningful encounters, with specific focus on the compound representation of Lisbeth Salander in the Larsson Millennium Trilogy. This will be achieved in a number of ways: through a discussion of the notion of remediation; through an account of the way the remake forms part of a remediated textual instance of adaptation; and by looking at ways in which, as Eco (1998) states, 'archetypicality' in narration generates audience interest and creates cult objects for cult audiences in repetitive textual circularity and incremental changes in narrative over time.

Remakes, remasters and remediations

Bolter and Grusin's conceptual framework of remediation (1999) is of particular use in understanding the reformatting of cinematic textual material in the ways people encounter films at an everyday level. This may take a number of forms, but fundamentally may be understood in two ways: platform and textuality. It is worth pointing out that this kind of distinction between technological and textual production is only made to engage the interplay between levels of production and consumption that do not match up tidily, nor can be separated in any neat taxonomy of viewership. To say that films are remediated objects is to say that, in the first instance, film texts are consumed through other media forms and that, in the second, other media texts come to resemble specific filmic texts and employ cinematic aesthetics in fundamental ways that have been the subject of some discussion so far.

There are aspects of remediation and its relation to medium-specificity and audience reception that are foregrounded in discussions of film remakes. Jess-Cooke, for example, states that 'It is impossible and generally nonsensical to separate film production and consumption from the systems of convergence and electronic media that have consistently re-imagined the role of the consumer' (2009: 75). Indeed, this is not a new phenomenon by any means. According to Sven Lütticken, the practice of remakes is as old as industrial film itself, and this assertion is supported by the well-documented remakes of the Lumières' *Workers Leaving a Factory* (1894–1895). In fact, the film industry's appropriation of such models indicates a borrowing from literary and newspaper serialisations, suggesting a prehistory of cinematic remediation. For Lütticken, familiarity with formulae is a key feature of the market life of the remake. He writes that:

> Of course, the repetitions and returns of mass culture clearly entail a
> *Lustgewinn* [pleasure] for the viewer: although similarity must be

alleviated by variation, enjoyment comes at least as much from the reproduction of what is familiar as from its modulation by what is new.

(2004)

The cult of repetition, then, appears to be a key feature of popular cinema entertainment, as well as the more 'specialised' arena of fandom.

Constantine Verevis has written at length on the remake (1997, 2004, 2006), summarising the recognition at work in the cult of repetition in film culture (seeing the remake as both an industrial and critical genre) as being 'extratextual' in nature. He writes that the intertextual referentiality between a remake and the 'original' is located 'in historically specific technologies and institutional practices such as copyright law and authorship, canon formation and film literacy' (1997). The problem in thinking this through in terms of the way audiences engage with and use canonicity as a standard of reference is in the assumption that canon is in some way a 'fixed' phenomenon and not a warm, living psycho-cultural process. Yes, it is true that *Star Wars* fans, for example, see themselves as the faithful guardians of a massively complex, expanded narrative universe.[11] However, this does not mean that agreement on what constitutes canonicity and what constitutes originality or authenticity within the *Star Wars* universe is a matter of straightforward consensus. This is especially fraught when it comes to (even the proposition of) film remakes of beloved films. As Verevis states:

> In addition to problems of canonicity [...] textual accounts of remaking risk essentialism, in many instances privileging the 'original' over the remake or measuring the success of the remake according to its ability to realise what are taken to be the essential elements of a source text – the property – from which both the original and its remake are derived.
>
> (2004: 87)

Verevis suggests that remakes are textual structures but that film remaking also depends on the existence of an audience and audience activity (whether popular, cult, fan, or an admixture of these). Prior knowledge of the narrative world, and its intertextual relationships with broader categories of film culture, plays its crucial part in the cultural life of a film and any remakes it subsequently spawns. However, remakes are, for Verevis, additionally enabled (and limited) by institutional factors 'such as copyright law, canon formation, and film reviewing which are essential to the existence and maintenance – to the "discursivisation" – of the film remake' (2004: 87). The act of remaking films, then, is a somewhat secondary result of broader discourses on the political levels of what constitutes a remake, and how this is decided through time.

Broadly speaking, and in a similar vein to King's untidily layered categorisations of New Hollywood innovation (2002) and Jenkins' studies on media convergence (2006a), Verevis deals with the phenomenon of film remakes as three overlapping categorical types: *remaking as industrial category*, dealing with issues of production, including industry (commerce) and authors (intention); *remaking as textual category*, considering texts (plots and structures) and taxonomies; and, last, *remaking as critical category*, dealing with issues of reception, including audiences (recognition) and institutions (discourse).

In terms of remaking as industrial category, remakes are often seen thus: 'instantly recognisable properties, remakes (along with sequels and series) satisfy the requirement that Hollywood deliver reliability (repetition) and novelty (innovation) in the same production package' (Verevis 2004: 88). Tino Balio (1993) has also noted this tension between repetition and innovation, identifying it in the Hollywood output of the Depression era. In acquiring sources for remakes, two contradictory goals are often highlighted. First, by basing films on pretested material, producers create new material considered low-risk: already well known and well received by the public. Second, if producers acquire properties as inexpensively as possible, especially during declining or uncertain economic circumstances such as in the Depression era or the current recession, initial outlay is kept to a minimum before any 're-imagining' through potentially expensive special effects and marketing campaigns that necessitate budget expansion (1993: 99). The role that credits and promotions play in the identification of remakes, with high-profile titles sometimes remade to take advantage of new technologies and practices, or to exploit new stars or commercial tie-ins, is a long-established practice in Hollywood. By reworking pretested material, producers inevitably cut costs at the front end in order that this investment may be deployed in post-production and in the circulation of the narrative image of a film.

There is a tendency in textual academic approaches (as well as those taxonomic practices found in fandom) to confine film remakes, as with the more encompassing notion of genre, to a corpus of texts or relationships between intertextual archetypes, revealing a tension between what Rick Altman describes as 'sharable terms' and 'accurate designation' (1999: 87). This enables a canonical shorthand that producers, critics and audiences alike mobilise in their general categorisations of film; to write and speak in a consensual language on an agreed area for discussion. At the same time, more specific taxonomies relating to the intertextual relationships between an 'original' and 'its' remake help to create a sense of ownership and meaningfulness in a film and its extratextual discourses, its narrative image, in its reception.

This sense of collective ownership and participation has been further enabled through the technological changes that have occurred in recent years and that have slowly transformed the home-viewing experience, complicating the differences and similarities between definitions of 'cult' and 'popular' in the process. The manner in which massively popular films such as *Star Wars*, for example, have taken on the resonance of cult objects is significant because it reflects upon the *kind* of films that are now being made in Hollywood. It is worth quoting the semiotician Umberto Eco at length on this, as his words testify to the changes that have taken place since the time of his writing, in 1984:

I think that in order to transform a work into a cult object one must be able to break, dislocate, unhinge it so that one can remember only parts of it, irrespective of their original relationship with the whole. In the case of a book one can unhinge it, so to speak, physically, reducing it to a series of excerpts. A movie, on the contrary, must be already ramshackle, rickety, unhinged in itself. A perfect movie, since it cannot be reread every time we want, from the point we choose, as happens with a book, remains in our memory as a whole, in the form of a central idea or emotion.

(1998: 198)

This is a situation that has arguably changed in recent years, thanks largely to the capabilities of time-shifting devices, carrier media such as videotape and DVD, and streaming thanks in part to fast broadband provision. It is now possible to take a non-linear view of a film as consumers have done with books in the past, and such interactivity facilitates the cinephilic view of repeated viewing, pausing for detail, and the special features that help suture the film text into the extratextual cultural activities associated with fans, cinephiles and casual viewers alike, in terms of retelling their encounters with the film. As Eco suggests:

It [a cult film] must display certain textual features, in the sense that, outside the conscious control of its creators, it becomes a sort of textual syllabus, a living example of living textuality. Its addressee must suspect it is not true that works are created by their authors.

(1998: 199)

Thus, fannish appropriations of objects and their ownership of them exist beyond authorial propriety, and what audiences do with texts beyond watching and reading them is to express that sense of ownership in a meaningful, shared way. Testament to this is the clip culture of YouTube and aggregate content sites which feature re-appropriated and repurposed content, often created by fans independent of the source producers. Indeed, if Eco is to be allowed it, this expressive cultural phenomenon had, to an extent, already become the norm in postmodern film culture, by the end of the last century. In cases of intertextual archetypicality, 'we witness an instance of metacult, or of cult about cult – a Cult Culture' (1998: 210).

Cinephilia, the cult of repetition and
The Girl with the Dragon Tattoo

To summarise, the cult of repetition appears to be a key feature of popular cinema entertainment, particularly in its blockbuster franchise versions. As well as operating at the production–industrial end of the viewer–viewed spectrum, the cult of repetition operates as a 'specialised' arena of fandom that partakes of broader discourses on the political levels of what constitutes the 'authenticity' of a remake, and how this is decided through an extended duration of consumption. This includes, crucially, a tertiary level of production produced by fans themselves that has an appearance-form of autonomous meaning-making in fan and audience communities. Here, I am addressing elements of blogging and online reviews, spoofs and parodies of popular cinema properties (e.g. the extremely popular 'Potter Puppet Pals' on YouTube), fanfic and slash fiction.

To bring this back to the primary viewing level (i.e. the film texts and close analysis) I would like to return to the example of the character of Lisbeth Salander from the Millennium Trilogy. In particular, an instance of cinephilia that struck me (in both watching the two film versions of *The Girl with the Dragon Tattoo* and reading excerpts of the novel for the purposes of comparison) was the amount of attention placed upon Salander's appearance in general (which I have already mentioned) and, in particular, upon her clothing and hairstyles. It has been mentioned on a number of occasions in the literature on cinephilia that the focus on hair, clothing and a character's style are all prominent *punctum* points of the viewing experience – for example, Roland Barthes on the 'admirable face-object' of Garbo (1993: 56); Béla Balász on the 'lyrical charm of the close-up' (1999: 305–11); James Naramore on the colour of Cary Grant's socks in Hitchcock's famous *North by Northwest* crop-dusting scene (1988: 215).

It is no accident that producers of the US remake of ... *Dragon Tattoo* 'teamed-up' with clothing chain H&M and costume designer Trish Summerville (who worked on the film) to initiate a capsule collection based on the clothes worn by Rooney Mara in the films themselves. This kind of synergy, typical of the kind of high-concept strategies already discussed, feeds back into the dialectic of proxemics at the heart of such making and viewing. Again, there is a being-together, being-apartness at work. Viewers have the opportunity, through extra-textual consumption practices, to emulate the styles of Lisbeth Salander to the finest detail, but also partake in the emulation process that only ever simulates the approximation through replicas (Mara kept all of the costumes she wore for the film). Once more, I ought to emphasise the importance that approximation plays here: much as fans do not generally give much attention to wanting to affect production *per se*, the emulation of a screen hero is pleasurable in itself – a likeness and closeness very much attuned to processes of adaptation itself. Thus the mythology of Lisbeth Salander/Noomi Rapace/Rooney Mara is kept intact for the pleasure of the fans themselves.

A subtle but important difference between the Swedish and US versions of the first film in the trilogy, and admittedly one that is as much a wholly subjective point as it is a critically engaged one, is the difference in emphasis on hair. Ostensibly more *dressed* and 'costume-y', the Salander style in the US version feels much more exaggerated than that presented in the novel and in the Swedish film. The most notable element of this is the frequency with which Rooney Mara's hairstyle changes from scene to scene. It is pronounced, like a visible *trucage* in precisely the sense Metz (1977) described it: a trick or special effect that, in Barthes' language, acts as a *punctum* for the invested viewer. The two narrative points where this occurs to the same extent in the Rapace instance happen when Salander goes into hiding (she disguises herself by wearing a blonde wig and dressing in WAG-fashion) and when she appears in court for her final legal showdown with Teleborian (Anders Ahlbom) at the close of the trilogy. For Mara, this happens in many scene transitions throughout ... *Dragon Tattoo*, to the extent that one is encouraged to speculate on the affective outcomes of such production choices.

This fixation on hair, although not reducible to any single reason or outcome, is nevertheless interesting because of its deliberate, spectacular nature. Perhaps the most immediate thought that springs to mind here is the focus of classical Freudian interpretation on hair, particularly regarding its fetishisation in relation to castration anxiety. Perhaps at some level, one can see how the production design has co-opted many of these well-known fantasies which, nonetheless, symbolically might hold the key to expressions of deep impulses about power and hierarchical roles in both social structures and intimate relationships. Lisbeth's hair may be read in this light, as a way of at least supplementing this inequality, particularly in the rather aggressive way the narrative exaggerates gender politics.

I think that, as well as this powerful idea of potency and loss, the brazen gesture of repetitive hair alteration allows us as viewers to engage Salander's (and Mara's) hair on a symbolic, archetypical level: it is synoptic on the revealing nature of cinema as a viewed-view (the camera's seeming obsession with Mara's physical attributes) and as perception-expression (that we view the human body, normal and abnormal, with the greatest of interest, but with seemingly little effort). I return to this notion of interest and effort in attentive viewing in Chapter 5, but here I mention it to illustrate the irresistible foreclosure of looking and gazing encouraged through this regime of attention. Salander's sexuality, expressed throughout numerous choreographed sex scenes, explored in her perceptible bisexuality, and problematised through an extant androgyny, is given particular symbolic expression through this fetish of hair. Fetish, in this instance, need not partake of the Freudian sense (but may do, particularly in relation to the gaze, I admit here), but is even more akin to the Marxian sense of value, or the animist sense of magical attribute. It evokes meaningfulness, even as it slips through specific meanings and efforts to interpret fully. In addition, and more importantly perhaps, the *oddness* of Lisbeth Salander is given a frequent pronunciation through what appears through production design and style as (almost) direct address to the audience: 'look at this (my hair)'. She is tragic, cool in a nerdy way, seductive in her accomplished gifts of analysis and determination despite all that men in authority have thrown at her during the course of her life.

This organic, ecological view of media adaptations and remaking processes, and the affective ripples that result from such relationships, may be thought of as fundamental to the end results of the viewing–viewed dialectical encounter. In this chapter, I have explored some of these relationships, in the light of recent literature on the subject of adaptation and as a revision of (the somewhat unfinished business of) classical Althusserian takes on the relative autonomy of cine-subjectivity.

What results from such an exploration is the groundwork for rethinking incremental changes in narrative across media forms, and in migrations of content from screen to screen, platform to platform, in the formation of a new cinematic theory of the feeling of having – in other words, a theory of cinematic apprehension. What follows is a chapter that extends this discussion, elaborating the flirtation with compound representations and gender politics found in the current chapter with reference to the existential and affective elements of cinephilia, anima(tion) and transcendence in examples from popular indie cinema.

Notes

1 In private correspondence, Luke Hockley noted that, far from being confined to New Hollywood, this type of imagery concerning failed paternity and both its conflation and conflict with child-like innocence, corruption and power is fairly common in classical mythology. It is certainly an undercurrent running throughout this chapter in contemporary popular cinema and I am tempted to think that several key writers, including Bettelheim in his seminal work *Uses of Enchantment* (1976), point to the similar roles of emotional pain of fatherhood (as well as the occasional impotency to act) in fairy tales and myths. In addition, Andrew Samuels' work on the psychological aspects of the father (*The Plural Psyche*, 1989) addresses many of these key themes from a post-Jungian perspective. Although the thrust of my argument here is to emphasise the frustrations of fatherhood and masculinity in late capital, there are probably a number of related psychological images that I will discuss which provide thematic motifs reproduced through several quite distinct contexts and manifestations. I follow up on this in Chapter 3.
2 Several sources on a simple Google search reveal that it was Larsson's intention to bracket the entire series under that title. Whether true or not, the fact that this notion is so prevalent in popular film cultures says as much about the mythologies surrounding the phenomenon as it does the 'facts'.
3 The classic example would be Bordwell, Staiger and Thompson's lengthy discussion of a particular historical cinema, *The Classical Hollywood Cinema: Film Style and Mode of Production to 1960* (1985), and the many responses to that book which take in phenomena typical of the 'post-classical' and New Hollywood periods, including King (2000, 2002) and Miller et al. (2005).
4 The Expanded Universe – in fandom terms, its EU – through television, cinema, mobile apps, the graphic novel series currently being developed by DC Comics under their Vertigo imprint, and fan fiction.
5 It is worth noting, following Wright, two important Swedish precedents that provide culturally specific context – recent productions in an otherwise relative dearth of vampire narratives in Swedish cinema: *Frostbiten* (Banke, Swe./Rus., 2006) and *Not Like Others* (*Vampyrer*, Pontikis, Swe., 2008). Importantly, however, these films share common ground with vampire narratives that clearly have teenagers as their target audience, whereas *Let the Right One In* (although conceivably a hit with teenagers nonetheless) does not necessarily cater to a teen market specifically. Wright notes that this is evident in its high production values which contrast with these other examples, which presumably operate through an impact aesthetic of some kind – Wright is uncharacteristically non-specific on this point.
6 For example, Albrecht-Crane and Cutchins 2010; Andrew 2011; Aragay 2005; Cartmell and Whelehan 1999; Constantinides 2010; DeBona 2010; Hutcheon 2006; Leitch 2009; MacCabe et al. 2011; McFarlane 1996; and Naramore 2000. Also, two highly

regarded peer-reviewed journals dedicated to the subject: *Adaptation* and the *Journal of Adaptation in Film and Performance*.

7 I outline a detailed account of the separation of imagined popular and cult audiences, and the textual tendencies accompanying both, in my essay 'Cinephilia; or, Looking for Meaningfulness in Encounters with Cinema', in Hauke and Hockley (2011).

8 Dylan Clark is particularly illuminating in this regard, and he is worth quoting in full. Although talking about punk subcultures, his notion of subcultural self-perceptions of distinction from imagined hegemonic centres is useful for unpacking the everyday evocation of the 'mainstream'. In a footnote (2003: note 3), he writes:

> 'Mainstream' is used to denote an imaginary hegemonic center of corporatized culture. It is used here as it is used by many people in dissident subcultures: to denote hegemonic culture. It is, in this sense, an archetype, rather than something with a precise location and character. It serves to conveniently outline a dominant culture for purposes of cultural critique and identity formation.

9 In his essay, Jameson also notes the thematic and textual importance of doubling in *Solaris*. I pick up on this again in the Introduction to Part II of this book, where I return to themes of doubling and embodiment in relation to intersubjectivity and psychological proxemics of cinema, as well as to the uncanny nature of simulacra as emphatic embodiments of technological cinematic encounters. Indeed, Jameson points out the SF trope 'android cogito' as an uncanny other, which thematically explores what the cinema's technicity metatextually embodies: 'I think, therefore I am not (human)' (2011: 220).

10 The breadth and coverage of recent literature on this subject, taking the aforementioned approaches, is staggering: Albrecht-Crane and Cutchins 2010; Andrew 2010; Aragay 2005; Carel and Tuck 2011; Cartmell and Whelehan 1999; Constantinides 2010; DeBona 2010; Hutcheon 2006; Leitch 2009; MacCabe et al. 2011; McFarlane 1996 and 2008; Miller et al. 2005; and Naramore 2000.

11 These issues of faithfulness, originality and canonicity are not specific to the remake, but join up with discourses on adaptation. See above. For discussion on this, see among others, McFarlane 1996; Cartmell and Whelehan 1999; and Stam and Raengo 2005.

3

WHAT BECOMES OF THE TENDER-HEARTED

Transcendence, *Geist* and lifeworld in popular independent cinema

> It should not be denied [...] that being footloose has always exhilarated us. It is associated in our minds with escape from history and oppression and law and irksome obligations, with absolute freedom, and the road has always led west.
>
> (Wallace Stegner, *The American West as Living Space*, 1974: 22)

> It is not that what is past casts its light on what is present, or what is present its light on what is past; rather, image is that wherein what has been comes together in a flash with the now to form a constellation. For while the relation of the present to the past is purely temporal (continuous), the relation of what-has-been to the now is dialectical, in leaps and bounds.
>
> (Walter Benjamin, *The Arcades Project* [N3, 1], 1999: 463)

In the previous chapters we saw how, through engaging incremental narrative changes across adapted textual material with particular focus on compound representations, we may build a theory that begins to account for the ripples of affect and the feeling of having in the cinematic encounter. Aspects of cinematic meaningfulness that live on through adaptive regimes in contemporary media forms seem to actively seek out pleasurable spaces of recognition: a lived, warm psychological phenomenon that I have identified as occupying the 'in-between' of viewer and viewed, and the living dialectic of being-together, being-apart. These tendencies in the contemporary cinematic media landscape are common in their popular forms because of the overriding emphasis on transmediality. This is not to deny the storytelling and creative power of such phenomena, whose kernel can be found in both high concept and licensing forms of transmedia storytelling, and whose secondary and tertiary products are today highly successful in both turning profits and turning-on favourable critical success with large user-audiences on an international level. Having set this scene, the current chapter now seeks to elaborate on a couple of these themes within the context of slightly different cinematic products and experiences. This is necessary because not all cinematic experiences are *necessarily* transmedial, or, at least, their transmedial properties are sometimes not immediately apparent to audiences. The stand-alone film, a tradition associated with the notions of film-as-art and director-as-author, still holds strong in popular film cultures, and films are often discussed in such terms, as is the corpus of work produced by production teams, studios and directors. As is fairly apparent, the recognition of such instances of cinema remains important in film cultures and illustrates other aspects of cinematic encounter only touched briefly upon thus far in this study.

In this chapter, the question of gender representation is given further consideration, particularly in its presentation of masculinities, through discussion of what might be classed as a recent cycle of US films that engage wounded men and their relationship with their environment. This 'environment' might be taken to mean natural landscape and the vastness of the wilderness – a tradition closely associated with historical cinematic genres such as the western, and sometimes action-adventure, both concerned with the interests of masculinity and what are sometimes regarded as masculine spaces. Equally, however, the environment under discussion might be considered as intersubjective spaces: those spaces of interpersonal relationships, domicile or familial spaces more traditionally associated with melodrama, but which, as discussed in the previous chapter, find a precedent in hybridised genre forms such that these spaces are familiar in many films that may be classed as 'genre films' of one persuasion or another. In doing such exploratory work, I will draw upon depth psychology's rich tradition of tending to the living movement and reciprocation of inner and outer forms. In particular, I want to explore the myth of the 'wounded man' in relation to his world, and the affective properties of such images for viewers. In relation to this, I will also give further consideration to philosophical notions of embodiment, enworldedness and lifeworld. In so doing, I will tread a pathway upon which characters are used as vehicles to explore wider concerns and emotional stories of transcendence and redemption.

Cinematic masculinity: setting the scene

In March 2010, I was working on a paper on masculinity and anger in contemporary Hollywood, to be delivered at the Andrew Samuels Lecture at SOAS the following month. Writing about the angry on-screen persona of Adam Sandler, I had been looking to other films that evoked more unusual aspects of masculinity in the cinematic encounter. I found that Sandler's comedy vehicle *Click* (Coraci, US, 2006) radicalised an existential angst at what might be termed a general, representational 'crisis in masculinity', a crisis which appeared in less extreme ways in many of the contemporary films that nevertheless addressed such questions head-on. Indeed, this is a crisis that has been well documented in cultural theory, but there are one or two notable absences from orthodox discourse. Andrew Samuels has noted in his book *The Political Psyche* (1993: 101) that 'Not a lot has been written about the father's desire to be loved'; that discernible historical and material shifts in the role of men, particularly within the family, have an intimate relationship with both the way men see themselves and with the way they are represented. Indeed, Sandler's character, Michael Newman, is a caustic representation of the aggressive and reactionary response to the conflicting demands of men's social roles under late capital; and one of those aspects is, I argue, a fatherly desire to be loved. Under such material and political conditions, this is fairly understandable. It is the nagging need to assert control – over life choices, environment, loved ones and their place in the life of the father – that exposes the psychological reality of some rather painful decisions about masculine identity and its disunity. This pain and conflict is often found represented on screen, and is not restricted to major Hollywood studio output by any means.

Whilst researching for that paper, I had the rather striking good fortune to watch *The Wrestler* (Aronofsky, US, 2008) and *Zidane: A 21st Century Portrait* (Gordon/ Parreno, Fr./Ice., 2006), both for the first time and back-to-back on DVD. They are, superficially speaking, very different films charting different narrative trajectories and shot in very different styles. The former is the story of Randy 'The Ram' Robinson (Mickey Rourke), a broken hulk of a man who carves out a grim living as a semi-professional wrestler in the twilight of his career. The latter is a film that teeters on the boundaries between art cinema and broad popular culture, capturing (in real time) an entire football match featuring legendary French footballer Zinédine Zidane – 17 camera set-ups following his every move. Perhaps one of the key features that these films share, however, is a cinematic inquiry into masculinity, specifically on-screen, and how that masculinity is transformed through the phenomenon of being observed, through acts of viewing and through the self-reflexive consideration of its status in reduced circumstances. In the case of both films, these 'reduced circumstances' can be found in the representation of a masculinity that, by conventional standards, might be considered as past its prime.

Zidane has been the subject of a fair amount of popular criticism, and not all of it positive. For example, Boba_Fett1138 , a blogger on imdb.com, goes as far to say that 'This movie only serves an artistic purpose', as if art merely exists for its own sake, residing in a place outside of the popular imagination and the mass-cultural world of football. Well, yes, film can serve an artistic purpose, and this one in particular does inhabit a cultural space not normally devoted to subjects such as professional footballers. However, one could argue that this film's ambitions stretch much further than performing 'only' artistic functions, and there are a number of reasons for this. The flux of competing elements in this film mobilise an extraordinary array of cinematic devices to 'bring in' the viewer, to capture the imagination and the feeling associated with the adrenalin-infused ritual of football spectatorship. In particular, the sound design (supervised by Kevin Shields of the band My Bloody Valentine) engages in a distinctive choreography that brings sound and vision together holisitically. The crowd, the commentary, the on-field dialogue, even Zidane's breathing are all featured at different times; sometimes in various combinations and levels, splicing and grafting the sounds onto an avant-garde whole and integrating with the apparent specific intention of that whole not rejecting any of its parts. This sound design, nestled within the crystalline beauty of Mogwai's post-rock soundtrack, makes for compelling viewing at times.

Zidane shares another, very important link with *The Wrestler*: Zinédine Zidane was fast approaching the end of his professional and international career at the time of filming, and the choice of game featured in the film (Real Madrid v. Villareal) is a conscious attempt to make sense of the contradictions and ambiguities at play in the world of football and discourses of youthful prime. The specific masculinities that are mobilised by football culture are as much subject to colonisation and subordination by patriarchal power structures as any species of cultural identity. The several cultural studies on this subject (for example, Boyle and Haynes 2009; Messner 2007) take various theoretical approaches to addressing masculinity and sport. What is interesting about this film is how it alerts the viewer to an always-already prurience of such hegemonic forms of masculinity in popular culture: commentary, punditry, sponsorship deals for fashion accessories and male-grooming products, and other species of expectation operate at an everyday level and pervade all areas of sporting life (both participation in it as well as spectator activity). In *Zidane*, this all comes under visual scrutiny, often in close-up, and we see the face (and, at times, hear the voice) of such masculinity under the most extreme pressure to 'perform' and 'deliver' in front of a fan audience, in the figure of Zidane himself.

If Zidane is under pressure to perform in his film, then it might be fair to suggest that Mickey Rourke's performance in *The Wrestler* is even more weighted around the need to succeed. As expected of a man his age, Zidane's playing career is drawing to a close and as of all players the expectation is that his career will be necessarily short. However, Rourke's movie career (which could have potentially lasted several continuous decades, given its early promise) has undergone a number of changes in fortune in the last 20 years or so. He had to give the performance of a lifetime in order to justify what is, essentially, a comeback film about a comeback – a metacomeback. To encounter Rourke on screen, whose beauty was once celebrated so highly in Hollywood and beyond, and face up to the realities of fading youth, lost looks and emasculating cosmetic surgery is not without its difficulties. This is, after all, a redemption movie of sorts: the sound of rapturous applause in the intelligent sound design in both diegetic moments and moments of psychological realism give *The Wrestler* its genuine moments of pathos. It is also at the same time a more straightforward redemption narrative: Randy is 'betrayed' several times over: by wrestling audiences (his popularity wanes), his body (which gives in after years of physical and narcotic abuse), his daughter (who rejects him in the interests of sparing herself further emotional trauma) and his girlfriend (who lays claim to unavailability – which is probably just as well, given his track record in relationships).

Marisa Tomei, also Oscar-nominated for her role as the stripper-with-a-heart-of-gold, Pam (or Cassidy to give her stripper stage name), isn't just a love interest in the film. She performs too, as an example of the way image-driven culture confines models of beauty and purity to the young and the clean. Like her character, Tomei is too old to make the big money and be a star in Hollywood (like, say, the much younger Keira Knightley or Natalie Portman), yet she is too good a performer to entirely forget about. She is, to my mind, reminiscent of a latter-day Natalie Wood, whose screen presence was often given second-rate importance to her various leading men; despite her extraordinary beauty even in later years, she could never quite capture the interest of her early career appearances – a situation exacerbated by the gender politics of the time, perhaps, but oddly still dominant in contemporary popular cinema and television. Tomei's performance in this and other films is often brilliant but here her acting is overshadowed by the presence of Rourke. He does this, not exactly through performance chops, but more through a palpable or material presence on screen *as Rourke*. I argue that it is this presence, a powerful performed identity, with which the audience engages at many different levels. The closing speech that Randy makes in addressing his comeback audience helps to illustrate this materiality. It is apparent that Rourke might as well be talking about his own career and comeback here:

> As time goes by they said 'He's washed up, he's finished, he's a loser, he's all through.' Well, you know what? The only ones who are gonna tell me when I'm through doing my thing are you people right here.

Had the studio's rumoured insistence on casting much bigger star Nicholas Cage in the lead role gone through, this would have been a very different film, given the performance, style, budget and so on that would have followed. Could we imagine anyone other than Mickey Rourke playing this role? Ask anyone who watched and enjoyed the film, and they would likely tell you: probably not. Why?

To my mind, this is a question that goes beyond matters of performance. It tells us something about what is going on between viewer and viewed in a wider, social dynamic. I am interested in how cinema works culturally, as an ongoing expression of how we perceive ourselves and each other in the world: that is to say, the encounter with cinema not merely as an instance of experience with the moving image on various screens and in different contexts, but, superimposed upon that notion, the way in which such narratives operate psychologically. My argument in this chapter is very much influenced by not only the deep structures of psychological meaning illuminated through depth psychology, but also the politics of an *opera aperta* of cinema, to borrow a turn of phrase from the Italian semiotician Umberto Eco: the idea of the unfinished work. So, I am interested in the idea that cinema is culturally experienced as a warm, lived constellation of phenomena that reveals something about how we go about the business of our daily lives, how we iterate our feelings on an artistic and perceptive level, and how we tell our stories, on a mass scale, by *showing* what we mean in popular cinema.

Cinema is, after all, as many film-philosophers including Julian Baggini have noted, a medium that doesn't tell; it *shows*. Baggini (2011: 210) writes that films offer reasons to accept their visions of reality, of the world: that is to say, in philosophical terms at least, films do not ordinarily provide the basis for syllogistic argument (i.e. deductive reasoning). 'Any truths it reveals are shown not told'. Furthermore, we can say that this kind of showing brings attention to an aspect of human experience, most commonly thought of in moral philosophy as social being: an experience of the world shared in common (whether expressed in terms that are friendly, antagonistic or otherwise).

Baggini articulates this by noting that if films are compelling,

> then we simply *see* that they accurately capture something important about the world, in just the way we see that Descartes's proposition [the cogito – 'I am, I exist, is necessarily true whenever it is put forward by me, or conceived in my mind'] has captured something about the nature of first-person experience.
>
> (2011: 210 [emphasis in original])

Descartes's proposition is not really an argument; it's more like an observation, in fact. So too of cinema: its capacity to show us our story of the world is its way of expressing perception – in Vivian Sobchack's phenomenology of film (1992, 2004), it gives us a viewed view, and shows us a viewing view; or in Stanley Cavell's philosophical approach to film (1979), we are presented with 'a world viewed': full of evocation, stimulation and, in existential terms, the situation and present-ness of the viewer. Bearing this in mind, there are three epistemic dimensions of cinematic proxemics (intersubjective present-ness in the in-between space of viewer and viewed) that help characterise some of the themes discussed so far in relation to films concerning masculinity, and I explore these in depth through an analysis of three films: *Geist* and redemption in *The Wrestler*, fatherhood and cultural adumbration in *Click*, and lifeworld, soul-world and transcendence in Sean Penn's *Into the Wild* (US, 2007).

Geist and redemption in *The Wrestler*

To begin with, I propose three allegorical figures that have been returned to in various schools of analytical thinking because they help to unpick the underlying meaningfulness of intersubjective encounters, both in cinema and more generally. The figures that I find compelling in cinema embody traditions of thought on some very fundamental questions, but also, it seems to me, are expressed readily not only on screen but also in the lived dialogue of our cultural exchanges. These questions involve time, change and causality: three interrelated cinematic properties that find their expression in philosophical engagement in the three ghostly presences or allegorical figures within the proxemics of cinematic viewing: History (a ghost of time and memory, also reflecting a general state of the cinematic medium which is time-based and relies upon pre- and pro-cinematic recording), Death (a ghost of changes, endings and repetitions) and what we might describe as Anima (a ghost of movement and dynamics, of space and soul, of unresolved dialectics and causality).

Anima, in this configuration, is a bit of unfinished business here, and I leave this figure open and ambiguous (once again, *opera aperta*) because it partakes of a number of systems of thought. The most obvious application, perhaps, is the Jungian contrasexual archetype, but its meaning as I conceive it here also invades spaces of less abstract, deep, structural origin. In popular cinema, for example, Anima (whose literal meaning may be observed through its etymology – life-breath; feminine energy and so on) might be considered the basis for a meaningful engagement with narrative agency (cause and effect); with motivational, ideological imperatives (the place of woman on screen; the emotional content of the relationships between on-screen human characters; the dynamics and interplay of the various elements of narrative, setting, character and so on); and, of course, we may think of Anima more generally as a figurative expression of the cinematic apparatus itself (the idea of all cinema as a kind of exercise in animation – bringing to life that which lies still and lifeless: the still photograph; the inanimate object viewed in time). More recently in Jungian-influenced film criticism, Christopher Hauke has invoked the phrase from Jung (who himself had appropriated it from antiquity), *anima mundi*, to describe the presence of spirit in the world, and the cinematic representation of the sometimes antagonistic relationship that can exist between humans and the natural environment. His case study, the Coen brothers' adaptation of *No Country for Old Men* (US, 2007), is typical of a recent cycle of such films from the United States to find popular and critical success.[1] I return to this particular instance of *anima* in my discussion of *Into the Wild* below. It is enough here to note that this notion of 'soul-world' in the enworldedness of on-screen characters has found its success partly due to the accomplished filmmaking style of the filmmakers involved, and partly due to a nostalgic mode of evocative rhetoric integrating human being with natural phenomena that stems from traditions in American literature and philosophy traceable to Emerson. The transcendental element of reintegration of soul-world attributable to such tradition will form the basis for further discussion towards the end of this chapter.

To summarise, *anima* operates at multiple levels simultaneously: figuratively, structurally, metaphorically and generically. To illustrate this, one might refer here to *The Wrestler*'s self-conscious Christ-narrative: after Cassidy has given Randy a lapdance, he shows her the scars from his wrestling mishaps. She responds with:

> He was pierced for our transgressions, he was crushed for our iniquities. The punishment that brought us peace was upon him, and by his wounds we were healed.

When he asks what she is talking about, she replies:

> It's *The Passion of the Christ* – you have the same hair.

This is significant for a number of reasons that go beyond the mere narrative mirroring of the Christ-narrative. It refers to two important cultural productions: first, the reference to cinema, with its conventions, stars and repeatable tropes (for example, biblical epics such as Mel Gibson's *The Passion of the Christ*, 2004), and, second, wrestling as a cultural phenomenon, with its rituals of repetition and its troublesome celebration and commodification of systematic bodily punishment (most often in its popular form, dished out by men and dealt to men). It gives us a vista upon which we as an audience may glance over the various culturally meaningful thematic connections at play. In other words, it helps drive the meaningfulness of our encounter with the story – it *animates* the story.

It is doubly significant that this scene takes place in the strip club. In another scene set there, Cassidy can't get any of the customers to pay for a lapdance. The juxtaposition of this against the previous scene, in which Randy attends a wrestling merchandise fair with other wrestling veterans who display various stages of decrepitude, suggests that her trajectory mirrors Randy's: her profession centres on a notion of bodily perfection (of a certain type – flexibility, rhythm, toned musculature and so on) and an accompanying notion of beauty (youthfulness, fresh demeanour, peculiar mix of natural style and cosmetic artifice). This last allows one to speculate with greater assurance on the marketability of bodily perfection and beauty, bound together as commodity. It also indicates that although Cassidy's trajectory mirrors Randy, there are subtle ways in which the culturally gendered practices of male and female bodies are enacted upon and looked at in rather different ways. The conventions of distinction made between hard masculine bodies (which in this film often are sites of punishment and pain) and softer feminine bodies (generally associated with the notion of to-be-looked-at spectacle in many film theory traditions, but here strangely hardened by the fitness training and other health practices) are both maintained and disrupted in their portrayal. This may be complicated through the conscious associations made between their relationship and those found in popular tradition between Christ and the Magdalene (the divine and the sinful). Therefore, one could argue that bodies play important symbolic roles in this film which are multilayered and polysemic, and which are fairly easy to discern through even the most casual viewing.

When Cassidy and Randy meet away from the club to go shopping for a present for his daughter Stephanie (Evan Rachel Wood), he remarks that he almost didn't recognise her because she looks 'clean'. It is the first glimpse we see of Randy being anything like a 'regular Joe', and he very nearly alienates Cassidy before they have even begun to embark on a relationship. Her response is quite gracious given his *faux pas*, and she literally ushers in a new energy in his life: he is inspired to attempt a full reconciliation with his estranged daughter. In this scene, the notion of the commodification of the body is bracketed within the professionalisation of the characters' identities and the uses to which they put their bodies. Cassidy/Pam maintains the line between the world of work and the outside world by insisting that she be called Cassidy in the club, and Pam outside; it is the strategy that Randy/Robin fails to maintain – there is no distance between his professional persona and his past personal life. The closest he gets to a conciliation of persona and self is through his relationship with Pam, which remains in tension throughout the course of the film.

It is also relevant to note, in passing, a scene towards the end of the film, when Pam leaves the club mid-shift. Her boss calls out after her: 'Cassidy?! Hey, Cassidy! ... Pam!' To which she affirms 'Pam' under her breath, reclaiming an identity outside of the club and the 'unclean' world of topless dancing. 'Pam' is a 'clean' identity: the identity of an individuated person who exists in real relationships with others in the outside world (outside of the club, and outside of relationships marked by commodified, secretive transactions), one which Randy of all people had endorsed through his approval. It is also a reaffirmation of her own personal history: where the inevitability of time counts for less because her identity is less contingent upon having a certain kind of body and inhabiting a certain persona. It is, following Walter Benjamin, a rejection of her own self-mythologising as a rational agent (as well as the mythology placed upon her) while cast in the role of 'tart-with-a-heart'. She reconciles this new Pam with a need to recognise the Cassidy of her past as a *present* concern, not an attempt to recapture a mythological past. As Benjamin would write: an 'image of the past that is not recognised by the present as one of its own concerns [...] threatens to disappear irretrievably' (1973: 256–7). She is thus eventually able to walk away from this identity as Cassidy with her dignity fully intact, integrating and accommodating aspects of all the roles she has had to perform (as mother, as worker and material provider, as love interest).

Randy lives in a past that never existed, and this is ironic, precisely because he bears the marks of a lived, mythological history: physical scars, eyeglasses, hearing aid – all visible traces of the ravages of violence visited upon a prematurely aged body over time. To deny this discrepancy, to mythologise this past, he actively engages in a cover-up operation; significantly, a *beauty* regime: self-medication, body sculpture, hair dye, tanning salon. This regime is, of course, tied in with the notion of commodified femininity in contemporary popular culture. Often trivialised and scorned, such male-grooming techniques reflect the notion of the 'new man' phenomenon so familiar in contemporary popular culture, and so alienated from the natural world of elements, wilderness and environment associated with rugged masculinity in other parts of that very same culture. Little wonder, then, that the 'crisis' in masculinity remains so tenacious a complex in cultural theory and in the everyday. In Randy's case, of course, his regime has rather more serious repercussions that, somewhat ironically, mirror the more serious political implications of commodified male beauty in everyday life. Following what is known as a hardcore match (a no-holds-barred, full contact wrestling bout), we are shown in graphic detail the effects of bodily mutilation and repair. Randy's decades-old regime of patching himself up results in shakes, convulsions, physical sickness and cardiac arrest: all accompanied by 'sick' sound design – a feedback sound of some kind, that signifies the inevitable intervention of Death itself.

Death is another figure that features powerfully in moving-image cultures, precisely because it seems to embody the idea of change and of repetition. This emphasis on the ability of time-based media to enable the cultural experience of repetition in a more literal sense is conjoined with (and in struggle with) the more metaphysical idea that we experience Death as a harbinger of change. The adage *plus ça change, plus c'est la même chose* – the more things change, the more they stay the same – sums up the cultural appearance of Death as an imminent figure from which there is no escape, but with which we may experience the world and our place in it many times over.

The film-philosopher Havi Carel has noted on a number of occasions (2006, 2011) the way in which Death is experienced cinematically mirrors quite closely the way that Death as an idea is experienced in the world more generally, and the way this has been articulated in the history of philosophy as one of its central concerns. This follows Heidegger's notion, summarised in his *History of the Concept of Time* (1992), of the *moribundus*, the certain function of Death as a structuring principle of being: being-towards-death. One of the most important features of this philosophical approach is that it questions the idea that Death is the negation of life. In many ways, of course, Death plays an active role in life; it structures life in the way that we form both practices to allay our fear of it (i.e. religion, ritual, symbolism) and physically avoid it (reduce the number of things that may go wrong in life to 'cause' death). Therefore, philosophically speaking, we might say that Death structures our self-understanding, through the struggle between self-determination and contingency of being-in-the-world. That is to say, it is a brute fact, BUT it is never something that we can directly experience of ourselves, at least to express. Death therefore has meaning beyond its certainty: it is imminent, but is also the structuring principle of human mortality and finitude.

It also forms a structuring principle in the psychological world. For Jung, the certainty of approaching Death, and the anxiety springing from an uncertain knowledge of the nature and time of its arrival, casts an anticipatory shadow over the life and the dreams of Death's victims (i.e. it is a part of human experience), an emotional turbulence he described as adumbration (1964: 63). Ironically, although one would think this anxiety finds a natural home in the psychological lives of the elderly, or those who are otherwise approaching death, Jung noted that it also occurred at key moments in the development of adult life, particularly in adolescents and others experiencing cardinal life changes. Such adumbrations lend themselves to repetitions of behaviour of the sort that classical Jungian thinking might describe as juvenile: defiant and wilful.[2]

We see its representation repeatedly in *The Wrestler*. For instance, when Randy needs to pay his overdue rent, he picks up some extra work at a supermarket deli counter. A customer asks Randy to slice some cheese for him and then recognises him as 'The Ram'. The sound of the mechanical cheese slicer gets audibly louder, and the feedback sound that accompanied Randy's earlier collapse returns here, suggesting a reprise of the bodily mutilation trope, prefiguring actual mutilation when he deliberately jams his thumb in the slicer in frustration. This scene immediately follows Stephanie's final rejection of Randy after he stands her up. The pattern that inevitably emerges from this sequence of events is the conclusion (both ours and Randy's) of Randy's wilful pursuit of self-destruction and an active disavowal of finitude, a pattern that repeats itself through back-story intimations in the narrative. To paraphrase the existential psychotherapist Emmy van Deurzen (2010), Pam got better at living with her imperfections, recognising them for their constitutive rather than determinist aspects; Randy resigned himself to his.

The back-story elements intimated during the course of this film are important for a number of reasons, and can be thought of as the connecting principles between a parasocial bond with the characters (mirroring the kinds of bonds formed in everyday life with real people) and a meaningful feeling with the performers themselves in the act of viewing (an empathic feeling). Following cognitive film theorists such as Murray Smith (1995), as well as philosophers working in the field of cognitive science such as Currie and Ravenscroft (2002), one might say that such connections via back-story to the human figures and their actions on film are complex functions of social interaction, which afford the audience a vista on the world of the film in ways similar to real-world interactions. Without straying too much into cognitivist analysis here, one might suggest that this underpinning cognitive process is lived through, psychologically speaking, in the personal and collective histories of those doing the viewing, of those having a feeling with cinema. The case of Mickey Rourke here illustrates, in a rather easy way, how the blend of on-screen persona and diegetic narrative can tap into an audience's historical sensibilities, enabling a mapping out of psychological meaningfulness. What is interesting in this case is that it is complicated through the labyrinthine gender politics at play in both the film and the actors performing in it, such that it becomes difficult, as a viewer, to unpack that politics in any straightforward demarcation: it happens on-screen, but also epistemologically in the interplay of character and performer histories, and the audience's knowledge of the conventions of pathos, both parasocially and generically, at work in that interplay.

So, perhaps, it is not a case of masculinity in crisis after all? The sophistication to which actors such as Rourke and Tomei are put to work in film narratives and the display of nostalgia-saturated filmmaking evidenced by the work of Aronofsky and others working in popular cinema today betrays a self-reflexivity and awareness of how audiences are able to discern pathic structures in their own acts of viewing. The present cultural turn in masculinity (its 'crisis') might be rethought, then, as an example of cultural and historical awareness on the part of filmmakers and audiences alike of those same shifts. It might also be thought of as the manifestation of a 'working through' of the cultural adumbrations associated with gender politics, and how a perceptible breaking down of structures of masculinity might be regarded as an event of historical and psychological importance. In what follows, I offer a further example of how such shifts in masculinity in contemporary popular cinema are both deftly exploited and palpably felt as cultural adumbrations.

Geist, fatherhood and cultural adumbration in *Click*

As noted towards the beginning of this chapter, Andrew Samuels (1993: 101) wrote in *The Political Psyche* that the traditional facets of men and particularly their role as the father within familial relationships – authority, a position as head or 'king' of the family – can be seen as a contribution to their psychological wounds, and 'hence, as something to be healed'. The complexity of this is in the awkward rejoinder to the scenario: 'Not a lot has been written about the father's desire to be loved.' What we seem to be seeing in contemporary popular cinema, however, is a direct addressing of this question. Perhaps it is true that there has not been so much written about this, but it is a key subject of contemporary popular cinema, and a theme to which it enjoys returning. A powerful example of this kind of film can be found in *Click*. It is my contention that in the character of Michael Newman, a middle-class professional architect who works for a corporate firm, this exposure of everyday material reveals that popular cinema is a suitable arena to play out, culturally speaking, such an important issue close to the interests of a popular audience.

What is quite interesting about this example – *Click*, a fantasy comedy about a man who is given a remote control that empowers him with the ability to govern his own life and those around him – is that his choices become *automated*. At the beginning, Michael uses the remote to choose how scenarios will play out – in order to get on with his work, he 'fast-forwards' through many different aspects of his family life: time spent with his loving parents (played by Henry Winkler and Julie Kavner), looking after the family dog, playing with his children, and even making love to his wife, Donna (Kate Beckinsale). Thus, he manages to fulfil the familial responsibility of career-building and providing a solid income, whilst at the same time shirking off several other familial responsibilities. However, his life takes on the appearance of an ability to balance several roles at once (a man *in control*) that would be impossible were it not for his fantastic universal remote control: as father, breadwinner, lover and devoted employee. The plot twist centres on the remote control itself – it does its work based on a 'personal preferences' setting. Every exertion of control over events Michael attempts leads to a transformation of each of his relationships into an alienated state: these transformations contradict his acts of male assertion, leading to destructive irreconcilability, exacerbated through his reactionary, aggressive persona. Although it is quite difficult to love someone like Michael Newman, it is not necessarily that he's a bad man, perhaps, but his coping strategies of denial and 'fast-forward' leave much to be desired and tell us something about everyday strategies that we have generally come to rely upon in order to cope with the anxiety of alienation.

The basic premise of this film is laid out plainly in its opening expository scene: Michael Newman is a commercial architect, married to a beautiful wife, and together they live in the suburbs with their two children and pet dog. Michael is obsessed with control (or the lack of control) in both his working and domestic lives. The uneasy split between his down-trodden subservience at work at the hands of his corporate-bullying boss (David Hasselhof) and the role of absent breadwinner at home (an image of traditional familial gender division if ever there was one) generate for Michael a crisis in his identity as a modern everyman. The generational divide is also made explicitly clear in the opening scene – the familiar trope of youth understanding technology in a way that the older generation can't hope to is directly associated with competitiveness and material acquisition: the O'Doyles next door have a universal remote that controls everything in the house in one handy box, and young Kevin O'Doyle points out his family's affluent material status at every opportunity he gets during the course of the film.

This complex of technology, gender division, generation gap, work and familial responsibility, and domestic consumption seems to be at the heart of problems that we might say characterise late capital and its competing demands. *Click*'s opening scene tells the narrative of everyman in a highly condensed way: Michael can't control his eating habits, defending his Twinkies from his children in a playful but ogre-like fashion. However, we might speculate that really this aspect of (lack of) control is related to an amplification of image, particularly self-image, and its commodification in today's world. It is ultimately a response to the pressure of the cultural image of masculinity as pillar of strength, and its discrepancy with how men really are psychologically. I will return to this particular theme momentarily as I think that it holds a key to the underlying psychological narrative of the division of masculine and feminine, the competing roles of the father and the reflection of persona as cultural adumbration that occurs in popular cinema.

The scene in which Michael first encounters Morty (Christopher Walken) and is given the universal remote control in a free trial gives the viewer a first sense of these psychological realities, as represented in this film. It is worth noting the kinds of spaces in which this scene occurs, in addition to the dialogue and what is said in a literal sense. Set in a domestic wholesalers called Bed, Bath and BEYOND, Michael collapses into a heap on one of the display beds. In exasperation, he mutters, 'I'm so tired of my life.' A chorus of synthesised angelic voices and muzak anticipates a zoom shot towards a sign that says 'BEYOND' above a doorway leading from the main open-plan of the store. Michael staggers tiredly through the doorway and encounters a rather different environment: in contrast to the bright electronically lit store, this BEYOND is a dimly lit workshop, complete with solitary technician Morty (Christopher Walken) dressed in laboratory overcoat and sporting technical equipment. When Michael tells Morty that he is looking to purchase a universal remote, he is led though yet another door into a huge, dark warehouse full of shelves with untold anonymous cardboard boxes, to a shiny aluminium shelving unit marked 'really new stuff', where they find the new universal remote that can 'bite the O'Doyles' ass, hard', according to Morty. It is an advanced piece of technology that promises to make Michael's life a little easier, quicker and less complicated, thus solving all of his problems at once. There is a catch, however – Morty explains to Michael that the store operates a strict 'no returns' policy.

There are a number of ways in which to read the first encounter between the two characters, and, to start, we might consider more obviously literal interpretations of the space of the action in order to deconstruct the multiple narratives at work. The warehouse, like all unseen aspects of the service economy, is something that is deliberately kept from the consumer's view. It is the underbelly of slick corporate America, if you like: all dust, wires and internal machine parts and metal-shop tools. This is an exposure of the inner workings, a hypermediacy where the glossy veneer of late capitalism is stripped away to reveal the hidden labour within. Yet, despite this, and Michael's privileged (and, for Morty, playful) glimpse at this 'other side' of commercial activity, he is still bound by its rules (i.e. the no returns policy).

In some ways, this is a literal rendering of Jung's 'dream house', as told in anecdotal form in his *Memories, Dreams, Reflections* memoir (1989). It is a deliberate evocation of imagery that, at its core, holds the truth about the dialogue between history and psychology (the collective and the personal) and a descent into the unconscious, the 'inner workings', so to speak, of our lives, that often remain hidden away, unseen. Postmodern theorists such as Frederic Jameson (1991) have noted that this invisibility of history is more like a 'disappearance' in its form under late capital: that is, a society whose economy is dominated by the commodification of service and consumerism itself. The inner workings of capital (in other words, its own history) disappear beneath the veneer of the twin rhetoric of technological progress and innovation on the one hand and alienated individualism on the other.

Mike Featherstone has commented that 'Any reference to the term "postmodernism" immediately exposes one to the risk of being accused of jumping on a bandwagon, of perpetuating a rather shallow and meaningless intellectual fad' (1988: 195). This is something to bear in mind, no doubt. However, the twin mercurial and hermetic nature of the postmodern – a periodisation concept of a world, not necessarily beyond or after the modern period, but a world enamoured by its own modernity – is such that it seems ripe for reading through the filter of the dialogue between history and psychology in relation to its representations on film. The operations, processes and mechanics of alienation and the prurient occupation with consumerism that are represented in various ways in *Click* are, in principle, similar to what the late-nineteenth-century sociologist Max Weber termed in his book *The Protestant Ethic and the Spirit of Capitalism* (1996) a 'calling' or duty of the individual: self-reliance, work ethic and the accumulation of material wealth.

It is worth noting the extraordinary insight that Jung's psychological reading of the idea of spirit or *Geist* lends to this area of representation. Jung saw *Geist* as an archetypal evocation of the background complex of the father-image, the mercurial aspect of the unconscious that binds convictions, prohibitions and decision-making in one authoritative psychic figure. This figure was, for Jung, a powerful enabler for actions both constructive and detrimental to psychic accommodation. It happens that so much cultural theory has identified these principles as the drives of constructions of masculinity that we know operate in today's society, reproduced repeatedly in representations of masculinity in moving image cultures, and principally governed by the laws of productivity that such diverse realms of the social sphere as the family, the economy, education and the arts maintain. The transformative aspect of the notion of spirit, in philosophical traditions as much as in the psychological sense following Jung, takes both positive and negative guises. When most ghostly and invisible, it can be a deceptive and insidious force on behaviour and attitude. Recognised in familial relationships of tyrannical paternity or images of abandonment, on a more collective level, it has led to the kind of economy of psychic health that has resulted in a privatisation of lifestyle choices and the inevitability of an atomised, monadic existence.

In such a guise, the Spirit of Capitalism has enabled near-universal commodification, reflected in the kinds of representations of masculinity in popular cinema that, in Jungian parlance, take on a juvenile, Trickster quality. Bernie Neville, writing for an online journal dedicated to the image of Trickster, in his piece 'Taking Care of Business in the Age of Hermes' (2003), outlines the narratives associated with late capital. He writes:

> We hear that the information society is enmeshed in a fantasy of the marketplace, in which everything is a commodity, exchange is an end in itself and the only value is market value. [...] We find Hermes getting by very well in the oppressors, in spite of his lack of commitment to the patriarchy.

This mythological mobilisation of Trickster, Hermes, is (to use the terminology of historical materialism) the embodiment of hegemony: multifarious, shape-shifting, excessive, insidious, powerful, deceptive, inspirational, irrational, commonsensical, nonsensical, eloquent and eminently forgivable. Neville goes on to state that:

> Our business culture has recently been worshipping the god of the marketplace with an excess of devotion. We still see an infatuation with the magic hand of the marketplace [...]. The consequences have been catastrophic for national economies, for public morality, for countless unemployed and for the political system. Nevertheless, the myth has not lost any of its power. It is rationalized into a belief that the unregulated marketplace is the source of growth, prosperity, freedom and democracy. The fact that governments have been acting on this belief for a quarter of a century with few positive results to show for it does not inhibit their faith.
>
> (2003)

Essentially, what Neville is doing is taking a psychic image and working with it to find its basis in a collective, archaic form that manifests as a contemporary faith narrative in today's world. The narratives with which late capital justifies itself are self-evident in the actions, thoughts and representations of father-images, and their own self-images projected large in the politics of gender.

Another scene in *Click* serves as a vivid example of such projections. It is a fairly incidental segment in the overall plot of the film and at first glance seems to have very little to do with aspects of control and Michael's amplification of father-image identity, but on closer inspection it becomes one of the key scenes of the entire movie. It reveals both the film's most reactionary element as a reinforcement of gender divisions and the twin concerns of gender politics that seem to preoccupy contemporary popular culture: the obsession with commodified self-image and, importantly, its verbalisation. Donna's best friend Janine (played with zest by improvisational comedienne Jennifer Coolidge) has come around to the Newmans' to share breakfast with Donna before they both head off to the gym. Michael walks in as Janine is explaining about her forthcoming cosmetic surgery procedures that will provide her with 'a face and a body that's gonna get me to places where I wanna be'. She bemoans the perception that her cheekbones are 'too Slavic' as the reason for the procedures as Michael sits at the table. They obviously have a fierce dislike of each other, and an argument about Janine's infidelity in three marriages with each of her ex-husbands' unemployed brothers leads to a screaming match where Janine outlines her 'self-esteem issues'. It leads Michael to use the universal remote yet again to control the actions of those around him, this time with a parody of a picture-in-picture feature, silencing Janine's tirade and showing a baseball match in the corner of the screen.

The interstices between gender divisions here and the commodification of self-image are give-away elements of *Click*'s attempts to engage meaningfully with the alienated coping strategies of both Michael and Janine. Michael's obsession with self-improvement is in the realm of production and material status (in competition with the O'Doyles next door, for example). It is in keeping with a rather perfunctory masculinity: a performance of convention, expectation and value that contravenes and yet underpins the privatised experience of married life. He therefore does what any husband is expected to do in such movies – he switches off many of his emotional faculties in order to get the job done. This is achieved in this case quite literally, through the use of a nifty remote control to change the ontology of his domestic situation. Christopher Hauke's work on masculinity and fatherly roles in the films of Steven Spielberg (2001) helps us to negotiate this path of persona: a masculine persona policing contrasexuality through tragicomic means. Hauke wrote that in cases which emphasise 'the loneliness of those who find themselves in unique, individual circumstances which are both unexpected and outside personal control' are compelled to 'act outside conscious, conventional, "civilised" standards' (2001: 156–7).

In this case, an obverse of this psychology is brought into play: Michael's cruel reaction to Janine's tragic circumstance is to exert control the way he is *expected* to – by using his universal remote, he ironically acts out the very convention that he seeks to avoid. Even though he may want the best for his family through adhering to the convention of work and obeying the call of the Spirit of Capitalism, by mobilising the technological means at his disposal (acquired through consumer culture) he accelerates his own alienation by acting within expectation, but outside 'civilised' standards. Essentially, he is being tricked and in his turn takes on the characteristics of the trickster.

Such representations in popular film comedies usually manifest in oppositional structures. One such structure is the rather reactionary one of family values vs. homosocial space. The internal logic of late capital suggests that this opposition of reproduction/true-love narratives, with their emphasis on privatised mono-gamous experience versus equally privatised, exclusively all-male environments, has led to a rather unhealthy splitting of masculine and feminine worlds. Certainly, as several commentators working in psychosocial or educational settings have noted,[3] there is much to be gleaned from the particular pleasures and discourses of multiple feminine and masculine spaces. However, very recent film comedies such as *I Love You, Man* (Hamburg, US, 2009) demonstrate the ability of men to laugh at their own folly in attempting to perform 'manliness' and at the recognition of the work of persona in all-male spaces. Whereas it could be argued that this is a lucky one-off in a raft of juvenile and irresponsible images of maleness, I will argue in Chapter 4 that we need such rich representations in popular culture, as exemplified in *I Love You, Man*, to stand apart from the formula. Somewhere in the comedy of recognition lies the political power of laughter, and, as far as the constructions of gender are concerned, this is an essential part of detaching oneself from the alienating 'angry man' phenomenon.

Lifeworld, soul-world and transcendence in *Into the Wild*

Before I go on to discuss this in detail, there is one last aspect of the concerns of the current chapter that needs to be addressed. The transcendental aspects of integration between psyche and world (in Jungian terminology) and the transcendental movement beyond the oppositional structures outlined above in gender politics in late capital are also represented in recent contemporary US cinema as a kind of rediscovery of lifeworld, of reintegration into the world of nature. In many ways moving beyond the clinging need for control and dominance of one's surroundings (a theme iterated so plainly in *Click*) or the need to redeem oneself in the eyes of another in order to resign oneself to the alienation of modern life (as painfully portrayed in *The Wrestler*), the reconciliation with a perceived authentic soul-world finds its expression in a number of recent US films.

Two of the Coen Brothers' most recent films, for instance – the aforementioned *No Country for Old Men*, and their remake of the classic western, *True Grit* (US, 2010) – both rely upon the landscape of the frontier, in the literal, ecological and philosophical senses, to outline their usual authorial concerns regarding the ethical status of money, amongst other concerns. Of these other concerns, the imminence of human being and death, contingent upon the natural world, seems to be paramount: where nature not only provides the spaces within which we may roam and carve out a living but also acts in seemingly random and utterly remorseless ways. Indeed, the 'force of nature' that is Anton Chigurh (Xavier Bardem) is, of course, a man who acts of his own volition and also out of a perverse sense of ethical responsibility; equally, his only human psychological quality seems to be his joy in pursuit and murder. We never really know his reasons for pursuing Llewelyn Moss (Josh Brolin) other than vague references to professionalism and reclaiming the money in Llewelyn's possession (even though Chigurh clearly isn't interested in the money at all). This leads one irresistibly to infer a dark, sinister driving motive at work; the very unknown in this situation is enough to make us unsure. The reason I bring this up is that this film is among the recent cycle of similarly environment-focused films, typical in its accentuation of *imminence* – Death approaches and has the capacity to happen at any time, by accident or deliberation, through natural or supernatural forces beyond the control of mere human beings. Thus the anxiety seems to be a fascination and, to me, is part of recent cinema's focus on the human–environment relationship.

However, aside from the concerns about Death, there are other important aspects of this kind of relationship between the human and natural world that are revealed in such films. Sean Penn's directorial debut, *Into the Wild*, tells the story of the real-life adventures of a young man, Christopher McCandless (Emile Hersch), and his escape from the contemporary world of consumerism and alienation. McCandless, a high-achieving Emory graduate, is a loner who finds it easier to relate to the characters and values of American literature than with other people. His parents are upper-middle-class professionals whose hatred for each other animates McCandless' memories of home life when both he and his younger sister witnessed their quarrels spill into family disputes, daily violence and holding the children to ransom against one another. Given this personal and familial history, it is little wonder that he seeks a life beyond the interpersonal. However, there is more to this than straightforward generational rebellion. The adventure borne out through McCandless' sheer determination to avoid the trappings of capital is to escape the obsession of his parents' neurotic bourgeois lifestyle and is ostensibly an attempt to get back to nature, to rekindle an authentic relationship of some kind with one's surroundings; to achieve a communion with the natural world that has very little to do with his troubled family history.

The trajectory of such aims bears remarkable resemblance to American philosopher Ralph Waldo Emerson's vision of 'the transcendentalist', found in his famous essay of the same name, originally published in 1842. Originally a term taken from Kant's reply to scepticism, where imperative ideas were intuitions of the mind itself (and not intellectualised results of external or sensual stimuli, or, indeed, of history), transcendentalism was a state of being which came through Emerson and his peers to refer to a person whose connection to the natural world is stronger than his connection with the social world, particularly where those rules of society infringed upon the sovereignty of the individual. The transcendentalist's longing for the company of oneself is guided not through a triumph over nature through the sheer force of hand, although a vulgar interpretation of Emerson might infer such; for example, in exploiting nature's bounty as in other Western traditions of colonisation and manifest destiny or in this case the McCandless parents' obsession with 'the next step' and material acquisition. To the contrary, solitude is given by the grace of nature to belong to (and with) it through self-reliance and self-determination. It is to escape from the 'facts' of history, as Emerson would put it, and unchain oneself from the social bonds of class, prejudice and cultivation to individuate in ways that traditional philosophies of the Old World were to that point (circa 1840s) unable to conceive.[4] It is to engage in a more holistic sense, the world unbound by faiths, dogma, government and the 'portable and convenient cakes' (Emerson 1982: 251) of modernity that compromise one's ability to see beyond petty materialist existence, and prevent our ability to perform actions that may move us beyond it. In a strange quirk of such philosophy, a philosophy that is indigenous to European America, Emerson's transcendentalism performs a doubling of consciousness similar to that found in Hegelianism.[5] However, in Emerson, the transcendentalist reckons the world (the prevailing modern state of 'buzz and din') an appearance, that distracts from the true relationships at work in the world (that of soul, serenity and independence). These states of thought diverge and contrast wildly, and, as in Hegel, lead ultimately to an instance of sublation of one in the other leading to an inauthentic existence not of one's own choosing or volition, or a synthesis of the two that stands uneasy and characterises modernity. Unlike Hegel, however, Emerson's thrust appears to favour the state of the ideal, of the soul, and it seems that he presumes a hierarchy that champions this as the desirable state of being.

With this in mind, there are certainly instances in the film *Into the Wild* that seem to ask similar questions of the state of contemporary America, and this is no accident: McCandless was, in real life, an avid reader of Thoreau (a contemporary of Emerson), as well as several American writers whose recurrent occupations included transcendentalist themes on nature, truth, the land and the relationship of the American subject to the state, recurring themes of later writers such as Wallace Stegner and Jack London. In the above description of the film, I have already laid the foundations for some of its meditations on the state of twentieth-century America, and the themes of the film that try to address this aren't always successful. I would like to furnish this evaluation through an anecdotal example from my own cinephilic experience.

My first viewing experience of this film was quite harrowing. The duration of watching it came and went with a little pang of admiration for Penn's first directorial effort, but nothing more especially. It is in what happened next in my emotional response to the film that made me think again about what the film was trying to do. I spent the next three days with an underlying and sickening sense of dread. I didn't realise at first what might be causing this, and then I thought back to the film, to McCandless and his own efforts to live a more authentic life. The prospect of having to remain a fairly anonymous drone for the rest of one's life is a gruesome one, and one that I am personally quite resistant to, and therefore I became quite aware of a significant empathy with McCandless. A dawning realisation that this is probably one's lot isn't the most positive reaction to a film, but I find it quite affirming in a sense. For me, this is popular cinematic storytelling at its best, because even though there is a Romantic veneer on the surface of this account of Christopher McCandless, there is also the sense of a moral tension in the film: his wilful flight from society, laden with tragedy and rapture in equal measures, tends to a nagging sense that he is shirking responsibilities to himself. His is ultimately a selfish juvenile act and, in this, almost unforgivable. Having said that, being true to authentic individuality, the transcendentalist worries little about these consequences in the faith that his actions show the way. What I find so touching about this portrayal is that, through tragedy, the McCandless parents rediscover their commonality – they cease fighting and become close, finding once more the things that are important in the life they had chosen. Not that this is a great outcome, of course, because they still lose their son, but a degree of meaningfulness re-enters their lives.

There are a number of ways that one can approach this film in order to unpack what it is showing. One may think of this process as peeling layers off an onion: densely packed meanings, opaque layers, revealing once-hidden insights. What is interesting about this film in particular is that it doesn't make this process a straightforward one, and even a brief analysis reveals an interconnected set of ideas and propositions for its audience to go away with, to think about and to discuss. At the most superficial level, one could suggest that this film is, to some extent, a descendant of 1960s countercultural values. McCandless' adverse reaction to the excesses of consumerism – shown here to be the mind-numbing effects of boredom, conformity and collusion with capitalism – is one with which many of us can sympathise. It may be easy to rush into criticisms of him shirking responsibility, throwing away opportunity and behaving just like the privileged young man he is attempting to leave behind. In acting on his desires to drop out of a cruel and alienating society, McCandless is fulfilling his own uniquely placed destiny as an adolescent with the capacity to think outside the limitations of the system – ironically, the same system that allows him to think like this in the first place. The film places this reaction in a Romantic mould: it is ennobled, an act of selflessness in a world that thrives on selfishness, and pits the world of soul against the world of understanding and predestined paths. On one level the film tells us this, but through further analysis what it shows us is something rather different. How does it achieve this?

The most obvious thing to notice is the interplay of references to popular culture that occur in this film. One might say that I am certainly a desirable element in the target audience for such a film: for example, as a thirty-something man I had an instant recognition of the music featured in the film. With songs composed and performed by Eddie Vedder of the Seattle rock band Pearl Jam (who found enormous popular success on the crest of the 'grunge' movement in rock music in the early 1990s), this music is evocative of a mood in the film, but also gives it a sense of *time*. Vedder's vocal is one of the most distinctive in recent popular music – instantly recognisable, particularly to a certain demographic who came of age during the period in which the film is set (again, the early 1990s). The film's strategy to address a particular audience through music suits the story's message of the aforementioned transcendentalist brand of individualism. Sean Penn, the film's director and screenwriter, is a well-known Hollywood player in his own right and was obviously able to draw from his resources in choosing any songwriter he wanted for this project. He chose well, for in the atmospheric, pared-down Americana of Vedder's songs we are able to access the visual landscape in musical terms: a film-poem whose total picture of the American frontier is as much about the inner world of intuition as it is the environmental and social worlds of America itself. Vedder, whose music is forever associated with the early 1990s in the popular imagination, is perceptibly engaging, through extratextual associations, with the film's audience. All of this in aesthetic terms means that the fitting soundtrack to the story itself, the cinematic sound, the appropriateness to the historical period in which the story takes place are complementary to the appeal of using this particular artist to reinforce the feeling of the story being shown.

Into the Wild is a kind of road movie. Road movies, brought to prominence in US cinema in the late 1960s and early 1970s (precisely around the time of the countercultural movements of Leary, Woodstock and Civil Rights in the United States), drew from earlier cinematic traditions of the western film and literary traditions of the beat writers (particularly Kerouac, Kesey and Burroughs), which in their turn drew on the myths of the frontier, of the pioneering adventurers of the post-colonial period and of the earlier European explorers who discovered and mapped the landscape of America in the first place. Road movies (and in this sense *Into the Wild* is firmly and unmistakably among them) therefore embody a heady mix of tradition and myth, history and nostalgia, and political energy. *Into the Wild* explores a journey into what might be thought of in the popular imagination as the 'real' America, and all that this ideal embodies, even as the ideal is revealed as a deception rooted not in the real world but in the world of abstract well-wishing. The idea of what this 'real' America might be has a very seductive, powerful and clear identity, because US cinema and US history are unique in their contemporary mutual development, and the cinematic representation of history in the US has followed closely the path of historical phenomena themselves. For example, the frontier was deemed to have officially finally closed in the 1890 US Census – just a handful of years before the first western films mythologising the frontier were produced. US history and US film history have remained intertwined as narratives of a country in evolution at least ever since.[6] American movies have always attempted to depict the 'real' America as popularly imagined, and *Into the Wild* is no exception, although one might also suggest that it is also a sort of *anti*-road movie. That is to say, it is ultimately all about the destination (Alaska) and not the journey (America) – a reversal of Jack Kerouac's famous dictum in *The Dharma Bums* (1958). It is, in the final analysis, about living space, both real and imagined.

Into the Wild explores one individual's efforts to lead an authentic life, to seek living space within which the intuitive forms of intellect may be nurtured. The film itself even quotes, in one particular voice-over, the American travel writer and historian Wallace Stegner, reproduced in the epigraph to this chapter. The idea of being footloose, the romantic notion of ultimate freedom, limited not by government, nor social bonds, nor religious dogma, is as seductive today as it was in Stegner's twentieth century, and indeed in the nineteenth century of Emerson and Thoreau. This path of individuation and personal freedom, portrayed so powerfully in *Into the Wild*, does not sit easily with either modern democratic protocol such as the 'irksome obligation' of voting, or of any strong form of government, including welfare systems; but neither does it sit well with the radical free-market capitalism, rejection of *a priori* knowledge, and the emphasis on the primacy of reason (rendered as 'understanding' in Emerson's essay) found in objectivism. In fact, the particular form of transcendentalism represented in the film ultimately remains unfinished, as with so many of the forms of personal and shared histories discussed in this chapter. It is an open space, where the final phrase found in McCandless' writing, that 'happiness is only real when shared', leans against his earlier foundational apprehension about the limiting nature of human relationships. In psychological terms, the McCandless 'great adventure' uncovers an image of inspiration: not to shed social obligation and human relations as he did, but rather to re-imagine one's life as *both* a continuing and living relationship with personal, interpersonal and transpersonal history, *and* as a present-ness with all of the new and the novel that such an experience has to offer. It seems, then, that in order to fully apprehend the soul-world that inspires such stories, we need to emancipate the living dialectic of consciousness: an accommodation between soul and understanding in Emerson's terms, or, as Merleau-Ponty describes in *Sense and Non-Sense*, 'the union of mind and body, mind and world, and the expression of one in the other' (1964: 58) which, he argues, movies make manifest.[7] This takes into account the reasonable notion that one's consciousness is both of and in the world; that intuition in the sense of spontaneous intellectual production, as well as the sense of intuitive feeling, is both individual production and has an intimate relationship with the material conditions of one's own existence which are historical in character. The relation of present to past is, just as Benjamin acknowledges in the epigraph to this chapter, a temporal relation of continuity between what-has-been to the now that is fundamentally dialectical, and partakes of an ongoing dialogue between viewer and viewed of which, as in Merleau-Ponty's vision, the image (in this case, the moving image and the psychological 'feeling-image') makes manifest. Just as his parents grow to accommodate the wrongness of their relationship and unsuitability for one another, so too, McCandless came to realise, tragically too late, the lopsided relationship he had embarked upon: that natural space has also come to mean human space, and this space is fundamentally social.

In Part II of this book, I elaborate upon this living dialectic, beginning in the following chapter with an analysis of the massively popular phenomenon known as 'frat pack' cinema. In particular, we will see how notions of masculinity touched upon in the current chapter are both clichéd and conventional as well as being the fabric through which satirical material is interwoven, with both hilarious and meaningful results.

Notes

1 These are films that depict representations of the flawed nature of 'unreconstructed' masculinity and its imminent relationship to the natural environment (in particular, the American wilderness or frontier). Such examples as the Coen brothers' remake of *True Grit* (US, 2010), P. T. Anderson's adaptation of *There Will Be Blood* (US, 2007), *Crazy Heart* (Cooper, US, 2010) and *Into the Wild*.

2 Again, I return to this theme in my discussion of *Into the Wild*, below.

3 Clarissa Pinkola-Estes' *Women Who Run with the Wolves* (2008) springs to mind here.

4 That is until the European upheavals of 1848, where responses from the likes of Marx and other thinkers advanced the intellectual engagement with revolutionary action, and such political philosophy entered a new phase of maturity – see Hobsbawm (1996) *The Age of Revolution* and (1995) *The Age of Capital*.

5 I discuss some of these issues in depth in *Film After Jung* (2009: 154–8), particularly in relation to the philosophy of W. E. B. du Bois.

6 This is in addition to the precedent in dime novels, comic serials and other literary output in the late nineteenth century that romanticised the frontier, the West and the folk heroes who, fictional or real, populate the popular imagination about such things.

7 I elaborate upon these ideas further in the final two chapters of this study.

Part II

THE SURROUND
OF CINEMA

INTRODUCTION TO PART II

Adventure is out there (where I see):
the surround of cinema

> For his love is a creative means of *making* her more worthy – in the sense that he invests her with greater value, not in making her a better human being. That may also happen. But significantly, the lover changes *himself*. [...] In making another person valuable by developing a certain disposition within oneself, the lover performs in the world of feeling something comparable to what the alchemist does in the world of matter.
>
> (Irving Singer, *The Nature of Love Vol. 1: Plato to Luther*,
> 2nd edn, 2009: 15)

> Love takes hostages. It gets inside you. It eats you out and leaves you crying in the darkness, so simple a phrase like 'maybe we should be just friends' turns into a glass splinter working its way into your heart. It hurts. Not just in the imagination. Not just in the mind. It's a soul-hurt, a real gets-inside-you-and-rips-you-apart pain. I hate love.
>
> (Neil Gaiman, *The Sandman Vol. 9: The Kindly Ones*)

In Part I of this book, I explored the relationship between viewer and viewed in the cinematic encounter. I discussed and explored ways in which complex and sophisticated models of different kinds of feelings in the field of human experience have been accounted for in some philosophical and psychological traditions. I also offered discussion on certain specific sites of philosophical and psychological approaches – namely, Leibniz and his notion of 'little perceptions', Merleau-Ponty's existential phenomenology, and post-Jungian depth psychology – and the ways in which these approaches provide insights into the experience of various kinds of feelings within the cinematic encounter. Through a number of examples in popular cinema, I outlined aspects of cinematic meaningfulness – for example, in adaptation, transmediality and sequelisation, representation of gender. Particular to Chapter 3, I offered examples of representations of gender relative to the concomitant representations of on-screen relationships with both other characters and the environments they inhabit in the world of the films themselves. In a sense, what I have attempted to do is to clarify for the reader certain facets of the cinematic encounter that seem to exemplify what some film-phenomenologists such as Vivian Sobchack and Greg Tuck, and some practitioners of depth psychology perspectives on cinema such as Luke Hockley, have recognised as an inhabited dialogue between viewer and viewed. This is what I describe as the lived, warm psychological phenomenon occupying the 'in-between' of viewer and viewed, and the living dialectic of being-together, being-apart.

I would now like to expand that discussion further. By engaging a self-reflexive view of that encounter within inhabitations of cinema, we may begin to furnish conventional thinking on the impacts that extratextual materials have upon our approach (so to speak) to that encounter. In sum, what I have described in Part I of this book is that the emotional work of cinema, far from operating as mere on-screen content for scrutiny, is a far more ambiguous and emergent process between viewer and viewed. This is something that is to an extent widely recognised in cinema studies today, but perhaps is not given the emphasis that I believe it deserves in orthodox film theory and criticism. In this Introduction to Part II, I wish to explore a specific recent example of popular animated cinema, the Disney Pixar animated feature *Up* (Doctor and Petersen, US, 2009) to think through some of the implications already discussed in Part I which dealt with the cinematic encounter in its anticipatory and afterlife modes. That is to say, the cinematic encounter as narrative image, in the thinking of Stephen Heath and John Ellis, tends to foreshadow audience expectations of a given film's problematics (and indeed how those problematics are sometimes confounded and far from *faits accomplis*). But also, in thinking in more detail about that encounter as a form of afterlife, I will begin to unpick some of the ways (already alluded to in Part I) the cinematic encounter is enriched through cinema's migrating content from screen to screen. In this discussion I will consider how that content emerges through different spaces of access, various technologies and the different ways various audiences engage with that content in, for example, blogging culture and other social media practices.

It isn't my intention to place too much emphasis on the perceived newness and open nature of such engagements. What I wish to bring to the reader's attention here is that such spaces foreground many of the fannish and cinephilic practices of popular review that have been in existence for decades anyway, and that by itself is probably good cause for taking them seriously. I think that the importance of these phenomena is that they enable the critic to engage with everyday passions, feelings and emotional engagements that popular film viewing, and 'talking up' a film, brings to the cinematic encounter. The next few pages will highlight some of these issues in the context of a particular example, in this case *Up*, with a view to placing into context some of the issues raised so far in this book.

About this book, Part II: the surround of cinema

In order to give this discussion context, and outline its importance for the following chapters, I wish to emphasise here three aspects (to which I return in summary at the end of this introduction). These are themes which, when considered in sum, I describe as the 'surround of cinema'. By this, I don't necessarily mean that we as viewers are always subject to the sort of massive wrap-around cinema screen typically found in cinemascope or IMAX exhibition technologies when we engage with popular cinema (although, of course, this is a going concern for critics who are interested in that kind of spectacular screening experience). In addition, I am not necessarily stating by using this term that we are constantly surrounded by screens – although it ought to be acknowledged, in the context of the contemporary media environment and the recent arguments concerning media saturation, that this is a vital factor in contextualising much of what follows in Part II of this book.[1] In fact, I briefly return to this particular issue in Chapter 6, in my discussion of the cinematic glance.

The first of the themes I would like to discuss here relates to some of the issues of gender that have been raised so far, and, in particular, to the complexities of shifting masculine identity in late capital. I discussed some of these issues in Chapter 3 in relation to representations of the human body, to fatherhood and labour, to age and to environment. Some of these issues are reprised in the *Up* case study below, particularly concerning age (here, old age and its relation to nostalgia and youth, and the process of getting older, plays a crucial role) within the context of environment, the wilderness and adventure. The play with such notions in cinematic texts is one dimension of this, certainly. However, again it is worth emphasising the importance that we as viewers bring to the act of viewing a sense of worth to the sentiments being communicated (feeling as evaluation, a judgement; feeling as a dawning realisation, an intuition) as much as the intentional meanings of the filmmakers could ever make clear in their own storytelling methods. We must bear in mind the importance here of both the stories being told and how they are told cinematically, itself a story-making and telling process placed within the context of psychological material that is brought to the act of viewing, and that which emerges in the inhabited spaces of co-production, before, during and after the screening of a film. The emotional resonance of this model of meaning-making is surely a prominent element of such experiences within a popular film culture that seems to place (not altogether unduly, perhaps) an importance upon both emotional turbulence (one of the key drivers of drama and disequilibrium in a narrative arc) and happy endings.

With this in mind, I also wish to take account of the ways in which masculinity is often presented within an emotional foreground: one of *Up*'s central operations, for example, is a 'tugging of heartstrings' in the film's discernibly exploitative use of familial romance, nostalgia and narrative themes of death and loss. Some of these issues, in particular growing older and the shifts of emphasis upon expectations of ageing masculinity, including the role of emotion and talking about feelings, are explored further in Chapter 4. In relation to the 'Frat Pack', and, in particular, recent examples such as *I Love You, Man* (Hamburg, US, 2009) and *This is 40* (Apatow, US, 2013), there I discuss how the misunderstandings involved in some of those shifts in emphasis are used to heighten the comedic aspects of everyday relationships, both intimate, fraternal and familial.

The second theme that starts to emerge in discussions of the surround of cinema refers to the ways that contemporary technologies both shape and are shaped by the ever-increasing emphasis on extratextuality. It is not necessarily the aim of this book to categorise the kinds of innovations that have the most apparent impacts upon the viewing experience. Nevertheless, what Chapter 5 seeks to disentangle are the ways in which the spectacle of the cinematic encounter endures across the aforementioned multiple access points, the migratory content of which seems to increasingly address itself in a self-reflexive culture of the spectacular and through narratives of spectacle. I re-engage notions of cinephilic response to film culture already discussed at length in Part I within this particular context, seeking to critique the rhetoric of innovation that shapes and in many ways over-determines a popular view of what popular cinema is and can be. I revisit some of the more problematic notions of technological (and other) determinist positions in order to discuss the notion of competing elements in the act of viewing at the multiple and often overlapping levels of on-screen action and visual style, viewing pleasures and the attention economy of contextual networks within popular film cultures. I close that particular discussion through a critical disquisition of cognitivist–phenomenological accounts of the cinematic encounter in relation to a number of interesting and extreme examples of cinema which exemplify very different kinds of spectacle.

The final chapter brings all of the threads together from the preceding chapters to build upon a theory of the cinematic glance, which will carry this study forward into the realms of film-phenomenology. In that chapter, I flesh out the details of what I consider the work of cinematic narrative in the extended duration of the cinematic encounter: a cultural afterlife of cinema, if you like. My aim there is to re-evaluate the role and richness of the glance from a specifically phenomenological perspective, in order to provide an insight into how the momentary stays with us, psychologically speaking, in the emotional resonance of experiences; but, more than that, how the momentary pleasures of the cinematic encounter, sometimes quite fleeting and brief, endure through their retelling, in an extraordinary number of meaningful ways. I also return briefly to the discussion found right at the beginning of this book, looking at the qualitative differences between the cinematic and the televisual in order to explore their repercussions in a film culture which relies so heavily upon different-sized screens as well as varying formats and definition standards.

Lovefilm, and the love film

The two epigraphs to this introductory chapter draw forth an ambiguity at the heart of one of the key human emotions: love. In Chapter 4, I will return to this discussion of love in some detail, noting its eminence for and within popular filmmaking. I will also continue this discussion of love within cinema in relation to the love *of* film, or cinephilia as it is sometimes referred to, in Chapter 5. The fact that love is such an apparent universal phenomenon (certainly within the realms of popular narrative cinema, at least) is at once comforting, alienating and distracting. I say this for the following reasons. As Gaiman observes above, love is not merely a thing of the mind, but is also a thing of the heart: it makes one feel both alive and in the moment (as a sublime aesthetic of knowing one's humanity) but also acutely aware of one's fragility and the notion that one's beloved-ness could at some point be forever rejected and thus lost. It is at once the cause of aspiration and hope; this site for the miraculous union between persons that has been the subject of philosophy and psychological thought for centuries. As Singer implies in the first epigraph, love is the site of a mutuality and recognition that gives rise to an intersubjective sensibility, a kind of evaluation-feeling that Singer describes elsewhere as 'bestowal'. This is an aspect of intersubjective relations that is quite palpable and sensibly felt as being created by the affirmative relationship itself: 'by the very act of responding favourably, giving an object emotional and pervasive importance regardless of its capacity to satisfy interests' (Singer 2009: 5). Therefore, bestowal is an aspect of love that lies beyond both emotional objectivity and beyond self-interest. It is a transcendent moment that is suited to both the recognition of one in the other in the sense of love as sexual (Eros) and love as brotherly (agape). Bestowal is imbued with an evaluative aspect that enables maturity in the sense that Aristophanes meant in Plato's *Symposium*, where he describes the quest to restore human being to its wholesome, ancient state through the bestowal and reciprocation of love. Plato's motivation here is to point out the transformative aspect of love (in the sense of agape and Eros) through such bestowal and recognition.[2] This mythological narrative is replayed in classical and archetypal Jungian psychology, not only in the literal sense of interplay between expressions of archetypal material and imagery, but also in the sense of accommodation of such material for psychological growth. In other words, the appraisal of love might be framed as the acceptance of one's own flaws and the possibility of change through the affirmative relationship itself. Of course, the obverse of this relation can result in the kind of self-loathing and bitterness found in Gaiman's sentiments, where love sails precariously close to obsession. In its turn, this ambiguity in the idea and in the material relations of love would be fairly familiar territory for Jungian analysis, particularly in Singer's alchemy metaphor – the transformative and transcendent aspects of such affirmative relationships, which find common ground in the material articulations of mind, body and world.

Love, in this respect, is as subject to imminence as is any part of one's life, body and all. In other words, love is, like life itself, both felt (or endured) in the psychological state of the one and visibly apprehended in the eyes of the beholder, because the one 'doing the having' in this loving-feeling can feel it in their heart and gut, and the beholder recognises the resulting adumbrations of love. It is, therefore, both a deeply personal, subjective feeling and one which may be thought of as universally recognisable in an intersubjective sense. It is for this reason that love is treated with both comedy and with menace in dozens of familiar narratives in science fiction cinema and television, where the attractive 'female' robot is taught to love by her human inventor, and as a result either runs amok with jealousy or whose mechanical heart is broken by her unreciprocated advances.

If this reads a little Lacanian, it possibly ought to: having read Žižek and the way he repeatedly[3] returns to this theme in a number of publications, it becomes clear that the frustrated narrative of love is part of the life-lesson that we are, psychologically speaking, doomed to repeat. However, I think that there are clearly also links to a more Jungian approach to the feelings of love here that are just as useful, and to a Jungian framework fundamentally informed by phenomenology. For example, the idea mooted earlier in the book, of being 'had' by the feeling of love, possessed by it; an invasion beyond what one might describe as mere affect, certainly, through repetition, despite one's misgivings or even prior knowledge. A reproduction, it seems, of the impossibly high standards of Arthurian romanticism, whose idealised vision of romantic love was held in such high esteem by the Victorians; an impossibility for us to attain and yet we are under such great cultural pressure to do so.

Romantic comedy films in particular seem to know this, or at the least show this, in their uncanny ability both to reflect that supposed universal intersubjective recognition and, more unconsciously, to underpin the notion that the aspirational values of personal love are fundamentally at odds with its universal counterpart. This might reasonably be argued to be because the interests of universal love and personal love do not easily live side by side: the comedic aspects of romantic comedy often rely upon this observation in order to carry the film through the twists in plot. I return to this theme in the following chapter (and, indeed, to the theme of doomed repetition), but it is worth flagging up the observation again here: how often in romantic comedies does the man in the couple (and the couple is, in the overwhelming majority of cases in popular cinema, heterosexual) need to resolve a conflict between the love of the woman and some aspect of his lifestyle? This cliché is parodied with extraordinary effect, for example, in *Ted* (MacFarlane, US, 2012), itself a romantic comedy (with the emphasis here on comedy in place of much romance). In this story, John Bennett (Mark Wahlberg) has to decide between his girlfriend Lori (Mila Kunis) and his best friend Ted, a talking stuffed teddy bear (CGI-animated, and voiced by Seth MacFarlane). Very often in such films, of course, the problem is not resolved by the man, but is resolved for him, when the woman accepts the man for who he is, and the initially objectionable friend/hobby/lifestyle becomes subsumed into a new accommodation. In this particular example, it is Lori's wish to save Ted's life that secures the couple's future together. After such an observation it becomes quite apparent that *Ted* is a film that reinforces sentiments of personal heterosexual love rather than critiques it, and, arguably, ends up reproducing some of the tired uneven power relationships in the resulting heterosexual couple that we are used to seeing in popular cinema. Even in a scenario, such as in *Ted*, where the female lead has the power to grant or deny the male protagonist access to both her own intimate space and to the level of romantic commitment, it seems that she is only empowered on the terms of idealised romantic love in such situations – a deeply problematic situation that appears to offer a wholesale adoption of normative capital (i.e. empowerment as some sort of consumer choice).

With so much popular cinema (even in the case of clear parodic examples such as *Ted*) reproducing this notion and championing the personal over collective issues, the notion of universal love at the level of wider family, or community, nationally, globally and so forth tends to look faintly ridiculous. At best, it could be considered a matter of ethics in such a context. As such, is there an argument to be met that the idea of universal love, which seems to be an unrealistic requirement for all modern democracies (particularly given the relatively recent violent histories of such societies) and personal romantic love are entangled in a somewhat antagonistic relationship with one another?

The other aspects of this argument fundamentally relate to this question: the apparent (universal) recognition of universal love as comforting is, at the same, time an alienating and distracting one. I say this because it seems impossible to universalise such a fundamental experience, when much of what we experience in real life does not accord with the representations of ideal and idealised love in cinema. We do not all look like Mark Wahlberg and Mila Kunis for a start (nor Paul Rudd and Rachida Jones in *I Love You, Man*, for that matter), and certainly do not share some of the problems associated with their lifestyles. Invariably, most couples in romantic comedies seem to be rather well-to-do, unless the source of the humour expressly comes from the differing lifestyles of the protagonists, and the nub of their problems seem to stem from what can often be thought to be fairly trivial issues to an outsider.

I mentioned just a moment ago that love, although certainly a feeling that covers wide ground in terms of values and resultant emotions, is often seen as a miraculous union of some kind, between persons. Certainly, it would seem that much of the light-hearted treatment of the subject by Hollywood accords with this notion of love. I chose that description quite deliberately. As Rachel Moore has noted, in modernist versions of wonder, there are two particularly 'well-worn apothegms' in cinema history: 'that love is magic, and that technology is magic' (2004: 3). It is not the case necessarily that such magic moments of cinema possess particular emphases upon love and technology, but more a case where cinema (and all cinema, to an extent) serves through its material elements to 'give technology a key part in any movie' (2004: 7). When taken in context, it is often cinema's role to reveal love, in the sense that 'In movies where people are shown getting to know each other and falling in love, the magic moment in which love is mutually acknowledged is often confirmed by some kind of attention to technology' (2004: 3). It is significant here that Moore is taking on these wide themes of love and technology (themselves themes so *beloved* of popular cinema) to think through the implications of tactility and the touching materiality of love films for cinema more generally. At the same time and of even more interest is the way she uses the vehicle of historical cinema, citing examples from Dutch colonial cinema through to Scottish social realist films of the interwar period, and thence to recent Hollywood examples which use aesthetic devices and visual styles of cinema past to deliver their narrative conceits. In doing so, Moore manages to illustrate how the twin magical expressions of love and technology have been dealt with throughout cinema's history. Opening her essay with what is very much a giveaway line – 'Old films and footage are fascinating not just because they are old, but because they look old' – Moore foregrounds the affective properties of *patina* in cinema. This is a powerful phenomenon that recent CGI animated features desperately (and not without success, it ought to be acknowledged) seek to simulate in various ways. Patina as a cinematic phenomenon has been the subject of some debate in film histories and equally has formed part of historical filmmaking practice: Tarkovsky (1986: 59) springs to mind here with his evocation of the Japanese notion of *saba*, which roughly translated means the 'rust of time' – a fascination, of fundamental cultural importance, with the evidence of age; the care-worn face of a living ancestor. I use the phrase 'care-worn' here because it seems to embody the precise nature of love as an ambiguous, yet tangible, feeling. It is heartfelt and thoughtful even, and yet is fundamentally tied up with psychological well-being and can be seen visibly on the face of the bestower. *Ted*'s uneasy rendition of such sentiments is a case in point: the CGI technology allows the filmmaker to show an aspect of childhood love that is lost to the adult – a boy's love for his teddy bear, and the imagined reciprocal love from teddy. Here, that the bear is magically animated (through, predictably enough, a little boy's wish for a best friend) through both love and through technology is doubly significant because of the attention to detail. The detail in mastering and satirising the repeatable trope of the power of a child's imagination, coupled with the detail in rendering Ted himself as an uncannily photorealistic teddy bear lends the film a kitschy but nonetheless nostalgic register that reflects upon cinematic nostalgia in a number of ways.[4]

Up the (grey) revolution: 'technological' film and the spectacle of nostalgia

Up is notable in the context of this book and lends itself to this particular discussion for a number of reasons. To begin with, it engages a sense of cinema that is both historical and contemporary. It is, following Rachel Moore, a film that is fascinating not because it is old but because it looks old. Let me qualify that – it actually doesn't look old, because the CGI aesthetic is perceptible in its visual make-up; rather, it *feels* old. In its turn, the CGI aesthetic being employed here is one that attempts to elicit the feel of age and a patina of the passage of time in a peculiarly self-reflexive and spectacular fashion, whilst at the same time being perceptibly contemporary to popular digital cinema.

One might argue, of course, that all contemporary popular cinema tends to do this in the arrangement of institutional and apparatus elements, or at least has within its remit the potential to do so. The conventions of popular cinema attest to this notion: editing (montage in particular, and other 'invisible' continuity techniques), narrative trajectory (for example, the classic three-part structure), characterisation (human characters acting out of familiar psychological, emotional or reactive motivations), camera work (certain traditions in popular narrative cinema such as tracking, the 180-degree rule, establishing shots and so forth). These conventions, familiar in so many contexts to cinema-goers that we scarcely think about them or even notice them in everyday viewing, are the building blocks of narrative cinema, and our familiarity with them enables a certain technicity of understanding and meaning-making as it is shown for us on screen.

As the first three chapters of this book have helped to illustrate, this is not a simple matter of a unidirectional experience of what unfolds for us on the screen, or indeed during the screening of a film, but is a co-creational and psychological encounter between viewer and viewed, rich in meaningful resonance and often highly emotive and affecting in the experience. It lives beyond the duration of the film's screening in the anticipatory sense of a film's narrative image, including all manner of marketing materials, previews, cross-promotional materials, visual cues including posters, trailers and the like (found in the theoretical approaches of, for example, Stephen Heath 1981 and John Ellis 1992). It also finds a living and lived afterlife in the way that people tend to 'talk up' the film, reviewing it, re-viewing it and engaging with the materials of the story-worlds in a number of highly creative and pleasurable ways. Blogging and blogging culture play a major role in this, but also here I am thinking of the kinds of tertiary production processes often described as forms of user-generated content that are now so widely and deftly exploited in the transmedial and convergent mediascapes of contemporary popular film cultures.

At this point, one must be careful not to write off the idea of a singular cinematic experience altogether: the pleasures afforded a distinct screening uninformed by promotional materials, and the ways that some cinephiles sometimes actively seek to avoid as much of the contextual promotion materials as far as possible, are important. Within the contexts of the big-budget megapictures found in contemporary popular cinema, this is no mean task, and the avoidance of extra-textual encounters has a value unto itself by virtue of its perceived rarity (whether this is actually the case or not). Having said this, it seems particularly difficult to avoid, and indeed film creatives at a number of levels actively embrace such extra-cinematic pursuits in the interests of telling rich and compelling stories within multilayered media environments. This layering of materials, and the awareness and engagement with such materials in the process of consumption, is related to the key differentiation that I mapped in the Introduction to Part I of this book, between 'film' and 'cinema'.

Up attempts (and we may say, to an extent, succeeds) to articulate much of this in the course of a stand-alone animated narrative feature film. Of course, there are endless promotional materials and merchandising opportunities exploited in the film's marketing, and fans have clearly been busy generating all sorts of visual content featuring characters and ideas from the film itself (including poster art and so on) if web searches are anything to go by. What I mean by stating that this is articulated through the course of the movie is that it tends to over-determine the articulation between telling and told; between its story and presentation. *Up* is by no means an isolated example of this – Moore's observation that the material elements of cinema tend to serve to give technology a role in all cinema seems particularly apt here. What this film does do is to invite the viewer *in*, to its world of unabashed nostalgia and yearning for a lost love. I mentioned a moment ago that *Up* feels old. How and why does this happen; or, is it just me?

I have to confess at this point that, yes, it is in a sense me projecting much of my own personal cinephilic and idealist views of cinema upon the reading of this particular film. Nonetheless, I am not entirely alone in thinking that *Up* seems to embody a feel of the old. When, in *Acting in the Cinema* (1988), James Naramore relates his fascination with Cary Grant's socks in the famous crop-dusting sequence in *North by Northwest* (Hitchcock, US, 1959), he reports his own delight at the idea that fascination with the most mundane and incidental of details should also be the object of fascination for someone else. It turns out that others have noticed and are fascinated by Grant's socks, and that although these details aren't necessarily open and shared, they are nonetheless known within cinephile circles. Naremore states that:

> In the overall economy of the film, the visibility of such minor details is little more than an instance of how stardom, acting and photographic imagery tend to 'outrun' narrative; if I am subjectively aware of Grant's clothing, that is simply because fragments of coloured fabric, in dialectical relation to flesh, constitute an elemental lure.
>
> (1988: 215)

Not minor details of *Up*, the sequences that I would like to flag up seem to have been major talking points of the film in general. During a recent television broadcast, my own Facebook news stream was inundated with status updates and comments within the first 15 minutes of the film's screening. Almost uniformly, these comments were of the variety 'I've blubbed already', 'The beginning gets me every time', 'So sad. Crying already :'(' and so on. There were at least 20 status updates, and these from a wide range of people from different backgrounds. Some were hardened film academics, others fashion buyers, teachers, photographers, shopkeepers, bar tenders and so on – men and women, young and old. Whilst this observation hardly constitutes strong empirical evidence or a reliable sample, it does illustrate what I mean by shared objects of fascination. Certainly, *Up*'s opening ten minutes are discernibly geared towards eliciting that sort of emotional response, and in this sense are a success. However, there are other more interesting things occurring here.

The film opens with simulated footage of a newsreel. The moving image is in grainy black and white, and, in the style of the *March of Time* reels, features an exposé on Charles Muntz (voiced by Christopher Plummer), an explorer who is decorated for his contribution to science. The report features shots of his dirigible, *The Spirit of Adventure*. We track out of the newsreel's screen space to see that it is being played in a movie theatre. A shot of the projector beam tilts down towards a young Carl Fredricksen in the cinema audience, enthralled and delighted at the images he sees of Muntz and his adventures. We are also shown Muntz's decoration by the authorities and subsequent self-imposed exile to Paradise Falls to prove his innocence when accused of falsifying scientific evidence. Ignoring his hero's fall from grace, we then see Carl playing in the street, pretending to be Muntz having an adventure. He meets a young Ellie (voiced by Elie Docter) who shares his passion for adventure, and who, on pain of making him swear that he will not tell a living soul, shows him her adventure scrapbook. Ellie makes Carl promise that when they grow up he will take them to Paradise Falls.

This childhood meeting sets the scene for a prolonged montage sequence without dialogue in which we are shown Carl and Ellie's wedding and married life together. They are happy and plan a family together but are unable to have children. Seeing Ellie distraught at this prospect, Carl resolves to keep his childhood promise and to take them to Paradise Falls. Over time, they attempt to save up the air fare to go, but various mishaps and life's necessities get in the way so that saving becomes impossible. Decades go by, and their savings are forgotten until one day, when they are in their dotage, Carl remembers his promise and buys two air tickets to Paradise Falls to surprise Ellie. Tragically, she suffers what appears to be a heart attack and passes away before he can deliver the tickets to her, leaving Carl alone. This is the point at which the main body of the film begins.

There are a few things to note about this sequence. First, although setting up large chunks of back-story through the newsreel, and through the childhood romance and married life of Carl and Ellie, it operates quite apart from the main body of the film. In essence, it would work very effectively as a stand-alone story.[5] One of the key elements that distinguishes this sequence from the remainder of the film is that Carl doesn't speak at all. In fact, this is one of the things that Ellie finds attractive in him: 'You know, you don't talk very much. I like you!' He is figured as a rather sensitive boy who becomes a sensitive young man, prone to accidents and bad luck as much in adulthood as he was as a child. Young Ellie speaks at length, not really giving Carl the opportunity, and she is clearly coded as a spirited tomboy with a taste for adventure and rough 'n' tumble; a coding complete with red hair, dungarees and missing teeth. The possibility that Carl mistakes her for a boy upon their first meeting adds to this image, and this is perfectly in keeping with what we are later shown about Ellie, where she is practical, creative and energetic. The glimpse that we are afforded of their family backgrounds (the only evidence of any family, until – possibly – the later adventure book scene) at their wedding is telling: Ellie comes from what appears to be a family of freewheeling homesteaders, who cheer as she leaps upon Carl for their first kiss; Carl, by contrast, seems to come from rather more sober, Lutheran stock, somewhat in keeping with his Scandinavian name.

Everything in the first moments of the film (including a rather excellent playful score composed by Michael Giacchino) is geared towards an aesthetic of the old, the lost and the innocent. The caption in Ellie's adventure scrapbook, 'Paradise Falls, a land lost in time', points to the recurring motif of the film. By removing, in a physical sense, the Fredricksens' house to a location 'lost in time', we are in a sense transported from the cares and woes of contemporary life for the remainder of the film. We are shown a fantasy space where dogs can talk, dirigibles are a modern form of transport, and the concerns of adulthood are stripped of their everyday value.

This is consistent throughout the film. The Paradise Falls fantasy space values the peculiar antiquated technologies employed by Carl compared to the more contemporary GPS technologies used by the Wilderness Explorers: when Russell (voiced by Jordan Nagai) reveals his Wilderness Explorer GPS navigation unit, he almost immediately tosses it out of the window of the floating house accidentally. It is almost as if something has unconsciously prompted him to disregard the cold and somewhat empty feel of twenty-first-century technologies, and the perceptibly empty values that this film associates with them. The retro-futuristic technologies that enable Muntz's dogs to speak English allow the narrative to move on the premise that whilst the story is contemporary to the present day, it is expressed through the dream machines of high modernity. All of this is quite in addition to the more general inter-generational miscomprehension between the curmudgeon Carl and the ever-optimistic, plucky Russell. This miscomprehension finds its mirror expression in the way that the dogs are anthropomorphised in their capacity to speak English, even though their use of it extends the expression of dogs-as-dogs: 'I like you, temporarily!'; 'The small mailman smells of chocolate!' This is doubly significant because it makes present the different kinds of 'magic' that Moore relates to the fascination with emotive filmmaking: the lost fantasy space of talking dogs and the magical technologies (both diegetically in the dogs' collars and the CGI animation technologies themselves) that enable the dogs to talk in the first place.

The title sequence, such as it is, consists of two production credits, rendered in what could be described as a vaguely art deco typographic style – a nod certainly to the period in which the childhood section of the opening sequence is played out, which, according to the Pixar wiki, is 1939.[6] For the postmodern Marxist thinker Frederic Jameson, this amounts to pastiche that reinvents the experience of 1939 in the way the film is attempting to convey a feeling of 1939-ness. Significantly, he writes at length on this subject in relation to another film with critical roots in 'technology-as-magic': *Star Wars* (Lucas, US, 1977). He writes of this landmark film that:

> It is a complex object in which on some first level children and adolescents can take the adventures straight, while the adult public is able to gratify a deeper and more properly nostalgic desire to return to that older period and to live its strange old aesthetic artefacts through once again.
>
> (1997: 24)

It seems reasonable enough to assume at first glance that this state of affairs is equally applicable to *Up*, so appropriate it seems to this case. However, there is another, more striking dimension of nostalgic register which allows us to take this a step further. The crucial point here is that Jameson is alluding to a memory of adventure movie serials, which older audience members at the time of the first screening of *Star Wars* in 1977 were almost certain to have experienced first-hand. Lucas and his team were attempting to reinvent the experience within a single movie context, which afterwards became the mega franchise that we are familiar with today.

Nostalgia films usually attempt to recreate an historical period, or at least the sense of one, that is either within living memory or beyond. *Star Wars* occupies a strange place here in that its historical conceits are both fictional and impossible: its nostalgic aspect lies in the recreation of the aesthetics found in artefacts that are within living memory and testimony of at least some of its audience. These artefacts (in this case, movie serials of the early to mid-twentieth century) are simulated in order that the film act as a metonym for oldness; for a representational regime that is now lost, and that itself perhaps only hinted at an historical truth.[7] This remove from historical truth is related to a similar notion I hinted at in relation to the postmodern in Chapter 3, and I return to this in some detail in Chapter 5, in relation to revisionism in Hollywood. For now, it is worth mentioning in relation to a feel for the past or a sense of the past, regardless of whether or not it is an accurate or somehow truthful representation of history. As Jameson continues: '[...] by reinventing the feel and shape of characteristic art objects of an older period (the serials), it seeks to reawaken a sense of the past associated with those objects' (1997: 24). In many ways, like *Star Wars*, *Up* seeks to nurture this feeling through its attempts to simulate the feel of adventure movie serials both overtly (in its repeated verbalisation, 'Adventure is out there!') and rather more subtly in its oblique and direct references to the aesthetics of cinema history.

Our 'readiness' to accept some of *Up*'s more perceptible overtures to nostalgia is clearly encouraged through the device of the old versus the new, and this is played out throughout the film. A prominent example of this occurs when we are shown the encroaching presence of property developers and big business upon the rather more sedate village life seen in the opening sequence. Almost immediately in the main body of the film, the visual language of the juxtaposition of the rather quaint, small-town, old Mom 'n' Pop America, symbolised by the Fredricksens' little wooden house, is pitted against a newer, slick corporate operation, involving high rise steel and glass structures and rather faceless men in suits. What seems obvious to me is that both the narrative and the visual juxtaposition presented here so closely resemble the opening moments of **Batteries Not Included* (Robbins, US, 1987) – a similar tale of encroaching mortality, love and 'magic'. I mention this as significant because the similarity between the two films does not end there. The presentation of advanced technologies (in this case, alien technology) is shown through matt work and animation, and has a peculiarly retro feel: one of the aliens is 'repaired' from old spare parts and mechanical detritus. The retro feel of

Batteries Not Included is underpinned quite noticeably through a score that is reminiscent of dance hall and big band music that was *the* popular music of the 1930s and 1940s. I am not necessarily suggesting that elements of *Up* directly plagiarise *Batteries*, or at least pastiche them (although, of course, this is a possibility). Rather, I am concerned here that both films seek to evoke a specific feeling, a sensibility of nostalgia, and that, perhaps operating unconsciously, such films negotiate their sense of history at similar, highly affective, gut-levels, using audio and visual strategies that are at once quite familiar and quite noticeable.

One way in which this becomes highly visible in *Up* is in the scene directly following Carl and Russell's falling-out over Carl's refusal to rescue Kevin, the 'Beast of Paradise Falls', from the clutches of the villainous Muntz. He finally reaches the falls featured in Ellie's scrapbook, having dragged their house there, and thus fulfils her childhood dream. He tidies up the house, positions their chairs in their customary place, takes a large breath and closes his eyes, and sits with a sigh of relief. The relief is short-lived, however – he immediately opens his eyes and stares into space, and then to the chair beside him where Ellie used to sit. In his haste to fulfil what he imagined to be Ellie's life-long dream, he has stumbled upon the same realisation that McCandless did at the end of his own adventure. As stated in Chapter 3, McCandless realised, at the end of things, that 'happiness is only real when shared'. Carl's journey has been anything but fulfilled. He picks up the scrapbook that lay on the table at his side, reinserting the torn-out page featuring 'Paradise Falls, a land lost in time'. He slowly turns the old pages, and here, once again, we are shown the relationship between degraded technology and age.

In the sound design, audibly we are able to perceive the surface of paper, as the sound of rough fingertips caressing the surface of the heavy paper in the scrapbook itself palpably expresses for us the act of touching and being touched, as well as the sensation, the *feeling* of being touched, both physically and emotionally. As Moore points out, the expressive relation between degraded technology and age is a powerful element of the tactility of cinema, and its ability to express the perceptive and perceptible feel of surface, of skin. She writes that:

> The power of degraded technology to create intimacy does not go unnoticed by filmmakers today where its use extends from the avant-garde to popular cinema. [...] The intimacy-effect of degraded technology operates within these modern films, but old film draws out a similarly stirring effect when the material detritus of time, in the form of patterns, changes of colour, and ageing's various haphazard scars' surface [...]
>
> (2004: 1–2)

As Carl flicks through, we are shown various pictures, old photographs and objects that Ellie collected as a child, and he comes to the page where the young Ellie scrawled 'Things I am going to do' in black crayon. The very term 'scrapbook' is suggestive of a more intimate, *actual* cut-and-paste relationship between the memories, dreams and feelings that Ellie had, and her effort to express and preserve these for Carl (and, hence, for us). In her book *Love, Mortality and the Moving Image* (2012), Emma Wilson writes about the way that 'the labile moves between time sequences, between childhood reconstruction, citation, and present footage in a film' can enable a director (and I would argue, viewer) to conceive of a non-linearity of time (2012: 30). *Up* has all of these things, embodied in the two sequences I am pointing to. Wilson is here describing the films of Agnès Varda, an altogether different tradition in cinema, but she is articulating a more general point concerning emotional time: a much more sporadic, spontaneous and circular time, which is made up of firm and loose associations connected to memories, dreams, aspirations, experiences and endings. This is, to put it in psychological terms, a kind of mythic time: a time of the imagination, full of resonance that seems to transcend the superficial significance that we might ordinarily accord everyday, ordinary time.[8] It is, in other words, an acknowledgement of the mysteries of everydayness – a rich tapestry of ordinary knowledge which, in the clutter of our lives, tends to get lost.

The existential psychotherapist Emmy van Deurzen champions the reconnection with this everyday time to the extent that it provides the key to unlocking the difficulties of psychological disquiet. She writes that 'It is only with an attitude of openness and wonder that we can encounter the impenetrable everyday mysteries, which take us beyond our own preoccupations and sorrows, and which by confronting us with death, make us rediscover life' (2010: 5). Wilson's rich description of Varda's work gives us further insight into the power of film to reveal the workings of such mysteries, particularly in this 'scrapbook' approach to building up images from various sources and times, made through very different technologies, to make visible such emotional time. She suggests, in much the same vein as Moore's apothegms concerning technology, love and magic, that 'Film is cherished as a medium that can hold different moments of being all at once, that can animate and renew the transcription of experience' (2012: 30). That transcription enables us to 'decode' the everyday and enter into an accommodation with its messy, but revealing, insights.

This is a rather cinephilic description of film if ever there was one – strongly reminiscent of the kind of thick description found in phenomenological accounts of the moving image. It is a self-reflexive viewing-view of film, engaging both the act of viewing and that which is being represented for viewing, in an anthropocentric sense. I would argue that *Up* is a definitive, if extreme, example of the ways that digital simulation of memory-making and recollecting are foregrounded in cinematic narratives of ageing, in this sense. The images in the scrapbook are rendered through the CGI to be flawed, to have something of what might be described as 'character', or even, dare it be said, 'soul'. Once again, we are brought into the realms of the interplay between the very modern (contemporary CGI technologies) and the antiquated objects these digital means render: older visual technologies, such as black and white photographs, and Polaroid pictures, many of them grainy, blurred and dotted with 'imperfections'. In addition, to return to an earlier point, these scratchy, faded images offer up for our vision aged faces, lined and worn with the cares of life. They are views of human relationships for our vision, and thus enable, in an intersubjective sense, the emotional objects there on the screen, where we see, from the here of where we look. This is further foregrounded because it is quite unclear who in the world of the film took all of these photographs of Carl and Ellie throughout their marriage – they have no children and are, as far as we are aware, both only-children, and so it is difficult to work out if these were taken by family, friends or whatever.

What is a little less ambiguous is the sense that these photographs play a crucial narrative role in terms of our understanding of Carl's inner feelings. Other than the adumbrations indicating his affective state such as tears welling, wobbly chin and so forth, it is through touch (and the sound of touch) that these feelings are cued for us more fully. This is expressed in the tenderness through which Carl's emotions are visibly stirred whilst revisiting them, and the physicality of contact between hand and page. The final photograph in the scrapbook, showing Carl and Ellie sitting in their chairs, happy in their dotage, has a handwritten note that simply reads: 'Thanks for the adventure – now go have a new one! Love, Ellie.' The 'scrapbook' embodies the notion that memories, tended through antiquated visual technologies, may be seen, therefore, as a sort of 'labour of love' – and in this, of course, I am aware of unabashedly reproducing *Up*'s nostalgic sentiment here – and I bring this up because of Carl's reaction to the handwriting. We are shown the writing in close-up, and then we see Carl's hand caress the writing, as if feeling for the indentations that the pencil markings have made and the trace of Ellie's hand: the gentle sound of scratching the surface lower in the mix now, but still audible, and perceptibly present for us.

Notes

1 Slightly outside of the remit of this book, nevertheless I note the importance of these issues here, as they provide vital context for the discussions to follow, particularly in the final chapter. I wish to note four major new media theorists whose work has influenced my thinking on these peripheral issues. First, in her recent study *Alone Together* (2010), Sherry Turkle outlines the psychological implications of being 'always-on'. Similarly, danah boyd's work on this subject (2012) has implications in terms of lifestyle and lifestyle choices within always-already connected contexts. Third, Howard Rheingold's earlier, more utopian take on the 'always-on' phenomenon as part of his *Smart Mobs* study (2002) and more recent critical reappraisal (2012). Finally, Siva Vaidhyanathan's recent book *The Googlization of Everything (and Why We Should Worry)* (2011) examines some of these issues from a politically aware anti-corporate stance.

2 It is thus a fascinating model for thinking through representations of both Platonic and Sapphic love on-screen, their differences and continuities, and love's ability as an act and as a feeling to both transform the self through bestowal and to enable a transcendent movement form the erotic to the sublime. This is the topic of some detailed discussion in Chapter 4, but I should also point out that this has repercussions that go beyond questions of representation and are intimately tied up with the prospects of transcendent movement between viewer and viewed in that other kind of love in the cinema – cinephilia. These are issues that I raise in Chapters 5 and 6, in relation to the surround of cinema.

3 In particular, I am thinking here of his book *Violence* (2008), which contains a critique of love in both idealised personal forms and in its broader sense. In addition, there is a rather well-known sequence from the biographical documentary film *Žižek!* (Taylor, US/Can., 2005) in which he describes the idea of universal love as 'evil'.

4 I have discussed many of these issues elsewhere as a peripheral concern about archetypical narratives and characters (2011) but also in some detail with regards to CGI to simulate patina for nostalgic purposes (2012). In the case of *Ted*, this kitschy use of nostalgic references even extends to a cameo appearance by Sam Jones as himself, who most notably played the lead role in *Flash Gordon* (Mike Hodges, US/UK, 1980), a high-camp tribute to the classic movie serial from the 1930s.

5 In private correspondence, Luke Hockley quite rightly pointed out to me that this feature is something of a nod to *Citizen Kane* (Wells, US, 1940), at least for the cinephile. Such practices are, I would add, fairly commonplace in the artisanal directorial work of filmmakers such as the Coen brothers, and, of course, a number of Bond movies, including *Casino Royale* (Campbell, US/UK/Ger., 2006).

6 http://pixar.wikia.com/Carl_Fredricksen (accessed 19/03/13). In fact, more evidence may be found in the newsreel reporter's reference to the size of *The Spirit of Adventure*, which he describes as being the equivalent length of 'twenty-two prohibition paddy wagons' end to end. Incidentally, the year in which *Up*'s opening moments are set, 1939, seems to be very significant. In my essay 'The Kitsch Affect; or, Simulation, Nostalgia and the Authenticity of the Contemporary CGI Film' (2012), I discuss the setting of *Sky Captain and the World of Tomorrow* (Conran, US, 2004); the New York premiere of *The Wizard of Oz* (Fleming, US, 1939); and the fact that New York, 1939 was the location of both the World's Fair and the first major science fiction convention. I return to some of these points briefly in Chapter 5 in relation to that film.

7 I elaborate upon the affective properties of retrofuturism in my essay 'The Kitsch Affect' (2012), as well as the way a lost past is relived, particularly through science fiction and action-adventure.

8 This is a dawning awareness of a kind of afterlife that resonates with the everyday, to which I devote much discussion in Chapter 6 and in the Conclusion to this book.

4

I LOVE YOU, MAN

Mandate movies, bromantic comedies and the 'Frat Pack'

Robbie Klaven:	A 'mandate' [...] casual lunch or after-works drinks, ok? No dinner and no movies – you're not taking these boys to see *The Devil Wears Prada*.
Peter Klaven:	Oh god, I LOVE that movie!

(*I Love You, Man*, Hamburg, US, 2009)

Supplementing Socrates with Alcibiades reveals the multiple possibilities of love and its perplexing articulation of the carnal and the ethereal, of voluptuousness and torment. Abstracted love and passionate love are not wholly opposed in Plato's text but are instead interrelated: love of knowledge develops from erotic experience.

(Linnell Secomb, on Plato's *Symposium*, 2007: 19)

In the Introduction to Part II of this book, I relayed the rather touching story of geriatric adventurer Carl Fredricksen, the love of his life, Ellie, and his pursuit of their childhood dream after her death. The story itself, though perhaps admittedly exploitative, is told in a thoroughly moving way: a love story between two childhood sweethearts separated by death, lovingly told through references to childhood games, traditional animation aesthetics (as well as, of course, CGI) and nostalgic references to the cinema of days-gone-by. In its expression of perception (a dream that is shared) and its perception of expression (living the dream), *Up* embodies for the viewer a view of that most palpable and yet elusive of cinematic themes: love. Love is a kind of feeling expressed in and expressible through cinema, that (at the risk of sounding trite and sentimental) seems to reach out and touch us, just as hearts in the audience crave it. It has, historically speaking, therefore been at the forefront of cinematic expression, in the stories of people and their lives, in the driving theme of even the most heartless big-budget action movies, and in the stylistic rendering of these love stories. Thinking back to *Cinema Paradiso* (Tornatore, It./Fr., 1988), a film about love in general as much as about the love of cinema, the montage sequence towards the end reveals the cares of the filmmaker Salvatore (Jacques Perrin) as he measures his life and his love through love-clinches throughout cinema history. The film's point is to remind us that we live and love vicariously through cinema with such feeling that we are, psychically speaking, in accord with it. Love is feeling *par excellence*, the emotion that much emphasis is placed upon and that has the most cultural value invested in it; and cinema, in its own way a domineering force within audio-visual cultures, is often love-shown-for-us.

Throughout his great work, *Thus Spake Zarathustra*, Nietzsche made grand flip-flop movements between radically different positions on love, ultimately identifying, as with all things in Nietzsche, a conflict of opposites in one and the same phenomenon. He wrote that love is inherently paradoxical: at once a search for fulfilment and a painful lack; it is effort and yearning at one and the same time, intoxicating in both its allure and its obsessive demands. It is a confusing and confused language in itself that intertwines the great love of mankind with a conditional Christian love of God, and the unhappy, yet passionate cravings of distant love in solitude (summarised in *Ecce Homo*, 1979: 108). Therefore, it is something of a miracle, perhaps, that we ever come to love; that we actively seek it out in order to experience it at all.

I bring up this rather unlikely expert on love because Nietzsche's amoral approach to the subject seems to echo down to our own time, to our own popular cultural artefacts. The paradoxical nature of what we might describe as love has within it the ingredients that are discernible in many examples of popular film genres today. The romantic comedy, for example, is a truly hybrid genre that foregrounds the comedic situations that arise from the mutual and fundamental misunderstandings that occur between the sexes and, as is becoming more frequent (if still uncommon), misunderstandings that occur in same-sex relationships. Most often, such misunderstanding is figured in instances of a 'battle between the sexes': *The War of the Roses* (DeVito, US, 1989) is a well-known replaying of the on-screen chemistry of Michael Douglas and Kathleen Turner, whose previous outings in the action-adventure romantic comedy vehicles *Romancing the Stone* (Zemeckis, US, 1984) and its sequel *The Jewel of the Nile* (Teague, US, 1985) are given a darker treatment in the later DeVito film. The perceptible on-screen chemistry, even if experienced vicariously through its articulation in popular film review and not necessarily the views of cinema-goers themselves, is rendered more palpable through the generic formal elements of romantic comedy associated with misunderstanding and reconciliation. Of course, as I write these accounts of 'on-screen chemistry', 'misunderstandings' and even 'romance', I become aware of their illusory aspects; thoroughly in keeping with a Nietzschean backdrop of internal opposites, such popular cinema tends to repeat the mistakes of the past *ad nauseum*, like some sort of mass cultural parapraxis. It is as if none of the characters featured in these films have ever seen a romantic comedy themselves, and do not understand the pitfalls (and pratfalls) of such entanglements.

Then again, neither do we, as cinema-goers, mind the pitfalls; even though we have certainly seen romantic comedies. Since antiquity, following Plato and Sappho, there have been fables and morality tales regarding the follies of love, even down to the misunderstanding of *which* love one is referring to in discussion. At the same time, these stories celebrate love and hold it up as a feeling in great esteem; often, our acceptance of being beloved, and our ability to return love, becomes the standard whereby our humanity is measured. Indeed, as pointed out with reference to the work of Irving Singer in the Introduction to Part II, the acts of bestowal are transformative; and the relationship between the lover and the loved is an intimate, one might say magical, intersubjective bond that has the power to change people dramatically. Historically, therefore, love has featured as one of the most important emotional and psychological feelings, and its political and ethical implications have been contested time and again in philosophy, art production and fiction.

So far, I have written about lost love, remembered love and conventional romantic love, usually figured through the perceived natural coupling of two members of opposite sexes. To this we need to add other kinds of representations of love. Same-sex relationships, for example, are now fairly conventional in mainstream Hollywood film (although still usually treated with suspicion, either in the sense that they are a source of comedy or otherwise a force of danger to be contended with and, even now, subject to arbitrary censorship by the MPAA and other political reactionaries in the US and beyond). The odd thing about this kind of representation is, once again, in the complex nature of how revising for an imagined marketplace tends to disturb the surface of a film, to send ripples out into the emotional and affective fabric of film-viewing. An example of this may be gleaned from a repeated viewing of the two cinema versions of *The Girl with the Dragon Tattoo*. In the Swedish version (and even more evident in the TV mini-series from which the cinema trilogy was edited down), the relationship between Lisbeth and Miriam/Mimi Wu (Yasmine Garbi) not only proves crucial in the plot intrigues of the later instalments, but is figured as the most important and stable of Lisbeth's relationships. We can tell this through Rapace's gestures – a look here, a deft but reassuring hand-hold there – when Lisbeth is with Miriam. For all we know, they are *lovers* in every sense of the word. We only get to glimpse Miriam briefly in ... *Dragon Tattoo*, at Mikael and Lisbeth's first meeting, when Mikael enters her flat, unwanted and unannounced, and Lisbeth just happens to be in bed with Miriam when he calls.

In the US remake, an altogether different effect is created through the preamble to the same scene. In this version, Lisbeth goes out to a club and picks up a stranger. At the time of writing, we are unsure as to how this relationship might develop in the US remakes of the sequels, because they have yet to be made, and various Web guesses (including Wikipedia and imdb) state these sequels are unlikely to go into principal production until 2014 at the earliest. However, we may speculate that either the sequels would need to introduce a new character called Mimi or the stranger that we meet in the first film is developed into a more significant character who takes on some of the attributes and plot roles of Mimi later on.

This matter is complicated, however, when one starts to unpick same-sex relationships as not merely sexual (whether casual encounters or in the context of stable monogamy) but, in the traditional sense of the word, 'Platonic'. For, although for the Greeks tended to champion the love of knowledge over and above the earthly pleasures of the flesh, Plato took on board and developed the teachings of Socrates, and there is evidence that he was very familiar with Sapphic, fleshly love as a value concept. As Linnell Secomb writes in the epigraph to this chapter, 'Abstracted love and passionate love are not wholly opposed in Plato's text but are instead interrelated: love of knowledge develops from erotic experience' (2007: 19). This is not quite the same as the opposites found in Nietzsche's love, but it lays the foundation for both the tension between the two loves and their union in a dialectical flowering where one may articulate the other. Here, I am referring back to the version of dialectics I mentioned in the Introduction to Part I, the version of dialectics that Merleau-Ponty describes as 'hyperdialectic': a suspension of struggle, an opening-out or bursting forth; a dynamic between interior and exterior aspects which 'provides the global and primordial cohesion of a field of experience wherein each element opens onto the others' (1973: 293).

Indeed, if seen reflexively, this dialectic of the passionate and the ethereal is the epitome of the dialectics of embodiment, and is eminently applicable to the phenomenology of film viewing. For the following of a film's narrative course is often an exercise in intellectual and emotional engagement. *Bicentennial Man* (Columbus, US, 1999), for example, is a film that engages speculative accounts of technology and the possibility of artificial intelligence as a kind of human intelligence (and artificial life forms taking on the spiritual characteristics and moral status of humanity). Once again, there seem to be strong narrative and emotive parallels between technology and love, articulated as kinds of 'magic', as described by Rachel Moore, referred to in my Introduction to Part II. Based upon an Isaac Asimov short story and novel ('The Bicentennial Man' and *The Positronic Man* respectively), *Bicentennial Man* is fairly complex in its ambitions to achieve the task of philosophical proposition (can artificial life be considered human life?) through cinematic storytelling, and requires intellectual speculation on behalf of the viewer as to the nature of humanity and what it is and means to be human. Speculation on such a fundamental subject is, unsurprisingly, a highly emotive one too, and is precipitated by scientific inquiry and philosophical treatments (Mori's notion of the Uncanny Valley (1970) springs to mind here). With this in mind, it should come as no surprise that *Bicentennial Man* is characterised by emotionally charged scenes throughout, brought about largely through an exploitative and saccharine music score that underpins the emotional message. The film portrays the story of Andrew Martin (Robin Williams), a robot who shows signs of humanity (creativity, emotion and self-awareness) and, over the course of several decades, eventually replaces all of his body parts with an artificially created organic body in order to experience life as a human and be legally declared a man. This is finally achieved towards the end of the film, when Andrew decides to alter his positronic brain so that it decays, much like the human brain, and he becomes mortal. In a state of empathy, we can view this story as a 'tug-of-loves': an evolution of both the heart and mind; an emotional and intellectual speculation on human identity told through a metanarrative of the particular story forms of emotional filmmaking and speculative fiction.

In common with *Bicentennial Man*, *Robots* (Wedge and Saldanha, US, 2005), like many Disney/Pixar, Dreamworks and Fox Animation CGI features, portrays mechanical technologies rendered through digital animation in similar retro-nostalgic register. Indeed, some of these issues were explored in the Introduction to Part II of this book. Likewise, *TRON: Legacy* (Konsinski, US, 2010), another Disney production (and the sequel to *TRON*, Lisberger, US, 1982), in common with many science fiction narratives of machines-going-wrong, features artificial intelligence which becomes malign through self-awareness. In an ecological spin on this kind of narrative, *TRON: Legacy*'s main contribution to the genre is the inclusion of artificial intelligent beings called ISOs (isomorphic algorithms), who are spontaneously brought into existence without programming or user intention. The two strands of big-budget science fiction here – artificial intelligence as both human-like and capable of love, and inhuman, dangerous and incapable of decision-making beyond pure logics and calculation – are the stuff of reflection upon the nature of our own humanity. In other words, as countless commentators on (and writers of) science fiction have noted, science fiction is not really about machines and future speculation. At its most fundamental, science fiction is most often a vision of human stories and is about the now, positing ideas as to how the human condition might be changed through the intervention of time and technology.

This retro-nostalgia is not unique to digital animation features nor to action-adventure and science fiction films, but, as we shall see, finds a powerful medium in the recent cycle of films made by and featuring Hollywood players known as the 'Frat Pack'. It is no accident to identify such a nostalgic register in fairly widely diverse kinds of films. Science fiction and action-adventure are, in the popular imagination, often thought of and described as masculine genres, and feature such tropes as violence, explosions, technology and homosociality often equated with all-male interests. There may be some truth in the attributing of such tropes to the cultural interests of men in Western societies, but this, of course, does not equate them necessarily with essential or genetic qualities we might associate with maleness or with the experience of men. One of the ways that this relationship is represented, questioned and parodied is through Frat Pack movies.

The Frat Pack

The apparently sudden and meteoric rise of the so-called Frat Pack cycle of films in the past decade has brought an urgency to certain questions regarding the representation of homosocial relationships, spaces and stories: questions that have perhaps always been there, but now come to the fore in respect of the popular cinematic treatment of different kinds of love, and in the specific context of romantic comedies. The Frat Pack is a term largely spawned by the popular press, but is also widely used in film blogging and review culture to badge a loose network of directors, writers, producers and actors. These are key figures in contemporary Hollywood who have pursued activities both on screen and behind the scenes during the last decade or so. Subject to arguments concerning inclusion and criteria, this group might be said to include major writer–directors and producers such as Ben Stiller, Judd Apatow, Todd Phillips and John Hamburg (and perhaps more loosely, Wes Anderson and Adam Sandler). It also includes actors such as Owen Wilson, Luke Wilson, Will Ferrell, Steve Carrell, Paul Rudd, Seth Rogan and Jason Segal. Many of these actors write or produce the material they appear in and have become (or are in the process of becoming) major stars and Hollywood players in their own right.

What makes this group and the films they are associated with important for this study is that not only does it represent some of the most popular cinema of the present day in the English-speaking world, but it has also helped innovate the romantic comedy form beyond a simple hybrid of two genres into a complex and emotionally sophisticated narrative platform to represent many of the key concerns and anxieties of contemporary America. The importance of the nomenclature 'Frat Pack' is up for debate, although it is notable that it embodies allusions to past cycles and movements in Hollywood which have proved historically significant, particularly in keeping the star system buoyant. As may well be familiar to the reader, the term is an allusion to the Rat Pack: the group of superstar singers and actors in the 1960s that included, most famously, Peter Lawford, Dean Martin, Frank Sinatra, Sammy Davis Jr and Joey Bishop. Together, these stars appeared in a number of feature films in various combinations, and some of them recorded and toured together at various stages of their singing careers. What is probably more significant, however, is the more 'knowing' comparisons made between the current Frat Pack and a later popular reference to the Rat Pack, known as the Brat Pack. This later group consisted of a number of young actors who regularly appeared in popular coming-of-age films in the 1980s – often, but not exclusively, hit films directed by John Hughes, whose stylistic and thematic influence is discernible in much of the Frat Pack output.

Another notable feature, and one that is immediately obvious in the above list of Frat Packers, is that although women do feature prominently in these films and 'women's issues' are often treated in sympathetic terms in plotlines, the overwhelming sense is that what we are dealing with here is a kind of boys' club. I use this term deliberately, because many of the films in this cycle are dominated by their male lead characters' anxieties surrounding impending marriage (*I Love You, Man*), fatherhood (*Knocked Up*, Apatow, US, 2007) or even terminal illness (*Funny People*, Apatow, US, 2009): all life-changing events that most men of certain ages will have to face. The comic and occasionally slapstick or gross-out treatment of such serious and everyday themes revolving around the anxieties of commitment and familial responsibility may be easily misinterpreted as juvenile, irresponsible or otherwise immature. *This Is 40* (Apatow, US, 2013) is a very recent case in point, concerning marriage and the perceived encroachment of middle age upon family life: Pete and Debbie, the couple featured in the film, are played by Frat veterans Paul Rudd and Leslie Mann, wife of director Judd Apatow. Their two children, Sadie and Charlotte, are played by Maude and Iris Apatow, daughters of Apatow and Mann. Mann and her daughters have appeared in a number of films directed by Apatow, including the film's prequel, *Knocked Up* (where the family featured in supporting roles rather than as the main focus). The ensemble casting of friends and family in the film may be overdetermined, but it isn't necessarily nepotistic: this film shines with performances that engage the detailed minutiae of family life and, arguably, the materials drawn from the performers' real lives can be seen informing how Debbie and her daughters would interact in a plausible manner. The ensemble performance engages with how such revelation is a part of the discovery of new and surprising things about loved ones whom we think we know inside and out (a situation that seems self-evident, and yet it reveals something about how we present ourselves in even the most intimate of relationships).

Some of these details include the darkest confessions of death-wishing imaginable: at one point, Pete confesses to his friend that he has often thought his life would be so much easier if Debbie were dead, the black humour evident in Rudd's deadpan delivery, and the way that Pete would want to cause this – nothing violent or painful, but slipping away gently over a period of months, 'in a coma, you know?' The other important details include frequent references to the familiar misunderstandings that occur between generations whose points of reference are worlds apart: Sadie's notable disgust at the confiscation of her IT hardware (laptop, phone, iPad) is met with the rather incongruous suggestion from Debbie that she ought to combat boredom by 'building a fort'. Debbie makes the fundamental error at not associating Sadie's need for communication and entertainment through various media with the way of life that teenagers lead today, and Sadie's total and complete incredulity that anyone would want to build a fort as an activity to pass the time ('A fort? A fort?! And what would I do with this "fort" once I built it?!') is met with Debbie's stonewall refusal to engage with Sadie's needs, even though they have from their own perspectives the best of intentions.

Reflecting upon this state of misunderstanding and the very fact of the way such themes are emphasised in romantic comedy, a genre often thought of as trivial or disposable, will be useful in gaining insight into where the burgeoning feelings of different kinds of love emerge through character interaction. The other side of this is an element covered in relation to previous chapters' considerations of the epistemological spaces around character and performer/star and audience prior knowledge of both particular instances, and more general generic expectations – in this case, of romantic comedy. Through a familiarity with the members of the particular ensemble cast in this and other Frat films, certain patterns may be discerned in the relationships within the narrative world of the film, particularly in relation to extratextual knowledge. I will now discuss these ideas through a case study of the John Hamburg Frat film, *I Love You, Man* (US, 2009).

Mandates and mancaves: awkward homosocial love in *I Love You, Man*

The male lead character in the film, Peter Klaven, is an estate agent living and working in Los Angeles. He is played by Paul Rudd who, up until *I Love You, Man*, was mainly associated with a number of slacker characters and supporting roles in Frat Pack movies. Prior to this cycle, he was notable for playing the romantic lead in *Clueless* (Heckerling, US, 1995). This is worth mentioning because Rudd's involvement in cult romantic comedies seems to set up a reference that some rom-com fans would appreciate. In the wider sense, this might be less relevant, but it clearly points to the star potential of Rudd, and his record since attests to his wider appeal as a male lead. Peter's girlfriend, Zooey, is played by Rachida Jones, previously notable for her performance as Karen Filippelli in the US version of *The Office* (incidentally with Steve Carell in the lead role in the first few seasons of that show – Carell himself a veteran of several Frat Pack movies).

In the opening scene of the film, set after several establishing shots of the city, Peter proposes to Zooey on the site of some real estate that he wants to buy and develop once he has saved up enough money. At this point, it is clear that he has a possible upcoming commission from a real estate deal, referred to as the 'Ferrigno deal'. The significance of this deal becomes more apparent as the story unfolds (I return to this as a point of discussion later). Zooey accepts his proposal. On the drive home, the couple conference-call her girlfriends to deliver the news. This helps to set up the entire film's premise of misunderstanding between the sexes (not genders in this particular instance, for which there are some complexities to be addressed later). During the call, certain back-story components are revealed, and these are carefully managed within the device of confiding with friends. For example, during the conversation it transpires that the couple spent a romantic holiday in Santa Barbara, early on in the relationship. Zooey's friend Hailey speculates that this was where Peter and Zooey first had sex, speaking frankly and unaware that the call is on speakerphone and that Peter can hear every word. Peter is shocked that Zooey had told her friends about their most intimate encounters in detail. He disapproves, revealing a discernibly prudish, sensitive persona that foregrounds the premise of misunderstanding and incomprehension. This works to complicate the notion of an easily gender-focused division between the sexes represented here, a theme that is amplified in the frank discussions between the all-female and all-male groups later in the movie, as well as the misunderstood encounters with homosexuality and homosocial relationships throughout.

It should be stated here that, at the beginning of the film, Zooey is under the impression (not exactly mistaken, but slightly misconstrued) that Peter has an all-male bonding group in the fencing club that he attends every week. However, it soon becomes apparent when we are shown scenes of the men fencing that Peter has little emotional openness with these men and doesn't even consider them as close friends. In fact, it would be fair to say that Peter has no close friends. This revelation sets up a number of 'rules' that are examined throughout the film, particularly in the ways that different kinds of relationships are articulated. Examples of this include the logic, verbalised in the film but not often spoken about in real life, that single men are supposed to have friends. Like so many of these Frat Pack examples, the unspoken is verbalised, to set up a comedy of error and embarrassment: *This is 40* is another prime example of verbalised interior monologue resulting in very dark humour and observation. As an extension of this logic that single men are supposed to have friends (or otherwise assumed to be rather sad individuals), we can pursue how such assumptions are worked out in *I Love You, Man*: this group friendship ought to be bonding and 'tight'; this friendship ought to bond through shared activity; this shared activity ought to consist of something considered classically 'masculine' such as sports, health and fitness, rock music, poker nights, drinking, practical jokes and so forth; and this shared, classically masculine activity ought to take place in an exclusively male, homosocial space that does not include women and ought not to entertain the idea that women should be included. Although this is expressed openly by male characters at various points in the film, as we shall see, the sexuality of such gender-specific spaces can be contestable and context-dependent.

Bringing these 'rules' into conscious consideration and verbalisation ('outing' the rules of gendered spaces and activities, so to speak) raises a number of questions. Some of these questions are played out with quite hilarious results on screen, whilst others are left more open to a psychological interpretation of the unspoken. These are most often leftover elements that are brought to the narrative through its observation and encounter. The definitions and ownership of masculinity, and the sexuality of homosocial activity, are under scrutiny here: occasionally painfully detailed, in which the conflation of masculinity, assertiveness, and heteronormative gender roles are brought into sharp relief.

This is made most apparent in a very early scene in the film, when Peter and Zooey take a trip to Peter's parents' house for dinner to celebrate the news of their engagement. The house is dotted with family photos, but these seem to be all featuring Mr Klaven (J. K. Simmons) and Robbie (Andy Samberg) sharing traditionally masculine activities such as fishing. There are no photos of Peter and his father. There are, however, pictures of Peter with the women in his life: a portrait of him and Zooey, and another photograph of him with his mother Joyce (Jane Curtain) in a celebratory pose at what we might assume is an early real estate sale for Peter. What emerges quite quickly in the flowing dinner conversation is that, contrary to Peter's experience, Robbie had lots of friends growing up. It is soon also revealed that Robbie is gay, a detail that is dealt with at speed in the film, as his sexuality (rather predatory, as it turns out) is never judged negatively or harshly by any of the characters. However, there are several clear indications that, however positively Robbie's sexuality might be portrayed, the representation is drawn as a caricature in order to heavily contrast Peter's awkwardness with Robbie's utter self-confidence.

Although the predatory character of Robbie's sexuality is brought to the fore and commented upon later in the film, the humour around this doesn't necessarily arise from ridicule. This complexity is further coloured through the film's strategies to represent the difficult relationship between homosociality and homosexuality, the overlaps between the two discursive spaces, and the somewhat traditionally radical notion that the two phenomenon are, in fact, mutually exclusive but mutually reinforcing. In Robbie and his various attitudes, we are presented with a challenge to an archetypical gay versus conservative dyad that still seems to permeate popular representations in the US, despite several years of liberalisation (including Obama's U-turn on same-sex marriage policy).

In her thorough article, 'Producing Containment: The Rhetorical Construction of Difference in *Will & Grace*', Danielle Mitchell (2005) details a historical and political critique of representations of homosexuality in popular texts, citing the hit TV series *Will and Grace* as an example of the contradictions inherent in the shame/invisibility dyadic presence that dominated discourse on same-sex relationships in the late twentieth century. Mitchell's claim that the liberal inclusivity of such mainstream popular media texts where, in this particular case, the show's 'inclusionary cast of characters and its homocentric plots function to perpetuate inequity' (2005: 1052) may seem out of step with the progressive arguments of inclusion, even unfashionable, and certainly politically incorrect. However, one might describe such apolitical correctness as a prime target of such a claim, where mere inclusion is simply not enough to assuage the sometimes violent or apolitical appeal of both 'screaming queen' and 'invisible' archetypical tropes of gay representation. The appearance of Robbie as out but matter-of-factly 'straight' in his approach to platonic male relationships is a clear progression from the containment strategies found in Mitchell's reading of *Will and Grace*. Rather than his mannerisms being a point of ridicule or humour in the sense that they are overtly effeminate as in so many cinematic and televisual representations of homosexuality, Robbie's mannerisms, behaviour and language are coded as laddish and heteronormative – straight. What results may, in fact, be read as a containment in itself – that, as one of the boys, Robbie is assuredly and reassuringly not one of *those* boys. However, my contention, and the one in which the meaningful association of open and unfinished narrative work here is centred, is that in the context of homosocial representations in this film (and the Frat cycle more generally) sexuality is far from a clear-cut issue. In the case of Robbie Klaven, the content (dialogue) refers to his homosexuality, but the form (particularly the visual and verbal cues) seems to conform to highly heteronormative conventions of straight masculinity – even hypermasculinity. One exchange which is particularly revealing here, and which adds to the campness of the humour offered throughout the film, is particularly telling in this regard. At the dinner table, Robbie's sexuality has been openly acknowledged:

MR KLAVEN: My son is a gay man and I embrace his lifestyle.
ROBBIE: It's true. Dad loves the gays. I actually made him an honorary homo last month.

The laddish use of the word 'homo' is slightly different to the ways that the term 'queer' has been re-appropriated as a term of empowerment or identity in gay culture. Here, it is used in a kind of humorous 'spin'. It is a deliberately provocative use of a derogatory term to positively promote an alternative lifestyle (in similarity to the use of the term 'queer'), but (rather differently to the somewhat familiar term 'queer') within the alien context of a term not ordinarily used for such counter-purposes, and casually dropped into an open conversation. It may even be reasonably considered as the obverse of the relatively recent counter-appropriation of the term 'gay' to refer to anything in derogatory terms, not limited to matters of sexuality. After the exchange, Robbie and his father enjoy a bonding moment, clearly in attuned to one another's sensibility on the subject, even going as far as bumping fists in celebration, a typically laddish gesture and one that Peter is uncomfortable with watching and would be even more uncomfortable with performing.

The dinner scene is also notable for the rather more subtle ways that these themes are explored. For example, Robbie and Mr Klaven drink beer from the bottle; Peter, Zooey and Joyce drink wine from the glass. This in itself, although an expression of a simple difference in taste, suggests a lifestyle divide that lies uneasily in the sexuality divide that is being offered. It is exacerbated through the ways that Robbie eats meat off the bone, where the others are using knives and forks. The conventions of dinner etiquette, so recklessly ignored by Robbie, are a foreshadowing of other notions of male etiquette and the complicated relationship this has with the representation of male sexuality. This is made even more complex through the sublation of the conventions of class difference with certain notions that are often associated with gender norms – a theme to which I return momentarily.

However, it is these moments of subtle difference in the way that Peter and Robbie behave and are treated by others in the family environment that lend the representations more than a hint of repressed anger and psychic disquiet. Mr Klaven's open remarks about Peter's development as a boy visibly embarrass Peter, and it is on this point more than any other that the sum of a somewhat Lacanian sense of Oedipal frustration becomes clear as the source of the comedy. Mr Klaven's open remarks, as well as the extremes of difference in his treatment of Robbie and Peter, institute and confer the very different masculine identities of his sons. This is confirmed in Robbie's status as favourite: Klaven declares that Robbie is one of his two best friends, along with his best man, Hank Mardukis. Peter is aghast at this revelation. He isn't exactly jealous of his father's affection for Robbie, but there is a sense that Peter was always a bit of a disappointment, to the extent that Robbie's alternative sexuality is not under question or subject to disapproval – his gender alignment is solidly 'straight' and traditionally masculine.

Peter's sexuality, whilst affirmed as straight through his relationship with Zooey, is figured in an altogether complicated gender alignment, confirmed through some of the rather camp ways he behaves and the way he expresses his feelings on occasion – as is the case in the first epigraph to this chapter. When he declares a love for *The Devil Wears Prada* (Frankel, US, 2006), he rolls his eyes upwards, exclaiming, 'Oh god, I LOVE that movie!' His love for the film (and for another favourite, *Chocolat* (Hallström, UK/US, 2000), is felt and expressed as a physical gesture, it so powerfully felt.

It could be suggested that one of the ways Peter seeks to remedy this lack of approval from his father is through his efforts at work to succeed. Peter reveals himself to be a popular office colleague, at least with the several women who work at his agency. In the first scene at work, he regales his female colleagues with the details of his proposal to Zooey. They are impressed by his unabashed romanticism, although, knowing what we know about the way that women talk about men and masculinity in the world of this film, we can never be sure that they then don't talk amongst themselves about some of his effeminate habits. These are later commented upon as 'clingy' and 'needy' in Zooey's group of friends. In his working life, everything hangs on Peter selling the Ferrigno estate – his first big estate deal. The significance of the cameo appearance of Lou Ferrigno should not be underestimated, particularly in relation to the masculinised world of work (incidentally, we never seem to see Zooey at work or know what she does for a living). Although Ferrigno is a minor Hollywood star compared to contemporary A-listers, his role in the 1970s TV series *The Incredible Hulk* (1977–1982) is very well known and his popularity as a result is iconic in the sense that he is fundamentally associated with it. This is the subject of humour in the way the characters in the film tend to refer to him as 'Hulk': to which the on-screen Ferrigno objects, stating that, as a person, he has feelings – 'the Hulk was a character I played on TV'. The mismatched superhero presence of Ferrigno as a kind of human special effect here, with his expressions as a sensitive human being with feelings (but who is not averse to placing people in a 'sleeper hold'), is a self-reflexive means by which the film continues to foreground the hypermasculine. This is a clear line of logic that continues through Peter's work colleague, Tevin.

Tevin is very quickly painted as a cocksure, aggressive and selfish man whose main goal is to muscle in on Peter's Ferrigno deal. When we first see him, he is watching a Quicktime file of some pornographic material a friend sent to him. He shows it to Peter, who is repulsed. Tevin, delighted by the clip and by Peter's reaction to it, describes the clip as 'sick' in a colloquially affirmative way. Peter agrees with the word, but employs it in the conventional negative. Tevin's over-exaggerated and misogynist view of women and female sexuality is important for a couple of reasons. As Richard Dyer has written (1993) on representations of sexuality, the 'Cartland' model of heterosexuality is a familiar one which 'luxuriates in power difference' (1993: 119). This is topical today with the rise of post-feminist blogging and the *Fifty Shades* phenomenon, with its innumerable imitators still fresh in the popular imagination. What Dyer suggests is that it is difficult to disentangle the representations of heterosexuality from the knowledge and weight of prejudice involving the inequality and difference of men and women colouring our attitudes towards such representations. He writes that such a notion of sexuality 'does not even seem to want that basic context of freedom and equality, it wants the full weight of coercion and inequality in heterosocial relations reproduced in heterosexual ones' (1993: 120). Hence, the narrative role that Tevin plays is to highlight both the effort that Peter is going to, to maintain a sense of equality in his courtship with Zooey, and his discomfort at the thought of having to distance himself from this position in order to perform the masculine role accorded him by accepted norms of sexual practice.

I remarked earlier that, at the beginning of the film, Zooey is under the impression (not exactly mistaken, but slightly misconstrued) that Peter has an all-male bonding group. Every week he meets up with 'Gill and the boys' for a fencing club. Why fencing? This is not a typical sport that features in romantic comedies, nor, indeed, might it be considered a particularly popular form of sport and entertainment. Fencing is a peculiar choice of sport to include here, but its appearance is no accident. The clues concerning its inclusion may have something to do with the perceived effeminacy associated with fencing and its somewhat prohibitively expensive trappings: the French terminology, the delicate poses and the elegant uniform of fencing sets it quite apart from American football, certainly, but there are also associations with class identity that are cued by these elements that ought to be considered. Taken in sum with many of the earlier notions of etiquette at the dinner table, these make for powerful confirmations of how we are being encouraged to think about Peter and make judgements based upon real-world experiences of these ideas. It perhaps ought to be acknowledged here that modes of verbosity and broad vocabulary, signs of intelligence or the perception of knowledge acquisition, are, as the satirical science fiction comedy *Idiocracy* (Judge, US, 2006) so carefully observes, often associated with both effeminacy and homosexuality. Sometimes this is coupled with outright class suspicion and anti-intellectualism, and this is a fairly familiar socio-political phenomenon in the US and beyond. It is an attitude sometimes found in GOP rhetoric and anti-intellectualist utilitarianism in public policy in the US and occasionally the UK. Therefore, although some of the connections noted here between gender construction and notions of queered bourgeois culture are perhaps not explicitly stated, they are nevertheless referred to in oblique, visual and verbal terms.

One of the fencing group, Eugene, announces that he's getting married next Sunday. Peter did not know Eugene was engaged to be married prior to this, nor is he invited to the wedding even when the information comes out. More tellingly, he is not even invited to the bachelor party the others are going to that evening. When he reveals his own wedding plans, the others respond politely but somewhat unemotionally, suggesting that although Peter is participating in a shared sporting activity in an all-male group, the homosocial bonds supposed to naturally emerge in such situations are absent. This exchange, which is followed by an awkward moment of silence in the locker room, confirms Peter's status as untypically masculine, and in the situation where, without real male friendship, he is coming up short (more appropriately, he is underperforming in his role as a single man). If nothing else to signify, this alone sets up the premise that he, like all single men, is in need of a 'best man'. The plot device of the imminent wedding sublimates this in a plot twist where he has to hunt for an actual best man for his wedding. But this is a sleight and doesn't manage to fully mask what seems to be an underlying implication: the universalisation of best friendship and its consideration as an, albeit unreliable, measure of masculinity.

After fencing, Peter comes home early (having been passed up on a celebratory drink with the fencing group that he had anticipated) to Zooey's 'ladies' night' at their home. He comes in quietly, without being noticed, and overhears Zooey and her friends taking about him. The theme of conversation, rather appropriately, given the fencing-buddies debacle, is that he has no friends. After an awkward moment where they hear him in the kitchen and he has no choice but to come into the room (with root-beer floats prepared for the ladies – a sweet gesture that is acknowledged through a close-up of Zooey's appreciative look), he retreats sheepishly to the kitchen, and declares to himself as if in a mission statement: 'I gotta get some fucking friends.'

Peter thus embarks on a quest to acquire a new best friend through a series of 'mandates' at Robbie's suggestion. As is implicit in the opening epigraph to this chapter, Robbie attempts to make a clear distinction between this idea of meeting strangers with the express purpose of getting to know them as friends and going on a date with women in order to embark upon a sexually intimate relationship. There is a clear line being drawn in the rules of engagement between Platonic and Sapphic encounters. Yet, he refers to the first as a process that could be described as a kind of 'date'. Many of the rituals undertaken are the same: the date is arranged through the introduction of a mutual third party; or the date is made after meeting on an introductions website; the date happens through accompanying an established couple in a 'double-date' or group night out; or simply through meeting and 'hitting it off'. In the montage sequence that follows, we are shown examples of all of these kinds of mandates, their distinction from straight romantic dates and the confusion that arises from miscommunication or, once again, dis-obeying or misinterpreting the 'rules'.

As highlighted in the epigraph, the idea of a mandate – that is to say, an appointment made between men to meet and get to know each other on a Platonic basis – is governed as much by what is unspoken as it is by what could be vocalised or formally agreed. Despite Robbie's warning about having dinner with prospective best friends, Peter ends up meeting for dinner with Doug, an architect who turns out to be gay. Misreading their mandate for a same-sex romantic date, Doug somewhat assertively French-kisses Peter at the end of the evening. Peter, while he hasn't consented to this, responds with surprise and is lost for words. He is in a state which Doug, incidentally, doesn't read in the negative way that Peter presumably intends. Rather, he gives Peter another quick peck on the lips and confirms that they will meet up again. Whereas the mandate with Doug was set up by Joyce as a mutual introduction, the mandate with Mel, a 91-year-old pensioner, was arranged through the online introductory service, friendfinder.com. Thinking that Mel is around his age, Peter goes along until he realises upon seeing Mel that he lied about his age on the form and posted a photograph of a much younger man on the site.

When one of Zooey's best friends, Denise (Jaime Pressly), strong-arms her husband, Barry (Jon Favereau), into letting Peter join in with his weekly poker night, promising him sex with the light on 'just like in Mexico', it ends in disaster. Peter takes part in a boat race beer drinking contest and, later confessing that he just doesn't drink that much, projectile vomits into Barry's face. This scene is made all the more significant for film aficionados who might recognise Favereau – far better known for directing the big budget action movies *Iron Man* and *Iron Man 2* than acting in small-budget romantic comedies. His tough, though comedic, on-screen persona here is exaggerated to the point of loutishness. Bearing this in mind, Peter's *faux pas* seems doubly vengeful. In the midst of these social-life disasters, Peter still needs to sell the Ferrigno estate. He holds an open-house viewing event, laying out an impressive buffet for prospective buyers. Quite incidentally to his plans to make a new best friend, Peter meets freeloader Sydney Fife (Jason Segal), whose pastimes include attending open-house viewings to get free food and opportunities to hit on newly divorced women.

Peter and Sydney hit it off immediately, and purely by chance.

The 'mandating' and other forms of social introduction and professional online services have not worked for Peter, and this might be seen as an offhand commentary on the artificial nature of socialising online: it seems that the boundaries in online and offline social communications are far from blurred here, as the authentic meeting by chance and without the pressure of *having* to create a friendship allows a bond to organically develop as Peter' and Sydney's personalities seem eminently compatible. This idea of introductions, dating and compatibility is not too far removed from the way that such operations exist in the social etiquette of meeting sexual partners. As we have already seen in the case of Doug, any distinctions drawn between the two experiences as different and, functionally speaking, serving an altogether different purpose are difficult to maintain, subject to misinterpretation and may be overlooked in any case. In these scenarios, the comedy of errors proceeds from both the unspoken rules and those articulated in casual conversation, as was the case in the above epigraph on 'mandates'. On many occasions throughout the course of the film, Peter expresses his uneasiness about making friendships, saying things like: 'There are no rules for male friendships', at least none comparable with the protocols of family relationships or sexually intimate ones.

What is interesting in the initial meeting between Peter and Sydney is, once again, the contravention of what might be expected in a heteronormative all-male introduction. When they meet, Sydney embodies elements of Robbie's laddishness in his open sexuality (although avowedly straight in Syndey's case) and his evaluation of the body language of one of the other open-house guests – he is correct in guessing that the guest wants to break wind but can't do so for fear of putting off the woman he is trying to impress. However, this is not the only sign of character depth here (which plays with the awkward comparison to Robbie's laddisms) as Sydney has a tendency to say things which are firmly in the realm of Peter's references to high culture (fencing, French terminology) and fondness for dinner etiquette (wine with dinner). For example, when they part and exchange business cards, Peter thanks Sydney for coming and Sydney replies: 'Thank you for the sundried tomato aeoli, because it's a revelation.' So, Sydney's way of being is a mixture of assuredly unreconstructed masculine enough to persuade Peter that he is best man material and unapologetically camp and open enough for Peter to like him and be able to, eventually, mesh with his personality.

Sydney can communicate with Peter in terms that he readily understands, and this is one of the reasons why, when they meet again for a 'mandate' (as well as at other points later in the film), he is able to make Peter feel so at ease that, relatively quickly, he gets him to reveal intimate details about his life with Zooey: how they met, what their sex life is like and so on. Peter is at ease at first, but, on realisation that he has let his guard down and revealed these details to a stranger he just met, he immediately withdraws into his guarded default. When Sydney spontaneously nicknames Peter 'Pistol' after the tennis player 'Pistol' Pete Sampras, Peter attempts to reciprocate. Again, quite sweetly and in a child-like manner that endears him to Sydney, these repeated attempts throughout the course of the film to give Sydney a nickname ('Joben', 'Magooch', 'Siddy Slicka') are clumsy, ill-judged and nervous. It confirms what we already know about Peter: conventional laddish behaviour, joshing and joking, don't come easily or naturally to him. It seems that he really has to force himself into that homosocial role, and on a number of occasions forces banter and small-talk with unintentionally (for the character) hilarious effect. On such occasions, it is noted and verbalised by several of the characters (including himself) that he sounds a bit like a leprechaun. In another scene, where Sydney is concerned that Peter hasn't embraced his masculinity fully, he insists Peter take part in an impromptu primal screaming session under Venice Beach boardwalk. In this Peter seems to succeed, at least more than he had done in previous attempts such as at the poker night.

Eventually, Sydney introduces Peter to his den: a mancave appropriated from a wooden outbuilding or garage around the back of his beach house. Here we see Sydney's bachelor lifestyle in its fullest expression: inside, we are shown a full drum kit and backline, permanently set up. Behind the kit, a prominent Rush *2112* poster covers the entire back wall. The fact that the band featured in the film (they actually make a live appearance, as does their music on the soundtrack) is significant in the rippling ways similar to the appearance of Eddie Vedder in *Into the Wild*. Rush, described widely by the music press as the biggest cult rock band in the world, are notorious, as are most prog-rock bands, for having an overwhelmingly male-dominated fan-base. This observation is played upon to devastatingly comic effect in *This Is 40* (with pub rock veterans Graham Parker and the Rumour staging a cameo comeback performance), where the divisions between men liking serious music and women liking partying music is satirised. Here, the division is exacerbated through the fact that Rush have this notoriety in music fandom, and the choice of this particular band is well-judged: when Peter attempts to show Zooey how good they are, he plays a track through laptop speakers and the resulting sound is comically disappointing. It sets up the gender-divided spaces of passing the time in the film, to the point that, when Zooey tags along with Peter and Sydney at a Rush concert, they spend all of their time pulling ridiculous poses, simulating fellatio on air-guitars and generally letting their hair down. Zooey, far from impressed by their behaviour, is actually disturbed and voices her concerns about the side of Peter she is seeing for the first time. It leads to the first of their quarrels that will lead to the inevitable separation and, ultimately, their reunion (both theirs, and Peter and Sydney's).

This discrepancy and misunderstanding of gendered space is vital. Of equal importance is the tendency to keep the spaces as separate as possible, in order to reduce the chances of such misapprehension and, therefore, hurt feelings. Sydney's shack is littered with drug paraphernalia and expensive stereo equipment, and next to his chair, on a table, Peter spies lotion and a box of unused condoms. When Peter spots this, Sydney openly and quite casually informs him, 'Oh, this is where I jerk off.' This revelation is neither particularly mad, bad, nor sad: although it may be argued that the idea that Sydney is trapped alone and masturbating in his mancave is an ultimately sad predicament, clearly from the way he entertains women at his beach house he is far from lonely or alone, at least in sexual terms. In fact, there is a distinct feel about the scene that this impression of male masturbation is given a peculiarly empowering treatment. This is especially so, given the way that masturbation is openly discussed as a normal and healthy activity, and that it can provide the opportunity for pleasure that extends beyond the act itself and into the variety that consumption around the act can provide. Sydney states quite openly that he uses condoms in his masturbatory acts because he likes it and it saves cleaning up afterwards.

This may appear at first to be quite strange: male masturbation as a serious topic of conversation, described expressively as a healthy act which enables one to explore an aspect of one's sexuality and as an activity that can be enhanced through acts of consumption. However, on reflection, these ways of representing masturbation are actually fairly common, albeit in different contexts, in popular culture. The element that provides an estrangement factor here is in the way these sentiments are expressed by men, in a frank manner, and masturbation is not dealt with as a smutty or juvenile practice to be ridiculed or judged negatively. Popular culture happens to be riddled with these kinds of references, but specifically related to the female practice – women's empowerment through the exploration of their sexuality, talking through their experiences frankly and engaging in a fulfilled and fulfilling sex-life with a partner: these are all familiar tropes and have found a clear path of expression as an entire industry has sprung up around the sale of sex toys, cosplay and erotic literature which have commodified the experience and led to the commercialisation of female masturbation.

Self-love is fundamentally different from interpersonal love, but is not evaluated or particularly judged in harsh comparative terms in this film. However, distinctions are maintained between the two experiences of sexuality, and yet another set of rules is revealed to Peter in his quest to understand male friendship. Once again, Sydney persuades Peter to confide to him an intimate detail of his sex life: the last time he masturbated. Sydney's somewhat prurient interest in this activity is tested when he pries further, only to have Peter tell him that he used a picture of Zooey as his masturbation material. Sydney is visibly repulsed and, to Peter's surprise, calls the activity 'sick', and in that moment Peter's bemusement at the various complicated social rules of discussing such subjects is foregrounded: Sydney asked, he risked ridicule through telling him and is rewarded with the rebuke.

Fratriarchy and love: a cinematic conclusion

As mentioned in the Introduction to Part II, the resolution of miscomprehensions and differences in romantic comedies often falls to the women in the film to achieve. In this, *I Love You, Man* is no exception. Throughout, the tension between Peter's need to perform as a single man (with a group of friends and a best man) and his wishes to perform as a husband (sexually, romantically and financially) drives the comedy forward. This tension reveals an uneasy conflict of interests and pressures: most tellingly and problematically, emanating from the featured woman's desire for her leading man to have it all. It is a familiar tension that may be described through the conflict between fratriarchy and the institution of marriage (which fratriarchy both supports and undermines equally). On the phenomenon of fratriarchy and the mancave or 'men's hut', Jonathan Remy writes:

> Fratriarchy implies primarily the domination of [...] young men who have not yet taken on family responsibilities. Marriage frequently gives rise to divided family loyalties on the part of the groom. His duties towards his family often conflict with his allegiances towards his fraternity 'buddies'. Many men attempt to preserve something of the atmosphere of the stag night well into middle age. Some, to not put too fine a point on it, simply never really grow up, and remain psychologically trapped in the *fratriarchal men's hut* for the rest of their lives.
>
> (1990: 45 [emphasis in original])

This notion that the bachelor lifestyle is a juvenile pursuit or a moribund dead-end for emotional growth ought to be fairly familiar to the reader. It may well be associated with some of the sentiments I've expressed in relation to Sydney's mancave. This may have some elements of truth to it; however, in the case of Frat Pack films such as *I Love You, Man*, it does not really tell the full story. The need for friendship, to bond and to be sociable is rather powerful in Western societies, and it may well have been ever thus. Indeed, it may be the case that such needs are pursued at the cost of other kinds of friendships and relationships (as happens in the case of Peter and Zooey); that it sours friendship that can and does occur between men and women; or even that it is blind to and denies (and yet reinforces) the links between the Platonic and the Sapphic that were once recognised in antiquity.

It is my contention that, just as women's spaces are seen as important and life-affirming social support spaces by analysts such as Pinkola-Estes (and rightly so, in my opinion), so men too have access to and are enriched by their own social spaces. The Frat Pack cycle of films show us these kinds of spaces and offers a somewhat critical (if sometimes celebratory) view of the challenges and pitfalls of gender identity and identification in contemporary popular culture. This is not unproblematic and raises a number of questions involving a review of the kinds of statements involved in Remy's (and others) perspective on dismissing such social practices generally as unproductive and somewhat immature. Surely, the performances of men in these films often involve buffoonery of the kind that we laugh at their misfortune. However, I would argue that this is a spectacle of the overdetermination of emotive representation that drives both the comedy and the drama of these films. The men depicted, often childlike in their innocence or ignorance, or overly sensitive (Ferrigno's demands to be treated like a person; Owen Wilson's emotionally sensitive on-screen persona in nearly all of his Frat output), act as canvases upon which broad, silly strokes are painted. Nevertheless, their efforts are rewarded by traditional romantic denouement, but these men are also not merely the cosmetic 'new men' of the 1990s; they also reflect the burgeoning awareness in late capital, of the need to engage with emotions as powerful psychological objects for growth. If this seems to place too much emphasis on fictional characters to bear the burden of this task, it may be worth a reminder that these representations exist within the complicated worlds of set and setting, the layers of context and text competing for our conscious attention as viewers, and therefore are reflexive indicators of a specific kind of spectacular cinema that involves the ongoing relationship between viewer and viewed. It is in this spirit that I now move my discussion of the surround of cinema forwards.

5

THE ALL-AROUND-ALL-AT-ONCE

Innovation and attention-seeking in the surround of cinema

> The world is already constituted, but also never completely constituted; in the first case we are acted upon, in the second we are open to an infinite number of possibilities. But this analysis is still abstract, for we exist in both ways at once. There is, therefore, never determinism and never absolute choice.
>
> (Maurice Merleau-Ponty, 2002: 527)

So far in this book, I have explored notions of feelings and the co-productive, intersubjective relation between viewer and viewed in terms of perception and emotional registers, taking into consideration the manipulation (whether intended or not) of this relationship in terms of revisionist filmmaking, adaptation and the appropriation of philosophical models of worldview in constructing basic relations between representation of human action and the environment. These are issues that have traditionally been associated with some of the more familiar problematics of cinema, involving amongst other things characterisation, strong role models and identification, fidelity to source material, and knowledge about how the film was made.

I contend that all of these problematics exist within a cultural framework of spectacle. Even in the previous chapter, where the discussion took a detour into the detailed world of character identity and gender representation in the specific genre phenomenon of bromantic comedy, spectacles are discernible. The kinds of spectacles found in such cinema may be ordinarily treated as quite apart from other kinds of cinematic spectacle (special effects, grand narrative arcs, action blockbusters and so on). But even here, in so-called 'small' pictures, the performances betray a tendency for the actors to literally make spectacles out of themselves for the sake of comedic or dramatic effect. This chapter seeks to move the discussion on by engaging questions of spectacle in order to tease out how evaluation operates in the surround of contemporary cinematic technologies. It takes in some of the problematics associated with technological innovation, but also seeks to establish evaluative structures in the relationship between production and consumption of cinematic product, as well as in the cinematic encounter. I will do this through a critical exploration of the relationships between various economies at work: in particular the political economy, the psychic economy, and the textual economy of the cinematic encounter.

I may risk a tautology here by stating that Hollywood has always relied upon developments in technology to facilitate the production of its spectacles. In turn, an emphasis upon the novel in popular media cultures (also led by televisual, online and advertising production) has led to marketing strategies and consumption patterns that proliferate a rhetoric of innovation. This tendency to place value upon innovation seems to be all-pervading and ubiquitous, especially as far as blockbusters are concerned. For example, as Bennett et al. state in their introduction to *Cinema and Technology*:

> Writing about new developments in cinema technology can convey the seductive impression of currency in documenting technological change as it happens, but the fact is that all too often such writing is complicit with or suborned to the neoliberal capitalist spectacle of radical progress [...] failing to address or dispute the very logic of the rhetoric of innovation.
>
> (2008: 5)

The ubiquity of such logic renders it difficult to be recognised for what it is, and makes it difficult to separate technicity and artistry as creative categories. As discussed in Chapter 1, the example of manipulating already-existing cinematic materials (for commercial as well as artistic reasons) in Spielberg's *Close Encounters of the Third Kind* was a re-visioning in an attempt to enable revisionism in narrative terms, which had a knock-on effect in terms of the various representations operating in the film. This had repercussions in terms of the available problematics of the film. In turn, this facilitated the marketing process, arguably producing more marketable commodities to suit the climate at the time.

However, whereas it is common to find emphases on technical virtuosity, special effects and other evidence of budgetary expense in popular and academic film criticism, it is not universally the case that audiences rely solely upon spectacles for viewing pleasure. Even though technical and technological expertise (reflected in, for example, special effects or spectacular cinematography) is often prized in popular culture as a signifier of accomplishment, there are different criteria of success mobilised for different purposes. Box-office success, for example, is often cited as a measure of value by studios, critics and audiences alike – understandable, given the financial risks undertaken in investing in popular film entertainments. Occasionally, 'small films', such as the recent *Crazy Heart* (Cooper, US, 2010) or *Moon* (Jones, UK, 2009), are noted as worthy by critics and audiences, and such plaudits are mobilised by studios and financiers to extend the economic afterlife of the film.

Another criterion of success might come from the way that film is sometimes judged as art. Indeed, it is tempting to take a critical viewpoint towards popular entertainment forms as reflecting a critical hierarchy of purist film art – one of the reasons why the notion of film authorship has had such a lasting impact upon the way that critics and audiences judge a film and filmmakers. Although this is not the place to expound upon what may and may not be deemed as 'film art', let alone 'art', this strand of film appreciation has been present in film scholarship and theory at least since Ricciotto Canudo's 1911 manifesto, 'The Birth of a Sixth Art', claimed that film extended the aesthetics of realist and formalist aspects of art photography.[1] In relation to this tradition of thought in film theory, the writing that comes to mind would include, in addition to those opinions expressed in previous chapters (Bordwell, Epstein, etc.), that of perceptual psychologist Rudolf Arnheim (1957) and art critic Clement Greenberg (1961). They described the industrialised art forms of the twentieth century as being 'brutal', in Arnheim's opinion, or 'kitsch', in the words of Greenberg.

To be fair, in *Film as Art*, Arnheim looks back upon his early writing to recontextualise it as the writings of an enthusiastic 'monomaniac', in later years transformed into a 'stray customer, who gratefully enjoys – a few times a year – the screen performances of intelligent artists' (1957: 2). In other words, his early thoughts on the ideological formation of film have been revised, underpinned by an acceptance of the place and importance in theory of *viewing pleasure*. This mellowing did not reflect a completely forgiving attitude towards industrialised filmmaking – he also stated in the same essay that 'When the eyes and ears are prevented from perceiving meaningful order, they can only react to the brutal signals of immediate satisfaction' (1957: 7). What it did reflect centred around contemporary (early 1930s) concerns of gestalt psychology, the modernist fascination with observable effects, and phenomenology's crossover from psychology into existentialism – from Titchener (1908) and Pillsbury (originally 1913) to Maurice Merleau-Ponty (*The Phenomenology of Perception* was first published in 1945): a shift of concern, one may describe in retrospect, from one with perception (in the sense of the classical stimulus–response model of perception) to one with meaningfulness (or meaningful, whole-body perception – a topic of the final chapter of this study).

It may be argued that, even in the most spectacular effects-laden blockbusters such as *Close Encounters*, one may find a meaningfulness that engages the viewer in quite unexpected ways: meaningfulness that implies that such a phrase as '*even* in the most spectacular effects-laden blockbusters' becomes a value-laden, redundant term. A cinephilic view, or what Roger Cardinal (1986) describes as a 'panoramic perception', may enable one to start to explore the unlooked-for in encounters with cinema, related in many ways to the cinephilic or photogenic gaze that Epstein (1978) outlined in his 'condiments of cinema' idea, discussed in Chapter 1. This seems to suggest that there is value in the incidental, the everyday, and in meaning-making processes that go 'against the grain' of what might be commonly thought of as universal responses to massively popular films. Even more so, through repeated viewings, one starts to find that certain unlooked-for aspects of the film's composition leap out of the screen in the sense of Barthes' *punctum* – disturbing and puncturing the (idea of the) unity of an ideologically and culturally fixed text (1981: 55). As viewing subjects, therefore, in Merleau-Ponty's formulation of embodiment and enaction, we are 'acted upon' and 'open to an infinite number of possibilities' at one and the same time (2002: 527). The encounter with the screened film is, therefore, characterised by a dialectic of intersubjectively being-with-the-film (viewers physically sharing a space with images and, in the meaning-making process, consuming ideological objects) and being differentiated from the film in negotiated ideological perspectives (taken from Hall 1981); and as what Vivian Sobchack has described as a 'viewed view' (the film existing for human viewing, an anthropocentric view, an 'image of the seen') (2004: 150). Furthermore, what this reading strategy enables is a different kind of revisionism – one that is more provisional, viewer-orientated, self-conscious (and less contingent upon the ideological), whilst at the same time incorporating and embracing the subjective and knowingly pleasurable viewing practice of the cinephile.

The final chapter in this study will return to Sobchack's notion of 'viewed view', in relation to affect and embodied viewing practices, and, in particular, to a revised notion of the glance as a regime of looking in contemporary film cultures. The current chapter will expand upon the 'knowingness' of viewing practice in a discussion of cinephilic fascination, with the intention of grounding the contemporary experience of film narrative in relation to currents in the field of perceptual psychology in order to facilitate that discussion of 'viewed view' and a phenomenology of the glance. In particular, I will elaborate upon notions of attention and distraction in viewing practice within the surround of cinema – notions that are currently under-theorised in film theory[2] – whilst thinking through the impact of film technologies upon aesthetics in the viewing experience. I shall do this by extending my analysis of *Close Encounters* from Chapter 1 to draw comparisons with popular examples from non-Hollywood and classic Hollywood production.

The rhetoric of innovation and a political economy of 'cinema as a technology'

Lev Manovich, in *The Language of New Media*, suggests that 'As traditional film technology is universally being replaced by digital technology, the logic of the film-making process is being redefined' (2002: 300). This suggests that changes amounting to a 'new language of cinema' operate upon a stylistic level, necessitating the need to reorganise production methods and choices, whilst also disorganising the notions of pure cinema (now presumably 'old' notions). Ultimately, the implications of Manovich's statement suggests that critics as far back as Arnheim, Epstein and Dulac in the first half of the twentieth century were always-already dealing with a hybridised form: newer sound technology incorporated into film art changed the popular silent form, at the same time keeping some of its fundamental aspects (i.e. the visual) more or less the same. It also highlights, however, this 'more or less' element, because film did change visually. For example, intertitles and other textual elements became largely redundant with the introduction of sound, but the fact that such textual elements were part of the visual make-up of popular cinema in the first place[3] indicates a hybrid pictorial–text form that problematises the notion of formal purity. Manovich's position seems to cohere with the notion that a purist position on cinematic form is, historiographically speaking, erroneous.

However, there are two main problems with Manovich's position. First, he suggests that there was a cohesive 'old language of cinema' at some point in film history; and, second, that cinema is basically a technological phenomenon, and that changes at the level of technology determine institutional, aesthetic and formal changes. The idea of determination often accompanies such historical shifts – either in general mass media discourse or in specific marketing materials. However, the determinist relationship is much more complex. It is negotiated and mutually contingent between different levels of production, distribution, exhibition and use more than is often acknowledged in histories of technological innovation. Furthermore, it is fundamentally a narrative and narrativising phenomenon.

In 'A Note on Terminology', a qualifying sleeve note to his book *Film Noir* (2005), Mark Bould states that 'Determination argues that the state of a system at one moment gives rise to the state of that system in the following moment' and is therefore causal in its nature. However, causality, as it is commonly understood, works in a slightly more direct sense within narrativised accounts of a system. As Bould continues, 'Cause-and-effect is a narrative technique by which we make sense of the transition of a system from moment to moment. It is always a retrospective and partial account, an abstraction which marginalises or ignores the totality of a system.'

Therefore, it is possible for Raymond Williams, for example, to assert that the arts and popular cultural objects in general are not merely passively dependent on (economic) social reality. Such a position would be simplistic and indicative of a 'mechanical materialism, or a vulgar misinterpretation of Marx' (1968: 266). After all, Engels himself wrote of this mechanical transposition: 'According to the materialist conception of history, the determining element in history is *ultimately* the production and reproduction in real life. More than this neither Marx nor I have ever asserted' (Engels, cited in Williams 1968: 260). Here, Engels refutes what would later be commonly referred to as 'vulgar' Marxism, which over-emphasises economic determinism as a causal factor of transition in the social apparatus (a typical example of what Bould describes as 'system'). We can clearly see in such vulgar accounts that a narrativised retrospective which fixes the point of determination and therefore prefigures the impossibility of change via other means is overly simplistic. It is to misinterpret determinism as fate or fatalism. Bould comments that:

> The ability to construct cause-and-effect chains implies that it should be possible to extend their construction into the future; this is an error based

on forgetting that cause-and-effect is a retrospective abstraction. A deterministic system does not require fate, inevitability, predictability or cause-and-effect.

(2005: n.p.)

Therefore, as with a political economic determinism, it is equally inappropriate to assume a vulgar position in terms of cultural determinism: art objects, cultural traditions and identification practices do not by and of themselves determine human consciousness. However, this does not negate the deterministic relation between culture, art and human proclivity, but instigates a deterministic relation that occurs spontaneously, not directly.

The same may also be said of technological determinism. When writing specifically about television and the reciprocity of technology and cultural form, Williams (1990) is most exacting in his engagement with this very problem. He specifically engages with versions of cause-and-effect that emerge from deterministic statements such as 'television has altered our world'. Indeed, one may say that, based upon this statement, the ubiquitous presence of television has influenced our relationship with the world in the most general sense, but this presupposition is the kind of philosophical error, a misinterpretation through grammatical presumption or a tautology, that constitutes self-proof.

It follows that the formal and commercial aspects of mainstream film production reflect such shifts to accommodate the foregrounding of technological change evident in film culture more generally. Bolter and Grusin, for example, note that cinema has tended to 'absorb computer graphics into its traditional structure' (1999: 147). Thus, contemporary popular cinema seems to make technology itself a visible theme and reiterates cinema's status as a type of technology. Their statement is, perhaps, too general by itself to be of use in describing such phenomena, but this subject has been addressed in much film scholarship since the common appearance of digital cinema production and consumption technologies in popular film (see Pierson, 1999a and 1999b, for example).

Inevitably, this appearance of digital technology has led to something of a technological convergence in audio-visual media. However, more specifically, one might add that this complicates the notion of medium-specificity. Anne Friedberg, for example, has written: 'The movie screen, the home television screen, and the computer screen retain their separate locations, yet the types of images you see on each of them are losing their medium-based specificity' (2004: 914). This is typical of the way that the VCR, for example, transformed domestic viewing experiences ('both the cinematic and the televisual past became more easily accessible and interminably recyclable'), except that in the current technological climate this effect has become more pronounced, particularly with the advent of online video tube sites.

As a crucial desiderata, Friedberg also goes on to state in the same essay that this opens up fundamental questions concerning the art of historiography within film studies, how film history (and our individual experiences of world history) is conducted, the ideological effects of such experiences, and what that looks like in the current audio-visual landscape. She writes that:

> As the field of 'film history' has flourished in its vitality, the concomitant changes to our concept of the past produce a reflexive problematic. Cinema spectatorship, as one of its essential features, has always produced experiences that are not temporally fixed, has freed the spectator to engage in the fluid temporalities of cinematic construction – flashbacks, ellipses, achronologies – or to engage in other time frames (other than the spectator's moment in historical time, whether watching the diegetic fiction of a period drama or simply a film from an earlier period).
>
> (2004: 923)

This postmodern phenomenon correlates with Frederic Jameson's 'ideological containment' – a containment that accompanies digital production and (specifically) manipulation of images; and, in particular, the digital revising of already-existing material. For Jameson, this revisionism is tantamount to no less than a re-materialisation of history through purely visual means, a vicarious experience of history as image/image as history. He writes that: 'Our entire contemporary social system has little by little begun to lose its capacity to retain its own past, has begun to live in a perpetual present and in a perpetual change that obliterates traditions' (1983: 125). It is, to borrow Metz's term, an extension of cinema as a 'vast *trucage*': only, in this instance, ideologically charged in similar fashion to the classical Marxist notion of ideology as specifically class-based, exploitative false-consciousness. As these ideas were published well before digitisation of the cinema had even begun to realise itself as a realistic proposition, and given that this question seems to be as urgent as ever, Jameson's work suggests that the idea of the digital 'revolution' is a mere effect of more fundamental seismic (ideological) shifts within the social sphere that have been taking place for far longer than the rhetoric of innovation will admit.

This is partly due to the way such rhetoric, particularly in its popular forms, insists on the 'revolutionary' model of technological development. John Belton (2004) questions the status of the evolution of digital technologies in image production and consumption as a 'revolution'. The recent development and adoption of digital cinema is taking place at a substantially slower pace than that of previous stages of technological innovation (the coming of sound, colour, etc.) for a variety of commercial, technological and marketing reasons. For example, the digital special effects boom is a highly visible and long-established one now, and the use of digital sound has followed, based on the commercial successes of CGI and digital editing in popular cinema. The current evolution, moreover, is not so much a break from previous technologies as a continuation of innovation logic. As Friedberg has stated: 'There were a number of pre-digital technologies that significantly changed our concept of film-going and television-viewing before the digital "revolution"' (2004: 916). The VCR was perhaps the most prominent of these in the 1980s and 1990s, because of its time-shifting capabilities, and because of its massive take-up as a domestic entertainment technology.

What seems to be clear, for Belton at least, is that this digital 'revolution' is being driven by Hollywood corporate synergy – a synergy that did not exist with such concentration during previous eras of cinematic innovation, nor in the form that currently exists. The market appears to be driving the current wave of innovation, and the market that connects the movie screen, the television screen and the computer screen (and, increasingly, smaller mobile screens of various kinds) is that of privatised, domestic consumption.

Clearly, Manovich's position is tenable insofar as cinema may be considered as a technology. However, recent scholarship on the status of cinema has sought to engage with the technical and infrastructural dimensions of cinema as an industrial, commercial and cultural phenomenon (e.g. Ndalianis (2000) on the transitional phase of technological innovation in recent Hollywood production). As Bennett et al. state, much of this scholarship is concerned with 'the relationship between cinema *and* a broader domain of technology, or as one particular site within extensive technological configurations or broader networks of technological activity or interaction' (2008: 2). In other words, following Bennett et al., much of the recent scholarship on cinematic technologies, in the context of popular commercial cinema in particular, may be broadly ring-fenced into three critical tropes:

1   The struggle for dominance of technological formats (film gauges, distribution technologies, delivery platforms, etc.).
2   The aesthetic and evaluative status of animation in cinematic media (both traditional forms such as stop-motion, and CGI) and the related questions of textuality and film viewing/experience.
3   The representations of technology, and films that address technology as a socio-cultural theme (often concentrating on genres such as SF, fantasy and so forth, but not exclusively).

This is not to say that issues relating to these tropes have not previously been the subject of debate. Indeed, as far back as 1980 Stephen Heath was writing accounts of historical and stylistic change in relation to very early cinema technology: 'In the first moments of the history of cinema, it is the technology which provides the immediate interest' (1980: 1).

Cinema as a technology, therefore, may be thought of more productively as 'an array of effects, affects, and narrative and aesthetic frameworks that are adopted and deployed in different media (contexts) such as, for example, video games, websites, TV programmes and gallery installations' (Bennett et al. 2008: 2). This feeds into the constant shifts in technological transformation that seem to pervade cinematic technology, the critical discourse that accompanies them, as well as the rhetoric of innovation. Cinema, therefore, provides an ideal example of the way that the rhetoric of innovation and technological progress becomes visualised (through visual technological means as well as traditional critique and word-of-mouth discourse).

Cinema in some ways seems to reflect the modernist fascination with technological innovation that characterises psychological concerns of modernity. The analyst Pat Berry has noted that 'Perhaps film emerged when it did because it was just the therapy people needed to bind into manageable form the chaos of modern overstimulation' (2001: 71–2). She points out that, significantly, film began around the same time as depth psychology, so that, for the very first time, the external world presented to its inhabitants coincided with the presentation of their inner worlds in fine detail. In turn, Berry's approach to film is coloured with allusions to the simulational function of cinema as somehow embodying loss. That is, nature (an event) has been transformed into art (an aesthetic form), but in that transformation 'the life water, flesh, here-and-now tangibility of the actual event is sacrificed, creating perhaps a vacuum, an emptiness, in the event itself' (2001: 71).

It is unclear to what 'event' Berry is referring to here: the event that was filmed; the event of spectatorship, perhaps? Aside from imprecise critical discourse, however, what is useful in Berry's approach is that it reflects the modernist impulse to conflate innovation, development and improvement. It does so through a lens of modern psychology and a kind of account for existential states within modernity. A critical eye can identify Berry's concerns with some early strands of film theory, where the concerns around technology, psychology and film art are similar (Epstein 1978; Dulac 1978; Münsterberg 1999; Arnheim 1957).

What seems to be fundamental to the critical tropes concerning digital cinema technologies is the way that themes from the modernist discourse on cinema and psychology, particularly in relation to the recognition of value in commodity exchange, persist today. Indeed, there is a tendency, according to Bennett et al., that:

> Announcements of innovation and radical change, in the press and in promotional material, are taken at face value. By the time the manifest-ations of technological transformations become more 'visible', the shifts have already taken place, generating the desire to account for this apparent change.
>
> (2008: 5)

This seems typical of the kinds of synergy that proliferate in Hollywood; typical of contemporary models of supply-side economics, whose appearance-form suggests the fetishisation of consumer choice, but whose real site of exchange is based upon what Cubitt has referred to as conditions 'not of our own choosing' (1991: 20). This is an echo of Metz's notion of cinematic landscape as a vast *trucage*, a site of knowledge of popular films that, subjectively, audiences feel they have propriety over and yet do not themselves set the terms of their own consumption practice.

This view of technology is of concern to the historian: in his history of global technologies, David Edgerton outlines this relationship, stating that: 'Too often the agenda for discussing the past, present and future of technology is set by the promoters of new technology' (2006: ix). Edgerton argues instead for a 'history of technology-in-use' to focus on the fact of duration over the moments of invention and innovation: 'By thinking about the history of technology-in-use, a radically different picture of technology [...] becomes possible' (2006: xi). This becomes possible to visualise by turning to Marx's model of exchange, regarding the commodity form, to illuminate what I referred to above as the 'appearance-form' of the site of exchange: the viewing process as technology-in-use. A brief overview of this model is necessary to pursue this visualisation in order that the either/or aspect of liberatory/repressive discourse (of, say, uses-and-gratifications models) be properly examined as a dialectical struggle between technology as a pleasurable consumable and technology as an ideological marketing tool.

After his discussion of the nature of value within capitalist economies in *Capital*, Marx goes on to discuss the commodity form, regarding it as principal in the transference of value from subsistence to transcendence. In the production of human labour, presented as a social relation 'existing not between themselves, but between the products of their labour', commodities take on a specific character. This character Marx termed fetishism, which invests a resonant value in the product, akin to magical properties, so that the products of human endeavour, whether of the brain or by hand, appear as 'independent beings endowed with life, and entering into relation both with one another and the human race' (Marx, 1999: 43).

Historically, various forms of domestic viewing and cultures of media consumption developed within specific commercial and industrial contexts. Each of these media technologies grew in response to the demands of consumer sensibilities, as well as reacting to fluctuations in the industrial concerns of cinema, whilst importantly shaping and defining those sensibilities through rules of supply, corporate concentration and other economic factors. What emerges from the economy of domestic viewing is, arguably, a culture from and through which a sense of retrospection is fostered, Doane's 'loved again' aspect of film consumption (2002: 229); a nostalgia that manifests itself not only in patterns of consumption on a mass scale, but also through a negotiation of texts by individual consumers in specific ways.

This negotiation – a cinephilic negotiation, one might argue – takes on the character of consumer valuation, in precisely the manner to which Marx referred. It reveals the commodified nature of media objects: objects that may be seen to be of *value*, but a value that needs to be defined, not merely in terms of the commodity's actual utility (what it is supposed to be for, in marketing or institutional terms) but in terms of the way that it *may* be used. Or, as Marx put it, *in* use: 'that by its properties it is capable of satisfying human wants, or from the point of view that those properties are the product of human labour' (Marx, 1999: 42). That is, value in *exchange*.

In his essay 'Cinema and Fetishism', Sean Homer outlines this relation, which develops from the social character of labour. He notes that: 'The value of a commodity does not reside in its utility but in the magnitude of labour time to produce it, and this is realised only through its exchange' (2005: 100). This echoes the classical Marxist approach to production, labour and value in capitalist society, where it is 'only by being exchanged that the products of labour acquire, as values, one uniform social status, distinct from their varied forms of existence as objects of utility' (Marx, 1999: 44). As a result of this, the human equation is essentially erased as social relations between producers take on the character of objective relations between things.[4] Therefore, in order to explore in detail the issues of both commodity fetishism and contemporary consumerism in film culture, a brief reappraisal of Marx's terminology of value and commodity form is necessary, as well as the notion of economic determinism within the context of the current discussion of a surround of cinema.

To clarify, the idea of a 'uniform social status' is not to suggest that the arts and popular cultural objects in general are merely passively dependent on social reality. Such a position would be simplistic and, as was discussed earlier, indicative of what Raymond Williams described as 'mechanical materialism, or a vulgar misinterpretation of Marx' (1968: 266). Conversely, and as discussed previously, it is equally inappropriate to assume a vulgar position in terms of any determinism, including cultural determinism: art objects, cultural traditions and identification practices do not by and of themselves determine human consciousness, even though through the act of consumption one may find a meaningful site of exchange. Equally, whereas it is *possible* for 'good' art to make social commentary, this does not bear out as a matter of course and is a problematic position in terms of its arguably idealist valuation of art. Again, usefully, Williams notes that this is a proposition that the Romantic poets sometimes advanced, thus highlighting the difficulty in tackling this question from a truly Marxist position.

Finally in relation to this outline of exchange, Williams devotes space to the definition of Marxist positions in literary and other cultural criticism, because at various times critics make use of the different propositions (either cultural or materialist) as the need fits. He does, however, offer a third proposition, which at first seems a compromise between the first two:

> The arts, while ultimately dependent, with everything else, on the real economic structure, operate in part to reflect this structure and its consequent reality, and in part, by affecting attitudes towards reality, to help *or hinder* the constant business of changing it.
>
> (1968: 266 [emphasis in original])

This is in part a commentary on the complexity of critical reflection, either in professional/academic terms or on the part of the consumer more generally. Williams is putting forward a rather provocative position, when he suggests the ultimate underlying structure of cultural production is economic. However, as has been the case with several of the film theorists discussed so far, contemporary film theory has sought to refigure these relations of exchange in more mechanical terms: the market, synergy, supply-side economics, branding, and so forth. This not only helps to contemporise the discussion of cinema as technology but lays the groundwork for further exploration of the viewing experience under conditions not necessarily of one's choosing, but under which meaningful negotiations of plot, character and story may take place.

Indeed, this position may be relayed through traditional concerns within histories of film, as viewing experiences are often figured as features of contemporary psychological concerns of the periods under discussion. Berry's statement (above) is more a reflection of her own agenda as a clinician rather than as a film scholar, but it demonstrates the problem of retrospective speculation concerning viewing sensibilities within film history. That these sensibilities are fundamentally bound up with (and, to an extent, shaped by) the technological concerns of the time as much as with psychosocial and economic concerns further complicates matters. For example, David A. Cook summarises the beginnings of film history as the end of another history: that of Victorian concerns with optical devices for the simulation of convincing representations of empirical reality in motion (1996: 1). However, it is not the mere periodisation of optical simulation technology at stake here: rather, the aesthetic possibilities that emerge in relation to experiences of technology and the psychosocial implications of such experiences that inevitably feed back into cultural production. Aesthetic possibilities in the sense of the aesthetic-as-present-ness, of being alive in-the-moment: what the phenomenologist Edward S. Casey calls the all-around-all-at-once. This is a mode of viewing and viewed to which I shall return towards the end of the current chapter and expand upon in Chapter 6.

For now, it should be noted that Cook's historical account is an established position that asserted its dominance early in the history of the film medium, as well as in film theory: the move from technology to art, from technical wonder to aesthetic sensibility. Bennett et al. criticise this teleology by asserting that innovation and change is constant, and that space for critical reflection is opened up only after such an assertion is acknowledged. They identify in textualism – the attempt to analyse the film text on its own merits and isolated from the technological, social and political determinants – a general tendency that has '[p]ushed technological questions to the margins of film studies, as it has sought to describe cinema in formal, aesthetic or social and cultural terms, which have been understood as distinct and separate (or separable) from technological issues' (Bennett et al. 2008: 9). This position on the importance of the role of technology in questions of the formal, aesthetic and cultural aspects of film underscores many of the points raised in the last chapter in relation to the fluid nature of cause-and-effect within the social sphere. It also raises the question not only of the role of technology in this process but also of the status of technology itself: what it is, and how it asserts its identity, within visual culture.

Competing elements, peripheral details

Technology is notoriously difficult to define. I outlined a number of phenomeno-logical and philosophical strands of thought in relation to the embodiment of technology in its nostalgic and kitsch aspects in the Introduction to Part II of this book. However, in film theory at least, philosophical and theoretical debates over the term 'technology' and the values, meaning and scope of technological phenomena are ongoing and multifarious. Ursula Franklin, for example, has defined technology as a 'multifaceted entity' that includes 'activities as well as a body of knowledge, structures as well as the act of structuring' (1999: 5–6). Bennett et al. contend that things tend to be 'technological [...] while their value and meaning are still being contested' (2008: 2). That is, technological things tend to become invisible *as* technology once this negotiation has settled, but in an intervening period of negotiation, whilst meanings and values are in a state of flux, the technology tends to announce itself or discernibly reflect upon its processes, its origins. It relies upon the *novel* as an instance of visibility. The appearance of CGI in live-action cinema during the 1980s provides a stark illustration of this reflexivity. In particular, during the late 1980s and early 1990s, when Hollywood was still suspicious of the market potential of a technology which was underdeveloped, expensive and conspicuous, a number of interesting examples emerged.

Several of James Cameron's films, including *The Abyss* (US, 1989), *T2: Judgment Day* (US, 1991), and culminating in *Titanic* (US, 1997) and the IMAX 3D documentary *Ghosts of the Abyss* (US, 2003), are examples that reflect Hollywood's changing aesthetic priorities during the course of the 1990s. Cameron's latest release, *Avatar* (US, 2009), reflects similar concerns with technology, high-definition and visible budgetary concerns that are easily discerned in some of his earlier films mentioned. Although not part of the cycle of films discussed because it falls beyond a specific late 1980s/early 1990s period of 'CGI wonder', *Avatar* nonetheless utilises the same rhetoric of innovation, an instance of novelty Pierson (1999b) associates with Hollywood CGI products from this time, and is a logical extension of the discussion. 'Indeed', as Michael Allen has put it, 'it could be said that the dominant identity of mainstream big-budget film-making of the past decade [the 1990s] is one framed by such images and such image-making technologies' (2004: 109). *The Abyss*, in particular, proved a testing ground for the new CGI technologies being developed in the late 1980s, with the filmmakers, according to Allen, uncertain of the capabilities of CGI – hence, the reason for the relative brevity of CGI material compared to live-action shots in the film's one CGI sequence, when the audience is given a glimpse of a water-like submarine life-form and witnesses its encounter with the crew of an underwater search-and-rescue mission (2004: 111).

This famous sequence is, formally speaking, 'bracketed off' from the rest of the live-action sequences in the film, according to Pierson (1999b: 172), having the effect of drawing attention to the origins of the visual make-up of the sequence – technological origins that have been commented upon widely within film culture and criticism. This bracketing is made more pronounced through the choice of shots used to present the creature in its relationship within the space of the frame, to the human actors and other real-world objects: the subjective shots from the creature's point of view are fluid, probing; the hand-held shots following the human crew investigating the disturbance give these elements a sense of urgency and realism; the shots partially made up using CGI material are static, giving a sense of awe, of wonder. With the very brief exceptions of slight tracking movements following the CGI creature in two of these shots, the overall emphasis of the CGI's presence is in its presentation. It is there to-be-looked-at in a way that other sequences in the film are not: true to the world of the film, the creature evokes a sense of wonder in the human observers within the diegesis, whilst, at the same time, the means by which it is rendered cinematically provide a focal point of wonderment for the cinema audience, whether they are aware of its precise production origins or not.

Once created and inserted into the frame, the CGI elements of *The Abyss* are free to be read as a part of the action just like any other element of the *mise-en-scène*, and at the same time are differentiated entities, free to be read as such by audiences. This example highlights generic and stylistic conventions, crucial to the consumption of cinematic spectacles that accompany technologies at such transitional, historical moments of production (and any textual interpretations that the audience might be inclined to establish). This dialectic of simultaneous cinematic spaces (of spectacle and affect), particularly at such transitional moments, demonstrates the importance of cinema's technological character without necessarily relying on technology as a purely determining factor, whilst also recognising its importance in the affective experience in the act of viewing films.

One of the key ways in which film theory has responded to this simultaneity is through the debate on film spectacle, and especially its tense relationship to narrative. One might say that both spectacle and narrative elements, whether competing or complementary, are able to solicit emotional and/or affective responses from the audience. In the most general sense, this relationship is often characterised by the technological and technical means by which these effects are solicited. This does not mean, however, that traditional forms of textual analysis are redundant in this view. In this regard, Bennett et al. state that 'The practice of looking at films usually involves the cognitive and emotional work of following stories, identifying with characters, studying performances and immersing ourselves in the *mise-en-scène*' (2008: 125 [emphasis in original]) .

This is one of the reasons why close analysis of *mise-en-scène* is still a useful strategy for teasing out relevant textual themes in overtly technologically inflected films, and is demonstrated through the above example. In *The Abyss* CGI sequence, all of the shot types mentioned frame the CGI as a presence, but also are thoroughly justified in their function to drive the narrative of the film and provide depth of characterisation in line with conventional film language. The crew panic, reflected through hand-held camerawork; the creature is awe-inspiring, reflected through a series of static shots; the creature is sentient and alive, reflected in the fluidity of subjective camerawork and shots from the creature's own point of view. However, in critically evaluating this textual material through analysis, and in considering its relationship to the ways a viewer practically engages with it (cognitively, emotionally) and responds to it (affectively), the analysis needs to incorporate another level of audience engagement. To do this, it may be useful at this time to consider alternative or complementary approaches to more traditional film studies methodologies.

For example, Aylish Wood's notion of competing elements (2007) can be aligned with a refusal of the hierarchical ordering of narrative significance in terms of impact aesthetics (of spectacle), and the drawing of attention towards the 'peripheral detail' of the edges of the frame. This idea was discussed at length by Roger Cardinal (1986) in his essay 'Pausing over Peripheral Detail', and the term 'peripheral detail', as he uses it, is taken from psychology and forensic psychology to determine the effectiveness of eye-witness testimony in both stressful and non-stressful contexts. In recent studies in the field of forensic psychology conducted by Castelli et al. (2006), they concluded that 'Crime witnesses are most likely to encode and remember what is often called the core event [...] compared to more peripheral details. This trend holds for stressful as well as nonstressful events and for adult and child witnesses' (2006: 247).

It is significant that a large number of experiments cited by Castelli et al. used film and photographic media to test the hypothesis. Their hypothesis suggests that 'the emotional content of an event may draw attention to central information of the traumatic event, to the detriment of more peripheral aspects that are left outside the focus of attention' (2006: 247). Hence, seemingly the everyday scenes in the *Close Encounters* example discussed in Chapter 1 do not appear to compete with the spectacular climax in the popular imagination and are not remembered in the same way that other scenes more pertinent to 'core events' in the narrative might be. Castelli et al. base their position (although with certain contingencies) upon the so-named 'Easterbrook' hypothesis. This is a classic eye-witness testimony study which suggests that 'As stress increases, the individual's attention is progressively restricted to the more central features of an event, at the expense of memory for information that falls outside the range of attention' (2006: 251).

To what extent this may be useful for thinking through the attentive relationship between viewer and screen is a debate that falls outside of the present study, but the fact that experimental psychology makes such wide use of film and screen media to test such hypotheses does give some scope for the film theorist to evaluate the usefulness of such findings. What is useful in this approach is that it enables the film theorist to engage the notion of shifting attention in terms of heightened emotional and affective states in psychological reality – states that could be said to be elicited through the dynamics between highly spectacular material and that of the mundane (in both aesthetic and thematic senses). It clearly relates to notions of attention and competing elements within the frame, such as those found in the sequence from *Close Encounters* discussed in Chapter 1. If one bears in mind that spectacular scenes of effects in popular cinema often rely on aesthetic novelty (e.g. the use of the iconic musical motif, along with giant lighting units at the climax to *Close Encounters*) to solicit the viewer's 'undivided' attention, then this has a direct bearing on the opportunity for film theory to engage with attention and distraction as useful phenomena.

It does not mean, however, that recollection of such fleeting or peripheral detail does not occur. The private experience of such moments may equally hold significance for the film-goer as an emotionally intense negotiation and co-production of meaning. This notion has been supported by psychotherapeutic uses and has consequently been appropriated for the criticism of film viewing, particularly within contemporary post-Jungian film scholarship. For example, Luke Hockley has argued that in the viewing process there is a participative relationship between the spectator and the screen which can be highly personal, as well as unexpected, in terms of the meaning outcome. Very often, in this relationship, the consensual encoding is secondary to a more spontaneous one. For Hockley, this means that 'as such, the plot is "lost" both in terms of the film and also in the extent to which, a consensual view of the film is abandoned in favour of a personal and affect laden response' (2009).

In some ways, this ambivalence is similar to more traditional approaches to film, in that often viewing experience is characterised by both an acceptance of the film (by the audience) as a constructed phenomenon and its ability to represent the world realistically, whether this is figured in terms of a photorealism or a psychological realism. In both cases, a kind of representational function is being performed by popular cinema, whereby the audience is able to tap into its familiar, formal conventions. When compounded with moments of technological transition, this can often have far-reaching implications for the viewing experience, as the audience is invited to suspend disbelief in enjoying escapist narratives, whilst simultaneously finding the pleasurable spaces of technical appreciation and a sense of wonderment.[5] As Angela Ndalianis, following Brooks Landon, has observed, 'This combination of the irrational with the rational is experienced as the ambivalent tension that tugs at the spectator: the oscillation between emotion and reason – between the sensory and the logical' (2000: 260).

More recently, Wood (2008) has commented upon the way that the cinematic encounter is being increasingly defined through competing elements within the frame and competing experiences of the interface. More and more, the relationship between viewer and viewed as a reflection of a much broader relationship between human subjects and the world has come to be defined through 'a multiplicity of interfaces'. Communications technologies in particular seem to have taken on a more intense mediating role through their proliferation and increased importance in everyday activities such as information retrieval, shopping and identity mobilisation through branding. Whilst it may be said that this role is not as determinist as Wood perhaps implies, in turn it has coloured audiences' relationships with the cinema screen, feeding into viewing sensibilities in popular culture more generally. Wood suggests that '[o]ur more long-standing moving image technologies such as television and cinema are also marked by this proliferation and so stand as indices for our experience of the expanding media terrain' (2008: 129).

Indeed, this view resonates with some of the convergence themes mentioned previously. Long-standing technological developments have meant that, alongside the transitional moments of technological evolution, other media exist and do so as a means of comparison for the production, distribution and consumption of images. Competing images/competing elements are therefore *de rigueur* in establishing references between texts in film culture generally, and indeed, intratextually within individual instances themselves. The impact of such competition upon viewing, articulated as an engagement with moving image technologies (themselves reflecting a broader, phenomenal change in the landscape of media technologies) is crucial, and may be illustrated through a selection of extreme examples.

Timecode (Figgis, US, 2000) is one such example of an internally cohesive film text using split screen techniques throughout its duration to engage the viewer in a story from four different but simultaneous viewpoints, in real-time. It is an extreme example of competing images within a single frame, perhaps, but Figgis is self-consciously commenting upon the proliferation of images in urban life (even going as far as to emulate CCTV aesthetics and conventions in some moments of the film). *Timecode* is not an isolated example of this kind of self-reflexive engagement with the notion of competing elements in visual culture, and indeed, contemporary television series such as *24* (Fox Network, 2001–2010) have embraced split-screen as an aesthetic driver for pivotal points in their narrative.

Run Lola Run (*Lola rennt*, Tykwer, Ger., 1998), although not often employing split-screen to emphasise its competing elements, uses competing timeframes to tell the protagonist's story in three narrative sequences, replayed to give three different outcomes. Lola (Franka Potente) has 20 minutes to find 100,000 Deutchmarks to give to her boyfriend to pay off a gangland debt, or he will resort to robbing a supermarket and be killed in the process. In this film, slight changes in timing at the beginning of each sequence cause huge alterations later on, resulting in alternative endings, reminiscent of multiple possibility outcomes in videogame play. The narrative as a whole relies on the viewer's memory to establish what 'went wrong' in previous sequences, and how Lola is 'fixing' the problem, in order to maintain coherence in a classic narrative sense to achieve a desired outcome (Lola gets the money and saves her boyfriend). That the filmmaker has chosen to use a variety of styles and aesthetic conceits to tell the story (animated sequences, drum and bass music video aesthetics, still photography and so forth) gives the film a sense of pastiche; a loose collection of vignettes forming a patchwork narrative, yet still maintaining a linear form.

Demonlover (Assayas, Fr., 2002) is another extreme example of such play with narrative cohesion, with the plot this time centring on corporate intrigue, media convergence and extreme pornography as themes for exploration, in a setting of competing diegetic realities. The identities of the main characters become blurred through confusion as to what reality (videogame/interactive media text, big business, subterfuge) is the stable, 'real' one in the world of the film. Such exploration of confusion through mediated identities has been explored before in, for example, *Videodrome* (Cronenberg, Can., 1983), and in both cases the competition focuses upon the relationship between humans and images, how humans use images and are in turn 'used' by them in order that coherent social identities can be maintained and/or transgressed.

Avalon (Oshii, Jap./Pol., 2001) uses similar conceits to explore the relationship between alienated youth, communications and gaming technologies, and reality. However, the aesthetic employed in *Avalon* visibly deconstructs image production itself, inviting the viewer to question the reliability of digitised images in mass media generally, whilst at the same time offering an existential critique of human relationships with technology. The thematic emphasis here is on addiction and legality, whilst the visual tropes employed to draw attention to such themes centre around the deconstruction, layering and revelation of imagery. Such visual tropes self-consciously add another dimension to the viewing experience of the film and offer up a further theme: the nature of the competition of images itself.

These examples all explore those aspects of popular film that highlight the particular conditions of encounters between humans and audio-visual technology, revealing this encounter to be peculiarly spatio-temporal and focused upon image production and consumption as functions of the rhetoric of innovation in popular culture. In doing so, such commentary draws attention to the way that popular cinema performs such functions, but does so representationally, in the service of narrative conventions. Even so, Wood contends that a key aspect of contemporary feature films facilitates the spatio-temporal function of competition: 'When competing elements exist in an image, a viewer's "eye" is drawn in more than one direction. Sometimes this capacity to split a viewer's focus is obvious' (2008: 130). Such obvious instances may be found in those extreme examples just cited, although this is also more subtly inculcated in popular cinema in general. Although discernible in such cinema, competition between visual (and audio-visual) elements forms part of a more general propagation of human–technology interaction, in which, Wood suggests, viewers have adjusted to shifting and competing interfaces, and from which they synthesise meaning. Thus, Wood is mapping out the ground for an account of viewing in the contemporary media landscape, shaped by modes and multiples of interface, and in doing so attempts to articulate the encounter with the interface as a site of 'emergent human agency' (2008: 129). She goes on to suggest that:

> In making sense of the world through interfaces of moving imagery, we directly experience the spatio-temporal incursions of technologies. These incursions take us to places we could never otherwise go, but in doing so also deny us the ability to exert full control over that experience. This is the compromise at the heart of our engagements with technologies.
>
> (2008: 131)

In straightforward terms, Wood here identifies a compromised relationship between humans and interfaces, and in so doing, implies a contradiction (even though Wood herself seems to err on the side of a positive outlook on human–interface potential in her argument in this essay, and in her book *Digital Encounters*, 2007). What characterises this compromise? What forms can this contradiction take? How has this contradiction been identified in media and film theory? How might this impact on the viewing experience? As Wood herself admits, in screen studies the most common way to understand textual organisation has traditionally been through discussion of linearity of narrative, although there have recently been radical interventions, other than Wood's own notion of competing elements, that incorporate a critique of such traditions.[6]

Dimensions of media convergence, history and determination all impact on the popular discourse of film and film culture, affecting commercial and artistic decision-making, marketing and distribution strategies, criticism and its concomitant problematics (plot, stars, directors, genre, etc.). To some extent, the consumer viewing experience is shaped as a result. These dimensions should be properly considered as extratextual competing elements that can shape the act of meaning-making, at various levels of production and consumption, and for the various bodies involved, investing as they do their particular interests. Genre, for example, can identifiably mean different things to different people (or groups of people/stakeholders) and at different times. Additionally, these groups and interests are not discrete. Sometimes they converge, sometimes they compete. The implications of Wood's argument have, therefore, consequences that reach far beyond textual interpretation and into industrial and institutional contexts. However, as already implied, the self-reflexivity of popular cinema towards a tendency to foreground human–technology relationships in its visual make-up can be illuminating in this respect.

As discussed at various points so far in this book, contemporary mediascapes have mainstreamed transmedia storytelling and expanded narrative experiences for the viewer. Digital effects in the cinema and on television are, arguably, a visual manifestation and representation of the kinds of worlds made possible through such enhancements. Often, more traditional, linear and hermetic narrative elements co-exist with or alongside such expanded narrative spaces: expanded narrative space extends to the paratextual material found on, for example, DVD special features via extratextual technological interfaces such as the partially interactive DVD root menu. Such co-existence attends to the competitive nature of visual elements, extending this into narrative structures, and thus feeds into an economy of attention and exchange in the cinematic encounter.

Economies of attention and exchange in the cinematic encounter

Attention, as a term, exists in conjunction with concepts that were the staple of Frankfurt School political economy; concepts that may be distilled in the terms 'distraction' and 'absorption' in a viewing process involving an (at least partially) passive viewer, and the proliferation of hegemonic ideological constructs at political and aesthetic levels. More usefully, however, attention also suggests an active process that relies on the 'blissful' relationship between what Barthes (1981) described as *studium* and *punctum*, both crucial to the notion of cinephilia as a method and concept. The paradigmatic definition of attention in cognitive science suggests that it is best understood as the process by which individuals attend to particular elements within their perceptive field. Whether this is shaped by ideological constraints or not is a separate question often ignored in this particular field, hence its ostensibly apolitical appearance (and therefore its conduciveness to the post-theorical discourse of anti-politicians such as Bordwell and Carroll). However, this does not mean that such politics should be ruled out en masse, but that perhaps they should be qualified through taking into account ideological forms (such as the rhetoric of innovation, or the reliability of experimental psychology, or the infallibility of the media-effects paradigm in some sociologies of the media).

Far from what might be considered a 'natural' ally with approaches that tend towards passive viewing models, some contemporary cognitivists are exploring attention in viewing as a highly active and high-ordered process. Harold Pashler (1995, 1998), for example, describes attention as an active process as it involves being *selective*, whether on a cognitive, affective, or emotional level, or in some combination of these levels of experience. Because it is a selective process, in popular discourse attention is also often understood to involve compromise on what is being attended to. In short, attention is often thought to be *divided* between cognitive tasks undertaken – hence, the phrase 'divided attention'. It is also worth mentioning that in popular discourse attention is often associated with effort, hence the term 'pay attention' – suggesting an exertion, commutation or exchange of some kind.

Pashler's account of this logic is summarised as follows: 'Selection is most obvious when it is difficult, as for example when we strain to listen to one voice in a crowd while ignoring other, perhaps louder voices' (1995: 72). He critiques commonsense or 'folk psychology' interpretations of attention, however, where the notions that are not generally accepted in contemporary attention research ('paying attention', 'divided attention' and so on) nevertheless formed the basic assumptions and problematics for early psychologists (influenced by phenomenological accounts of experience such as those of William James, Titchener, Pillsbury, etc.) and exert their influence in the field to this day. There still exists a commonsense view that an individual can devote their attention simultaneously to stimuli, to memories (and associations) and to activities, but that, in so doing, less of that individual's attention remains available for other experiences or activities at that time. Laurence R. Harris and Michael Jenkin (2001) confirm Pashler's critique, stating that:

> Attention implies allocating resources, perceptual or cognitive, to some
> things at the expense of not allocating them to something else. This

definition implies a limit to the resources of an individual such that they cannot attend to everything at once, all the time. In one sense this is obvious in that the senses already provide a filter. [...] But attention [actually] refers to selection from the array of information that is arriving at the brain and is potentially available.

(2001: 1)

Wood's position on competing elements seeks to challenge the commonsense assumptions that form a false economy of attention, assumptions that Pashler has (and by implication, Harris and Jenkin have) identified in popular discourse. Wood cites the example of *Timecode* as a film that cues and distributes attention nevertheless demonstrating that attention is as much analytic as it is synthetic simultaneously. Wood is here citing concepts of attention drawn from the early psychology of W. B. Pillsbury, who differentiates analysis and synthesis of elements competing for attention thus: in analysis, one part of a whole is more prominent, and, through its prominence, one is able to examine its constituents; in synthesis, the whole is attended to, rather than its components, so that in attention the whole is given prominence rather than its elements (Pillsbury 2008: 106–7). Wood's conclusion is a useful weapon in the challenge to commonsense assumptions on attention. It is also a challenge that is taken up by other research in contemporary cognitive science. For example, Harris and Jenkin suggest that 'The term "attention" suffers from the fact that it is a word in both common and scientific usage, and the common and scientific meanings only loosely overlap' (2001: 1).

Therefore, the term 'attention' as it is referred to in the discourse of my own work exploits this overlap in the same way that Kracauer in *The Mass Ornament* (1994) used the terms 'boredom' and 'distraction' to articulate alienation and critique the bourgeois fiction of self-identity. Competing elements in the field of experience, when viewing films, are intimately connected with both the psychological, cognitive process of selection and the social, political character of agency, viewed selectively in the act of meaning-making to incorporate analytic and synthetic modes, registers of meaningfulness, and on multiple levels (the textual, the political/ideological, the institutional).

As Harris and Jenkin state, 'None of the processes of "visual" attention are exclusively visual: they are neither driven exclusively by visual inputs nor do they operate exclusively on retinal information' (2001: 1). Stimuli are not purely visual, nor are they either pure physiological phenomena restricted to the private or personal, but are shaped through social production of meaning and meaning-making (as whole-body perception in Don Ihde's Body One and Body Two). In addition, the consensus in the fields of cognitive and experimental psychology on the matter of attention can be interpreted critically to lend support to many of the claims of 'embodied viewing' that exist in contemporary film phenomenology and theory (including Angerer 2008; Casey 2007; Ihde 2002; Manojlovic 2008; Moore 2004; Singh 2007, 2009; Sobchack 1992, 2004; Tuck 2007; Wood 2007, 2008) giving these largely theoretical approaches a practical habitus. Therefore, rather than simple stimulus–response models that are often associated as drivers of cognitive psychology, as Pashler contends: 'For the most part modern cognitive scientists take it for granted that unobservable internal structures and processes are important' (1995: 72).

How may the film theorist usefully appropriate such views on attention in the act of viewing? Following a study of the importance of unique visual experiences in the process of attention responses, Pashler and Harris concluded that 'Commonsense suggests that unique and/or abruptly changing stimuli sometimes seem to grab our attention "automatically"' (2001: 747). This lends credence to the (again, commonsense) notion that contemporary effects-driven spectacles, impact aesthetics, the garish and 'brutal', are more likely to grab the attention of viewers than a more contemplative or somehow poetic cinema. It follows over a century of such views in orthodox psychology, led by Edward B. Titchener (1908), whose early work on attention and feeling drew heavily from phenomenology.

Titchener wrote of attention that 'A stimulus that is repeated again and again is likely to attract the attention, even if at first it is altogether unremarked' (1908: 191). This makes sense in the light of the way that the recognisable and the repeatable in popular cinema has traditionally drawn both large box-office success (because of the attraction of the familiar, the conventional) and critical accusations of popular cinema as formulaic – in Arnheim's words, 'brutal'. What is interesting about Titchener's claim is that he immediately qualifies it with exceptions, stating that any sudden change would provide distraction for an individual who was focusing on something else (1908: 192). Hence, the value of the novel, of the individual or cinephilic view again pulling into focus as aspects of memorable cinema, pleasurable or otherwise.

Let us consider a memorable example from Hollywood's 'classical' period: Natalie Wood's initial appearance as Judy in *Rebel Without a Cause* (Ray, US, 1955) dressed in a brilliant red coat, sitting in a police station. Because of the way Technicolor enhances the appearance of reds and other tints between red and yellow, Wood's coat and lips markedly stand out against the rather drab, brownish interior of the police station and the milky complexion of her skin. Even when appearing towards the edge of the frame, her appearance in such a form is not accidental, and the then-new Cinemascope ratio allowed the inclusion of elements disparate enough to be housed in different rooms, but within the same frame (Wood and James Dean either side of Plato (Sal Mineo)). Of course, the connotations of a woman in red are not lost on the viewer: as a juvenile delinquent dressed in pillar-box red, Wood's appearance is intended to signify 'bad girl'. However, even without such connotations, the visual make-up of the scene facilitates a shifting attention between Dean as star, Mineo as the focus of dialogue in the centre of the frame, and Wood, who is first seen at the left edge of the frame in another room.

As demonstrated in this classical example, competing elements within the frame (as well as extratextual knowledge of the film, its production, its visual and cultural make-up) bring together a co-production of meaning, to borrow Hockley's phrase. In this case, for example, the fairly common knowledge within film culture surrounding the relatively early deaths of each of its young stars adds to the mythos of the film's production and subsequent cult status. Attention is cued not only through its aesthetics but also through its cultural impact as a nostalgic text. This helps to lend credence to Aylish Wood's claim that 'All cinema cues attention' (2008: 136). In other words, attention is not solely contingent upon the overtly technological and the spectacular, particularly in retrospective viewing, where once cutting-edge technologies (such as Technicolor and Cinemascope in the above example) are now seen as commonplace, tame even.

So far, contemporary examples from so-called 'second cinema' (e.g. *Timecode*, *Avalon*) outside of Hollywood production, as well as examples from latter 'New' Hollywood (e.g. *Close Encounters*) have been cited to demonstrate competing textual and extratextual elements. In *Rebel Without a Cause*, an example exists to demonstrate this cueing of attention existed in classical period Hollywood, and together, these examples collectively suggest that Wood is correct in identifying the phenomenon as characteristic of narrative cinema in its most general sense. However, whereas Wood's own approach emphasises aesthetic concerns as well as the phenomenological aspects of interactivity in the 'viewsing' process, the emphasis in the argument of the current study lies in the manner in which popular cinema cues attention through both peritext (within the aesthetic make-up of the film itself, but embodying discernibly intentional meaning beyond denotation, e.g. Natalie Wood's red lipstick and clothes, connoting her as 'bad girl') *and* extratextual or epitextual means (e.g. in *Rebel*, the appearance of rising star James Dean in the lead role, embodying the then relatively new phenomenon of teen angst in late capital). In Genette's terms (1997), both of these vestibular types of textuality that compete along with elements of the *mise-en-scène* constitute paratextual material.[7]

Paratextuality is a concept that has been discussed already in Chapter 1, in relation to *Close Encounters*. The definition of paratexts in relation to film and film viewing may be briefly expanded upon here as liminal devices (such as title sequences, DVD commentaries and reviews) that orientate the consumer around the narrative and mediate the object of the film to the viewer. Of course, there are links between this concept, taken from Genette's literary theory, and that of Wood's competing elements, taken largely from a transdisciplinary media study. This comes to light particularly when Wood's observation that all cinema cues attention is followed up by her statement that this disposes the viewer 'in different ways to what is occurring on the screen as the tactics of textual organization determine the viewing experience, interrupting engagements with characters, genres and so on' (2008: 136). This was demonstrated in Chapter 1, where the example of everydayness in the different versions of *Close Encounters* enables a particular engagement with the narrative that is brought forth through the various edits and the (albeit subtle) changes to narrative and visual elements that manifest as differing ideological contents in the film's climax as a result.

For example, in the scene where Roy has had a breakdown and constructs his living-room sculpture, TV broadcast, mountain and phone conversation all vie for the viewer's attention, enabling a sophisticated negotiation of meaning to take place where Roy's character is fleshed out through dialogue, behaviour, gesture, environment and his relationship to both that environment (the mess, the sculpture, the TV broadcast and the suburban scenes outside) and to his estranged wife. Where this process becomes more subtle lies in the way that such competition allows for competing views of the same event, depending on what element is directly attended to and which are left for a more peripheral, secondary attention. In this process, idiosyncratic viewer response to intentional meanings and their own negotiated meaning-making evolve into more complex forms of co-creation, which in turn problematise universalisation of meaning and interpretation of film narrative.

As the early cognitive psychologist W. B. Pillsbury wrote in *The Essentials of Psychology*, 'One of the much discussed problems of attention concerns the difference between the sensation that is directly attended to and the others that constitute the background of consciousness' (2008: 105–6). Whereas this may suggest a primary and secondary attentiveness in viewing an event (or indeed a filmed event), this cognitive approach does not fully account for an affective approach that deals with embodied viewing (such as those espoused by Ihde, Wood, Sobchack, etc.) that co-creative schemas such as those suggested by Hockley and by Hauke attempt to account for. Nevertheless, there is a clear link between Pillsbury's early cognitive work and the influence of phenomenology that still held sway in the field of psychology at the time (i.e. 1913) which may be of use in creating a dialogue between these two positions.[8] It is worth quoting him at length here, on his discussion of the separate definitions of attention through 'interest' and 'effort':

> If one should ask the average non-scientific individual why he attends, he would answer in practically every case that he attended because he was interested or because he forced himself. If we examine our own consciousness, it is evident that attention from interest and attention from effort are natural divisions. [...] To say that attention is due to interest is merely to say that it is due to some one of the subjective conditions other than social pressure. [...] The attention that is said to be due to effort falls almost universally under the socially conditioned.
>
> (2008: 117–8)

This, it must be argued, simplifies the manner in which subjective states and social pressures are separated in attitudes towards intention, and it is far from clear that Pillsbury was entirely satisfied with this distinction. For example, he states that 'It is generally asserted that attention increases the clearness of a mental state. The state becomes clearer, its details more prominent, it can now be easily used and understood.' Importantly, however, Pillsbury goes on to write that 'this quality of clearness is [...] different from intensity in spite of the fact that both make a mental state more important' (2008: 106). This suggests two principles of attention in the encounter with an event (intensity, clearness) that separate the 'merely' spectacular ('brutal', 'kitsch') from the meaningful (the 'cinephilic moment'). In that separation, however, rather than a gap, void or split, one might say that a site of agency may be identified, whether the attention is gained through 'interest' or 'effort'. As Wood states, 'Making sense of the elements requires a viewer to synthesize a meaning, and the freedom offered to a viewer to make this synthesis is a site of potential agency' (2008: 137).

In fact, Pillsbury (2008: 118) himself distinguished three forms of attention, forms that 'cannot always be distinguished':

a   Voluntary: conditioned by social pressure and accompanied by *effort*, social incentive and a sense of duty.
b   Non-voluntary: conditioned by the idea in mind, attitude, education and heredity, and accompanied by *interest*.
c   Involuntary: conditioned by the character of the stimuli that are presented, 'and either is accompanied by interest or is the distraction that gives occasion for effort'.

These different forms, perhaps, always-already constitute a dialectical form of attention that includes attention, distraction, interest and effort, the form that Merleau-Ponty describes as the site of acting and being acted upon. This is usefully articulated in an affirmative form in Wood's approach as a mediated form of potential agency and teases out the provisional, viewer-orientated, self-conscious viewing strategies alluded to at the beginning of this chapter. Cognitively speaking, Pillsbury's model demonstrates the interaction between sensory stimulation, viewer intentionality and the ideological status of the viewed text: clearly having some shared attributes with Ihde's notion of whole-body perception and the superimposition of Body One, Body Two. This interaction becomes clear when a text knowingly draws attention to its competing elements through reflexive, intratextual and intertextual references to its production origins, as well as to its conceptual origins. Often, as in the case of *Avalon* and other similar contemporary CGI films, the retrogressive deconstruction of images as a storytelling strategy allows the viewer to interact with those elements competing for attention through what could be described as a kitsch mode of storytelling.

One such example is *Sky Captain and the World of Tomorrow* (Conran, US, 2004), a film employing CGI elements throughout to depict a science-fictionalised world of the 1940s. Radio communications are represented through concentric circles emanating from giant communications towers (so large, in fact, that the circumference of the Earth is visible in shot), reminiscent of the RKO Pictures studio ident of the classic Hollywood period. Of course, the illustration is not a photorealistic depiction of radio communications, yet is a suitable representation given the narrative context in which it is set. Based on a retro graphic novel series featuring Sky Captain (Jude Law), a daredevil fighter pilot during the Second World War, *Sky Captain* uses such kitsch representations to underscore its story-world. Radio waves are not visible; radio transmitters are not that big; if there were such things as giant flying robots and death-rays, surely more sophisticated means of communication could be invented alongside these wonders of science fiction? Yet, these kitschy elements of *Sky Captain* maintain the integrity of the film's aesthetic viability, appropriateness to the film's story-world, and institute immediate apprehension of the film's narrative conceits on those terms. Therefore, the notion of kitsch as a sensibility discernible in the encounter with the film text seems to point to Merleau-Ponty's dialectic of action and being-acted-upon and Jameson's re-materialisation of history as a vicarious experience, that both demonstrate Arnheim's frustrated experiences of watching films that bring only 'immediate satisfaction', and provide Wood's site of potential agency.

In what follows in the final chapter, I will extend this discussion in relation to currents in film-phenomenology, noting the ways in which the arc of narrative operations in contemporary cinema extends across multiple sites of access. I will also discuss the extension of narrative through extratextual time and space in the contemporary cinematic encounter. In this sense, I will offer some thoughts towards what Casey (2000, 2007) identifies of the act and procedure of the glance and its all-at-once-ness. I will engage this notion phenomenologically, in terms of a cinematic glance which partakes of an arc of operations running parallel to those of narrative, extending the duration of the cinematic encounter in what I describe as a cinematic afterlife.

Notes

1 For a thoroughgoing commentary on the impact of Canudo's work, see Susan Hayward's entry on 'Theory' in her *Key Concepts in Cinema Studies* (1999). See also Tredell (2002).

2 Although only recently a point for discussion in film theory as outlined in this chapter, processes of attention and distraction have been addressed at length in television studies. The qualitative differences between gaze and glance, attentive cinematic spectatorship and inattentive (or distracted) television viewing will be the subject of lengthy discussion in Chapter 6. I note recent examples from television studies here to contextualise the present discussion, in preparation for its theorisation and illustration later. The problem of defining 'quality TV' is most acute here, in relation to re-evaluation of the televisual viewing experience and secondary markets in the wider remit of multinational media conglomeration, the horizontal integration of industrial organisation and the distribution of media properties. For a detailed overview of this, see MacCabe and Akass (2007); also, Buonanno (2008); Hammond and Mazdon (2005); Turner and Tay (2009); and, of course, John Ellis (1992).

3 According to Ben Brewster and Lea Jacobs, in *Theatre to Cinema: Stage Pictorialism and the Early Feature Film* (1997: 54–7), one of the first major productions to use intertitles, rather than simple 'freeze-frame' tableaux as transitions, was Edison's version of *Uncle Tom's Cabin* (Porter, US, 1903). This is confirmed by Lee Grieveson and Peter Krämer in their introduction to 'Storytelling and the Nickelodeon' (2004: 80).

4 Although outside of the immediate concerns of this study, it is worth noting that this position was taken up more forcefully by Georg Lukács in *History and Class*

Consciousness (1971) in his notion of reification – the processes and state of consciousness in capitalist societies by and through which its subjects are reduced to the status of relations between 'things'. This was also the subject of development in sociology, in terms of Weber's theory of instrumentalism and social uniformity, put forward in *The Protestant Ethic and the Spirit of Capitalism* (1996), which breeds an equivalent relationship between consumers.

5 As already alluded to in my essay 'The Kitsch Affect' (2012), this sense of wonderment, so important in traditions in SF literature and cinema, is connected to the sense of nostalgia that accompanies the knowing consumption of kitsch artefacts. It should also be noted, in passing, that this wonderment is also associated, in a depth psychology sense, with a knowing loss of innocence in the face of technological and aesthetic innovation, and a concomitant underlying re-sacralisation of culture. For more on this aspect of depth psychology, see the first chapter in Samuels' (1993) *The Political Psyche*. Although some over-simplification of the technological is evidenced, this text nevertheless provides a crucial link between psychological theories and the politics of technological discourses (in particular, for the sake of the present study, the aforementioned rhetoric of innovation).

6 In particular, I refer the reader to Miller et al. (2005), *Global Hollywood 2*. Here, the authors explore a radical political economy of Hollywood production–distribution–consumption systems. Whilst incorporating critical textual interpretation, they reject determining textualism in favour of socio-economic criticism to produce leftist-liberal discourse on representation analysis itself and the studio system as a global economic force.

7 Additionally, it should be noted here that both George A. Wilson's *Narration in Light: Studies in Cinematic Point of View* (1986) and John Gibbs' *Mise-en-Scène: Film Style and Interpretation* (2002) (following and critiquing Wilson) have noted the importance of the relationship between costume and narration in *Rebel Without a Cause*. What is useful to note here is that the close readings that Wilson and Gibbs perform are in line with the kinds of attentive viewing that accompany moments of cinephilia, providing an academic precedent to the approach to this particular film, as suggested in this current chapter.

8 Although it should be noted here that some of Pillsbury's terminology is fairly antiquated, and that some reinterpretation is required in order for his psychology to be understood in contemporary terms, it still addresses the interstitial spaces between mind and body in perceptual psychology, and is therefore useful here. The 'mental state' he mentions, for example, refers to the relative importance, at the time of encountering an event or stimulus, of the cognitive states of perception, attention, cognition and memory of an individual. 'Interest' here includes attention that has been 'grabbed' through sensory stimulation, similar in some ways to orthodox phenomenological accounts of the 'gripping' of intentionality. 'Effort' and 'social conditioning' should be taken to include ideological, political as well as cultural and technological elements, competing 'for' the attention of Ihde's Body Two (2002).

6

ADVENTURES IN THE CINEMATIC AFTERLIFE

A phenomenology of the cinematic glance

> A movie has meaning in the same way that a thing does: neither of them speaks to an isolated understanding; rather, both appeal to our power tacitly to decipher the world [of] men and to coexist with them.
>
> (Maurice Merleau-Ponty, 1964: 58)

> By glancing, I enter into a gleaming realm. I look from the darkness of not knowing into the light of knowing: knowing places and surfaces that gleam sufficiently to attract my glance, placial surfaces off from which the glancing rays of dawning ken may bounce. I move from *here* and *now* into the glistening horizon of being *there* and *then* – into the glint of space and duration.
>
> (Edward S. Casey, 2000: 159 [emphasis in original])

A number of technological developments have signalled the rise of digital cinema during the last 25 years or so that have contributed to its exponential growth in the industrial landscape of popular cinema. Digital sound configurations such as Dolby and THX have enabled filmmakers to design soundscapes to match spectacular visual creations. Digital, non-linear editing formats such as Avid and Final Cut Pro have utterly transformed the assemblage of the moving image, and have affected production decisions from storyboard through to post-production and promotion. The affordability of scaled-down versions of such industrial-standard packages has contributed to the continued rise in semi-professional and amateur film production cultures. More recently, the development of digital film distribution has once again foregrounded the commercial need for the conservation of copyright and the elimination of film and video piracy. Perhaps the most visible signifier of digital cinema for the spectator, however, can be found in the proliferation of CGI in mainstream film.

In Chapter 5, I discussed the rhetoric of innovation in digital cinema cultures, the accompanying phenomena of competing elements across various levels of viewsing, and the various interrelated economies of the contemporary cinematic encounter. Often highlighted through transitional technological developments, as well as the accompanying critical discourses of cinema as technology, such competing elements are memorable through moments of spectacle, when they seem to 'grab' one's attention. In this way, cinematic spectacle, particularly in popular cinema, can often seem to be overwhelmingly 'brutal', in Rudolf Arnheim's words; soliciting attention in order to provide immediate satisfaction, as a reward for attention paid.

However, recent developments in the field of cognitive psychology (as well as in post-Jungian film analysis) have made something of a return to that discipline's origins as a phenomenology of meaningfulness, existing within social and cultural contexts: contexts that shape and colour encounters with cultural artefacts. Such a return to a 'co-production of meaning' within film theory, as well as the theory of psychology in the context of film viewing, demonstrates that the economy of effort in attention is not as simple or straightforward as popular discourse or folk psychology would suggest. The assumptions providing the foundation for the economy of attention therefore need to be problematised for film theory to make use of it as a theoretical tool, in order to more properly situate attention within the material and political economy of consumption and exchange in film culture.

It was suggested that recent interventions, such as Aylish Wood's work on digital encounters and her notion of competing elements, provide insight into this area of film theory and I have argued elsewhere[1] that cinephilia as a concept, an object of study and a critical method could be a useful theoretical tool for this task. It would be crucial to engage, in addition to Arnheim's critique of popular cinema, not only the moments most 'memorable' in film culture (such as, for example, the spectacular climax in *Close Encounters of the Third Kind*) but also those moments incidental to those key, 'core' moments of the narrative. In other words, 'cinephilic' moments which capture the imagination of the viewing audience according to individual taste and pleasurable consumption. Such moments, following Roger Cardinal, are 'peripheral' in that they are highly contingent upon idiosyncratic interpretations of the film text and the viewing experience, and incidental in that they do not necessarily directly affect core aesthetic elements within the frame. However, as demonstrated through the example of everydayness in *Close Encounters*, discussed in Chapter 1, such subtle and otherwise unnoticeable elements can and do affect, in Althusserian terms, the problematics of narrative trajectory in a film's narrative.

This seems especially the case when dealing with a contemporary film culture that thrives on carrier media that provide information on a film's production processes, that act as reflexive commentaries upon the textual elements of the film itself (sometimes quite literally, in the case of DVD commentaries and alternative edits/endings) and afford the viewer opportunities for repeated viewings. Such practices are bound up in questions of the essence of narrative encounter in contemporary popular film culture, one of the driving theoretical problems to which this study seeks solutions.

When Christian Metz noted that 'A narrative has *a beginning and an ending*, a fact that simultaneously distinguishes it from the rest of the world' (1978: 17 [emphasis in original]) he was deliberately evoking a snapshot of cinematic narrative based upon textuality; that is, narrative discourse of the film's story-world as an act of telling a story, with a beginning and an ending. To be sure, Metz's approach offers film theory a defined structural model for analysing a film's meaning, its signification. In order for this to occur, however, one must perform a kind of bracketing-off of what I would argue are two interrelated phenomena: structurally determined closure, based on a film's enunciative style (the film's textuality or textual strategy, the way in which it tells and shows its story) and a sense of completeness (and obversely, I would further argue, incompleteness) of the world of the film (a sensibility of closure, the affective and felt relation of a film's audience corresponding to the film). In this chapter, it is not my intention to outline a lengthy semiotics of narrative discourse, although I will draw from the work of Metz (1977, 1978), Genette (1980) and Neupert (1995) in relation to this where appropriate.

The concern of this final chapter is to discuss and offer some observations towards a theory of what might be termed the 'cultural afterlife' of the cinematic encounter. Somewhat influenced by Rodowick's notion of the 'virtual life of film' (2007), this notion sees narrative as a rather more open system of telling and told, both textually and extratextually. It is part of the 'action' of narrative, or if preferred, the work of narrative in the act of telling and retelling, in which the film (when viewed, hypothetically, as a singular text) becomes subject to various kinds of discourses and commentaries, often accompanied by highly emotive responses to a film's narrative, characters or style. These are mobilised by both the industry itself (marketing, secondary and paratextual production, the narrative image) and audiences (the kinds of tertiary production, collecting, reviewing, word-of-mouth and participation culture that have been discussed at length in various parts of this book so far).

The role of cinephilia in this regard is fairly self-evident, judging purely by the activity of the cinephile in their cinematic encounter. In the duration of the initial encounter, the viewing methods employed by the cinephile, of negotiating the competing elements within the frame, necessitate a gaze-like viewing capacity, whose function is to watch avidly, take in details with precision, and take pleasure in the immersive properties of the film holistically. They also mobilise a glance-like capacity, a flirtatious encounter with the screen to manoeuvre around the incidental or inconsequential. In this way, the viewer does not necessarily dwell on these incidental moments in the duration of watching (although they *may*), but these are moments for reflection and for sharing in the retelling of the encounter.

As will become apparent later in this chapter, gazing and glancing are very different regimes of looking, often associated, respectively, with cinematic spectatorship and televisual viewing in film and television studies. To give the briefest of schema here for the purposes of outlining the argument (subject to revision later on), one might say that the gaze seeks mastery over that which it looks at, whereas the glance, as its etymological basis suggests, slides off the surface. The gaze attempts to penetrate the textual material it engages; the glance is *mere*: it inhabits the screen and perforates its surface in a softer incorporation to that sought by gazing. Yet, following both Edward S. Casey (2007: 5) and Jacques Derrida (1973: 104), the glance does not *abide*.

As touched upon elsewhere in this study, thinking about telling and retelling in this way extends the encounter beyond the frame. This, it could be argued, has always been a part of the cultural afterlife of a film, in that a film's reputation has always been subject to reviews and comments *a posteriori* the act of viewing, but, in its contemporary form, appropriates and therefore extends the narrative discourse in ways that, whilst perhaps not necessarily new to film cultures, nevertheless have come to take on a dimension of value and meaningfulness. The manner in which viewers extend these observations and commentaries through communications technology and platforms for expressions of taste (blogging and social media being particularly powerful tools in this regard) has meant that the materiality of the cinematic encounter is both enhanced and extended through more concrete, paratextual productivity. I argue that this broadens the definitions of cinephilia somewhat to (however occasionally) incorporate other kinds of audiences, be it a fan, cult or casual one.

It is in this vein that the current chapter proceeds. Richard Neupert's lengthy semiotic analysis of narration and closure in cinema (*The End*, 1995) seems to render the film a closed textual object (or system of objects) in order to fix its categories of signification for analysis. He states that the function of the narrator is an organising principle of narrative discourse, performing a bracketing function that 'operates on a large textual level, using textual and paratextual codes to address the spectator, begin the narrative, and eventually close off the narrative and the text' (1995: 26). This taxonomic approach, whilst useful for analysis purposes, is problematic because it does not address the rather more organic processes of reflection that inhabit the cinematic encounter. Although Neupert does attempt to address the problem of the spectator later in his discussion, his relationship between spectator and text is confined to categories for analysis rather than as a dynamic, intersubjective relationship between viewer and viewed.

As an alternative to Neupert, I propose that this chapter be read in light of recent work in the field of depth psychology and film theory on the notion of a 'third image' (Hauke 2009; Hockley 2009) where the participative relationship between viewer and viewed is underpinned through a co-creation of meaning that continues upon leaving the cinema theatre or beyond the end of the screening, as well as the cognitivist ideas associated with a critique of commonly assumed economies of 'effort' in the act of viewing, as drawn upon in Chapter 5. In his own account of spectatorship, Neupert seems to be inconclusive and, to an extent, needs to leave open the question of the work of spectatorship as an ongoing dynamic event in order that the textual material be analysed as a specific object of inquiry. Nevertheless, he states in his concluding remarks that:

The viewer, like the film critic, works by perception. Interpretation, hypothesis-making and retrospection to make sense of, and interact with, any given film text. Resolution and closure then become functions of the spectator, and, depending on background and past narrative experience, some of us will impose resolution where others will grant open ambiguity.

(1995: 180)

This suggests interpretative processes that occur in the work of the viewer, in the narrativisation of both the text's semiological strategies and the encounter with them. In fact, Neupert even goes as far as to state that the study of narrative has redefined the spectator:

From being an organic individual to an invisible and metaphorical position or place to an unconscious processor of the collective, cultural imaginary. The dramatic inroads made by cognitive psychology and reception theory within film studies offer strong evidence that structuralist, psychoanalytic, and semiotic conceptions of the spectator have proven incomplete.

(1995: 181)

Thus Neupert's conclusions, whilst self-admittedly non-exhaustive, are none-theless problematic, for the task he sets himself in his formalist approach would seem an impossible one. The ongoing work of narrative, the retelling of stories in a circular cultural exchange (the 'action' of the narrative), is thus a trope of the pleasurable journey: less a task than a part of the way narratives are passed from group to group, individual to individual, with each transition adding to (or editing) it. This action itself is probably worthy of a formal semiotic study itself, if one were inclined to perform such a task, although one would suspect that the rhizome-like, open-source tendencies of how information is exchanged and dealt with in contemporary popular culture would make this task an onerous one, and one that falls outside of the remit of the present study. I return to the (somewhat literary) notion of ongoing co-production of meaning – the 'action' of narrative – momentarily.

For now, it is worth mentioning that this closed–open aspect of cinematic textuality has been the subject of Gilles Deleuze's film-philosophy and subsequent commentaries (for example, Kennedy 2002; Totaro 1999). The recourse to the analogy of the rhizome as a visualisation of the activities of film culture in the previous paragraph is a deliberate one: philosopher Gilles Deleuze having (with anti-psychiatrist Félix Guattari) appropriated such multiply-networked, rhizomatic analogues to the point of re-imagining and mapping individual and collective psychological experience of late-capitalist culture in several of his works, as being 'oriented toward an experimentation in contact with the real' (1987: 12).

The aspect of Deleuze's work that is most pertinent here is that set out in his book *Cinema 1: The Movement-Image* (2004). Here, he delimits three interrelated

172

levels of the cinematic encounter, the first of which broadly corresponds with Neupert's efforts to engage textuality as a singular form. Deleuze describes this level as a frame, set or closed system, the determination of which '*includes everything which is present in the image* – sets, characters and props' (2004: 12 [emphasis in original]). At this level, the frame consists of a number of elements that may constitute sub-sets of interacting elements, thus allowing for analysis of the breakdown of the moving image, but where the relatively closed system is never in complete isolation from its outside, in its relation with other levels (2004: 17). For, as Deleuze states:

> Framing is the art of choosing the parts of all kinds which become part of a set. This set is a closed system, relatively and artificially closed. The closed system determined by the frame can be considered in relation to the data that it communicates to the spectators: it is 'informatic'.
>
> (2004: 18)

Donato Totaro, commenting upon this informatics, suggests that 'The set is more specific than a shot because it can include sub-sets in the case of moving camera shots that reveal new information' (1999). Although Deleuze is sometimes deliberately ambiguous in his delimitation of the terms 'set' and 'shot', his approach is nonetheless useful for attempting to uncover a movement between levels of the cinematic where relationships of framing connect with movement through cinematic space and the extension of such movement beyond the text and through the experiences of the viewer of the 'action' of narrative. As such, for example, he describes the third level of encounter with cinema as 'duration or the whole, a spiritual reality which constantly changes according to its own relations' (2004: 11). To my mind, this movement beyond the artificial slicing of time into framing, or sets, and into a warm relational body of meaning is key to understanding how meaning-making is sustained in a film's cultural afterlife. It is similar, in many ways, to close *mise-en-scène* analysis found in more traditional film criticism, although it moves analysis away from purely screen-based observation and towards a philosophy of the emotional relationships between viewer and viewed through time.[2]

Neupert's artificially closed text therefore might be rehabilitated to take into account the cinematic encounter as psychological experience of duration through telling and retelling of a narrative. For, as Totaro goes on to write about the notion of a 'set': 'If not a precise term, it does add an important component to a psychological consideration of filmic time in the notion of changing "informatics"' (1999). Those changing informatics, I argue, are mobilised as much by the actions of audiences as they are by the material of the cinematic texts themselves, and continue in an ongoing process of cultural exchange.

This bears close resemblance to the cultural life of literary narrative. Paul Ricoeur, in his book series *Time and Narrative* (1984), suggests that the functions of narrative in the act of storytelling and in the roles of teller and told become clear through the act of retelling. That is, retelling reconstructs narrative through the experience of extra-narrative time that passes between telling and retelling, through memory and hindsight; extending the duration of a narrative encounter beyond its initial telling. Ricoeur explains this through a hermeneutic approach which 'is concerned with reconstructing the entire arc of operations by which practical experience provides itself with works, authors, and readers' (1984: 53). If one considers this as a starting point from which to begin to examine the positioning of the text for an audience through acts of retelling, then one may revisit Roland Barthes' site of *jouissance* or bliss (1981) and the meaningful encounter with cinematic textuality as an exponent of narrative across various sites of consumption as well as within the duration of the viewing of texts as parts of the storytelling process itself, and how this process extends itself across time, as an extratextual duration. In other words, one may pose this as a question: how does the contemporary cinematic encounter succeed in incorporating the deferral of textual ending through multiple sites of consumption (extending the duration of textuality), whilst at the same time providing audiences with the denouement necessary to familiar narrative storytelling structures in order to highlight meaningfulness in encounters, such that audiences will return to experience them again (extending the duration of narrative on retelling through multiple and repeatable singular textualities)?

One might argue that such tension between deferral and satisfaction is one of the key ingredients in popular cinema today, particularly in relation to the blockbuster as discussed in previous chapters. Indeed, this tension was the subject of some discussion in Chapter 2, where I outlined a repetition discernible in popular film franchises and adaptations. This repetition finds expression in consumer passions for their favourite films, but, as I pointed out, many of the conditions for such consumption practices are maintained through corporate propriety and economic expediency, and through the flexible circularity of expanded narrative worlds. The audience's encounters with such expanded narrative worlds are important sites of pleasure.

This is, of course, not universal in its expression or how it is expressed. It appears as peculiar to such Hollywood blockbuster franchises as the *Star Wars* and *Matrix* series. However, an analysis that takes *obvious* sites of extratextuality as the only source of a film's narrative image (as exemplified in the aforementioned franchises and their secondary and tertiary sites of consumption) can only engage the narrative forms expressed through and across these franchises on a superficial level. One argument put forward in the current chapter concerning such superficiality is that what is revealed as apparent to the viewer in the act of viewing textual and extratextual material of these particular kinds of franchises (and the consumer in the act of consuming these materials) is hidden (but nonetheless still present in a film's narrative image) in a wider film culture where secondary and tertiary production is less obviously apparent. What is revealed is *meaningfulness* which is both visible and invisible in popular cinema.

The hidden work of cinema is not a new object of inquiry for film theory. 'Appearances can be deceiving', a popular colloquialism, might be used here to superficially describe the residue of ideological containment inherent in massively popular film franchises, for example – a subject of much debate in the history of film theory. A film's textual material and its narrative conceits (a film's story, and how that story is presented in that film's enunciative style) may be interpreted in various ways, revealing through close analysis of the *mise-en-scène* (or fan testimony, or merchandising practices for that matter) subtle inculcations of ideological material peculiar to that film and to its production and consumption. Indeed, approaches and conclusions such as these are the bread and butter of academic film studies, and have revealed throughout this book the commodity-identity of such cultural practices.[3]

However, one might just as easily negotiate this idea phenomenologically, by thinking through how *appearances can be revealing*. Phenomenology as a branch of philosophy (and their extensions in this context being the extant subdisciplines of film-phenomenology and film-philosophy respectively) is concerned primarily with appearances: how the world appears to and for us, how it perceives and is perceived, how it expresses and is expressed. This way of seeing in phenomenological thinking lends itself to contemporary thinking on film; after all, both hold in common their concern with appearances, images and intersubjective encounters with and in the world. As a method, phenomenology provides film theory with a powerful tool for engaging the field of perception in the act of viewing a text and the act of consuming extratextual material as appearances to and for us.

Such approaches, exemplified in Merleau-Ponty's essay 'The Film and the New Psychology' (1964), as cited in the epigraph to this chapter, and Vivian Sobchack's film phenomenology (especially 1992, 2004), reveal ways of engaging the appearance of film within the field of perception and experience such that the film theorist moves beyond what film analyst Don Fredericksen (2006) has described as (following the likes of Ricoeur and Jürgen Habermas) a 'hermeneutics of suspicion', towards something akin to a 'hermeneutics of amplification'. To it put another way, film-phenomenology moves towards a consideration of what Sobchack describes as a viewing-view and a viewed-view of film:

> Rather than merely replacing human vision with mechanical vision, the cinema functions mechanically to bring to visibility the reversible structure of human vision: this structure emerges in the lived body as systematically both a subject and an object, both visual (seeing) and visible (seen), and as simultaneously productive of both an activity of seeing (a 'viewing view') and an image of the seen (a 'viewed view').
>
> (2004: 150)

That is to say, following Merleau-Ponty in the above epigraph, film's appearance brings us as viewers closer to our intersubjective relations with the world, our co-existence with and in the world, through various activities of seeing. For Sobchack, viewing film is an anthropo*centric* activity,[4] in that cinema's principal function is to show the activity of seeing, as well as the seen, to and for the viewer whose viewing activity is expressed through the cinematic for the duration of viewing. It is here necessary to reiterate how I use phenomenology and its concomitant terms in the context of the contemporary cinematic encounter.

As phenomenology is concerned with appearances, so it lends itself to the idea that it can reveal much in the textual material that appears to us in the act of viewing film; that its primary concern is the image, representation. As the epigraph from Merleau-Ponty above suggests, the phenomenology of film is little different to the phenomenology of things because its primary concern is the perception and understanding of the world and being-in-the-world. Problems of representation obviously play an important role here, in that popular moving images most often attempt to reflect or show human action (whether fictional or not). The more important aspect of Merleau-Ponty's observation here is the implication that film operates within a process of ongoing meaning-making, the *ambiguity* of such narrative operations forming the anthropocentric view that Sobchack describes: of, to and for human vision and intersubjective co-production of meaning. As such, and in accord with earlier arguments put forward in this book that call for a subversion of the ocular–specular emphasis in film theory, appearances in phenomenology aren't merely references to what things look like or represent; nor are appearances solely the property of private individuals' experiences. Appearance is more akin to knowing, at an embodied, wilder level that pre-empts representational language, perhaps even visual language, in the senses in which this notion has been treated in film theory in the past. It is also part of a shared and lived experience of cinema outside of the contexts of the viewing process, and away from the cinema screen. In other words, in depth psychology's topology at least, the idea of 'human vision' is, in this sense, less to do with optical apparatus and more to do with the hidden realm of the psyche, and within the context of a shared cultural life of cinema.

It is true that phenomenology as a method can reveal the hidden elements of a representation in its apparency, the way it appears to us in the act of viewing. However, just as the cinephilic moment can reveal for the cinephile whole new layers of engagement that move beyond the text and into the wider cultural life of a film, so phenomenology as a method can help film theory move beyond what appears for us as immediate to the text and into the means by which such encounters endure beyond the text's momentary duration. They endure for us and through us (as viewers, as members of the audience) as acts of narration; as the 'action' of narrative in telling and retelling. One of the most apparent and visible platforms that facilitates this process of narrative action in recent history of popular cinema industries is the instance of DVD.

DVD telling and retelling: textuality and hypertextuality in the 'action' of narrative

Arguably, the most dramatic alteration of the viewing 'position' from traditional academic models of film-viewing is a rather obvious one, in that the DVD affords the viewer a level of interactivity not typical to viewing in a cinema theatre. Indeed, as outlined in some detail so far in this study, when it came into popular use in the late 1990s, the DVD was largely marketed upon its durability, its quality, definition and resolution of picture and sound, its non-linear accessibility and its data storage capacity, allowing more material and added features to be included in a single unit of production. At the same time, and perhaps more importantly for the context of this chapter, the DVD is a unit that need only be bought once in order that it enable repeated pleasures of viewing, re-viewing and sharing (whether in a viewing context or digitally copied sense).

In this sense, which is a word-of-mouth phenomenon as much as it is an act of viewing, I argue that contemporary cinematic time lends itself more to a literary condition of narrative. This follows certain aspects of Ricoeur's aforementioned work, as well as Gerard Genette's work on narrative discourse (1980) in literature. As Genette suggests, any narrative can do without anachronies (disruptions and discordance in the ordering of story and narrative) but not anisochronies (the effects of rhythm) (1980: 88). Anisochrony is an interesting phenomenon in the context of home viewing because it acts upon meaning-production both within the film's stylistic enunciation (its own narrative discourse) and without, in the afterlife of the cinematic encounter: in the cult of repetition and circulation of meaning found in fan cultures, for example – the subject of some discussion in Chapter 2.

DVDs have come to resemble and appropriate some of these literary tropes, as Parker and Parker (2005) observe. Some of these tropes are obvious, as in the labelling of DVD sections as 'chapters' or in the ambiguous status of commentary tracks as expositions of meaning and authorial intention, often in conflict. The notion of hypertext is also quite useful here to outline the limits of production intentionality in relation to the cultural activities of audiences and the afterlife of the cinematic encounter. I discuss this momentarily, when I return to Barthes' notion of lexia in relation to pleasurable viewing. However, I think it is useful here to note in passing one of the functional aspects of DVD as a type of hypertextual format (the ability to 'skip' chapters perhaps being the most obvious, as well as switching between different supplementary paratextual elements).

Hypertext can 'jump about', so to speak: the DVD viewer enabled to move around the linearity of the feature film text in an act of wilful disassemblage. However, this is not the same thing as anachrony. Re-ordering disassembles the linearity of the narrative discourse during the act of viewing, but in the aftermath of the cinematic encounter, rhythm, repetition, the circular forms of film culture become the predominant means by which narrative data is re-assembled to give account of the encounters themselves. In other words, one of the primary associations of DVD viewing and cultural commentary is with anisochrony; it is not a narrative re-ordering as such, but rhythm, or *pulse*. For, as Parker and Parker suggest, 'Meaning is not inherent to a text, but something a community of readers or viewers, acting in loose accord with various interpretative protocols, agree to infer' (2005: 126). In other words, I would argue, it is an ongoing, living, warm process of co-production of meaning-making, whose 'third image' inhabits the social-psychological re-enactments of story-telling as a communal activity. In Parker and Parker's terms, 'The DVD edition is essentially a reorientation of the film, often carried out by a variety of agents, and subject to a wide variety of choices made by the eventual viewers' (2005: 125). This reflects the medium-specific idiosyncrasies of the DVD as a format, but additionally, acknowledges the cultural activities of an imagined empirical audience.

The *Matrix* franchise was an example of this process writ large in millennial film culture, through the re-presentation of the 'original' cinematic texts on DVD, the multiplication process of three-part structure and the addition process of concomitant material (website, the *Enter the Matrix* and *Path of Neo* videogames, massively multiplayer online game, graphic novels, comic books, animated short films, documentary material, action figures and merchandise). What occurred as a result was a hypertextual augmentation of the three *Matrix* film texts through their relation to these additions: a kind of metacommentary upon the re-presentation process and the new formats through which the text may be accessed. The relative novelty (at the time) of such convergences between media platforms, in tandem with the relatively new format of the DVD, meant that this re-presentation process was a highly visible and, therefore, lucrative one.

'Capitalism', as Weber declares in *The Protestant Ethic and the Spirit of Capitalism*, 'is identical with the pursuit of profit, and forever renewed profit, by means of continuous, rational, capitalistic enterprise' (1996: 17). In the examples just given, where the narrative world of the *Matrix* franchise is extended through highly novel and therefore visible forms, contemporary cinema has lent itself to this Weberian form of capital, inasmuch as it is another example of the subject of my discussion on the rhetoric of innovation in the previous chapter. In the context of DVD mass production and consumption in general, the primary thing that is being sold in the *Matrix* franchise is *endings*, a continuous stream of technological products and goods sold to an increasingly media-savvy set of markets. This is accomplished through multiple aggregated sites of access, technologically orientated and privatised interventions into the institutional structures of cinema. Such intervention amounts to a plenitude of endings, in common with Peter Lunenfeld's 'sheer plenitude of narrative' (2004: 151). Narrative structure is 'played with' by filmmakers (as much as it is commented upon in secondary production and consumption sites such as blogs and discussion boards) in order to achieve this goal. Multi-stranded, multiple, repeatable endings, within a single, delayed, over-arching narrative closure, allow for traditionally linear, strong narratives to emerge as singular spaces of engagement and consumption for the casual viewer and also as one element amongst many for the buff or cinephile.

What is at stake then, is a flexible framework of textuality, narrative duration(s) and multiple platforms working to impose or foreclose narrative meaning upon the text. Whether consciously arrived at through an intention to do so or not is rather beside the point here: in the context of the rhetoric of innovation and marketing, this foreclosure of meaning *appears* to its audience as novelty, accessibility and, therefore, value. In terms of the collectability and value of media products in the marketplace, the further extension of marketing a property on newer digital platforms such as Blu-Ray and online streaming has preserved this movement of longevity in the franchise. Its narrative presence, as it appears, is not cheapened through its proliferation.

An interpretive theoretical model of this movement of longevity and proliferation would seem to (out of necessity) need to consider it as either an opening-up process[5] or as a process of foreclosure. This chapter argues for a dialectic which subsumes both positions in tension, therefore negating the need for an exclusively interpretive model (one that seeks to expound upon ideological textuality, for example) to re-engage a phenomenology of the glance in viewing practice: a way of seeing that seeks to bring the material of the text into closer proximity with the viewer.

Commercially speaking, one of the most useful things about DVD is its capability to render the cinematic text as a physical, purchasable, storable and repeatable commodity. This lends DVD a place in popular cultural history that has enabled the spread of various cinephiliac viewing practices. Indeed, as Barbara Klinger has stated of the longevity and duration of the textual life of contemporary films:

> Research into the reissue expands the parameters of historical inquiry by reframing questions about a film's historical meaning through analysis of its afterlife. Focusing on such a 'textual diachronics' allows us to track transfigurations in film meaning and in audiences as well as to examine procedures of canon formation in mass culture.
>
> (2006: 8)

In other words, the emphasis on secondary production as the profitable source of revenue of the life of a film allows one to think through textual duration in terms of meaningful consumption as much as an act of viewing and re-viewing. A 'textual diachronics', as Klinger puts it, is not artificially bound by singular, discrete modules of text (a film, a trailer, a poster, a DVD) but considers the circularity and circulation of a film's narrative image through time and through consumption. Carolyn Jess-Cooke also points out the circular nature of this cultural afterlife of film narrative as encountered by the audience, writing of film sequelisation that 'The circularity of repetitive forms deconstructs the authenticity of reality or, more exactly, is employed as a framework within which to consider a deconstruction of authenticity by technologies, genres of repetition and media intertextuality as an agent of artifice' (2009: 61).

If artifice is highlighted in the technicity of repetitive forms as Jess-Cooke proposes, it appears, to the specialist consumer at least, to be an element of consuming and viewing pleasure nonetheless. Such meaningfulness also expresses itself in narrative textuality that extends through multiple and additional textual material. The following passage from the philosopher and narratologist Paul

Ricoeur is suggestive of both functionality of narrative (what it is for) and aspects of readership, for which the medium expresses its contents:

> To follow a story is to move forward in the midst of contingencies and peripeteia under the guidance of an expectation that finds its fulfilment in the 'conclusion' of the story. [...] It gives the story an 'end point', which, in turn, furnishes the point of view from which the story can be perceived as forming a whole.
>
> (1984: 66–7)

Simply put, one may read the story in terms of the activity of telling a story and one's position in relation to it. Reading and re-reading are not merely dependent upon the textual material itself. Ricoeur does not establish a universality of contingency and peripeteia – that is, human action and sudden changes of fortune – as occurring in narrative content alone, or even narrative structure. He specifically states that the story-world is established through the guidance of expectation, and by this, one could argue for both generic expectation and expectation of the format's capabilities. This is because, when applied to specific media in the sense of audio-visual story-telling having to adapt its strategies according to the medium via which it is being transmitted, what occurs is a 'change of fortune', so to speak, in the ways in which the audience addresses the text in its retelling. That is, from the 'original' context of cinema, with its rarefied, 'event' phenomena ('going to the movies') to a domestic viewing context and the reconstituted interactive DVD version ('buying the film'). As a caveat, and perhaps an obvious point, one need not experience an encounter with a particular film in the cinema theatre in order to participate in its repeatability: one may purchase the DVD to experience that 'original' encounter vicariously and repeatedly.

This needs to be taken in the context of Ricoeur's concept that 'between the activity of narrating a story and the temporal character of human experience there exists a correlation that is not merely accidental but that presents a transcultural form of necessity' (1984: 52). One suspects that this statement places a vector of value upon narrative form and, in particular, narrative closure, for which the DVD form is particularly adept at deferring, delaying: simultaneously avoiding but delivering. Delivering, that is, in abundance through multiple-version releases, as in the case of the *Lord of the Rings* trilogy, for example. This, one could say, follows a model of capital accumulation, on the one hand, via a phenomenon of addition and multiplication (multiple film texts, with the addition of media texts and forms) which opens up spaces of consumption and points of access, but, on the other hand, also effects a foreclosure on meaning through textual proliferation. This phenomenon and effect signifies the commodity-identity of the cultural afterlife of the cinematic encounter: proliferation and meaning-making as an ongoing process.

Why does Ricoeur evoke a correlation of human temporal existence and storytelling as a 'transcultural necessity'? The literary critic Frank Kermode

(2000) regards this necessity as a 'need to speak humanly of a life's importance in relation to it [the world] – a need in the moment of existence to belong, to be related to a beginning and to an end' (2000: 4). Kermode insists that such is the need to relate to beginning and end that the dying do so in order to join the two together, to make sense of their life, permanently 'in the middest'. This suspension, of course, is susceptible to trauma because the beginning and end of one's life remain unremembered but are imaginable, and everything in between exists in relation to these imagined events. In other words, cultural practices of storytelling and retelling exist to satisfy a psychological need for origin and closure that does not occur in everyday life (at least, in the same way it does in narrative films and other storytelling forms). This phenomenon has also been identified by film theory: as previously stated, Christian Metz suggests that what constitutes a narrative as narrative is that it has '*a beginning and an ending*, a fact that simultaneously distinguishes it from the rest of the world' (1978: 17 [emphasis in original]).

This, it seems clear, is related to Ricoeur's notion of 'configuration'. For example, in the act of viewing a film, one may be aware of the origins of the text in terms of production, through the familiarity of narrative structure (simply beginning, middle and end), generic form, and through extratextual materials that make up a film's narrative image. One may also be keenly aware of the way in which sense is made of this information through the text's consumption and its accessibility, but one may only address these issues 'in the middest' of the reading process. Configuration is, therefore, the mapping of meaning as it occurs to oneself in the duration (the 'middest') of the act of viewing, much like the aforementioned rhizomatic relational state in Deleuzian relations between viewer and viewed. However, as already implied, this duration is extended beyond the singular text itself: the cinematic encounter encompasses the textual and the extra-textual in its duration. This is achieved through a system of negotiation: with the text itself (in the duration of viewing), with knowledge about the text (extra-textual extension of the story-world through multiplications, additions and commentaries) and with knowledge about one's position in relation to the text (as, for example, a casual viewer or as a fan and an awareness of one's own paratextual consumption and tertiary production practices).

This configurational dimension, which Ricoeur suggests is a fundamental part of the textual negotiation process, mediates between a prefiguration of the practical field (in the interests of this study, cinema as institution: genre cinema, convention, verisimilitude, the star system and so forth shaping Althusserian problematics of viewing) and its refiguration through reception of the work (genre expectation, pleasurable viewing, active viewing and interactivity, and fandom). He states:

> The configurational arrangement transforms the succession of events into one meaningful whole which is the correlate of the act of assembling events together and which makes the story followable [...]. The configuration of the plot imposes the 'sense of an ending' (to use the title

of Frank Kermode's well-known book) on the indefinite succession of incidents. I just spoke of the 'end point' as the point from where the story can be seen as a whole. I may now add that it is in the act of retelling rather than in that of telling that this structural function of closure can be discerned.

(1984: 67)

This is vital to a conception of hypertextual thinking, whereby any notion of a singular textual structure is disrupted, as is the case with most contemporary Hollywood franchises and popular cultural texts such as the *Matrix* and so forth. This suggests a complex system of 'authorship', via multiple sites and authors, multiple techniques, functions and intentions. It may therefore be useful to consider the notion of hypertextuality from literary studies and digital humanities models: it is a conceptual model that both relies on technological aspects in the sense that a book is a summation of writing, printing and reading technologies, and also on the notion that the reading process is a way of interfacing with the text, in several interrelated ways. As Foucault says in *The Archaeology of Knowledge and the Discourse on Language*, 'Frontiers of a book are never clear-cut [...] it is caught up in a system of references to other books, other texts, other sentences: it is a node within a network [... a] network of references' (1976: 23). The boundaries between texts and paratexts, between reader and read (viewer and viewed) are liminal, permeable, and the site of bliss: rich in connection and resonating with meaningfulness. Here, I expand upon the notion of bliss in relation to the operations of hypertext and lexia.

How does the hypertext operate within a transmedial film culture, and how is the film theorist able to apprehend such a conceptual model for contemporary viewing? '*Hypertext*', according to George Landow, 'denotes text composed of blocks of text – what Barthes terms a lexia – and the electronic links that join them' (1997: 3 [emphasis in original]). What hypertext refers to in wider media culture according to this model is the textual material itself; the breakdown and assemblage, or compartmentalisation of textual material into lexia; and the media through which this information is carried and is accessed by the user or viewer.

As Landow goes on to say:

> In *S/Z*, Roland Barthes describes an ideal textuality that precisely matches that which in computing has come to be called hypertext – text composed of blocks of words (or images) linked electronically by multiple paths, chains or trails in an open-ended, perpetually unfinished textuality described by the terms link, node, network, web, and path [...]. 'This text is a galaxy of signifiers, not a structure of signifieds; it has no beginning; it is reversible; we gain access to it by several entrances, none of which can be authoritatively declared to be the main one.'
>
> (1997: 3 [quote taken from Barthes 1990b: 5–6])

To what can extent can we consider this notion of hypertextual lexia as being applicable to the DVD text, in the most practical sense? To start with, one may argue that the DVD resembles a hypertextual form in its most basic manifestation: it is composed of a collection of interrelated words, images and sounds. Not only is the DVD text a time-based audio-visual text, it is also interactive in that its menus are composed of computer-generated words and images, as are the optional subtitles on many such texts. Intertextual and metatextual information is occasionally specifically produced for the format: director's commentaries and 'making-of' documentary materials, for example, are particular to the featured text, but refer explicitly to extratextual information not available elsewhere. This is also applicable to the way in which films are now produced specifically with DVD in mind.[6]

A fairly recent and visible example of this was the special edition DVD of *The Return of the King*. The 'normal' release featured two discs: disc one is the feature film; disc two has a collection of documentaries, featurettes, and trailers advertising the then-forthcoming trilogy box-set and the video game. The special edition featured a 'Specially extended Director's Cut edition of *The Lord of the Rings: The Return of The King*',[7] consisting of four discs, suggesting that a substantial amount of material was shot that could not reasonably be considered to have been used for mainstream cinema release, as the existing cinema version was already 201 minutes long. It is quite conceivable, however, that this material was always intended for secondary release, especially when one considers the extended version being referred to as a 'director's cut' was released so soon after the first version (rather than there being a rather public artistic disagreement between studio and director over the final cut, as famously happened with Ridley Scott's *Blade Runner* [US, 1982]). It suggests a branded-style directorial/authorial intention – a 'definitive' version. Also worth considering is the other special feature noted on the extended release, that of a 'bonus disc of value added material'.[8] This label identifies quite succinctly the conscious attribution of value towards special features within popular discourse.

Another way in which the DVD text might be considered hypertextual is that access is made available via several sites. As Michael Mateas puts it in his PhD thesis, 'Interactive Drama, Art and Artificial Intelligence', 'A hypertext consists of a number of interlinked textual nodes, or lexia. The reader navigates these nodes, selecting her own path through the space of lexia, by following links' (2002: 21). Perhaps the DVD is not as complex or as visibly intricate as an interactive literary text or hypertext novel, but there is something of a hypertextual interactivity at work in the experience of consuming the DVD text (particularly in box-set form) in a more hidden, invisible sense. This extends through the audio-visual text, into the format itself. Not only can DVDs be played on several different hardware types (DVD players, PCs, games consoles and so on), lending the DVD a kind of portability not afforded the videotape or other antecedent formats,[9] but the way in which one may navigate various menus from different digital spaces also lends itself to the concept of the hypertext: the remote control of a DVD player, for example, or point and click via personal computer. Hypertextuality lends the text a duration beyond singular textuality, beyond even physical format in the case of DVD, as its eminent portability makes DVD as a secondary cinematic platform invisible (yet present). It lends itself to consumption in the contemporary sense of *convenience*.

Glancing beyond the gaze: *televisuality* and the cinematic encounter

A moment ago I noted that, in wider media culture, hypertext refers to the breakdown and assemblage or compartmentalisation of textual material into lexia which may be reassembled and repurposed as a whole, and the media through which this information is carried and is accessed by the user or viewer. This is something akin to a gestalt textuality: a whole and the sum of its parts in relation. I would make one further note with regards to this definition of hypertextuality in the contemporary cinematic encounter. It seems to occupy a similar position to that of Deleuze, who, as mentioned earlier in this chapter referred to the cinematic level of *framing* as 'informatics'. I should note again here that whereas Deleuze points towards this informatics as an ongoing experimental mapping of relations, he tends to veer markedly away from compartmentalisation in the organisation of such relations. In this, there is common a debate in the Deleuzian approach with that of existential phenomenology. Barbara M. Kennedy, in engaging Deleuzian film-philosophy, suggests that:

> Rather than think only about the sign of the cinematic, or what a film 'means', we can also debate how the film connects across a diverse arena such as the mimetic, the pathic, the gestural, the cognitive, the affective. Cinema operates in non-teleological ways.

That is, as I discussed in Chapter 5, *around the periphery* of cause-and-effect and dimensions of determination (2002: 69). Merleau-Ponty, for his part, wrote that modern gestalt psychology shared, with then-contemporary philosophies:

> The common feature of presenting consciousness thrown into the world, subject to the gaze of others and learning from them what it is: it does not, in the manner of the classical philosophies, present mind *and* world, each particular consciousness *and* others.
>
> (1964: 58 [emphasis in original])

Merleau-Ponty sought to address the cinematic encounter as reflecting the existential fate of intersubjective relations, between human beings and human encounters with things. As will become clear, phenomenologists are not all in agreement concerning this issue. For example, Edward S. Casey suggests in relation to the glance that gestaltism:

[for] all its indisputable value, has the disadvantage of implying homogeneity among the parts, their mutual fittingness if not their outright similarity. The glance, however, can draw things of the greatest diversity together in an instant: this is the very source of its uniqueness.

(2000: 153)

Casey's approach illustrates a movement away from gestaltism and back some way towards the Deleuzian informatics approach. In doing so, one may glimpse some of the more subtle implications of John Ellis' own position on the glance as a somehow inferior embodiment of heterogeneity and segmentation. I would like to address these debates further in respect of the phenomenological notion of the glance.

Before I do, however, I would like to make one more note with regards to Deleuze's experimental mapping as a kind of glance. Casey states that 'The glance is subversive not just in its spontaneous but efficacious anti-establishmentarianism. It subverts in a positive way as well: by its experimentalism. To glance is to explore the environing world by sampling its surfaces' (2007: 146). This sampling is very much a part of wider film cultures and partakes of the cultural afterlife of the film. When one considers the implications of the subversive nature of different audiences and their repurposing of cinematic materials (online parodies, fanfic, slash fiction, etc.), one is compelled to acknowledge the attempted subversion of authorial propriety as a glancing blow against residual ideological containment. Glancing, sampling, using and repurposing are all subversive and potentially political acts of agency in film culture. It is with this in mind that this chapter proceeds.

I return to Christian Metz's notion of *trucage* here, this time applying it specifically to DVD in both the sense of text (imperceptible, invisible and visible 'tricks') and the sense of platform (DVD as a vast *trucage*) in order to begin to tease out aspects of the visible and invisible hypertext, how it appears to and for the consumer, and how it relates to pleasurable consumption. Metz identifies *trucages* as 'Various optical effects obtained by the appropriate manipulations, the sum of which constitutes *visual*, but not *photographic*, material' (1977: 657 [emphasis in original]).

What is useful for the discussion here is that, as Metz correctly points out, the *trucage* is an 'avowed machination [...] it is avowed in the film, even in the case of invisible but perceptible *trucage*' (1977: 664). Any disavowal that might occur could do so only through a process of complicity because of the effect's value as a commodity in itself. So, in what ways can the special effect, specifically related to the DVD, be regarded as commodity? In what respects is it subject to evaluation (that crucial aspect of feeling so integral to depth psychology and other models of affect discussed towards the beginning of this book)? In what ways do *trucages* illuminate the phenomenology of extended narrative duration and extratextual encounters? Metz elaborates on the 'avowed machination' of cinema, saying that '*Trucage* [...] avows itself, so to speak, in the periphery of the film, in its publicity, in the awaited commentaries which will emphasise the technical skill to which the imperceptible *trucage* owes its imperceptibility' (1977: 664).

This statement seems prophetic in the context of contemporary visual media. It bears itself out in the functionality of the DVD, facilitating a revelatory kind of viewing only hinted at in the cinematic release. The periphery to which Metz refers can be read in contemporary viewing cultures as: 'making-of' documentaries; Internet 'spoilers'; film reviews; leaked information from the studio/production team, subsequently reported in newspapers or journals; gossip columns and celebrity magazines such as *Heat* or *Tatler*; fanzines; and fan-based websites.

Significantly, when applied to the DVD text as a technology, segregation and compartmentalisation of various lexia (film text, commentaries, documentaries, etc.) is a process peculiar to the format in both industrial and consumer discourses. For example, the DVD release of *The Lord of the Rings: The Return of the King*, with its 'bonus disc of value added material' is a single physical object, but the information it contains is accessed by making a choice from a list or menu. Therefore, it is not necessarily treated as a singular object in its use. It may be treated as a segregated, compartmentalised collection of paratexts. It has simply gained currency as a convention with which both the DVD enthusiast and cinephile are familiar, and is a source of pleasure in familiar viewing strategies. Pleasure, in this context, comes from knowledge, from avowal of the 'trick'. Pleasure comes from familiarity with the format's capabilities and with the information carried through its compartmentalised processes. The value of such encounters, their appearance-form, is in the exchange of knowledge as a site of pleasure.

In the introductory section of this chapter, I mentioned that phenomenology as a branch of philosophy is concerned primarily with appearances: how the world appears to and for us, how it perceives and is perceived, how it expresses and is expressed. When applied to film theory, and in particular the area of film theory with which the current chapter is concerned (encounters with the cinematic afterlife across media forms and over time), phenomenology can further understanding of how cinematic textuality appears to and for the consumer on multiple sites, and the meaningfulness that is produced through the duration of that encounter. Phenomenology testifies to the power of *trucage* that Metz identified in his approach to cinema, but, in the context of the current discussion, one may say that fleeting glimpses of such phenomena in contemporary film cultures are encouraged through the extension of the duration of the cinematic encounter.

Maurice Merleau-Ponty wrote of film that '[Movies] directly present to us that special way of being in the world, of dealing with things and other people, which we can see in the sign language of gesture and gaze and which clearly defines each person we know' (1964: 58). This closeness of the essence of viewer and viewed is crucial to the understanding of how phenomenology has been used to engage film in the past. I, however, would argue for a phenomenology of the glance to unlock precisely how meaningfulness in the cinematic encounter comes into being through a duration of time, and how this encounter appears to and for the consumer as not one rarefied and singular text but as a paratextual and extratextual encounter through which commodity-identity of a cinematic property expresses and is expressed.

The theorised glance has appeared in film and television theory in the past as a particularly televisual way of looking and has been viewed as the location in which the differentiation between the televisual and the cinematic may be defined. My argument, as will become apparent, is that, due to essentialism in which the inherent properties of television and cinema have been delimited in past theories, contemporary theory now has to overcome some rather basic assumptions of the differences between televisual and cinematic viewing in a media landscape where both cinema and television do not exist in the same ways as even 10 or 15 years ago. Contemporary theory needs to accommodate for the apparent erosion of cinematic and televisual spaces (other than the physical places in which cinema and television traditionally occur – i.e. the cinema theatre and the living room, respectively) to more thoroughly engage the question of how popular film cultures embrace viewing contexts and platforms, for multiple purposes (whether considered 'cinematic' or not).

John Ellis (1992), for example, has written most famously (originally in 1982) in favour of differentiating between the cinematic gaze and the televisual glance. He wrote that:

> TV's regime of vision is less intense than cinema's: it is a regime of the glance rather than the gaze. The gaze implies a concentration of the spectator's activity into that of looking, the glance implies that no extraordinary effort is being invested in the activity of looking. The very terms we habitually use to designate the person who watches the TV or the cinema screen tend to indicate this difference.
>
> (1992: 137)

The distinctiveness of differences between the two media has been eroded due in part to the increasing ability to transfer textual material from one medium to the other. The TV, used as a monitoring platform for video and DVD (and online media: PCs and videogame consoles with Internet capability, for example) has often meant in practice that this 'handing down' occurs from cinema to TV. Very rarely is this situation reversed except under those relatively rare circumstances where a TV series has been adapted for cinema.[10] However, the aforementioned phenomena associated with 360-degree programming indicates that transmediality is much more integrated and nuanced in viewing practices than mere adaptation. In addition to textual convergences, 'home cinema' domestic set-ups are very much in vogue presently, testifying to hardware convergence on a popular scale. As mentioned previously in this chapter and elsewhere, such set-ups have a tendency to resemble the cinematic in various ways (plasma widescreen, HD, Dolby 5.1 sound, video projection, etc.). Furthermore, in relation to this erosion of differences, on an industrial level the term 'quality television' has in recent years come to designate US television programmes screened on on-demand services such as HBO and purchased worldwide on DVD – thereby eroding further the evaluative cultural barrier between TV and cinema, and lending 'quality TV' DVD box-sets an eminent collectability. Last worth mentioning here, the fact that texts are increasingly under the pressure of competing forms of participation culture: the convergence of media at multiple levels (industry, hardware, audience, experience) has led to the obsolescence of older models of medium-specificity, particularly in relation to cinema and TV.

In his work, Ellis equates glancing with television viewing, implying that the quality of the televisual glance is inferior to the quality of the cinematic gaze. He does not change his original (1982) position on this, either in the more recent 1992 edition of *Visible Fictions* nor in his later work *Seeing Things* (2000), when reflecting upon the subject: televisual graphics, he suggests, 'are used to summarise, and assemble within one frame or within a short sequence, providing layers of information in one frame, compressing material into a single but fractured space' (2000: 100).

This position, while useful, still maintains the qualitative caesura between cinema and television without allowing for the textual convergence and transmedial visual flourish of contemporary mediascapes. Here, I am not arguing *against* specialist regimes of looking or indeed against medium-specific qualities. Rather, I seek an affirmative approach to those regimes that are deemed inferior ways of looking and seeing in orthodox discourses (both popular and academic).

Increasingly, audiences, for a variety of reasons (expedience, convenience, economics, pleasure, etc.), are seeking out and experiencing different sorts of encounters with the cinematic that have little to do with the voyeurism and fetishism of Screen Theory's cinematic apparatus. This is not to say that such experiences are impossible or do not take place; there are clearly elements of fetishism and voyeurism in contemporary viewing practices within popular film cultures. Indeed, I have shown during the course of this study and elsewhere (2010, 2011) that a species of fetishism exists in cinephilic viewing models that expresses its intensity through commodity-identity and viewing pleasure. This is one of the reasons why I choose to use the terms 'viewer', 'user', 'audience' and 'consumer' throughout the current study to indicate the various parties consuming visual media, and rarely use the term 'spectator' unless necessary to address a phenomenon specific to the darkened cinema theatre. It is also the reason why a discussion of the glance is so crucial for film theory today: glancing may be momentary, but it is not 'lazy' or 'inattentive' as Ellis would have it. Indeed, Ellis states that:

> TV is a relay, a kind of scanning apparatus that offers to present the world beyond the familiar and familial, but to present them in a familiar and familial guise. Hence the lack of a truly voyeuristic position for the TV viewer. It is not the TV viewer's gaze that is engaged, but his or her glance, a look without power.
>
> (1992: 163)

This argument is not entirely convincing: that the glance is a look without power. Ellis assumes a rather passive model of viewing, and also suggests a diametric opposition to the powerful look of the spectator's gaze (ironically, a simplification of the *passivity* and immersion inherent in the scopophilic (male) gaze under phallogocentric patriarchal regimes of cinema as originally theorised by Mulvey in 1975 [1999]). Such separation is unlikely in contemporary viewing contexts, precisely because of the anisochronies (following Genette, the effects of rhythm within and upon narrative) of the viewing experience even if the quality or essential properties of such experiences differ from one medium to the next. The textual material's extended duration through repeated encounters with the narrative image enables the glance to move into what Casey has claimed, as stated in the above epigraph, a 'glistening horizon of there and then': to enable the cinematic encounter to endure through time (2000: 159). Rather than inattentiveness, the glance sparks a realisation of meaningfulness in the encounter, such that in the acts of viewing, re-viewing and exploring the extended extratextual material of popular cinema, the glance rests upon the surface of that material as it appears to us and for us. The 'placial surfaces off from which the glancing rays of dawning ken may bounce' that Casey mentions indicate an intersubjective expression that appears to and for our glance as viewing subjects; an instantaneous realisation of familiarity and the familial that Ellis writes about, but tends to reserve for the purely televisual realm; a coming forth into being, in the immanent cinematic encounter that in turn transcends the momentary through its extratextual extension in the retelling.

John T. Caldwell is most vociferous in the attack on Ellis's 'glance theory', as he puts it. He states that:

> Glance theory, perhaps more than any other academic model, sidetracked television studies from a fuller understanding of the extreme stylization emergent in television in the 1980s. The myth's most cherished assumption? That television viewers are, by nature distracted and inattentive.
>
> (1995: 25)

Indeed, as Milly Buonanno (2008) points out, this assumption is out of keeping with actual practices of televisual viewing that are as diverse as the textual flow of that medium would suggest. She states that:

> There is no need to mistake conditions of possibility for conditioning that is so conclusive as to rule out any theoretical or practical alternative. Even though it has been shown to happen very frequently, the 'subsidiary' use of television does not in fact represent the only possible use, or the only use made of it.
>
> (2008: 36)

Buonanno therefore leaves signposts towards an approach to televisuality, and viewing practices more generally, that would attempt to move away from a universalising account of viewing practices, whilst at the same time acknowledging the qualitative differences between viewing contexts. Somewhat in common with my own phenomenological approach to the glance, Caldwell suggests that contemporary televisual viewing is a rather more sophisticated affair than that suggested by Ellis. He states that:

> Contrary to glance theory, the committed TV viewer is overtly addressed and 'asked to start watching' important televised events. The morasslike flow of television may be more difficult for the TV viewer to wade through than film, but television rewards discrimination, style consciousness, and viewer loyalty in ways that counteract the clutter.
>
> (1995: 26)

I would agree with Caldwell here, as his critique attempts to cut through cultural hierarchies still often associated between cinema and its 'poorer cousin', TV. These hierarchies have inflected the theorising of viewing structures and practices throughout the history of film and television studies: qualitative differences in gaze and glance, associated with cinema and television respectively, indicating and prefiguring a mobilisation of value-responses without a thorough phenomenological account of the qualities associated with both. Indeed, as Buonanno goes on to suggest:

> The gaze (of the audience) is commonly associated with film-going. Such an elective affinity takes place above all through the descent from the empirical conditions of the cinema – sitting more or less still in darkness and silence – which certainly favours the immersion in the images of film. But it represents something more: the direct consequence of a high regard for the cultural and ethical values of the cinema.
>
> (2008: 37)

Buonanno is not the only commentator in film and television studies to have pointed this problem out. Joan Hawkins (2000) and Matt Hills (2005) have both pointed out the problems of essentialising TV and cinema as inherently different and mobilising inherently different viewing practices. Indeed, Caldwell suggests that much 'glance theory', as he puts it, sets up an opposition of glance and gaze, mostly in terms of inherent quality, thereby establishing evaluation based upon essential differences between cinematic spectatorship and televisual viewing, supported by an underlying psychoanalytic insistence on the importance of presence and absence in the viewing experience. This way of critiquing the state of gaze and glance has recently been taken up by philosophy and, in particular, the work of Edward S. Casey, who writes that 'Precisely because the gaze has been so often thematized in current debates – especially in the contexts of feminism and film – it is time to take up the glance anew and on its own terms and not as a weak sibling of an ostensibly more "legitimate" or normative" gaze' (2007: 24).

Caldwell suggests four corrective measures in reconsidering the glance in relation to the concentration of cultural theory upon the gaze. I would broadly endorse these, particularly in light of Casey's phenomenology of the glance (to which I shall return), as well as the evolution of the media landscape during the course of the last few years, and the increasing presence and sophistication of paratextuality and 360-degree programming that facilitates the marketing of a popular cinematic property. There are, however, some caveats that I believe should be maintained alongside each point in order to push the phenomenological properties of the glance into focus, which I outline here.

These measures are to reconsider that:

- The television viewer is not always, nor inherently, distracted (this is a rather obvious point, it seems, but has sometimes been ignored in television studies, and I discuss this matter in detail momentarily).
- Cinema and television viewing should be considered for their similarities as much as their differences. Rather than making the case for a medium-specific viewing strategy, or diametrically opposing gaze and glance, cinema and television, film theory should be striving to elaborate upon the sophisticated challenges brought to bear by contemporary everyday practices of information gathering, time-shifting, media stacking, and the admixture of attention and distraction that accompanies the encounter with the cinematic text and its narrative image across media forms and over time.
- Psychoanalytic and feminising theories of the gaze and glance tend to limit the potential of the glance to essentialist and gendered political roles. In other words, glance theory insists upon television as a serious, high-quality medium after all, and a liberating one for women. Whereas there may be some truth to these ideas, from the perspective of phenomenology, the glance is much more than limited to a mere essentialising or justifying role for the study of television, and is, additionally, not essentially a feminisation of the look for the empowerment of women (or for that matter, for men, for that particular reason alone).
- It is still in television's best interests to engage the viewer – and television works hard both aurally and visually to achieve this, no matter how inattentive the viewer may be. One could argue that duration of textual presence has a key role to play in the extension of the encounter through time, which ensures an enduring encounter, or one that may be brought forth at a future time through the proliferation of textual material that accompanies popular cinema today. Syndication, repeats, VoD, time-shifting, aggregation sites, file-sharing and access to home cinema technologies of various kinds all add to the possibility of the encounter with popular cinema: perhaps not in a cinema theatre, but elsewhere, and not under an essentially diminished quality of circumstances.[11]

What Buonanno proposes, somewhat in agreement with Caldwell, is that instead of assuming a conflict between glance and gaze, both are 'appropriate' and 'legitimate' modes of viewing. Therefore, the need to privilege cinema as the cultural touchstone of what legitimised viewing is or might be in theory should be seen as a reproduction of its *cultural* privilege over and above television. In light of this, theory needs to reconsider the importance of the glance in relation to the gaze. I would furthermore suggest that, in a dialectic of longevity (duration) and proliferation (multiple texts) in the contemporary media landscape, theory needs to appropriate a phenomenological model of the glance that can re-energise the debates on viewing without resorting to outmoded and unfounded cultural prejudices, such as the valuation of cinema over and above other visual media forms. In doing so, I would suggest that, effectively, one may be able to extend Aylish Wood's notion of competing elements even further, not only locating such elements within the frame, but also extratextually in secondary media sources, and over time in repeatable encounters with a cinematic property.

I would argue that ultimately Caldwell's ideas on 'glance theory' need updating in terms of the contemporary turn away from television as a broadcast medium and towards a viewing practice that is a privatised and interactive selection of competing textual elements and competing (convergent) media platforms. Caldwell writes that '[w]hereas viewership for film is a one-shot experience that comes and goes, spectatorship in television can be quite intense and ingrained over time. Any definition of television based on the viewer's "fundamental inattentiveness" is shortsighted' (1995: 26). There is much to agree with in this statement. However, viewership for film is clearly not a one-shot experience as far as the contemporary cinematic encounter goes (or, indeed, the encounter with the aforementioned 'quality TV' which is, as well as being a private phenomenon, also a shared one through box-set lending, file-sharing and so on). It may be said that if this intensity and ingrained viewership is a fundamental characteristic of specifically *televisual* viewing, then, to a degree, such viewing practices and experiences have migrated to the cinematic in its various guises and platforms, because of the erosion of viewing platforms and the extended narrative encounter over time. It may even imply that the cinematic seems to have incorporated the televisual, just as the televisual seems to have incorporated the cinematic. It is yet another instance of doubling, a dialectical suspension between cinema and television at multiple levels.

Textual material may rarely be transported to the rarefied arena of the cinema theatre, save occasional adaptations, but it appears that what may be deemed *cinematic* textuality, transferred to domestic and private consumption, has much in common with this view of *televisuality*. The glance is an appropriate concept for an act of viewing that seems to fit contemporary cinephilia. There is a danger here that the two terms – cinephilia, the glance – need to be conflated in order for this migration to make sense theoretically. This need not be the case, however. Returning to my tripartite notion (2011) of cinephilia as a framework for thinking through concept, object of study and as method for textual analysis, the glance may be re-appropriated to rethink the looked-for and the un-looked-for in relation to contemporary viewing as an illumination of the visual field as it appears to and for the viewer, and an inhabitation of the narrative world as it unfolds to and for the consumer in various spaces over time. In the following concluding section, I elaborate upon these notions in the dawning light of a phenomenology of the glance.

Notes

1 Singh (2011).
2 Although I am not suggesting that traditional film criticism can or has not accomplished this feat, it is worth noting that, very often, such close readings emphasise shot composition, movement and performance. The aesthetic is an important aspect of this kind of approach, but is sometimes reduced to its visual capacity, rather than its cognitive and affective functions as a sensibility.
3 I refer the reader to my previous note on *mise-en-scène*. There are parallels between the approach espoused in the current chapter and that of more traditional close readings. However, in taking into account extratextual accounts of interpretation and meaning-making (fan testimony, merchandising, etc., as described above), I seek to offer an intervention in approaches that takes account of how meaningfulness evolves over time. *Mise-en-scène* analysis in this regard is a useful critical and analytical tool, and one that I have mobilised in the discussion of specific textual examples where necessary in previous chapters.
4 Although, importantly, not anthropomorphic. In other words, Sobchack is not equating cinematic vision with human vision, but ways of seeing that appear to and for human vision. We view a film's act of seeing (a viewing-view) and the film's seen (a viewed-view). To make an anthropomorphic equation would be to misread Sobchack's position, a misreading championed foremost by Daniel Frampton throughout his book *Filmosophy* (2006).
5 As in much discourse on the hypertext and the implications of new media. For example, George Landow's *Hypertext 2.0* (1997); Lev Manovich (2002) *The Language of New Media*; Martin Dodge and Rob Kitchin (2002) *Mapping Cyberspace*; Howard Rheingold, various sources, but see especially 'Daily Life in Cyberspace: How The Computerized Counterculture Built a New Kind of Place', in *The Virtual Community: Homesteading on the Electronic Frontier*, available at: www.rheingold.com/vc/book/2 (accessed 27/08/04); and various ongoing articles in the *Media Guardian* newspaper supplement and *Wired* magazine.
6 It perhaps ought to be noted here that films are produced with post-DVD access points in mind also: it may be true that DVD is still a viable market at the time of writing (2012–2013), but one must speculate on its forthcoming obsolescence – such is the rhetoric of innovation and media change. Already evident as an example of obsolescence-in-action according to Bennett and Brown (2008), DVD is useful as an example of how the compacted media historiography of a fading media trend can illuminate more general and already-existing operations of narrative and hypertext.
7 Source: www.play.com (accessed 28/07/04).
8 Source: www.play.com (accessed 28/07/04).
9 This complicates matters somewhat, and whilst not really within the remit of this study, it is worth noting in passing that the possibility of DVD spectatorship moving closer to the experience of gaming and game culture is made more physical through shared hardware. For example, one may play games on an Xbox 360 console, or one may play online massive multiplayer games with the same console, or one may view DVDs. And this is but one example among many. This convergence of functionality into a single piece of electronic real estate has helped to accelerate the 'living room of the future' phenomenon alluded to in much popular cultural rhetoric, and needs to be addressed in

terms of media ownership, gaming economy, media convergence and media historio-graphy.

10 Examples include: *Miami Vice* (Mann, Ger./US, 2006); *Serenity* (Whedon, US, 2005) – the adaptation of Whedon's axed TV series *Firefly*; *Traffic* (Soderbergh, Ger./US, 2000); *Edge of Darkness* (Campbell, UK/US, 2010).

11 In addition to these problems, the importance of sound in glance theories, to command the attention of the casual viewer, precludes any further consideration or poetics of televisuality (ultimately, the poetics of a narrative image that extends across different screens, viewing contexts, visual scenarios and repurposed content over time). In claiming that sound tends to anchor meaning in TV, for example, Buonanno suggests that Ellis is universalising the phenomenology of domestic television viewing. In fact, this idea of inattentive, distracted domestic viewing has 'entered into our collective consciousness and created a corpus of anecdotes and case histories' that make such common sense as to often remain unquestioned (2008: 38).

CONCLUSION

The cinematic glance: commodity-identity, its afterlife and foreclosure

In the last chapter, I suggested that in order for film theory to move forward and face the challenges presented by a fast-changing media landscape, it would need to reconsider the importance of the glance in relation to the gaze in the cinematic encounter. The implication of migrating content from platform to platform, context to context, is that the cinematic seems to have incorporated the televisual just as the televisual seems to have incorporated the cinematic. Furthermore, I laid out a theoretical schema suggesting that, in a dialectic of longevity (duration) and proliferation (multiple texts) in the contemporary media landscape, film theory needs to appropriate a phenomenological model of the glance to re-energise the debates on viewing without resorting to outmoded and unfounded cultural prejudices, such as the valuation of cinema over and above other visual media forms. In the repetitive forms of encounter that I have discussed at various points in this book in relation to revisionism, extended narrative-building and tertiary production practices, an intense and ingrained viewership characteristic of specifically *televisual* viewing has migrated to the cinematic in its various guises and platforms because of the erosion of material and qualitative differences between viewing platforms and the extended narrative encounter over time.

Henry Jenkins has put forward ideas in his book *Convergence Culture* concerning this phenomenon of media convergence. In particular, one bald statement stands out as of particular importance for the future of film theory: 'We are in an age of media transition, one marked by tactical decisions and unintended consequences, mixed signals and competing interests, and most of all, unclear directions and unpredictable outcomes' (2006a: 11). This is important for film theory because it has become clear that 'films' are less defined in terms of their material differences from other audio-visual forms in an era where media technologies, industries and audiences have converged in myriad ways.

Indeed, to complicate matters, the materiality of 'films' and the manner in which the moving image is referred to in popular discourse are somewhat at odds. As shown throughout this book, by 'film' I mean that which is popularly called film in the UK, or feature film, even though 'film' has either little or nothing to do with a celluloid recording and exhibition medium and sometimes does not accord with the traditional 90-minutes-or-so duration of a main feature.

This illustrates that there is still a strong, passionate and recognisable film culture in the UK, despite or even because of such material ambiguity. As a subsidiary but no less important concern, this ambiguity suggests that declarations of film theory's limited capability to provide robust theorisation on contemporary media (in short, declarations of the death of film theory, along with the death of cinema itself), such as that found in Bordwell's 'middle-level' approach (1996, 2006), have proved premature. As such, the importance of material and qualitative differences between different audio-visual forms raises a number of questions in relation to the way consumers feel about their viewing practices, to which this book provides tentative answers. The most fundamental of these would be: do historical changes brought about by media convergence open new opportunities for a vibrant, meaningful film culture or expand the power of corporate media to the detriment of film culture?

I addressed this first question in my PhD thesis,[1] where I outlined the problems of writing media histories. In many accounts of recent histories of audio-visual media mentioned there, historiographical errors occur that make conclusive judgements about the determination of technology, economy or culture upon the evolution of cinema in its history. As shown in Chapter 5, such errors are common because they misunderstand the functionality of determination within a total system which has nothing to do with fate or destiny; such histories create a causality narrative that is easy to follow and which attempts to account for historical discrepancies and material ambiguities in the development of the medium itself. The causality involved between the various dimensions of convergence is rather more spontaneous, provisional, embodied and problematic than either technological determinism or cultural deterministic accounts imply. This causality is more suggestive of a 'remediation': a conflation of converging media forms and consumption patterns, a repurposing of content from platform to platform.

This is a problem that this book tackles in a number of ways. In relation to the problem of determination in the last instance, for example, some of Chapter 2 was devoted to the discussion of authorial propriety and ideological containment in popular film culture. There,[2] I outlined the factors within contemporary corporate media landscapes and, in particular, the relative dynamic relationships between producers and consumers that need to be taken into account in current film theory. What appears to be the case is that, in addition to primary cinematic production (the films themselves and other materials shown at cinema theatres) and related secondary production (secondary carrier media and other film-related ephemera produced through corporate activity), media corporations are moving into newer production territory. Tertiary production, which includes fan activities such as blogging and criticism, as well as other forms of critical material and the repurposing of content, has been contained and repackaged as another tier of production by media giants such as Lucasfilm and other international co-producers such as the various partners involved in the Millennium Trilogy, discussed in Chapter 2. I argue that the discursive premises of 'Web 2.0' and other forms of utopian imagining of participation culture – a meaningful instance of shared user-generated content – are caught in a dialectical tension with authorial propriety which seeks to protect intellectual property and copyright for the purpose of generating and recuperating profit. In this sense, then, the emotional investment and value that consumers place in their acts of viewing, repurposing and retelling has a material, historically concrete basis which provides crucial context for the more emotive and psychological bases that I have detailed throughout this book.

This reveals for film theory a rather traditional problem of relative autonomy – a mechanism that is ultimately political in character as corporations are legally obliged to protect shareholders' profits (an economic imperative in the last instance) whilst at the same time engaging the audience's sense of agency and commodity-identity by incorporating DIY subcultures, cinephiliac practices and fandom into models of revenue. This realisation of a rather old theoretical problem in a contemporary film culture inevitably leads to a second question that I ask in relation to Jenkins' work: what are the consequences of the changing relationship between participants (producers *and* consumers, stakeholders) for theories of, and approaches to, spectatorship in the cinematic encounter?

The consequence of changing relationships between stakeholders is a profitable one first and foremost, but this is not to deny that the cinematic encounter is any less aesthetically rich or phenomenologically pleasurable. It would be reasonable to suggest that the encounter with digital cinema has for some time now been one of the prime examples of time-shifting through secondary production and an effective economic model of marketing secondary products to a willing and demanding audience. Not only have we seen the medium- and long-term effects of home video and DVD upon this secondary market, but also the impacts of digitalisation (a digital aesthetics of cinema as well as its portability) and online media (itself partially formed through consumer practices of file-sharing and repurposing content) have led to the rise of what might be described as an 'ephemeral wrap' of secondary and tertiary products based upon a film's narrative.

This tends to extend the story-world of a film and provide numerous access points for consumers. It has itself in turn led to an ever-increasing sophistication of brand-identity for popular films. As such, one of the (often cited) implications here is that popular films, and films which belong to the spectacular genres such as SF, fantasy and action-adventure in particular, tend to have a sharper focus on impact aesthetics such as faster-paced plotting and editing, and spectacular scenes as cardinal points of the narrative. In addition, key elements of a film's narrative are repurposed for multiple media forms where the basic narrative structural elements are kept intact (here, I would include DVD extras as well as trailers and online phenomena such as webisodes and so forth). This is the case generally, although it is vital to bear in mind that such generalisations concerning spectacle and narrative are problematic, and more narrative through secondary materials contrarily tends to lead to a foreclosure on meaning. This leads to a third question implied in Jenkins' original statement: what are the implications for film theory, in its articulation of the audience's encounter with popular cinema narrative within this fast-changing media environment?

The implications of these factors for film theory come in the form of a number of subsidiary concerns. Overall, this book represents an intervention in film theory that, within the context of the emotional work of cinema, addresses such fundamental shifts in technological processes, rhetorical positions on innovative technologies and practices, and the contemporary encounters with film narratives that extend across media forms and beyond the duration of a single (and singular) film screening. Retrospectively, it enables film theory to challenge certain assumptions concerning narrative cinema, namely that classical narrative cinema was always cohesive; that, at some stage, film narratives began to fragment due to pressures external to the films themselves; and that contemporary, synergistic practices result in films having less narrative cohesion (and it is implied, therefore, have/are 'less' narrative in some way) than classic stand-alone film texts.

An illustration of these erroneous assumptions can be found in the dialectic of 'viewsing' that contemporary film viewing opens up as a potential site of agency, and as a site where viewers act and are acted upon through the consumption of competing textual and paratextual elements: such competing elements are memorable through moments of spectacle, when they seem to 'grab' one's attention. The subject of discussion in Chapter 5, cinematic spectacle, particularly in popular cinema, can often seem to be overwhelmingly 'brutal', in Rudolf Arnheim's words; soliciting attention in order to provide immediate satisfaction, as a reward for attention paid.

However, recent developments in the field of cognitive psychology as well as in post-Jungian film analysis complicate these simplistic mechanisms of attention economy, particularly in the retelling of the encounter with the film that takes place after the fact, whether by word of mouth, or through blogging and other tertiary practices. By offering notions of a 'co-production of meaning' or a warm, psychologically indeterminate space between viewer and viewed, such everyday acts of telling and retelling become more important in defining precisely what 'meaningfulness' as a critical and theoretical notion might mean, and the repercussions of such a notion for dealing with cinema and feeling. I argue that the indeterminacy and ambiguity implied in the notion of meaningfulness is a source of its strength as a theoretical term. Far from being flawed because of imprecise definite terms, meaningfulness is useful precisely because it embodies the ambiguity and indeterminacy of the cinematic encounter, as well as the richness of different kinds of feelings mobilised through it. Theoretical currents within both depth psychology and cognitivism suggest a return to meaningfulness as a useful term to describe the subjective and affective feelings that one forms in relationships with and in the world.

In applying such notions as appearance-form, commodity-identity and residual relative autonomy to the cinematic encounter, this book approaches the notion of cinephilia as both a material phenomenon that is grounded in economic, cultural and technological dynamics, but also located within the matrices of the psychological and the phenomenological. The analysis of *Close Encounters of the Third Kind* in Chapter 1 illustrated that meaningfulness in the cinematic encounter is facilitated through the jostling, viewsing dialectic of togetherness–apartness. The following chapters then discussed in detail how those aspects of cinematic meaningfulness engage the knowing pleasures of contemporary audio-visual consumption and the cinephilic tendencies that actively seek out such pleasurable encounters. The psychology of attention and distraction in such contexts, drawing from recent work in cognitivism and depth psychology, was shown to contradict many of the assumptions within folk psychology of how attention is solicited and held during the viewing encounter, assumptions that are often found in film criticism.

Indeed, one of the vicarious pleasures of film-viewing, and, in particular, attending the cinema theatre, is that conventional premise of letting the film 'happen to you', suggesting that viewing is not generally sought after as an attentive encounter at all. This is not to suggest that non-attentive viewing is in some way trivial and meaningless. On the contrary, as discussed at some length in the final chapter, what is needed in a theory of film that seeks to take into account the televisual character of contemporary cinematic encounters is a phenomenology of the glance, in order to tease out the momentary meaningfulness along an axis of extended duration: duration beyond the life of the film screening and into its cultural afterlife.

This book has proposed a number of ways to think about a cinematic cultural afterlife as a rich understanding of various kinds of feeling in the cinematic encounter. It is, to summarise, a presence, within the cultural sphere, that takes many forms, whether textual, verbal or economic. It can even be as *ghostly* as an intertextual nod, barely or 'not-present' in its presence. As textual presence, a film may be regarded as the film as encountered, the context-affiliation within which that encounter takes place and the format upon which it is consumed. Examples of these encounters were discussed particularly in Chapters 3 and 4, where anticipation played a key role in the expectation of how the films related to and revealed their own contextual framing. As a verbal presence, film partakes of everyday life: in popular culture as tales told and plots relayed; as myths about the filmmaking process and the wild real lives of its screen stars. As market presence, studios tend to release films according to an appropriate season in order to increase the market impact. Additionally, a market afterlife occurs through secondary production and, increasingly, tertiary production practices. These artefacts and practices form the objects through which audiences engage the films they love (or, indeed, hate) and reveal something of the passionate nature of the cinematic afterlife.

The remake is an example of a material presence of film, extended into a cultural cinematic afterlife, but remakes too often have something of the immaterial about them. Remakes are not just textual corpora but are located, much like genres, in audience expectations and institutional conventions. Intertextually speaking, for instance, the sheer availability of texts and the expanding use of extra-cinematic home technologies (including rather sophisticated archiving technologies associated with both cinephilic and popular collecting practices) need to be situated within an historically aware Hollywood: where filmmakers and audiences alike share the same intertextual references and demonstrate a shared cine-literacy. Constantine Verevis, for instance, has used the example of *The Thing* (John Carpenter, 1982) to illustrate how such expectations and textual knowledge can remain pleasurable over time. This is a film that establishes direct intertextual relations to the original film *The Thing From Another World* (Nyby, US, 1951) through quotations that act as pleasurable rewards for those in the know but that are not necessary to the understanding or continuity of the film and the audience's enjoyment (2004: 95). As such, whereas remakes are sometimes berated in popular critical discourse for 'cashing in' on a much-loved cinema classic,[3] there are occasions where the mobilisation of audience knowledge, the dedication of fans in prolonging the pleasure of watching and talking about such films, gives the remake cultural value.

Through close readings and contextual analyses of paratextual objects such as DVDs and so forth, this book has illustrated that in contemporary media contexts it has become very difficult to assume that hierarchies of importance are maintained between feature films and their affiliated textual products. The cultural afterlife of a film has become the grounding for the popular imagination, the idea of the film, its narrative image. A film's presence is not confined to its material textuality, as its textual identity and commodity-identity extend into an afterlife that partakes of a wider cultural remit that has its roots in the conventions and representational regimes of genre, parody and so on. Examples from 'Blue Harvest' (a *Family Guy* parody of the *Star Wars* films) to the *Harry Potter* spoof 'Potter Puppet Pals' clip series on YouTube (itself subject to Lego remakes from its own fans) show how duration plays a key role in the meaningfulness of narrative encounters. Fans (and fans of fans) within popular film cultures create and extend narratives far beyond the intentions of producers, and this has in turn stimulated creative innovations for the marketing of media properties through the containment and commodification of prescribed tertiary production practices. Slash fiction, for example, is a medium that is not encouraged within the fan domains of either *Harry Potter* or *Star Wars* properties by Warner Bros. or Lucasfilm, because of its subversive and intellectual potential (as well as, possibly, its feminine bias). Fan video, however, if still tightly circumscribed for copyright purposes, is broadly accepted.

Not economically subordinate to the theatrically released film text, the importance of secondary production and associated paratexts for the commercial success of both films and the corporations who produce them should not be underestimated. As I have shown, some theoretical approaches that tend towards artificially separating a film text as a singular object from its affiliated paratexts do not take into account the importance of how encounters with these paratexts themselves often given shape to the viewing encounter with the feature film. For everyday encounters with film, paratextual materials such as trailers, posters, accompanying music videos and other collectable goods inform and realise the consumer's needs, shaping the cinematic encounter and affording the consumer several concomitant avenues of pleasure.

Indeed, even if in practice as critics we find it expedient or indeed desirable to allocate attention to the feature film itself (examples of close reading practice are evident in Chapters 1 to 4), both theoretically and philosophically speaking it is impossible to separate the encounter of the feature film from encounters with its paratexts. The paratext's work is to give shape, identity and meaning to the text, to help the text reach its individuation as a cultural artefact. Even the enunciative function of a particularly effective title sequence or the emotional weight of a punchy official soundtrack, or even passing intertextual nods to fans through the course of a film, can give rise to a co-creative formation of indeterminate meaning between viewer and viewed, which in its turn can be communicated through word of mouth, or through further remediations such as blogs, mash-ups or other tertiary forms.

In addition, the economic effects of such relations within remediated secondary products are necessary for the survival of the industry as a whole and for the shelf-life of any given major-release film, given as they serve to shape the commodity-identity of the film brand. The importance of the digitalisation of portable sharing and self-distribution processes for repurposing and popular critique within a vibrant participation culture of film also should not be disregarded lightly. Portability leads ultimately to a further major problem concerning the theorisation of narrative theme, structure and presentation: how might one refit film theory to account for what appear in the cinematic encounter to be major formal shifts in these phenomena from classical, stand-alone texts, to synergistic, remediated hypertexts? How might contemporary theory account for what happens to a film's narrative?

Addressing this problem is both straightforward and complex, and reveals a contradictory tension at its heart. The remediation of film, enabled through digitalisation processes at the production stage, and further enabled through the film's dissemination into secondary and convergent forms, has something of the novel about it. Certainly, the technologies that enable such phenomena were not possible or available until relatively recently. To say that classical film theory is out of date because it has been somewhat reluctant to engage with these phenomena may be a legitimate criticism, but to say that theory is not useful or relevant would be unfair. As this book has illustrated, some of the key propositions of theory are still intact and in need of investigation. Indeed, one could argue that, with the emergence of such new technologies, the job of theory is to stay engaged with movements in film culture, aesthetics and technological innovation, and is as vital today as it ever was.

For instance, digitalisation has enabled filmmakers to pursue the 'types' of cinematic storytelling choices that have become commonplace in popular film cultures (and fan cultures in particular), and these choices have material consequences in the kinds of content that have emerged in contemporary popular film. In terms of narrative theme, structure and presentation, far from 'crumbling' as David Bordwell would have it, the experience of film narrative has been bolstered through strong multi-platform narrative building and enhanced or expanded story-worlds, dispersed through multiple access points. Such complex narrative architecture disrupts any strong claims of a singular, stand-alone film text. It may *appear* that narrative has been displaced, but even if this could be said to be somehow symptomatic of an actual narrative displacement due to the impact aesthetics of high-octane spectacle found in numerous contemporary popular films, one might equally admit that this displacement is only virtual. That is to say, narrative often appears this way because of the manner in which everyday configurations of technology, economy and taste happen to shape consumption patterns. As audiences, our first encounters with 'films' and subsequent repeated viewing, tend to take place within contexts other than a cinema theatre. Additionally, as often as not these encounters are fleeting and ephemeral, and may only obtusely relate (textually speaking) to the feature film itself in the way that its materials are repurposed for marketing and promotion.

So how does one go about theorising such encounters? The appearance of this aesthetic of the dispersed is the key to understanding how audiences consume contemporary cinema. The digitalisation of films has shifted everyday experiences of textuality and has led to an urgent need in film theory to re-examine orthodox definitions of cinema and the experiences that result from encounters with it. Here, I have not explored redefinition in a direct way as some contemporary theorists have attempted (particularly from the film-philosophy sub-discipline). What I have illustrated through a metacriticism of what film theory's objects of analysis are is that narrative dispersal, far from weakening cinematic encounters, actually works to bolster the narrative presence of a film – what Stephen Heath described as the 'narrative image' of the film, or the 'idea' of a film. I suggest that this would be more properly and usefully acknowledged as the film's commodity-identity. This is not to say that the experience of the film has been cheapened in some way. On the contrary, the expansive narrative worlds of the *Harry Potter* franchise or the *Star Wars* franchise, to cite two important examples, are very rich grounds for marketing their media properties and are important objects for the attention of film theory. Indeed, one might speculate that highly media-literate and media-conversant audiences, often with a strong passion for voicing their critical judgements, would expect a strong commodity-identity to associate with a film in their contemporary cinematic encounters. This is reasonable to suggest since a film's visual, verbal and narrative tropes, if instantly recognisable, are therefore attributed cultural value within popular discourses.

In addition one might suggest that such commodity-identity is far from meaningless. The triviality with which televisuality, glancing and inattentive viewing has been accorded in film and television theory is misleading and ultimately counter-productive. Indeed, the notion of the glance, brought to attention by key phenomenologists in recent years, is more complex and rich than much film and television theory has given it credit for. The glance, as Casey puts it, is a gathering and inhabiting process: '*The all-around is taken in all-at-once.*'

Given the promotional and ephemeral surround of contemporary popular film, it is little wonder that such cursory yet holistic viewing practices are mobilised in everyday life.

Film theory has often worked with a defined structural model for analysing a film's meaning, bracketing off the film into a singular, defined entity; regarding a film apart from its ephemeral surroundings and paratextual delimitations. Although this is useful for close reading purposes, I have shown that the cultural afterlife of the cinematic encounter is as important to the commodity-identity of the film as the feature film itself. It is part of the 'action' of narrative, or, if preferred, the work of narrative in the act of telling and retelling, in which the film (when viewed, hypothetically, as a singular text) becomes subject to various kinds of discourses and commentaries. The holistic inhabitation of the glance in consuming such expansive narrative and textual worlds is part of an appropriate and meaningful engagement with contemporary stories, fables and multi-media experiences more generally.

In taking this open approach to narrative, the point I want to make is that what is usually regarded as cinematic textuality is most often viewed within domestic and private contexts either for the first time or repeatedly. Although the material and qualitative differences between cinema and television may be deemed to be still intact in arguments concerning medium-specificity, these differences appear to have eroded and disappeared or have taken on a reduced level of importance in everyday contexts. The cinematic encounter has taken on the appearances of the televisual. As I have argued, the glance is an appropriate concept for an act of viewing that seems to fit contemporary cinephilia. Why turn to the glance, and, in particular, a phenomenology of the glance, to open up the cinematic encounter for analysis?

As mentioned previously, I turn to the phenomenology of the glance to tease out momentary meaningfulness of the cinematic encounter along an axis of extended duration – duration beyond the life of the film screening and into its cultural afterlife. So that film theory may deal appropriately with the residual relative autonomy that remains encrusted in popular film culture, foreclosing upon meaning and providing interference in meaning-making and evaluative processes (yet without defining or determining individual responses), the notion of the glance may be regarded as something of a political tool. The following statement from Casey is worth quoting in full, as it seems to summarise the political potential of the glance, a potential that is pregnant for application in the context of this book. Here, Casey engages the problems associated with the gaze – the regime of looking that has perhaps garnered the most critical attention in film theory to date:

> The gaze proves problematic. For the Open into which it looks so intently is closed from within regarding what is admitted into its bright circle, closed from before its opening, and closed from without by the force of the ways we construe it. All of these forms of foreclosure – which collude among themselves to the point where it is often difficult to distinguish

between them – arise in the very midst of the manifest virtues of the gaze: its conscientious attentiveness, its patience, its highly inflected thoughtfulness, its aversion to drawing hasty conclusions.

(2007: 138)

The glance, on the other hand, has a different kind of intensity. Note that, in the above quote, Casey fully acknowledges the virtues of the gaze. The glance is never set in opposition to this, but is appropriated as a momentary regime which complements gazing. If one regards the etymology of the glance – the German *glanz*, gleam, glide – one starts to understand my use of this term. In Casey's approach, glancing is not just a minor and indifferent perceptual act, but something special in its own right. The act of glancing illuminates and what is glanced at illuminates. A glance is met with a glance – it glances back. Not only is the glance a gleaming, comprehensive and comprehendible act of perception and perceptibility, but, as Casey suggests, 'When this gift for being comprehensive is combined with a particularly insistent now of mercurial speed, the glance emerges as something special in the array of perceptual acts' (2007: 12). It is meaningful, yet mercurial; it is flirtatious, yet comprehensive.

This realisation that the glance has the potential to be comprehensive, and quickly, is vital for a contemporary film theory that needs to account for engagements with the fullest array of textual and paratextual surrounds of film in order to thoroughly apprehend and critique the notion of a cultural afterlife of cinema and its importance to a meaningful encounter with film.

This brings me to my final point – a somewhat mercurial point in the spirit of the cursory-yet-holistic glance. Taken in sum, this book functions somewhat as a kind of metacommentary upon film theory and theorising. In order to fully acknowledge this, one has to assume that this book itself forms, along with numerous other tertiary practices and instances of cultural engagement, an example of the cinematic afterlife. I have engaged the contemporary cinematic encounter as well as the academic disciplines allied to film theory, but, in doing so, I have constructed a self-reflexive viewing of the cinematic encounter through another encounter with cinema itself. To further matters, the book that you are reading, subject to its own institutional scrutiny and a robust regime of examination, is itself viewed: a kind of tertiary encounter which represents something of the afterlife of several encounters with cinema as a formal practice, an institution, a hub of global and local cultural activities, as technology and as a way to engage with meaningful expressions through art, consumption, critique and emotional engagement. Therefore, this book is, to my mind, an artefact of cinephilia.

Much like Ellie Fredericksen's scrapbook of scrawled opines to adventure, scratched memories and blurred documentation that expresses *Up*'s viewing view to and for us, so too, this book is a labour of love. I hope that it has, in some ways, communicated for the reader a sense of how I feel 'about' cinema and what I feel 'cinema' is. The motivation behind this book is to reflect upon the ways that contemporary film theory and film-philosophy are seeking to engage meaningfully with various kinds of feelings in the cinematic encounter. There are a number of ways that one may meditate upon this and make connections with theoretical currents, in order to take these ideas forward. To me, the most obvious and exciting currents to do this involve the rather specialised world of film-philosophy and post-Jungian psychology. My own approach humbly borrows from both of these burgeoning movements, and I hope that I have shown in my own small contributions to these areas that the participatory elements of meaningfulness in the cinematic encounter rely upon an indeterminate, lived, psychologically warm space between viewer and viewed.

Notes

1 'Cinephilia, Meaningfulness and Commodity-Identity: Contemporary Encounters with Popular Film Narratives and the Cinematic Afterlife' (Reading, 2010).
2 As well as elsewhere – see Singh (2011).
3 Indeed, the 2011 prequel to the Carpenter version, also titled *The Thing* (van Heijningen, US/Can.) has generated mixed popular reviews on various online sites.

FILMOGRAPHY

NB: This list contains references to films, television programmes and interactive sources such as videogames. Given the argument embodied by this book, it would have been inappropriate to separate cinematic and other media properties into separate artificial lists. Details given for television programmes refer to country of origin and initial broadcast. Where franchises, trilogies or 'Expanded Universes' (EUs) are listed, the titles have not been italicised in order to distinguish from sources that are not discussed as part of EU encounters. Sources are listed alphabetically.

Batteries Not Included (Robbins, US, 1987)
24 (Fox Network, US, 2001–2010)
28 Days Later (Boyle, UK, 2002)
A-Team, The (Carnahan, US, 2010)
Abyss, The (Cameron, US, 1989)
Avalon (Oshii, Jap./Pol., 2001)
Avatar (Cameron, US, 2009)
Back to the Future franchise:
   Back to the Future (Zemeckis, US, 1985)
   Back to the Future Part II (Zemeckis, US, 1989)
   Back to the Future Part III (Zemeckis, US, 1990)
Basic Instinct (Verhoeven, US, 1992)
Ben Hur (Wyler, US, 1959)
Bicentennial Man (Columbus, US, 1999)
Billy Elliot (Daldry, UK/Fr., 2000)
Bits (Channel 4, UK, 1999)
Blade Runner (Scott, US, 1982)
Blue (Jarman, UK, 1993)
Body Heat (Kasdan, US, 1981)
Bonnie and Clyde (Penn, US, 1966)
Brainstorm (Trumbull, US, 1983)
Bram Stoker's Dracula (Coppola, US, 1992)
Brewster's Millions (Hill, US, 1985)

Casablanca (Curtiz, US, 1942)
Casino Royale (Campbell, US/UK/Ger., 2006)
Chinatown (Polanski, US, 1972)
Chocolat (Hallström, UK/US, 2000)
Cinema Paradiso (Tornatore, It./Fr., 1988)
Citizen Kane (Wells, US, 1940)
Clerks (Smith, US, 1994)
Click (Coraci, US, 2006)
Close Encounters of the Third Kind (Spielberg, US, 1977 [*Special Edition*
   released 1980])
Clueless (Heckerling, US, 1995)
Commando (Lester, US, 1985)
Crazy Heart (Cooper, US, 2010)
Dances With Wolves (Costner, US, 1990)
Dawson's Creek (WB Television Network, US, 1998–2003)
Demonlover (Assayas, Fr., 2002)
Devil Wears Prada, The (Frankel, US, 2006)
Dirty Dancing (Ardolino, US, 1987)
D.O.A. (Maté, US, 1950)
Doctor Who (BBC, UK, 2005–present)
Dog Soldiers (Marshall, UK/Lux./US, 2002)
Double Indemnity (Wilder, US, 1944)
Edge of Darkness (Campbell, UK/US, 2010)
Expendables, The (Stallone, US, 2010)
Family Guy (Fox Network, US, 1999–present)
Fatal Attraction (Lyne, US, 1987)
Firefly (Fox Network, US, 2002–2003)
Forrest Gump (Zemeckis, US, 1994)
Frostbiten (Banke, Swe./Rus., 2006)
Funny People (Apatow, US, 2009)
Gamesmaster (Channel 4, UK, 1992–1998)
Ghosts of the Abyss (Cameron, US, 2003)
Girl with the Dragon Tattoo, The (Fincher, US/Swe./Nor., 2011)
Godfather trilogy:
   Godfather, The (Coppola, US, 1972)
   Godfather Part II, The (Coppola, US, 1974)
   Godfather Part III, The (Coppola, US, 1990)
Gone with the Wind (Fleming, US, 1939)
Grindhouse project:
   Death Proof (Tarantino, US, 2007)
   Don't (Wright, US, 2007)
   Hobo with a Shotgun (Eisner, Davies and Cotterill, Can./US, 2011)
   Machete (Rodriguez, US, 2010)
   Planet Terror (Rodriguez, US, 2007)

Thanksgiving (Roth, US 2007)
Werewolf Women of the SS (Zombie, US, 2007)
Harry Potter franchise:
    Harry Potter and the Philosopher's Stone (Columbus, US/UK, 2001)
    Harry Potter and the Chamber of Secrets (Columbus, US/UK/Ger., 2002)
    Harry Potter and the Prisoner of Azkaban (Cuarón, UK/US, 2004)
    Harry Potter and the Goblet of Fire (Newell, UK/US, 2005)
    Harry Potter and the Order of the Phoenix (Yates, UK/US, 2007)
    Harry Potter and the Half-Blood Prince (Yates, UK/US, 2009)
    Harry Potter and the Deathly Hallows: Part I (Yates, UK/US, 2010)
    Harry Potter and the Deathly Hallows: Part II (Yates, UK/US, 2011)
    'Potter Puppet Pals' clip series, available at www.youtube.com (accessed
      10/08/10)
Heroes (NBC, US, 2006–2010)
Hurt Locker, The (Bigelow, US, 2009)
I Love You, Man (Hamburg, US, 2009)
Idiocracy (Judge, US, 2006)
Incredible Hulk, The (Universal TV/CBS, US, 1977–1982)
Into the Wild (Penn, US, 2007)
Jade (Friedkin, US, 1995)
Jaws (Spielberg, US, 1975)
Jazz Singer, The (Crosland, US, 1929)
Jewel of the Nile, The (Teague, US, 1985)
Jism (*Body*, Saxena, Ind., 2003)
Johnny Mnemonic (Longo, US, 1996)
Just Imagine (Butler, US, 1930)
King Kong (Jackson, US, 2005)
Kiss Me Deadly (Aldrich, US, 1955)
Knocked Up (Apatow, US, 2007)
Last of the Mohicans (Mann, US, 1992)
Let Me In (Reeves, US, 2010)
Let the Right One In (*Låt den rätte komma in*, John Ajvide Lindqvist, Swe., 2004)
Lord of the Rings trilogy:
    The Lord of the Rings: The Fellowship of the Ring (Jackson, NZ/US, 2001)
    The Lord of the Rings: The Two Towers (Jackson, US/NZ/Ger., 2002)
    The Lord of the Rings: The Return of the King (Jackson, US/NZ/Ger., 2003)
Magnificent Seven, The (Sturges, US, 1960)
Mama Mia! (Lloyd, UK/US/Ger., 2008)
Matrix franchise:
    Enter the Matrix (Atari, 2003)
    Matrix: Path of Neo (Atari, 2005)
    Matrix, The (Wachowski Bros., US/Aus., 1999)
    Matrix Reloaded, The (Wachowski Bros., US/Aus., 2003)
    Matrix Revolutions, The (Wachowski Bros., Aus./US, 2003)

Miami Vice (NBC, US, 1984–1889)

Miami Vice (Mann, Ger./US, 2006)

Millennium trilogy:

> *The Girl with the Dragon Tattoo* (*Män som hatar kvinnor*, Oplev, Swe./Den./ Ger./Nor., 2009)

> *The Girl Who Played with Fire* (*Flickan som lekte med elden*, Alfredson, Swe./Den./Ger., 2009)

> *The Girl Who Kicked the Hornet's Nest* (*Luftslottet som sprängdes*, Swe./ Den./Ger., Alfredson, 2009)

Minority Report (Spielberg, US, 2002)

Modern Times (Chaplin, US, 1936)

Moon (Jones, UK, 2009)

National Treasure (Turteltaub, US, 2004)

National Treasure: Book of Secrets (Turteltaub, US, 2007)

No Country for Old Men (Coen, US, 2007)

North By Northwest (Hitchcock, US, 1959)

Not Like Others (*Vampyrer*, Pontikis, Swe., 2008)

Passion of the Christ, The (Gibson, US, 2004)

Pinocchio (Luske and Sharpsteen, US, 1940)

Pirates of the Caribbean franchise:

> *Pirates of the Caribbean: The Curse of the Black Pearl* (Verbinski, US, 2003)

> *Pirates of the Caribbean: Dead Man's Chest* (Verbinski, US, 2006)

> *Pirates of the Caribbean: At World's End* (Verbinski, US, 2007)

> *Pirates of the Caribbean: On Stranger Tides* (Marshall, US, 2011)

Poseidon (Petersen, US, 2006)

Pursuit of Happyness, The (Muccino, US, 2006)

Raiders of the Lost Ark (Spielberg, US, 1981)

Rain Man (Levinson, US, 1988)

Rebel Without a Cause (Ray, US, 1955)

Regeneration (Walsh, US, 1915)

Robots (Wedge and Saldanha, US, 2005)

Romancing the Stone (Zemeckis, US, 1984)

Run Lola Run (*Lola rennt*, Tykwer, Ger., 1998)

Scarface (De Palma, US, 1983)

Scream franchise:

> *Scream* (Craven, US, 1996)

> *Scream 2* (Craven, US, 1997)

> *Scream 3* (Craven, US, 2000)

Searchers, The (John Ford, US, 1956)

Secret of My Succe$s, The (Ross, US, 1987)

Serenity (Whedon, US, 2005)

Seven Samurai, The (*Shichinin no samurai*, Kurosawa, Japan, 1954)

Shine (Hicks, Aus., 1996)

Shooting Fish (Schwartz, UK, 1997)

Short Circuit 2 (Johnson, US, 1988)

Shrek (Adamson and Jenson, US, 2001)

Sky Captain and the World of Tomorrow (Conran, US, 2004)

Solaris (Tarkovsky, USSR, 1972)

Solaris (Soderbergh, US, 2002)

Speed Racer (Wachowski Bros., US, 2008)

Spider-man franchise:

   Spider-man (Raimi, US, 2002)

   Spider-man 2 (Raimi, US, 2004)

   Spider-man 3 (Raimi, US, 2007)

Star Wars franchise:

   Lego Star Wars (LucasArts/TT Games, 2005)

   Star Wars Episode I: The Phantom Menace (Lucas, US, 1999)

   Star Wars Episode II: Attack of the Clones (Lucas, US, 2002)

   Star Wars Episode III: Revenge of the Sith (Lucas, US, 2005)

   Star Wars Episode IV: A New Hope (Lucas, US, 1977 [Widescreen re-issue 2004])

   Star Wars Episode V: The Empire Strikes Back (Kershner, US, 1980 [Widescreen re-issue 2004])

   Star Wars Episode VI: Return of the Jedi (Marquand, US, 1983 [Widescreen re-issue 2004])

Strange Days (Bigelow, US, 1995)

Stuff, The (Cohen, US, 1985)

T2: Judgement Day (Cameron, US, 1991)

Ted (MacFarlane, US, 2012)

There Will Be Blood (Anderson, US, 2007)

Thing, The (Carpenter, US, 1982)

Thing, The (van Heijningen, US/Can., 2011)

Thing From Another World, The (Nyby, US, 1951)

Things to Come (Menzies, UK, 1936)

This Is 40 (Apatow, US, 2013)

Timecode (Figgis, US, 2000)

Titanic (Cameron, US, 1997)

Top Gun (Scott, US, 1986)

Traffic (Soderbergh, Ger./US, 2000)

TRON (Lisberger, US, 1982)

TRON: Legacy (Konsinski, US, 2010)

Tropic Thunder (Stiller, US, 2008)

True Grit (Coen, US, 2010)

Two or Three Things I Know About Her (*2 ou 3 choses que je sais d'elle*, Godard, Fr., 1967)

Uncle Tom's Cabin (Porter, US, 1903)

Up (Doctor and Petersen, US, 2009)

Videodrome (Cronenberg, Can., 1983)

War of the Roses, The (DeVito, US, 1989)
Will and Grace (NBC, US, 1998–2006)
Wizard of Oz, The (Fleming, US, 1939)
Workers Leaving a Factory (Lumière, Fr., 1894–1895)
Working Girl (Nichols, US, 1988)
World of Tomorrow, The (Bird and Johnson, US, 1984)
Wrestler, The (Aronofsky, US, 2008)
Zidane: A 21st Century Portrait (Gordon/Parreno, Fr./Ice., 2006)

BIBLIOGRAPHY

Aarseth, E. *Cybertext: Perspectives on Ergodic Literature*. Baltimore, MD: Johns Hopkins University Press, 1997.

Adler, A. *The Individual Psychology of Alfred Adler*. New York: Basic Books, 1956.

Adorno, T. W. *Aesthetic Theory*. London: Continuum, 1997.

—— *The Culture Industry*. London: Routledge, 2002.

—— *The Jargon of Authenticity*. London: Routledge, 2003.

Albrecht-Crane, C. and D. Cutchens (eds) *Adaptation Studies: New Approaches*. Cranbury, NJ: Associated University Presses, 2010.

Allen, M. 'Talking About a Revolution: The Blockbuster as Industrial Advertisement', in Stringer, J. (ed.) *Movie Blockbusters*. London: Routledge, 2003.

—— 'The Impact of Digital Technologies on Film Aesthetics', in Harries, D. (ed.) *The New Media Book*. London: BFI, 2004: 109–18.

Allen, R. and M. Smith. *Film Theory and Philosophy*. Oxford: Oxford University Press, 1999.

Althusser, L. *Lenin and Philosophy*. Trans. B. Brewster. New York: Monthly Review Press, 1971.

—— *Essays in Self Criticism*. Trans. G. Lock. London: New Left Books, 1976.

—— *For Marx*. New York: New Left Books, 1977.

Altman, R. 'The Evolution of Sound Technology', in Weis, E. and J. Belton (eds) *Film Sound: Theory and Practice*. New York: Columbia University Press, 1985: 44–53.

—— 'Emballage reutilisable', *Iris* 20 (Fall 1995): 13–30.

—— *Film/Genre*. London: BFI, 1999.

Anderson, B. *Imagined Communities*. London: Verso, 1991.

Anderson, K. J. *Jedi Search*. New York: Bantam Spectra, 1994a.

—— *Dark Apprentice*. New York: Bantam Spectra, 1994b.

—— *Champions of the Force*. New York: Bantam Spectra, 1994c.

Anderson, K. T. and S. Hameed. 'Faithful to a Fault: Was it Really Necessary to Remake "Let the Right One In" in English?' 2010. Available at: http://works.bepress.com/kevin_taylor_anderson/8 [Accessed 29.10.13].

Andrew, D. *What Cinema Is!* Oxford: Wiley-Blackwell, 2010.

Ang, I. *Watching 'Dallas'*. London: Methuen, 1985.

Angerer, M.-L. 'Affective Troubles in Cinema', in Bennett, B., M. Furstenau and A. Mackenzie (eds) *Cinema and Technology: Cultures, Theories, Practices*. Basingstoke: Palgrave Macmillan, 2008: 214–40.

Anthony, A. 'Bobby Fischer: From Prodigy to Pariah', *Observer*, 15 May 2011.

Aragay, M. (ed.) *Books in Motion: Adaptation, Intertextuality, Authorship*. Amsterdam: Rodopi, 2005.

Arnheim, R. *Film as Art*. London: University of California Press, 1957.

Ashbee, B. 'Animation, Art, Digitality: From Termite Terrace to Motion Painting', in Thomas, M. and F. Penz (eds) *Architectures of Illusion: From Motion Pictures to Navigable Interactive Environments*. Bristol: Intellect, 2003: 1–50.

Astruc, A. 'The Birth of a New Avant-Garde: Le Caméra-Stylo', in Graham, P. (ed.) *The New Wave*. London: Secker and Warburg, 1968: 17–23.

Baggini, J. 'Serious Men: The Films of the Coen Brothers as Ethics', in Carel, H. and G. Tuck (eds) *New Takes in Film-Philosophy*. London: Palgrave Macmillan, 2011: 207–22.

Balász, B. 'The Close-Up', in Braudy, L. and M. Cohen (eds) *Film Theory and Criticism: Introductory Readings* (5th edn). Oxford: Oxford University Press, 1999: 304–11.

Balcerzak, S. and J. Sperb (eds) *Cinephilia in the Age of Digital Reproduction*. Vol. 1. London: Wallflower, 2009.

—— *Cinephilia in the Age of Digital Reproduction*. Vol. 2. London: Wallflower, 2010.

Balibar, E. *The Philosophy of Marx*. London: Verso, 1995.

Balio, T. *Grand Design: Hollywood as a Modern Business Enterprise 1930–1939*. New York: Charles Scribner's Sons, 1993.

Barbo, M. S. *The Pokemon Handbook*. New York: Scholastic, 1999.

Barker, J. M. *The Tactile Eye: Touch and the Cinematic Experience*. London: University of California Press, 2009.

Barker, M. and J. Petley. *Ill Effects: The Media Violence Debate*. London: Routledge, 1997.

Barlow, A. *The DVD Revolution: Movies, Culture and Technology*. Westport, CT: Praeger Publishers, 2005.

Barthes, R. *Image/Music/Text*. London: Fontana, 1977.

—— *Camera Lucida: Reflections on Photography*. New York: Hill and Wang, 1981.

—— *The Pleasure of the Text*. Trans. R. Miller. Oxford: Blackwell, 1990a.

—— *S/Z*. Trans. R. Miller. Oxford: Blackwell, 1990b.

—— *Mythologies*. Trans. A. Lavers. London: Vintage, 1993.

—— 'Myth Today', in Storey, J. (ed.) *Cultural Theory and Popular Culture: A Reader* (3rd edn). Harlow: Pearson, 2006: 293–302.

Baudry, J.-L. 'The Apparatus: Metapsychological Approaches to the Impression of Reality in Cinema', in Braudy, L. and M. Cohen (eds) *Film Theory and Criticism: Introductory Readings* (5th edn). Oxford: Oxford University Press, 1999: 760–77.

Bazin, A. 'La politique des auteurs', in P. Graham (ed.) *The New Wave*. London: Secker and Warburg, 1968: 137–55.

—— *What Is Cinema?* Vol. 1. Trans. H. Gray. London: University of California Press, 1967a.

—— *What Is Cinema?* Vol. 2. Trans. H. Gray. London: University of California Press, 1967b.

Beebe, J. 'Jungian Illumination of Film', *Psychoanalytic Review* 83: 4 (August 1996): 579–87.

Belton, J. 'Digital Cinema: A False Revolution', in Braudy, L. and M. Cohen (eds) *Film Theory and Criticism: Introductory Readings* (6th edn). Oxford: Oxford University Press, 2004: 901–13.

Bender, G. and T. Druckery (eds) *Culture on the Brink: Ideologies of Technology*. Seattle, WA: Bay Press, 1994.

Benjamin, W. *Illuminations*. Trans. H. Zohn. London: Fontana, 1973.

—— *The Arcades Project*. London: Harvard University Press, 1999.

Bennett, B., M. Furstenau and A. Mackenzie (eds) *Cinema and Technology: Cultures, Theories, Practices*. Basingstoke: Palgrave Macmillan, 2008.

Bennett, J. 'The Public Service Value of Interactive Television', *New Review of Film and Television Studies* 4: 3 (2006): 263–85.

Bennett, J. and T. Brown (eds) *Film and Television After DVD*. Abingdon: Routledge, 2008.

Ben-Shaul, N. *Film: The Key Concepts*. Oxford: Berg, 2007.

Berry, D. M. *Copy, Rip, Burn: The Politics of Copyleft and Open Source*. London: Pluto Press, 2008.

Berry, P. 'Image in Motion', in Hauke, C. and I. Alister (eds) *Jung and Film: Post-Jungian Takes on the Moving Image*. Hove: Brunner-Routledge, 2001: 70–79.

Bettelheim, B. *Uses of Enchantment: The Meaning and Importance of Fairy Tales*. New York: Vintage, 1976.

Bjorklund, D. F. and C. Hernandez Blasi. 'Evolutionary Developmental Psychology', in Buss, D. (ed.) *The Handbook of Evolutionary Psychology*. Hoboken, NJ: Wiley and Sons, 2005: 828–50.

Bogle, D. *Toms, Coons, Mulattoes, Mammies and Bucks: An Interpretive History of Blacks in American Films*. London: Continuum, 1994.

Bolter, J. D. and R. Grusin. *Remediation*. Cambridge, MA: MIT Press, 1999.

Bordwell, D. *Narration and the Fiction Film*. Madison: University of Wisconsin Press, 1985.

—— 'Contemporary Film Studies and the Vicissitudes of Grand Theory', in Bordwell, D. and N. Carroll (eds) *Post-Theory: Reconstructing Film Studies*. London: University of Wisconsin Press, 1996: 3–36.

—— *The Way Hollywood Tells It: Story and Style in Modern Movies*. London: University of California Press, 2006.

Bordwell, D. and N. Carroll (eds) *Post-Theory: Reconstructing Film Studies*. London: University of Wisconsin Press, 1996.

Bordwell, D., J. Staiger and K. Thompson. *The Classical Hollywood Cinema: Film Style and Mode of Production to 1960*. London: Routledge, 1985.

Bould, M. *Film Noir*. London: Wallflower, 2005.

—— 'The Dreadful Credibility of Absurd Things: A Tendency in Fantasy Theory', *Historical Materialism* 10: 4 (2002): 51–88.

—— 'On the Edges of Fiction: Silent Actualités, City Symphonies and Early Sf Movies', in Rhodes, G. and J. Springer (eds) *Docufictions: Mockumentary and Docudrama in Film and Television*. Jefferson, NC: McFarland & Company, 2006: 43–63.

—— 'Nothin Much to Phone Home About (with Exceptions): Four Books on Spielberg', *Science Fiction Film and Television* 1: 2 (Autumn 2008): 303–25.

Bould, M., K. Glitre and G. Tuck (eds) *Neo-Noir*. London: Wallflower, 2009.

Bourdieu, P. *Distinction: A Social Critique of the Judgement of Taste*. Trans. R. Nice. London: Routledge and Kegan Paul, 1984.

Bowen, J. L. *Anticipation: The Real Life Story of Star Wars: Episode I – The Phantom Menace*. Lincoln, NE: iUniverse, 2005.

boyd, d. 'Participating in the Always-On Lifestyle', in Mandiberg, M. (ed.) *The Social Media Reader*. London: New York University Press, 2012: 71–6.

Boyle, R. and R. Haynes. *Power Play: Sport, the Media and Popular Culture* (2nd edn). Edinburgh: Edinburgh University Press, 2009.

Branigan, E. 'Color and Cinema: Problems in the Writing of History', in P. Kerr (ed.) *The Hollywood Film Industry: A Reader*. London: BFI, 1986: 120–47.

Brantlinger, P. and J. Naremore (eds) *Modernity and Mass Culture*. Bloomington: Indiana University Press, 1991.

Braudel, F. *Capitalism and Material Life, 1400–1800*. Trans. M. Kochan. London: Weidenfeld and Nicholson, 1973.

Braudy, L. and M. Cohen (eds) *Film Theory and Criticism: Introductory Readings* (5th edn). Oxford: Oxford University Press, 1999.

—— *Film Theory and Criticism: Introductory Readings* (6th edn). Oxford: Oxford University Press, 2004.

Brewster, B. and L. Jacobs. *Theatre to Cinema: Stage Pictorialism and the Early Feature Film*. Oxford: Oxford University Press, 1997.

Brooker, P. and W. Brooker (eds) *Postmodern After-Images: A Reader in Film, Television and Video*. London: Arnold, 1997.

Brooker, W. 'New Hope: The Postmodern Project of *Star Wars*', in Brooker, P. and W. Brooker (eds) *Postmodern After-Images: A Reader in Film, Television and Video*. London: Arnold, 1997: 101–12.

—— 'Internet Fandom and the Continuing Narratives of Star Wars, Blade Runner, and Alien', in A. Kuhn (ed.) *Alien Zone II: The Spaces of Science Fiction Cinema*. London: Verso, 1999: 50–72.

—— *Using the Force: Creativity, Community, and Star Wars Fans*. London: Continuum, 2002.

—— *Star Wars*. London: BFI, 2009.

Brookey, R. and R. Westerfelhaus. 'Hiding Homeroticism in Plain View: The Fight Club DVD as Digital Closet', *Critical Studies in Media Communication* 19: 1 (March 2003): 21–43.

Bruno, G. 'Pleats of Matter, Folds of the Soul', in Rodowick, D. N. (ed.) *Afterimages of Gilles Deleuze's Film Philosophy*. Minneapolis: University of Minnesota Press, 2010: 213–34.

Brunsdon, C. *Screen Tastes: Soap Opera to Satellite Dishes*. London: Routledge, 1997.

Buckland, W. *Directed by Steven Spielberg: Poetics of the Contemporary Hollywood Blockbuster*. London: Continuum, 2006.

Buonanno, M. *The Age of Television: Theories and Experiences*. Bristol: Intellect, 2008.

Burgin, V. *The End of Art Theory: Criticism and Postmodernity*. London: Macmillan, 1986.

Buscombe, E. 'Sound and Colour', in Schatz, T. (ed.) *Hollywood: Critical Concepts in Media and Cultural Studies Volume III – Social Dimensions: Technology, Regulation and Audience*. London: Routledge, 2004: 16–26.

Buss, D. (ed.) *The Handbook of Evolutionary Psychology*. Hoboken, NJ: Wiley and Sons, 2005.

Caldwell, J. T. *Televisuality: Style, Crisis and Authority in American Television*. New Brunswick, NJ: Rutgers University Press, 1995.

—— 'Second Shift Media Aesthetics: Programming, Interactivity, and User Flows', in Caldwell, J. T. and A. Everett (eds) *New Media: Theories and Practices of Digitextuality*. London: Routledge, 2003: 127–44.

—— 'Convergence Television: Aggregating Form and Repurposing Content in the Culture of Conglomeration', in Spigel L. and J. Olsson (eds) *Television After TV: Essays On a Medium in Transition*. London: Duke University Press, 2004a: 41–74.

—— 'The Business of New Media', in Harries, D. (ed.) *The New Media Book*. London: BFI, 2004b: 55–68.

Caldwell, J. T. and A. Everett (eds) *New Media: Theories and Practices of Digitextuality*. London: Routledge, 2003.

Calinescu, M. *Five Faces of Modernity: Modernism, Avant-Garde, Decadence, Kitsch, Postmodernism*. London: Duke University Press, 1987.

Campbell, J. *The Hero with a Thousand Faces*. London: Fontana, 1993.

Cardinal, R. 'Pausing Over Peripheral Detail', *Framework* 30–31 (1986): 112–30.

Carel, H. *Life and Death in Freud and Heidegger*. Amsterdam: Rodopi, 2006.

—— 'In the Grip of Grief: Epistemic Impotence and the Materiality of Mourning in Shinya Tsukamoto's *Vital*', in Carel, H. and G. Tuck (eds) *New Takes in Film-Philosophy*. London: Palgrave Macmillan, 2011: 240–55.

Carel, H. and G. Tuck (eds) *New Takes in Film-Philosophy*. London: Palgrave Macmillan, 2011.

Carroll, N. *Mystifying Movies: Fads and Fallacies in Contemporary Film Theory*. New York: Columbia University Press, 1988.

—— *The Philosophy of Horror: Or, Paradoxes of the Heart*. London: Routledge, 1990.

—— 'Prospects for Film Theory: A Personal Assessment', in Bordwell, D. and N. Carroll (eds) *Post-Theory: Reconstructing Film Studies*. London: University of Wisconsin Press, 1996: 37–68.

Carson, D., L. Dittmar and J. R. Welsch (eds) *Multiple Voices in Feminist Film Criticism*. Minneapolis: University of Minnesota Press, 1994.

Carter, M. 'Coming Soon to Your Living Room', *Guardian*, Monday 26 July 2004.

Cartmell, D. and I. Whelehan (eds) *Adaptations: From Text to Screen, Screen to Text*. London: Routledge, 1999.

Casey, E. S. 'The World at a Glance', in Evans, F. and L. Lawlor (eds) *Chiasms: Merleau-Ponty's Notion of Flesh*. Albany: State University of New York Press, 2000: 147–64.

—— *The World at a Glance*. Bloomington: Indiana University Press, 2007.

Castelli, P., G. S. Goodman, R. Edelstein, E. Mitchell, P. M. Paz-Alonso, K. Lyons and J. Newton. 'Evaluating Eyewitness Testimony in Adults and Children', in Weiner, I. B. and A. K. Hess (eds) *The Handbook of Forensic Psychology*. Hoboken, NJ: John Wiley and Sons, 2006: 243–304.

Cavell, S. *The World Viewed: Reflections on the Ontology of Film*. London: Harvard University Press, 1979.

Chaney, D. *Fictions and Ceremonies: Representations of Popular Experience*. London: Edward Arnold, 1979.

Chomsky, N. *Necessary Illusions: Thought Control in Democratic Societies*. Cambridge, MA: South End Press, 1989.

Chomsky, N. and E. Herman. *Manufacturing Consent: The Political Economy of the Mass Media*. London: Pantheon, 2002.

Clark, D. 'The Death and Life of Punk, the Last Subculture', in Muggleton, D. and R. Weinzierl (eds) *The Post-Subcultures Reader*. Oxford: Berg, 2003: 223–36.

Collins, J., H. Radner and A. P. Collins (eds) *Film Theory Goes to the Movies*. London: Routledge, 1993.

Collins, R., J. Curran, N. Garnham, P. Scannell, P. Schlesinger and C. Sparks (eds) *Media, Culture and Society: A Critical Reader*. London: Sage, 1986.

Comolli, J-L. and J. Narboni, 'Cinema/Ideology/Criticism', in Braudy, L. and M. Cohen (eds) *Film Theory and Criticism: Introductory Readings* (5th edn). Oxford: Oxford University Press, 1999: 752–9.

Compaine, B. M. and D. Gomery. *Who Owns the Media? Competition and Concentration in the Mass Media Industry* (3rd edn). Mahwah, NJ: Lawrence Erlbaum Associates, 2000.

Constable, C. *Thinking in Images*. London: BFI, 2005.

Constantinides, C. *From Film Adaptation To Post-Celluloid Adaptation: Rethinking the Transition of Popular Narratives and Characters across Old and New Media*. London: Continuum, 2010.

Cook, D. A. *A History of Narrative Film*. London: W. W. Norton, 1996.

Cook, P. 'Whatever Happened to BFI Publishing?', *Cinema Journal* 47: 4 (Summer 2008): 140–47.

Corner, J. 'Finding Data, Reading Patterns, Telling Stories: Issues in the Historiography of Television', *Media, Culture and Society* 25 (2003): 273–80.

Cronin, A. M. *Advertising and Consumer Citizenship*. London: Routledge, 2000.

Cubitt, S. *Timeshift: On Video Culture*. London: Routledge, 1991.

—— 'Digital Filming and Special Effects', in Harries, D. (ed.) *The New Media Book* (2nd edn). London: BFI, 2004: 17–29.

Currie, G. and I. Ravenscroft. *Recreative Minds: Imagination in Philosophy and Psychology*. Oxford: Oxford University Press, 2002.

Darley, A. *Visual Digital Culture: Surface Play and Spectacle in New Media Genres*. London: Routledge, 2000.

Davis, A. *Women, Race and Class*. New York: Random House, 1981.

Davis, R. 'What WOZ: Lost Objects, Repeat Viewings and the Sissy Warrior', *Film Quarterly* 55: 2 (Winter 2001–2002): 2–13.

Davison, A. *Hollywood Theory, Non-Hollywood Practice: Cinema Soundtracks in the 1980s and 1990s*. Aldershot: Ashgate, 2004.

DeBona, G. *Film Adaptation in the Hollywood Studio Era*. Champaign: University of Illinois Press, 2010.

Debord, G. *The Society of the Spectacle*. Trans. K. Knabb. London: Rebel Press, 1983.

De Certeau, M. *The Practice of Everyday Life*. London: University of California Press, 1984.

—— *Heterologies: Discourse on the Other*. Trans. B. Massumi. Minneapolis: University of Minnesota Press, 1986.

de Lauretis, T. and S. Heath (eds) *The Cinematic Apparatus*. New York: St. Martin's Press, 1980.

Deleuze, G. 'Having an Idea in Cinema', in Kaufman, E. and K. J. Heller (eds) *Deleuze and Guattari: New Mappings in Politics, Philosophy and Culture*. Minneapolis: University of Minnesota Press, 1986: 14–19.

—— *Cinema 1: The Movement-Image*. Trans. H. Tomlinson and B. Habberjam. London: Continuum, 2004.

—— *Cinema 2: The Time-Image*. Trans. H. Tomlinson and R. Galeta. London: Continuum, 2005.

—— *The Fold: Leibniz and the Baroque*. London: Continuum, 2006.

Deleuze, G. and F. Guattari. *A Thousand Plateaus: Capitalism and Schizophrenia*. Trans. B. Massumi. London: Athlone, 1987.

Derrida, J. *Speech and Phenomena*. Trans. D. Allison. Evanston, IL: Northwestern University Press, 1973.

—— *Acts of Literature*. Ed. Derek Attridge. London: Routledge, 1992.

—— *Of Grammatology*. Trans. G. C. Spivak. Baltimore, MD: Johns Hopkins University Press, 1997.

Diawara, M. 'Black Spectatorship: Problems of Identification and Resistance', in Braudy, L. and M. Cohen (eds) *Film Theory and Criticism: Introductory Readings* (5th edn). Oxford: Oxford University Press, 1999: 845–54.

Dick, P. K. *Do Androids Dream of Electric Sheep?* New York: Doubleday, 1968.

Dixon, W. W. 'Twenty-five Reasons Why It's All Over', in Lewis, J. (ed.) *The End of Cinema As We Know It: American Film in the Nineties*. London: Pluto Press, 2002: 356–66.

Doane, M. A. 'Film and the Masquerade', *Screen* 23: 3/4 (September/October 1982): 78–87.

—— *The Emergence of Cinematic Time: Modernity, Contingency, The Archive*. London: Harvard University Press, 2002.

Dodge, M. and R. Kitchin. *Mapping Cyberspace* London: Routledge, 2002.

Dovey, J. and H. W. Kennedy. *Game Cultures: Computer Games as New Media*. Maidenhead: Open University Press, 2006.

Druxman, M. B. *Make It Again, Sam: A Survey of Movie Remakes*. Cranbury, NJ: A. S. Barnes, 1975.

DuBois, W. E. B. *The Souls of Black Folk*. Eds H. Gates Jr and T. H. Oliver. London: W. W. Norton, 1999.

Dufrenne, M. *The Phenomenology of Aesthetic Experience*. Evanston, IL: Northwestern University Press, 1973.

—— *In the Presence of the Sensuous*. New York: Humanity Books, 1990.

Dulac, G. 'From "Visual and Anti-visual Films"', in Sitney, P. A. (ed.) *The Avant-Garde Film: A Reader of Theory and Criticism*. New York: New York University Press, 1978: 31–5.

Dyer, R. *The Matter of Images: Essays on Representation*. London: Routledge, 1993.

Eagleton, T. *The Ideology of the Aesthetic*. Oxford: Blackwell, 1990.

—— *Ideology: An Introduction*. London: Verso, 1991.

Easthope, A. (ed.) *Contemporary Film Theory*. London: Longman, 1993.

Easthope, A. and K. McGowan (eds) *A Critical and Cultural Theory Reader.* Toronto: University of Toronto Press, 2004.

Eco, U. *Semiotics and the Philosophy of Language.* Bloomington: Indiana University Press, 1984.

—— *The Limits of Interpretation.* Bloomington: Indiana University Press, 1994.

—— *Faith in Fakes: Travels in Hyperreality.* London: Vintage, 1998.

Edgerton, D. *Shock of the Old: Technology and Global History Since 1900.* London: Profile, 2006.

Edwards, D. and D. Cromwell. *Guardians of Power: The Myth of the Liberal Media.* London: Pluto Press, 2006.

Ellis, B. J. and D. F. Borklund (eds) *Origins of the Social Mind: Evolutionary Psychology and Child Development.* New York: Guilford Press, 2005.

Ellis, J. 'Made in Ealing', *Screen* 16: 1 (1975): 78–126.

—— *Visible Fictions: Cinema, Television, Video* (2nd edn). London: Routledge, 1992.

—— *Seeing Things: Television in the Age of Uncertainty.* London: I. B. Tauris, 2000.

Elsaesser, T. and A. Barker (eds) *Early Cinema: Space, Frame, Narrative.* London: BFI, 1990.

Elsaesser, T., J. Simons and L. Bronk (eds) *Writing for the Medium: Television in Transition.* Amsterdam: Amsterdam University Press, 1994.

Elsaesser, T. 'Everything Connects, but not Everything Goes', in Lewis, J. (ed.) *The End of Cinema as We Know It: American Film in the Nineties.* London: New York University Press, 2002: 11–22.

Emerson, R. W. *Selected Essays.* Ed. L. Ziff. New York: Penguin Books, 1982.

Epstein, J. 'For a New Avant-Garde', in Sitney, P. A. (ed.) *The Avant-Garde Film: A Reader of Theory and Criticism.* New York: New York University Press, 1978: 26–30.

Fanon, F. *Black Skin, White Masks.* London: Pluto Press, 1986.

Featherstone, M. 'In Pursuit of the Postmodern: An Introduction', *Theory, Culture and Society* 5: 2 (June 1988): 195–215.

Flaxman, G. *The Brain Is the Screen: Deleuze and the Philosophy of Cinema.* Minneapolis: University of Minnesota Press, 2000.

Fordham, M. *Analytical Psychology: A Modern Science.* London: Karnac Books, 1994.

Foster, H. (ed.) *The Anti-Aesthetic.* Port Townsend, WA: Bay Press, 1983.

—— 'Yellow Ribbons', *London Review of Books* 27: 13, 7 July 2005.

Foucault, M. *The Archaeology of Knowledge and the Discourse on Language.* Trans. A. M. Sheridan Smith. New York: Harper and Row, 1976.

—— 'What Is an Author?', in Rabinow, P. and N. Rose (eds) *Essential Foucault: Selections from Essential Works of Foucault, 1954–1984.* New York: The New Press, 2003: 377–91.

Frampton, D. *Filmosophy.* London: Wallflower, 2006.

Franklin, U. *The Real World of Technology.* Toronto: Anansi, 1999.

Fredericksen, D. 'Jung/Sign/Symbol/Film', in Hauke, C. and I. Alister (eds) *Jung and Film: Post-Jungian Takes on the Moving Image.* Hove: Brunner-Routledge, 2001: 17–55.

—— 'Jung and Film'. Conference workshop. 'Psyche and Imagination' conference, IJAS/University of Greenwich, 6–9 July 2006.

Freeman, Gregory, 'LAEDC Study Concludes Redbox's $1 DVD New-Release Rentals Could Result in $1 Billion in Entertainment Industry Losses', 2009. Available at: http://laedc.org/2009/12/07/redbo/ [Accessed 20/09/13. Original LAEDC report no longer available.]

Freud, S. *Beyond the Pleasure Principle*. London: Penguin Modern Classics, 2003.

—— 'On the Universal Tendency towards Debasement in Love', in Easthope, A. and K. McGowan (eds) *A Critical and Cultural Theory Reader* (2nd edn). Toronto: University of Toronto Press, 2004: 148–56.

Friedberg, A. *Window Shopping: Cinema and the Postmodern*. London: University of California Press, 1994.

—— 'The End of Cinema: Multimedia and Technological Change', in Braudy, L. and M. Cohen (eds) *Film Theory and Criticism: Introductory Readings* (6th edn). Oxford: Oxford University Press, 2004: 914–26.

Friedman, L. *Citizen Spielberg*. Chicago: University of Illinois Press, 2006.

Frith, S. *Performing Rites: Evaluating Popular Music*. Oxford: Oxford University Press, 1998.

Frome, J. 'Representation, Reality, and Emotions Across Media', *Film Studies* 8 (Summer 2006): 12–25.

Frow, J. 'Intertextuality and Ontology', in Worton, M. and J. Still (eds) *Intertextuality: Theories and Practices*. Manchester: Manchester University Press, 1990.

Frye, N. *Anatomy of Criticism: Four Essays*. New York: Atheneum, 1966.

Fuery, P. *New Developments in Film Theory*. Basingstoke: Macmillan Press, 2000.

Furby, J. and K. Randell (eds) *Screen Methods: Comparative Readings in Film Studies*. London: Wallflower, 2005.

Gaiman, N. *The Sandman Vol. 9: The Kindly Ones*. Available at: www.goodreads. com/work/quotes/2647-the-kindly-ones [Accessed: 25/03/13].

Galloway, A. R. 'Playing the Code: Allegories of Control in *Civilization*', *Radical Philosophy* 128 (November/December 2004): 33–40.

Gauntlett, D. (ed.) *Web.Studies: Rewiring Media Studies for the Digital Age*. London: Arnold, 2000.

Gauntlett, D. and R. Horsley (eds) *Web.Studies* (2nd edn). London: Arnold, 2004.

Genette, G. *Narrative Discourse*. Trans. J. E. Lewin. Oxford: Basil Blackwell, 1980.

—— *Paratexts: Thresholds of Interpretation*. Trans. J. E. Lewin. Cambridge: Cambridge University Press, 1997.

Geraghty, C. *Women and Soap Opera: A Study of Prime Time Soaps*. Cambridge: Polity, 1991.

Gere, C. *Art, Time and Technology*. Oxford: Berg, 2006.

Gibbs, J. *Mise-en-Scène: Film Style and Interpretation*. London: Wallflower, 2002.

Gibbs, J. and D. Pye (eds) *Style and Meaning: Studies in the Detailed Analysis of Film*. Manchester: Manchester University Press, 2005.

Gibson, W. *Neuromancer*. New York: Ace Books, 1984.

Giddens, A. 'Introduction', in Weber, M. *The Protestant Ethic and the Spirit of Capitalism*. London: Routledge, 1996: vii–xxiv.

Giddings, S. '"I'm the one who makes the Lego Racers go": Studying Virtual and Actual Play', in Dixon, S. and S. Weber (eds) *Digital Girls: Growing Up Online*. New York: Palgrave Macmillan, 2007: 37–50.

Giddings, S. and H. Kennedy. 'Little Jesuses and *@#?-off Robots: On Aesthetics, Cybernetics and Not Being Very Good at *Lego Star Wars*', in Swalwell, M. and J. Wilson (eds) *The Pleasures of Computer Gaming*. Jefferson, NC: McFarland, 2008: 13–32.

Gledhill, C. 'Pleasurable Negotiations', in Pribam, E. D. (ed.) *Female Spectators: Looking at Film and Television*. London: Verso, 1988: 64–89.

Goldsmith, B. and T. O'Regan. *The Film Studio: Film Production in the Global Economy*. New York: Rowman and Littlefield, 2005.

Gordon, A. M. *Empire of Dreams: The Science Fiction and Fantasy Films of Steven Spielberg*. Lanham, MD: Rowman and Littlefield, 2008.

Graham, P. (ed.) *The New Wave*. London: Secker and Warburg/BFI, 1968.

Grainge, P. *Brand Hollywood*. London: Routledge, 2008.

Grant, B. K. (ed.) *Film Genre Reader III*. Austin: University of Texas Press, 2003.

Green, A. *The Fabric of Affect in the Psycho-Analytic Discourse*. London: Routledge, 1999.

Greenberg, C. *Art and Culture: Critical Essays*. Boston, MA: Beacon Press, 1961.

Grieveson, L. and P. Krämer (eds) *The Silent Cinema Reader*. London: Routledge, 2004.

Grodal, T. *Moving Pictures: A New Theory of Film Genres, Feelings, and Cognition*. Oxford: Clarendon Press, 1997.

Gross, L. 'Big and Loud', *Sight and Sound* 8 (August 1995): 6–10.

Guerrero, E. *Framing Blackness: The African American Image in Film*. Philadelphia, PA: Temple University Press, 1993.

Gunn, S. *History and Cultural Theory*. Harlow: Pearson, 2006.

Gunning, T. 'The Cinema of Attractions: Early Film, Its Spectator and the Avant-Garde', in Elsaesser, T. and A. Barker (eds) *Early Cinema: Space, Frame, Narrative*. London: BFI, 1990: 56–62.

—— *D. W. Griffith and the Origins of American Narrative Film: The Early Years at Biograph*. Urbana: University of Illinois Press, 1994.

—— 'An Aesthetic of Astonishment: Early Film and the (In)Credulous Spectator', in Braudy, L. and M. Cohen (eds) *Film Theory and Criticism: Introductory Readings* (6th edn). Oxford: Oxford University Press, 2004: 862–76.

Hall, S. 'Encoding/Decoding', in Hall, S., D. Hobson, A. Lowe and P. Willis (eds) *Culture, Media, Language: Working Papers in Cultural Studies, 1972–79*. London: Hutchinson, 1981: 128–38.

—— 'Cultural Studies: Two Paradigms', in Collins, R., J. Curran, N. Garnham, P. Scannell, P. Schlesinger and C. Sparks (eds) *Media, Culture and Society: A Critical Reader*. London: Sage, 1986: 33–48.

Hall, S. (ed.) *Representation*. London: Sage, 1997.

Hall, S., D. Hobson, A. Lowe and P. Willis (eds) *Culture, Media, Language: Working Papers in Cultural Studies, 1972–79*. London: Hutchinson, 1981.

Hambly, B. *Children of the Jedi*. London: Bantam Books, 1995.

Hammond, M. and L. Mazdon. *The Contemporary Television Series*. Edinburgh: Edinburgh University Press, 2005.

Harries, D. (ed.) *The New Media Book* (2nd edn). London: BFI, 2004.

Harris, L. R. and M. Jenkin. *Vision and Attention*. New York: Springer-Verlag, 2001.

Hauke, C. *Jung and the Postmodern: The Interpretation of Realities*. London: Routledge, 2000.

—— '"Let's Go Back to Finding Out Who We Are": Men, *Unheimlich* and Returning Home in the Films of Steven Spielberg', in Hauke, C. and I. Alister (eds) *Jung and Film: Post-Jungian Takes on the Moving Image*. Hove: Brunner-Routledge, 2001: 151–74.

—— 'The Six Thirds: Movies and the Third Image'. Conference paper. 'Screen' conference, University of Glasgow, 3–5 July 2009.

Hauke, C. and I. Alister (eds) *Jung and Film: Post-Jungian Takes on the Moving Image*. Hove: Brunner-Routledge, 2001.

Hauke, C. and L. Hockley (eds) *Jung and Film II: The Return*. Hove: Routledge, 2011.

Hawkins, J. *Cutting Edge: Art-Horror and the Horrific Avant-Garde*. Minneapolis: University of Minnesota Press, 2000.

Hayward, S. *Key Concepts in Cinema Studies*. London: Routledge, 1999.

Hearn J., and D. H. J. Morgan (eds) *Men, Masculinities and Social Theory*. London: Unwin Hyman, 1990.

Heath, S. 'Film and System: Terms of Analysis Part I', *Screen* 16: 1 (Spring 1975a): 7–77.

—— 'Film and System: Terms of Analysis Part II', *Screen* 16: 2 (Summer 1975b): 91–113.

—— 'The Cinematic Apparatus: Technology as Historical and Cultural Form', in de Lauretis, T. and S. Heath (eds) *The Cinematic Apparatus*. New York: St. Martin's Press, 1980: 1–13.

—— *Questions of Cinema*. Indianapolis: Indiana University Press, 1981.

—— 'Cinema and Psychoanalysis: Parallel Histories', in Bergstrom, J. (ed.) *Endless Night: Cinema and Psychoanalysis, Parallel Histories*. London: University of California Press, 1999: 25–56.

Heidegger, M. *History of the Concept of Time: Prolegomena*. Trans. T. Kisiel. Bloomington: University of Indiana Press, 1992.

Henderson, B. *A Critique of Film Theory*. New York: E. P. Dutton, 1980.

Hergenhahn, B. R. *An Introduction to the History of Psychology* (6th edn). Belmont, CA: Wadsworth, 2009.

Hillman, J. *Emotion: A Comprehensive Phenomenology of Theories and Their Meanings*. London: Routledge and Kegan Paul, 1960.

Hills, M. *Fan Cultures*. London: Routledge, 2002.

—— 'Star Wars in Fandom, Film Theory, and the Museum', in Stringer, J. (ed.) *Movie Blockbusters*. London: Routledge, 2003: 178–89.

—— *The Pleasures of Horror*. London: Continuum, 2005.

Hirst, P. *On Law and Ideology*. London: Macmillan, 1979.

Hobsbawm, E. *The Age of Capital*. London: Abacus, 1995.

—— *The Age of Revolution*. London, Abacus, 1996.

Hockley, L. *Cinematic Projections: The Analytical Psychology of C. G. Jung and Film Theory*. Luton: University of Luton Press, 2001.

—— *Frames of Mind: A Post-Jungian Look at Cinema, Television and Technology.* Bristol: Intellect, 2007.

—— 'Cinema and the Psychotherapeutic: In-Between the Screen and the Viewer'. Conference paper, 'Screen' conference, University of Glasgow, 3–5 July 2009.

—— 'Losing the Plot: A Story of Individuation and the Movies', *Quadrant* XXXX: 1 (Winter 2010).

—— 'The Third Image: Depth Psychology and the Cinematic Experience', in Hauke, C. and L. Hockley (eds) *Jung and Film II: The Return.* Hove: Routledge, 2011.

—— *Somatic Cinema: The Relationship Between Body and Screen – A Jungian Perspective.* Hove: Routledge, 2013 (in press).

Hollows, J. and M. Jancovich (eds) *Approaches to Popular Film.* Manchester: Manchester University Press, 1995.

Hollwitz, J. 'The Grail Quest and *Field of Dreams*', in Hauke, C. and I. Alister (eds) *Jung and Film: Post-Jungian Takes on the Moving Image.* Hove: Brunner-Routledge, 2001: 83–94.

Homer, S. 'Cinema and Fetishism: The Disavowal of a Concept', *Historical Materialism* 13: 1 (2005): 85–116.

hooks, b. *Black Looks.* Cambridge, MA: South End Press, 1992.

Hutcheon, L. *A Theory of Adaptation.* Abingdon: Routledge, 2006.

Ihde, D. *Bodies in Technology.* Minneapolis: University of Minnesota Press, 2002.

Izod, J. *Myth, Mind and the Screen: Understanding the Heroes of our Time.* Cambridge: Cambridge University Press, 2001.

—— *Screen, Culture, Psyche: A Post-Jungian Approach to Working with the Audience.* Hove: Routledge, 2006.

Jameson, F. 'Postmodernism and Consumer Society', in Foster, H. (ed.) *The Anti-Aesthetic.* Port Townsend, WA: Bay Press, 1983: 111–25.

—— 'The Vanishing Mediator; or, Max Weber as Storyteller', in *The Ideologies Of Theory, Essays 1971–1986 Volume 2: The Syntax of History.* Minneapolis: University of Minnesota Press, 1989: 3–34.

—— *Postmodernism, or, The Cultural Logic of Late Capitalism.* London: Verso, 1991.

—— *Signatures of the Visible.* London: Routledge, 1992.

—— *The Political Unconscious: Narrative as a Socially Symbolic Act.* London: Routledge, 1996.

—— 'The Nostalgia Mode and Nostalgia for the Present', in Brooker, P. and W. Brooker (eds) *Postmodern After-Images: A Reader in Film, Television and Video.* London: Arnold, 1997: 23–35.

—— 'Afterword: Adaptation as a Philosophical Problem', in MacCabe, C., K. Murray, and R. Warner (eds) *True to the Spirit: Film Adaptation and the Question of Fidelity.* Oxford: Oxford University Press, 2011: 215–34.

Jameson, R. T. 'Son of Noir', in Silver, A. and J. Ursini (eds) *Film Noir Reader 2.* New York: Limelight Editions, 1999: 197–206.

Jancovich, M. 'Screen Theory', in Hollows, J. and M. Jancovich (eds) *Approaches to Popular Film.* Manchester: Manchester University Press, 1995: 123–50.

Jenkins, H. *Textual Poachers: Television Fans and Participatory Culture.* London: Routledge, 1992.

—— *Convergence Culture: Where Old and New Media Collide*. London: New York University Press, 2006a.

—— *Fans, Bloggers and Gamers: Exploring Participatory Culture*. London: New York University Press, 2006b.

Jess-Cooke, C. *Film Sequels*. Edinburgh: Edinburgh University Press, 2009.

Jung, C. G. (ed.) *Man and His Symbols*. London: Aldus, 1964.

—— *Memories, Dreams, Reflections*. New York: Vintage Books, 1989.

—— *The Essential Jung: Selected Writings*. London: Fontana, 1998.

Kant, I. *Critique of Pure Reason*. Trans. J. M. D. Meiklejohn. London: Dent, 1974.

Kassabian, A. *Hearing Film: Tracking Identifications in Contemporary Hollywood Film Music*. London: Routledge, 2001.

—— *Ubiquitous Listening: Affect, Attention, and Distributed Subjectivity*. London: University of California Press, 2013.

Kaufman, E. and K. J. Heller (eds) *Deleuze and Guattari: New Mappings in Politics, Philosophy and Culture*. Minneapolis: University of Minnesota Press, 1998.

Keane, S. *CineTech*. Basingstoke: Palgrave Macmillan, 2007.

Keathley, C. *Cinephilia and History, or, The Wind in the Trees*. Bloomington: Indiana University Press, 2006.

Kennedy, B. M. *Deleuze and Cinema: The Aesthetics of Sensation*. Edinburgh: Edinburgh University Press, 2002.

Kermode, F. *The Sense of an Ending*. Oxford: Oxford University Press, 2000.

Kerouac, J. *The Dharma Bums*. London: Penguin Classics, 2000 [1958].

Kerr, P. (ed.) *The Hollywood Film Industry: A Reader*. London: BFI, 1986.

King, G. *Spectacular Narratives: Hollywood in the Age of the Blockbuster*. London: I. B. Tauris, 2000.

—— *New Hollywood Cinema: An Introduction*. London: I. B. Tauris, 2002.

King, G. and T. Krzywinska (eds) *Screenplay: Cinema/Videogames/Interfaces*. London: Wallflower, 2002.

Klein, N. *No Logo*. London: Picador, 2000.

Klinger, B. 'Digressions at the Cinema: Commodification and Reception in Mass Culture', in Brantlinger, P. and J. Naremore (eds) *Modernity and Mass Culture*. Bloomington: Indiana University Press, 1991: 117–34.

—— *Beyond the Multiplex: Cinema, New Technologies, and the Home*. London: University of California Press, 2006.

Kojima, H. *Monad and Thou: Phenomenological Ontology of Human Being*. Athens: Ohio University Press, 2000.

Kracauer, S. *Theory of Film: The Redemption of Physical Reality*. Oxford: Oxford University Press, 1968.

—— *The Mass Ornament: Weimar Essays*. London: Harvard University Press, 1994.

—— 'From *Theory of Film*', in Braudy, L. and M. Cohen (eds) *Film Theory and Criticism: Introductory Readings* (5th edn). Oxford: Oxford University Press, 1999: 293–303.

Krämer, P. 'Big Pictures: Studying Contemporary Hollywood Cinema through Its Greatest Hits', in Furby, J. and K. Randell (eds) *Screen Methods: Comparative Readings in Film Studies*. London: Wallflower, 2005: 124–32.

Kristeva, J. *Desire in Language: A Semiotic Approach to Literature and Art.* Trans. A. Jardine, T. Gora and L. S. Roudiez. London: Blackwell, 1980.

Kuhn, A. (ed.) *Alien Zone.* London: Verso, 1990.

—— *Alien Zone II: The Spaces of Science Fiction Cinema.* London: Verso, 1999.

Kuhn, T. S. *The Structure of Scientific Revolutions.* London: University of Chcago Press, 1996.

Kulka, T. *Kitsch and Art.* Pennsylvania: Pennsylvania State University Press, 1996.

Kundera, M. *The Unbearable Lightness of Being.* London: Harper and Row, 1984.

Lacan, J. 'Excerpt from *Écrits*', in Easthope, A. and K. McGowan (eds) *A Critical and Cultural Theory Reader* (2nd edn). Toronto: University of Toronto Press, 2004: 81–6.

Laine, T. *Shame and Desire: Emotion, Intersubjectivity, Cinema.* Oxford: Peter Lang, 2007.

Landon, B. *The Aesthetics of Ambivalence: Rethinking Science Fiction in the Age of Electronic (Re)production.* Westport, CT: Greenwood Press, 1992.

Landow, G. *Hypertext 2.0.* London: Johns Hopkins University Press, 1997.

Lapsley, R. and M. Westlake. *Film Theory: An Introduction.* Manchester: Manchester University Press, 1988.

Larsson, S. *The Girl with the Dragon Tattoo.* London: MacLehose Press, 2008.

—— *The Girl Who Played with Fire.* London: MacLehose Press, 2009a.

—— *The Girl Who Kicked the Hornet's Nest.* London: MacLehose Press, 2009b.

Leitch, T. M. 'Twice-Told Tales: The Rhetoric of the Remake', *Literature/Film Quarterly* 18: 3 (1990): 138–49.

—— *Film Adaptation and Its Discontents: From Gone with the Wind to The Passion of the Christ.* Baltimore, MD: Johns Hopkins University Press, 2009.

Lewis, J. (ed.) *The End of Cinema As We Know It: American Film in the Nineties.* London: New York University Press, 2002.

Littau, K. (2008) 'The Physiology of Momentary Angels: Towards Reception Aesthetics of Media'. Conference keynote. 'Philosophy and Film/Film and Philosophy' Conference, University of the West of England, 4–6 July 2008.

Lukács, G. *History and Class Consciousness.* London: Merlin Press, 1971.

Lunenfeld, P. 'The Myths of Interactive Cinema', in Harries, D. (ed.) *The New Media Book* (2nd edn). London: BFI, 2004: 144–54.

Lütticken, S. 'Planet of the Remakes', *New Left Review* 25 (Jan/Feb 2004): 103–19.

Lyotard, J.-F. *Libidinal Economy.* Trans. I. H. Grant. London: Continuum, 2004.

MacCabe, J. and K. Akass. *Quality TV: Contemporary American Television and Beyond.* London: I. B. Tauris, 2007.

MacCabe, C., K. Murray and R. Warner (eds) *True to the Spirit: Film Adaptation and the Question of Fidelity.* Oxford: Oxford University Press, 2011.

Malaby, T. 'Parlaying Value: Capital in and Beyond Virtual Worlds', *Games and Culture: A Journal of Interactive Media* 1: 2 (April 2006): 141–62.

Maltby, R. *Harmless Entertainment: Hollywood and the Ideology of Consensus.* Metuchen, NJ: Scarecrow Press, 1983.

—— *Hollywood Cinema* (2nd edn). Oxford: Blackwell, 2003.

Mandel, E. 'The Labor Theory of Value and *Monopoly Capitalism*', *International Socialist Review* 28: 4 (July/August 1967): 29–42.

Mandiberg, M. (ed.) *The Social Media Reader*. London: New York University Press, 2012.

Manojlovic, M. '*Demonlover*: Interval, Affect and the Aesthetics of Digital Dislocation', in Bennett, B., M. Furstenau and A. Mackenzie (eds) *Cinema and Technology: Cultures, Theories, Practices*. Basingstoke: Palgrave Macmillan, 2008: 142–67.

Manovich, L. *The Language of New Media*. Cambridge, MA: MIT Press, 2002.

—— 'Old Media as New Media: Cinema', in Harries, D. (ed.) *The New Media Book* (2nd edn). London: BFI, 2004: 208–18.

Marks, L. *The Skin of the Film: Intercultural Cinema, Embodiment and the Senses*. London: Duke University Press, 2000.

Marx, K. *Grundrisse: Foundations of the Critique of Political Economy*. London: Penguin, 1993.

—— *Capital (An Abridged Edition)*. Oxford: Oxford University Press, 1999.

—— *Capital: A Critique of Political Economy*. Vol. 1. Trans. B. Fowkes. London: Penguin, 2004.

Massumi, B. *Parables of the Virtual: Movement, Affect, Sensation*. London: Duke University Press, 2002.

Mateas, M., 'Interactive Drama, Art, and Artificial Intelligence', PhD thesis, Carnegie Mellon University, 2002.

McDonald, P. *Video and DVD Industries*. London: BFI Publishing, 2007.

McDonald, P. and J. Wasko (eds) *The Contemporary Hollywood Film Industry*. Oxford: Wiley-Blackwell, 2008.

McFarlane, B. *Novel to Film: An Introduction to the Theory of Adaptation*. Oxford: Clarendon Press, 1996.

—— *Screen Adaptations. Charles Dickens' Great Expectations: The Relationship Between Text and Film*. London: Methuen Drama, 2008.

McLuhan, M. *Understanding Media: The Extensions of Man*. London: Routledge and Kegan Paul, 1964.

McQuillan, M., G. Macdonald, S. Thomson and R. Purves (eds) *Post-Theory: New Directions in Criticism*. Edinburgh: Edinburgh University Press, 1999.

McQuire, S. 'Impact Aesthetics: Back to the Future in Digital Cinema?', *Convergence: The International Journal of Research into New Media Technologies* 6: 2 (June 2000): 41–61.

Meehan, E. R. '"Holy Commodity Fetish, Batman!": The Political Economy of a Commercial Intertext', in Pearson, R. E. and W. Uricchio (eds) *The Many Lives of Batman*. New York: BFI-Routledge, 1991: 47–65.

—— 'Ancillary Markets – Television: From Challenge to Safe Haven', in McDonald, P. and J. Wasko (eds) *The Contemporary Hollywood Film Industry*. Oxford: Wiley-Blackwell, 2008: 106–18.

Mercer, K. *Welcome to the Jungle: New Positions in Black Cultural Studies*. London: Routledge, 1994.

Merleau-Ponty, M. *Sense and Non-Sense*. Evanston, IL: Northwestern University Press, 1964.

—— *Adventures of the Dialectic*. Evanston, IL: Northwestern University Press, 1973.

—— *Phenomenology of Perception: An Introduction*. Trans. C. Smith. London: Routledge, 2002.

—— 'The Experience of the Body in Classical Psychology', in Fraser, M. and M. Greco (eds) *The Body: A Reader*. London: Routledge, 2005: 52–4.

Messner, M. M. *Out of Play: Critical Essays on Gender and Sport*. Albany: New York State University Press, 2007.

Metz, C. '*Trucage* and the Film'. Trans. F. Meltzer. *Critical Inquiry* 3 (Summer 1977): 657–75.

—— *Film Language: A Semiotics of the Cinema*. Oxford: Oxford University Press, 1978.

—— *The Imaginary Signifier: Psychoanalysis and the Cinema*. Bloomington: Indiana University Press, 1986.

—— 'The Imaginary Signifier', in Braudy, L. and M. Cohen (eds) *Film Theory and Criticism: Introductory Readings* (5th edn). Oxford: Oxford University Press, 1999: 800–17.

Michel, G. F. and C. L. Moore. *Developmental Psychobiology: An Interdisciplinary Science*. London: MIT Press, 1995.

Miller, T. (ed.) 'In Focus: The British Film Institute', dossier, *Cinema Journal* 47: 4 (Summer 2008): 121–63.

Miller, T., N. Govil, J. McMurria, R. Maxwell and Ting Wang (eds) *Global Hollywood 2*. London: BFI, 2005.

Mitchell, D. 'Producing Containment: The Rhetorical Construction of Difference in Will & Grace', *The Journal of Popular Culture* 38: 6 (November 2005): 1050–68.

Moore, R. 'Love Machines', *Film Studies* 4 (Winter 2004): 1–11.

Mori, M. 'The Uncanny Valley'. Trans. K. F. MacDorman and T. Minato. *Energy* 7: 4 (1970): 33–35. Available at: www.androidscience.com/theuncannyvalley/proceedings2005/uncannyvalley.html [Accessed: 22/03/13].

Morley, D. *The Nationwide Audience*. London: BFI, 1980.

Morley, D. and C. Brunsdon. *The Nationwide Television Studies*. London: Routledge, 1999.

Morris, N. *The Cinema of Steven Spielberg: Empire of Light*. London: Wallflower, 2007.

Muggleton, D. and R. Weinzierl (eds) *The Post-Subcultures Reader*. Oxford: Berg, 2003.

Mullarky, J. *Refractions of Reality: Philosophy and the Moving Image*. Basingstoke: Palgrave Macmillan, 2010.

Mulvey, L. *Visual and Other Pleasures*. London: Macmillan, 1989.

—— 'Visual Pleasure and Narrative Cinema', in Braudy, L. and M. Cohen (eds) *Film Theory and Criticism: Introductory Readings* (5th edn). Oxford: Oxford University Press, 1999: 833–44.

Münsterberg, H. 'The Means of the Photoplay', in Braudy, L. and M. Cohen (eds) *Film Theory and Criticism: Introductory Readings* (5th edn). Oxford: Oxford University Press, 1999: 401–7.

Naramore, J. *Acting in the Cinema*. London: University of California Press, 1988.

Naramore, J. (ed.) *Film Adaptation*. New Brunswick, NJ: Rutgers University Press, 2000.

Ndalianis, A. 'Special Effects, Morphing Magic, and the 1990s Cinema of Attractions', in Sobchack, V. (ed.) *Meta-Morphing: Visual Transformation and the Culture of Quick Change*. Minneapolis: University of Minnesota Press, 2000: 251–72.

Neale, S. *Genre and Hollywood*. London: Routledge, 2000.

Neale, S. and M. Smith (eds) *Contemporary Hollywood Cinema*. London: Routledge, 1998.

Negroponte, N. *Being Digital*. New York: First Vintage Press, 1996.

Nelmes, J. (ed.) *An Introduction to Film Studies*. London: Routledge, 1996.

Nelson, C. and L. Grossberg (eds) *Marxism and the Interpretation of Culture*. Urbana: University of Illinois Press, 1988.

Neupert, R. *The End: Narration and Closure in the Cinema*. Detroit, MI: Wayne State University Press, 1995.

Neville, B. 'Taking Care of Business in the Age of Hermes', *Trickster's Way* 2: 1 (2003). Available at: www.trinity.edu/org/tricksters/trixway/current/Vol%202/ Vol2_1/Bneville.html [Accessed 24/03/13].

Newman, J. 'Playing the System: Videogames/Players/Characters', *Semiotica* 173 (February 2009): 509–24.

Newson, E. 'Video Violence: And the Protection of Children', *Psychology Review* 1: 2 (1994): 2–5.

Nichols, B. (ed.) *Movies and Methods*. Vol. 1. London: University of California Press, 1976.

—— *Movies and Methods*. Vol. 2. London: University of California Press, 1985.

Nietzsche, F. *Ecco Homo*. Harmondsworth: Penguin Classics, 1979.

Nowlan, R. A. and G. W. Nowlan. *Cinema Sequels and Remakes, 1903–1987*. Jefferson, NC: McFarland, 1989.

Olson, S. R. *Hollywood Planets: Global Media and the Competitive Advantage of Narrative Transparency*. Mahwah, NJ: Lawrence Erlbaum Associates, 1999.

Osherson, D. N., S. M. Kosslyn and J. M. Hollerbach (eds) *Visual Cognition and Action*. Cambridge, MA: MIT Press, 1995.

Parker, D. and M. Parker. 'DVDs and the Director's Intentions', in T. E. Wartenberg and A. Curran (eds) *The Philosophy of Film: Introductory Text and Readings*. Oxford: Blackwell, 2005: 123–31.

Pashler, H. 'Attention and Visual Perception: Analyzing Divided Attention', in Osherson, D. N., S. M. Kosslyn and J. M. Hollerbach (eds) *Visual Cognition and Action*. Cambridge, MA: MIT Press, 1995: 71–100.

—— *The Psychology of Attention*. Cambridge, MA: MIT Press, 1998.

Pashler, H. and C. M. Harris. 'Spontaneous Allocation of Visual Attention: Dominant Role of Uniqueness', *Psychonomic Bulletin and Review* 8: 4 (2001): 747–52.

Pearson, R. E. and W. Uricchio (eds) *The Many Lives of Batman*. New York: BFI-Routledge, 1991.

Perkins, V. F. *Film as Film: Understanding and Judging Movies*. London: Penguin Books, 1991.

—— 'Must We Say What They Mean? Film Criticism and Interpretation', *Movie* 34 (October 1990): 1–6.

Perry, S. *Shadows of the Empire*. London: Bantam Books, 1996.

Perryman, N. '*Doctor Who* and the Convergence of Media', in Storey, J. (ed.) *Cultural Theory and Popular Culture: A Reader* (4th edn). Harlow: Pearson Longman, 2009: 472–92.

Phillips, P. 'The Film Spectator', in Nelmes, J. (ed.) *An Introduction to Film Studies*. London: Routledge, 1996: 92–3.

Pierson, M. 'No Longer State-of-the-Art: Crafting a Future for CGI', *Wide Angle* 21: 1 (January 1999a): 29–47.

—— 'CGI Effects in Hollywood Science-Fiction Cinema 1989–95: The Wonder Years', *Screen* 40: 2 (Summer 1999b): 158–76.

—— *Still in Search of Wonder*. New York: Columbia University Press, 2002.

Pillsbury, W. B. *The Essentials of Psychology*. Alcester: Read Books, 2008 [1913].

Pinkola-Estes, C. *Women Who Run with the Wolves*: *Contacting the Power of the Wild Woman*. New York: Rider Classic Editions, 2008.

Pribam, E. D. (ed.) *Female Spectators: Looking at Film and Television*. London: Verso, 1988.

Prince, S. 'True Lies: Perceptual Realism, Digital Images, and Film Theory', in Braudy, L. and M. Cohen (eds) *Film Theory and Criticism: Introductory Readings* (6th edn). Oxford: Oxford University Press, 2004: 270–82.

Propp, V. *Morphology of the Folktale*. Austin: Univeristy of Texas Press, 2000.

Pye, D. 'Genre and Movies', *Movie* 20 (Spring 1975): 29–43.

Rabinow, P. and N. Rose (eds) *Essential Foucault: Selections from Essential Works of Foucault, 1954–1984*. New York: The New Press, 2003.

Remy, J. 'Patriarchy and Fratriarchy as Forms of Androcracy', in Hearn J. and D. H. J. Morgan (eds) *Men, Masculinities and Social Theory*. London: Unwin Hyman, 1990: 43–54.

Rheingold, H. *Smart Mobs: The Next Social Revolution*. New York: Basic Books, 2002.

—— *Net Smart: How to Thrive Online*. London: MIT Press, 2012.

Ricoeur, P. *Time and Narrative*. Vol. 1. Trans. K. McLaughlin and D. Pellauer. London: University of Chicago Press, 1984.

Robertson, Toby, 'Advertising Effectiveness in UK Film Distribution: A report for the UK Film Council', 2003. Available at: http://industry.bfi.org.uk/publications [Accessed 20/09/13].

Rodowick, D. N. *The Virtual Life of Film*. Cambridge, MA: Harvard University Press, 2007.

Rodowick, D. N. (ed.) *Afterimages of Gilles Deleuze's Film Philosophy*. Minneapolis: University of Minnesota Press, 2010.

Ross, S. M. *Beyond the Box: Television and the Internet*. Oxford: Blackwell, 2008.

Rowland, S. *C. G. Jung and Literary Theory: The Challenge from Fiction*. London: Macmillan, 1999.

Ryan, M. 'The Politics of Film: Discourse, Psychoanalysis, Ideology', in Nelson, C. and L. Grossberg (eds) *Marxism and the Interpretation of Culture*. Urbana: University of Illinois Press, 1988: 477–86.

Samuels, A. *The Plural Psyche: Personality, Morality and the Father*. London: Routledge, 1989.

—— *The Political Psyche*. London: Routledge, 1993.

Samuels, A., B. Shorter and F. Plaut. *Critical Dictionary of Jungian Analysis*. Hove: Routledge, 1986.

Scarry, E. 'The Merging Bodies and Artefacts in the Social Contract', in Bender, G. and T. Druckery (eds) *Culture on the Brink: Ideologies of Technology*. Seattle, WA: Bay Press, 1994: 80–86.

Schamus, J. 'To the Rear of the Back End: The Economics of Independent Cinema', in Neale, S. and M. Smith (eds) *Contemporary Hollywood Cinema*. London: Routledge, 1998: 91–105.

Schiller, H. *Information Inequality: The Deepening Social Crisis in America*. London: Routledge, 1996.

Schatz, T. 'The New Hollywood', in Collins, J., H. Radner and A. P. Collins (eds) *Film Theory Goes to the Movies*. London: Routledge, 1993: 8–36.

Schrader, P. 'Notes on Film Noir', in Grant, B. K. (ed.) *Film Genre Reader III*. Austin: University of Texas Press, 2003: 229–42.

Secomb, L. *Philosophy and Love*. Edinburgh: Edinburgh University Press, 2007.

Shaviro, S. *The Cinematic Body*. Minneapolis: University of Minnesota Press, 1993.

—— *Post-Cinematic Affect*. Ropley, Hampshire: O-Books, 2010.

Shinkle, E. 'Gardens, Games and the Anamorphic Subject: Tracing the Body in a Virtual Landscape'. Conference paper. 'Melbourne Digital Arts and Culture' conference, RMIT, Melbourne, 19–23 May 2003.

—— 'Sensory Engagement and Affective Response in Digital Game Environments'. Conference paper. 'Synthetic Sensations: The Five Senses and New Technology', Kingston University, 30 June 2006.

Shone, T. *Blockbuster: How Hollywood Learned to Stop Worrying and Love the Summer*. London: Simon and Schuster, 2004.

Silver, A. and J. Ursini (eds) *Film Noir Reader 2*. New York: Limelight Editions, 1999.

Simons, J. 'Unwritable Films, Unfilmable Texts?', in Elssaesser, T., J. Simons and L. Bronk (eds) *Writing for the Medium: Television in Transition*. Amsterdam: Amsterdam University Press, 1994: 149–55.

Singer, I. *The Nature of Love Vol. 1: Plato to Luther* (2nd edn). Cambridge, MA: MIT Press, 2009.

Singh, G. 'CGI: A Future History of Assimilation in Mainstream Science Fiction Film', *Extrapolation* 48: 3 (Winter 2007): 543–57.

—— *Film After Jung: Post-Jungian Approaches to Film Theory*. Hove: Routledge, 2009.

—— 'Cinephilia, Meaningfulness and Commodity-Identity: Contemporary Encounters with Popular Film Narratives and the Cinematic Afterlife', Doctoral Thesis, University of Reading, 2010.

—— 'Cinephilia; or, Looking for Meaningfulness in Encounters with Cinema', in Hauke, C. and L. Hockley (eds) *Jung and Film II: The Return*. Hove: Routledge, 2011.

—— 'The Kitsch Affect; or, Nostalgia, Cinephilia and the Vicariousness of CGI Feature Film', in Sperb, J. and S. Balcerzac (eds) *Cinephilia in the Age of Digital Reproduction: Film, Pleasure, and Digital Culture*. Vol. 2. London: Wallflower, 2012.

Singh, Gurpreet, and M. Pickard. 'Using Knowledge of Vision Science to Inform Creative Image Design'. Conference paper. 'MeCCSA-PGN' conference, University of the West of England, 13 July 2007.

Sitney, P. A. (ed.) *The Avant-Garde Film: A Reader of Theory and Criticism*. New York: New York University Press, 1978.

Smith, A. *The Wealth of Nations*. Ed. A. Skinner. Harmondsworth: Penguin, 1974.

Smith, G. M. *Film Structure and the Emotion System*. Cambridge: Cambridge University Press, 2003.

Smith, M. *Engaging Characters: Fiction, Emotion and the Cinema*. Oxford: Clarendon Press, 1995.

Sobchack, V. 'The Virginity of Astronauts: Sex and the Science Fiction Film', in A. Kuhn (ed.) *Alien Zone* London: Verso, 1990: 103–15.

—— 'Child/Alien/Father: Patriarchal Crisis and Generic Exchange', in Penley, C., E. Lyon, L. Spigel and J. Bergstrom (eds) *Close Encounters: Film, Feminism and Science Fiction*. Minneapolis: University of Minnesota Press, 1991: 3–32.

—— *The Address of the Eye: A Phenomenology of Film Experience*. Princeton, NJ: Princeton University Press, 1992.

—— *Screening Space: The American Science Fiction Film*. New Brunswick, NJ: Rutgers University Press, 1997.

—— *Carnal Thoughts: Embodiment and Moving Image Culture*. London: University of California Press, 2004.

—— 'Fleshing Out the Image: Phenomenology, Pedagogy, and Derek Jarman's *Blue*', in Carel, H. and G. Tuck (eds) *New Takes in Film-Philosophy*. Basingstoke: Palgrave Macmillan, 2011: 191–206.

Sobchack, V. (ed.) *Meta-Morphing: Visual Transformation and the Culture of Quick Change*. Minneapolis: University of Minnesota Press, 2000.

Soloman, G. 'The Illusion of the Future', *Film Comment* 28: 2 (March/April 1992): 32–41.

Sontag, S. *A Susan Sontag Reader*. New York: Vintage, 1982.

Sperb, J. and S. Balcerzac (eds) *Cinephilia in the Age of Digital Reproduction: Film, Pleasure, and Digital Culture*. Vol. 1. London: Wallflower, 2009.

—— *Cinephilia in the Age of Digital Reproduction: Film, Pleasure, and Digital Culture*. Vol. 2. London: Wallflower, 2012.

Spigel L. and J. Olsson (eds) *Television After TV: Essays On a Medium in Transition*. London: Duke University Press, 2004.

Springer, P. *From Ads to Icons: How Advertising Succeeds in a Multimedia Age*. London: Kogan Page, 2007.

Stacey, J. *Star Gazing: Hollywood Cinema and Female Spectatorship*. London: Routledge, 1994.

Staiger, J. 'The Politics of Film Canons', in Carson, D., L. Dittmar, and J. R. Welsch (eds) *Multiple Voices in Feminist Film Criticism*. Minneapolis: University of Minnesota Press, 1994: 191–209.

—— 'Hybrid or Inbred: The Purity Hypothesis and Hollywood Genre History', *Film Criticism* 22: 1 (Fall 1997): 5–20.

—— 'Hybrid or Inbred: The Purity Hypothesis and Hollywood Genre History', in Grant, B. K. (ed.) *Film Genre Reader III*. Austin: University of Texas Press, 2003: 185–99.

Stam, R. *Film Theory: An Introduction*. Oxford: Blackwell, 2000.

Stam, R. and A. Raengo (eds) *Literature and Film: A Guide to the Theory and Practice of Film Adaptation*. Oxford: Blackwell, 2005.

Stegner, W. *The American West as Living Space*. Ann Arbor: University of Michigan Press, 1974.

Stewart, C. T. *Dire Emotions and Lethal Behaviours: Eclipse of the Life Instinct*. Hove: Routledge, 2008.

Storey, J. (ed.) *Cultural Theory and Popular Culture: A Reader* (3rd edn). Harlow: Pearson, 2006.

—— *Cultural Theory and Popular Culture: A Reader* (4th edn). Harlow: Pearson Longman, 2009.

Stringer, J. (ed.) *Movie Blockbusters*. London: Routledge, 2003.

Studlar, G. *In the Realm of Pleasure: Von Sternberg, Dietrich and the Masochistic Aesthetic*. Urbana: University of Illinois Press, 1988.

Sutton, D. *Photography, Cinema, Memory: The Crystal Image of Time*. Minneapolis: University of Minnesota Press, 2009.

Swalwell, M. (2003) '"This Isn't a Computer Game You Know": Revisiting the Computer Games/Televised War Analogy'. Conference paper. 'Melbourne Digital Arts and Culture' conference, RMIT, Melbourne, 19–23 May 2003.

Tan, E. S. 'Film Induced Affect as a Witness Emotion', *Poetics* 23 (1995): 7–32.

—— *Emotion and the Structure of Narrative Film: Film as an Emotion Machine*. Mahwah, NJ: Erlbaum, 1996.

Tarkovsky, A. *Sculpting in Time*. Austin: University of Texas Press, 1986.

Telotte, J. P. *A Distant Technology: Science Fiction Film and the Machine Age*. Hanover, NH: Wesleyan University Press, 1999.

Terranova, T. *Network Culture: Politics for the Information Age*. London: Pluto Press, 2004.

Thomas, M. and F. Penz (eds) *Architectures of Illusion: From Motion Pictures to Navigable Interactive Environments*. Bristol: Intellect, 2003.

Thompson, K. *Moral Panics*. London: Routledge, 1998.

Titchener, E. B. *Lectures on the Elementary Psychology of Feeling and Attention*. New York: Macmillan, 1908.

Tocqueville, A. de. *Democracy in America*. Vol. 2. London: Vintage, 1945.

Todorov, T. *The Fantastic: A Structural Approach to a Literary Genre*. Ithaca, NY: Cornell University Press, 1975.

Tong, W. L. and M. C. C. Tan 'Vision and Virtuality: The Construction of Narrative Space in Film and Computer Games', in King, G. and T. Krzywinska (eds) *Screenplay: Cinema/Videogames/Interfaces*. London: Wallflower, 2002: 98–109.

Totaro, Donato, 'Gilles Deleuze's Bergsonian Film Project', 1999. Available at: www.horschamp.qc.ca/9903/offscreen_essays/deleuze1.html [Accessed 20/09/13].

Tredell, N. *Cinemas of the Mind: A Critical History of Film Theory*. Cambridge: Icon Books, 2002.

Tuck, G. 'The Pleasure of Invisible Sex: Cinematic Meaning, Sexual "Metaphors" and the Phenomenology of Editing in Classical Hollywood Cinema', in Jeffers-McDonald, T. and E. Wells (eds) *Realities and Remediations: Film at the Limits of Representation*. Newcastle: Cambridge Scholars Press, 2007: 1–13.

—— 'Art, Cinema, Sex, Ontology: Maurice Merleau-Ponty and the In-Visible of Cinema', in Carel, H. and G. Tuck (eds) *New Takes in Film-Philosophy*. London: Palgrave Macmillan, 2011: 171–87.

Tudor, A. *Theories of Film*. New York: Viking Press, 1973.

Turkle, S. *Alone Together: Why We Expect More from Technology and Less from Each Other*. New York: Basic Books, 2010.

Turner, G. and J. Tay. *Television Studies after TV: Understanding Television in the Post-Broadcast Era*. London: Routledge, 2009.

Vaidhyanathan, S. *The Googlization of Everything (and Why We Should Worry)*. Berkeley: University of California Press, 2011.

Van Deurzen, E. *Everyday Mysteries: A Handbook of Existential Psychotherapy* (2nd edn). London: Routledge, 2010.

Vaz, M. C. *Industrial Light and Magic*. New York: Del Ray, 1996.

Verevis, C. 'Re-viewing Remakes', *Film Criticism* 21: 3 (1997): 1–19.

—— 'Remaking Film', *Film Studies* 4 (2004): 87–103.

—— *Film Remakes*. Edinburgh: Edinburgh University Press, 2006.

Vogler, C. *The Writer's Journey: Mythic Structure for Writers* (3rd edn). Studio City, CA: Michael Wiese Productions, 2007.

von Leibniz, G. W. *New Essays on Human Understanding*. Eds P. Remnant and J. Bennett. Cambridge: Cambridge University Press, 1996.

Walters, J. 'Repeat Viewings: Television Analysis in the DVD Age', in Bennett, J. and T. Brown (eds) *Film and Television After DVD*. Abingdon: Routledge, 2008: 63–80.

Wartenberg, T. E. and A. Curran (eds) *The Philosophy of Film: Introductory Text and Readings*. Oxford: Blackwell, 2005.

Wasko, J. *Hollywood in the Information Age*. Cambridge: Polity Press, 1994.

—— *How Hollywood Works*. London: Sage, 2003.

Wayne, M. *Marxism and the Media*. London: Pluto Press, 2003.

Weber, M. *The Protestant Ethic and the Spirit of Capitalism*. Trans. T. Parsons. London: Routledge, 1996.

Weiner, I. B. and A. K. Hess (eds) *The Handbook of Forensic Psychology*. Hoboken, NJ: John Wiley and Sons, 2006.

Weis, E. and J. Belton (eds) *Film Sound: Theory and Practice*. New York: Columbia University Press, 1985.

White, H. *Metahistory: The Historical Imagination in Nineteenth-Century Europe*. Baltimore, MD: Johns Hopkins University Press, 1973.

Wilkin, P. *The Political Economy of Global Communication*. London: Pluto Press, 2001.

Willemen, P. *Looks and Frictions: Essays in Cultural Studies and Film Theory*. London: BFI, 1991.

Williams, R. *Culture and Society 1780–1950*. Harmondsworth: Penguin, 1968.

—— *Television: Technology and Cultural Form*. London: Routledge, 1990.

Wilson, E. *Love, Mortality and the Moving Image*. Basingstoke: Palgrave Macmillan, 2012.

Wilson, G. A. *Narration in Light: Studies in Cinematic Point of View*. New York: Johns Hopkins University Press, 1986.

Winston, B. *Misunderstanding Media*. London: Routledge and Kegan Paul, 1986.

—— *Technologies of Seeing: Photography, Cinematography and Television*. London: BFI, 1996.

—— *Media Technology and Society, a History: From the Telegraph to the Internet*. London: Routledge, 1998.

Wollen, P. 'The Auteur Theory', in Braudy, L. and M. Cohen (eds) *Film Theory and Criticism: Introductory Readings* (5th edn). Oxford: Oxford University Press, 1999: 519–35.

Wood, A. 'Timespaces in Spectacular Cinema: Crossing the Great Divide of Spectacle versus Narrative', *Screen* 43: 4 (Winter 2002): 370–86.

—— *Digital Encounters*. London: Routledge, 2007.

—— 'Cinema as Technology: Encounters with an Interface', in Bennett, B., M. Furstenau and A. Mackenzie (eds) *Cinema and Technology: Cultures, Theories, Practices*. Basingstoke: Palgrave Macmillan, 2008: 125–41.

—— 'Encounters at the Interface: Distributed Attention and Digital Embodiments', *Quarterly Review of Film and Video* 25: 3 (May 2008): 219–29.

Wood R. *Hollywood from Vietnam to Reagan*. New York: Columbia University Press, 1986.

Worton, M. and J. Still (eds) *Intertextuality: Theories and Practices*. Manchester: Manchester University Press, 1990.

Wright, R. 'Vampire in the Stockholm Suburbs: *Let the Right One In* and Genre Hybridity', *Journal of Scandinavian Cinema* 1: 1 (2010): 55–70.

Zahn, T. *Heir to the Empire*. New York: Bantam Spectra, 1991.

—— *Dark Force Rising*. New York: Bantam Spectra, 1992.

—— *The Last Command*. New York: Bantam Spectra, 1993.

Žižek, S. *The Fright of Real Tears: Krzysztof Kieślowski Between Theory and Post-Theory*. London: BFI, 1999.

—— *Violence*. London: Profile Books, 2008.

INDEX

Note: significant references are **emboldened.**